W9-BCT-981

The
UNICORN'S
SECRET

Murder in the Age of Aquarius

A TRUE STORY BY

Steven Levy

PRENTICE HALL PRESS

New York   London   Toronto   Sydney   Tokyo

For my parents

PRENTICE HALL PRESS
Gulf+Western Building
One Gulf+Western Plaza
New York, New York   10023

Copyright © 1988 by Steven Levy

PRENTICE HALL PRESS and colophon are registered
trademarks of Simon & Schuster, Inc.

Library of Congress Cataloging-in-Publication Data

Levy, Steven.
    The unicorn's secret: murder in the Age of Aquarius / Steven
Levy.—1st ed.
        p.   cm.
    ISBN 0–13–937830–8 : $18.95
    1. Einhorn, Ira, 1940–   . 2. Crime and criminals—Pennsylvania—
Philadelphia—Biography. 3. Murder—Pennsylvania—Philadelphia—
Case studies. *I. Title.*
HV6248.E55L48   1988
364.1'523'0924—dc19

[B]

88–11726
CIP

Designed by Irving Perkins Associates, Inc.

Manufactured in the United States of America

10   9   8   7   6   5   4   3   2   1

First Edition

ACKNOWLEDGMENTS

It is difficult enough to piece together a story when one subject is dead and another is a fugitive. It would be impossible without the generous cooperation of many of those who were close to the principals. During the course of my research more than 250 sources unselfishly participated in this project, and I thank them all.

The Maddux family has my special gratitude. Undoubtedly my questions and requests brought painful memories to them, yet they never complained, instead asking what else they might do to help. Their warmth and candor toward a stranger will not be forgotten.

The notes, interviews, and contacts of Greg Walter, who wrote about Einhorn in *Philadelphia Magazine*, were the materials with which I began *The Unicorn's Secret*. Greg not only provided me with otherwise unavailable documents and a long taped interview with Einhorn after his arrest but also contributed valuable background from his years of interest in the case. His work allowed me a tremendous head start. In addition, several other journalists who had done work on the Einhorn case shared their labors or impressions with me, including Howard Shapiro, Don DeMaio, Claude Lewis, Bernie McCormick, Gaeton Fonzi, and especially Al Robbins.

During my travels I benefited from the hospitality of Steve Fried, Jane Friedman, Katie Hafner, Bill and Susan Mandel, John Markoff, and Eileen Wise. Diane Ayres performed some research work and Wendy Scheir cheerfully undertook the monstrous task of transcribing hundreds of hours of tapes. Alan Halpern provided wisdom and assistance at a key point. The good offices of Glenn Horowitz provided a port in a clerical storm. My agent Pat Berens helped get the project underway and Flip Brophy adopted it with equal enthusiasm. At Prentice Hall Press, Michael Moore aided in innumerable tasks, and Pam Thomas provided help in the final stages. My editor Phil Pochoda, who believed in the project from the very beginning, was always there with suggestions and feedback.

I would also like to acknowledge the support of my family and friends, in particular Bruce Buschel, John Brockman, Helen and Lester Levy, Diane Levy, William Mooney, David Rosenthal, Randall Rothenberg, David Weinberg, Tim Whitaker, and Deborah Wise. Finally, I was lucky in having the companionship of Teresa Carpenter, who had been down this path before; besides her constant love and patience, I was able to get free advice at odd hours.

STEVEN LEVY
New York City, 1988

CONTENTS

Prologue:
Of Excellent Reputation

First to take the stand was a corporate attorney. Like the others, he seemed steeped in an air of unreality. He had known the defendant since both were boys. Now, two decades later, he was called on to defend his friend, under oath. He had never dreamed such an endorsement would be required of him, especially in circumstances such as these.

Would you say his character is poor, mediocre, or excellent?

"He is of good—*excellent*—character."

Next to testify was a lecturer at an Ivy League university. He, too, had discounted the charges against Ira Einhorn as not only untrue but impossible.

How would you characterize his reputation?

"He has the highest level of integrity. A man who goes out of his way to help people, a man who keeps his word, a man who in his feelings is compassionate and loving."

It was Tuesday, the third of April, 1979, in a Philadelphia courtroom, and Ira Einhorn's friends had come to verify his reputation as the benevolent, energizing spirit of his generation. The witnesses were sober, substantial members of the community, described in the newspapers the next day as "upper-crust professionals." Prominent as these citizens were, they represented only a tiny fraction of the important people the defendant had come to impress in the course of his unique career. One by one these witnesses made their way to the stand and swore before God to tell the truth. Then the defense lawyer would ask them questions. The lawyer was the city's former district attorney, and within two years he would be sitting in the United States Senate.

Now he addressed a reverend of the Episcopal Church known for his work in the peace movement.

What do you know of Mr. Einhorn with respect to his reliability to keep commitments or dates or obligations of that sort?

"I learned to rely on him absolutely. If he said he'd do something, he'd do it. . . . His reputation is excellent. He is a man of non-violence. That's the way he's known in the community."

In all his years on the bench, the judge had never seen such an impressive array of volunteers testifying to the character of a defendant. There was a vice-president at Bell Telephone describing Ira Einhorn's reputation, again, as "excellent." And here was an economist, the former London bureau chief of the *Wall Street Journal*:

What is his reputation in the community?

"The finest, as far as I'm aware."

The economist was followed by the dermatology consultant, who was followed by the businessman, who was followed by the playwright, who was followed by the restaurateur, who was followed by the minister—a daisy chain of accolades that seemed to have no end. So many prominent people were ready to bestow equally vigorous sworn honorifics that the lawyer had them stand up at their seats and acknowledge that their experiences of the defendant, Ira Einhorn, were congruous with the testimony thus far.

There simply was not enough time for all their praises.

Meanwhile, the man in question seemed to be following the proceedings with steady confidence, bordering on idle amusement. At thirty-eight, he was wide featured and burly, with a checked flannel shirt, a bushy, graying beard, and a ponytail. He was known for his blazing blue eyes, and even today they were not dim. He smiled as his friends shuttled to the stand. You would not think that the crime he was charged with, this man who moved the community to such respectful odes, was premeditated murder. A generous, peace-loving paragon such as the witnesses described would not, as the State charged, kill a thirty-year-old woman whom he loved, and thereafter cold-bloodedly cover up his fatal deed. An act like that would not only be a crime against a fellow human and a crime against the State but a violation of all the righteous values the defendant had come to stand for in the past fifteen years.

But Ira Einhorn was not an ordinary defendant. And this was certainly not an ordinary case.

The
UNICORN'S
SECRET

1

A CONDITION
OF MYSTERY

Less than three weeks before he would be sitting in a courtroom seeking bail as a defendant on a murder charge, the man who called himself the Unicorn flew home to Philadelphia. It was March 15, 1979, the cusp of a new era, and the Unicorn was ready for it. He had spent years embracing the future. A survivor from the sixties, he was a man who had stood shoulder-to-shoulder with the top Yippies when the antiwar protesters levitated the Pentagon in 1967, but only two days earlier he had been rubbing elbows with Prince Chahram Pahlavi-Nia, nephew of the Shah of Iran. They had driven back to London together after the Unicorn addressed an intimate gathering sponsored by the prince. The conference, attended by an elite corps of heavy thinkers, was touted "a focal point where environmental, ecological, and spiritual concerns meet internationally." The Unicorn's turf.

A month before that, he was in Belgrade, meeting with government officials to help promote relations between America and Yugoslavia, and arranging a centenary celebration for Nikola Tesla, a legendary Yugoslavian inventor.

And just months before *that*, the Unicorn was at Harvard, lodged in the Establishment's belly as a fellow in the Kennedy School of Government.

The whole thing verged on a goof, a cosmic giggle, a sudden hit of irony unleashed by cannabis truth serum. Yet Ira Einhorn, who had adopted the "Unicorn" nickname in the sixties, was utterly

1

serious. He had gone from a media guru who promoted LSD and organized Be-Ins, to an Establishment-approved self-described "planetary enzyme," a New Age pioneer who circulated vital information through the bloodstream of the body politic. Through his networking, consulting, lecturing, and writing, Ira Einhorn was doing his best to inject the values of the sixties into the global mainstream, and amazingly, he was making some headway. Without making compromises in his outlook or life-style, Ira Einhorn and his pro-planetary vision had attracted the attention of some very powerful people—leading-edge scientists, influential politicians, and captains of industry.

Not bad for a bearded-and-ponytailed former hippie still casual enough to greet callers to his home buck naked. He had plenty to congratulate himself on as he rode home on the TWA Heathrow-Philadelphia flight. He could ponder his burgeoning career or his ballooning list of powerful contacts. Or the future. Instead, he watched the in-flight film, *Comes a Horseman,* and, being an amateur movie critic, considered it "dreadful."

Having drawn his schedule with typical optimism, Ira Einhorn had a speaking engagement the very night he arrived home from England. The flight arrived late, but there was enough time for him to clear customs and return to his West Philadelphia apartment before he had to go crosstown to speak.

Einhorn was a natural choice to address the London Group. The radical psychiatrist who organized the semiregular discussion sessions, Ross Speck, tried to challenge the imagination of the mental health professionals who comprised the group. In the first few sessions, the London Group had entertained healers, drug cultists, and a doctor who treated cancer victims by attempting "retribalization" based on anthropological work with African tribes—the therapy included chanting and all the primitive trimmings. It was fitting to present Ira Einhorn to the fifteen or so members who would gather in the living room of the Specks' South Philadelphia townhouse during the middle of March in 1979.

The invitation Speck had sent out read,

> *The London Association*
> *Presents*
> *Ira Einhorn*

He is a poet, a philosopher,
a physicist.
Topic: Politics and Dada

Einhorn appeared at the townhouse just a few blocks south of the historic district in time for the scheduled 7:30 meeting. The four-story structure was on a tiny cobblestone street in a recently rejuvenated area.

Twelve years after the publicly declared "Death of the Hippie," Ira Einhorn looked more like a sixties' creature than ever. One would not call it a defiant pose, because he seemed so comfortable with it. The long brown-to-gray hair knotted in a ponytail, the thick, graying Santa Claus beard, the loose-fitting dashiki, and the somewhat ratty corduroy pants . . . these were not social gambits as much as physical facts. Comment on those appurtenances, at least direct comment, would be as unlikely as someone making a face-to-face remark on a deformed physical feature.

Of course, those living in Philadelphia for any period of time would not need to question the striking look of this man only two months from his thirty-ninth birthday. The answer to the puzzle was tautological. Ira looked that way because he was Ira. And everybody, it seemed, knew Ira. In a city still formal enough to call its major figures, even in casual conversation, by their surnames (the charismatic mayor would be forever "Rizzo" but never simply "Frank"), Ira Einhorn was someone known in circles journalistic, cultural, even legal and financial, by first name alone. Even those of ephemeral acquaintance with him long recall his greeting: a buoyant, "Hi, I'm Ira!" and a sudden launch into a mind-blowing topic that ordinarily would be dismissed as palaver, but somehow, from the mouth of this person of such confidence, was thrillingly plausible.

This was a process begun in the days of the counterculture, when the life-style of Ira Einhorn made news. His fame spread by television interviews, radio talk shows, poetry in underground newspapers, sponsorship of Be-Ins, and broad flaunting of his friendships with the national oligarchy of anti-Establishment figures. In the alternative United States, there was Rubin, Hoffman, Leary, Ginsberg. In alternative Philadelphia, only Ira.

During the past few years Einhorn had faded somewhat from the public eye. But the London Group soon learned of what Ira Einhorn had been up to in the seventies. Sprawled on the couch of the Specks' living room, a cozy space decorated with primitive artifacts collected by anthropologist Joan Speck, Einhorn related his recent adventures to the receptive after-dinner aggregation. He spoke in a soft voice, often punctuating his speech with the characteristic Einhorn laugh—a wild, nervous giggle, almost as high-pitched as a gleeful roar bleated out with aid of helium. He said that for years he had been primarily interested in the relation of nonphysical entities to the physical world. This led him to revelations, he explained, that had startling consequences for our civilization.

A prime example was Uri Geller, the Israeli psychic. Einhorn told the London Group that he had spent years working to inform the world of the significance of Geller's powers of metal bending, remote viewing, and divination. These powers indicated that our current scientific "paradigms" were inadequate. Likewise, the well-known controversy over UFOs was another indicator of how our long-held perceptions of reality were crumbling. Evidence existed that Western intelligence agencies were actively suppressing information about UFOs—not because of any grand plan but due to their inability to cope with such information. The Russians, on the other hand, were conducting some troubling studies in the paranormal, particularly using the technological ideas of Tesla, the genius who devised alternating current. There were experiments in controlling the weather, in sending deadly beams across oceans to affect behavior.

The Unicorn's news was strange indeed. And he knew it. Yes these things are incredible, he told the London Group, yet the world *must* come to grips with them soon. Einhorn's implications, presented in his upbeat manner but not without the dramatic emphasis required by their dire content, were apocalyptic.

"Anyone who is in a government structure knows their days are numbered," the Unicorn noted matter-of-factly. "Most people in power are waking up not knowing if they're going to wake up [tomorrow] in the same bed. It's as true in the United States as it is anyplace else."

The London Group learned of the conference Einhorn had just attended, and his unofficial diplomatic mission to Belgrade just weeks earlier. The members heard of his tenure at Harvard's Kennedy School of Government. And Einhorn told them how he had been sending carefully selected missives from reality's fringes to his personal network of significant figures in science, philanthropy, business, and parapsychology. The network was financed by the world's largest corporation: the telephone company.

The men and women in the London Group seemed disoriented by these facts. Just who *was* this person? His life seemed more far-out than his rap. He obviously could draw on an encyclopedic storehouse of cultural knowledge. Though not a degree-holding physicist, he could rattle off any number of esoteric scientific formulas, applying them with what would certainly be metaphoric brilliance, if anyone knew what he was talking about. He seemed plugged into the workings of global strategy, expounding on items as obscure as Chinese movements into Vietnam. On any subject of consequence he not only had personal command but apparent access to key figures. When talking about the niceties of arms control, for instance, he casually referred to a recent conversation he had with Paul Warnke, the country's chief negotiator.

Uri Geller, the shah, the family who owned Seagram liquors, the vice-president of AT&T, top NASA officials, Timothy Leary, Krishnamurti, the Trilateral Commission—a dazzling display of names and institutions. The name-dropping built to a crescendo when Ira Einhorn mentioned that "I was very surprised recently when I was approached by the Rockefellers and offered whatever amount of money I wanted to run for public office." When a woman pointedly asked just why the Rockefellers would ask this guru-with-portfolio to do a thing like that, Ira was undaunted.

"They need a front," he said. "Very badly. They're constantly hunting for people." Their efforts previously had been confined to more conventional potential candidates, he claimed. "It's not succeeding!" he said. "That's why they're looking other places. That's why they would come to some crazy like myself." A Rockefeller aide had approached Einhorn at a party and, said Ira, "gave me this incredible harangue how I had to go eat rubber chicken all over the country and really become a politician and get out front." Einhorn declined gracefully. "I had already been through that process, and I felt I had a lot more power doing what I was doing."

The London Group continued to press for clarification. The questions posed by the liberal social scientists were tentative—no one seemed really unwilling to let go of the titillating possibility that this fellow was for real. The prospect stirred the imagination—a figure born of the sixties, still in period garb, insinuating himself as sort of a free-floating Rasputin to power brokers and opinion makers, lobbying for humane treatment of human beings. Exposing what he called a "psychic Watergate" of mind weaponry in order to make real the clichéd cry of "Give Peace a Chance." But the group could not easily accept its outlandish lecturer, and the polite inquiries between the clinking of cups, saucers, and dessert spoons had a skeptical undercurrent. Ira—explain, please, your *identity!*

"I'm at the point now where the question of identity is mythic," Ira Einhorn proclaimed. "It doesn't matter. It disappears. I cannot give it any form except through the way I live."

The London Group did not let him escape just yet. They asked about the meaning of his *commitment.*

"I can't even use those words anymore," said Einhorn sadly, as if assuming his listeners would commiserate at the failure of language. "It's just action. I don't have very good words. Because I've gotten to the point where words do not really describe what I'm experiencing. I stay away from most religious words now. I don't use the word *love* very often. I'm in a condition of mystery most of the time."

And then he began talking about cattle mutilations.

It was, all in all, a boffo performance. Though he had undergone an exhausting round of motion and activity in the past few weeks— "How difficult it is to travel when you're going through this explosion of consciousness!" he exclaimed at one point—his energy seemed boundless. To promote the cause of peace and nonviolence, he could go on forever. When Ross Speck suggested, several hours into the meeting, that it was a natural time to quit, and perhaps those who wanted to stay a little longer might talk more to Ira, if Ira were not too tired, the words hardly escaped his mouth when Einhorn burst out, "I'm not tired at all! No, no problem!" So the session continued.

Einhorn remained in Ross Speck's house until the last guest left, and it was just Ira, Ross, his wife, Joan, and their twenty-three-year-old daughter, Diane, who had listened with wonder to the speaker's exhortations. And then, to Ross Speck's amazement, Ira Einhorn made a pass at his daughter. Not blatant, but certainly not subtle, sitting next to her, his arm up over the back of the couch, and using the momentum of his bravura performance to charge into an unmistakable flirtation. Nothing came of it, but as Speck later said, "it was kind of inappropriate for him to be putting the make on my daughter in my own house."

The London Group's failure to pin down Ira Einhorn on the particulars of his existence was only to be expected. Einhorn's life defied labels, and he was perfectly accustomed to the bogglement of listeners when it dawned on them that the person they were speaking to had no antecedent in their experience. For years, Einhorn had been shaping his work to fit not only his ideals and visions but his own uncompromising life-style. In doing this, he confronted the frustrations of an upstream swimmer with a robust sense of humor. Now that he was finally succeeding at his lifelong career, was it any wonder that this career was so complex that even Einhorn was unable to easily enlighten the puzzled minions who could not grasp exactly what it was that he did?

Why couldn't they accept the simple explanation? That Ira Einhorn had made a career of being Ira Einhorn.

Just what that entailed can best be understood by noting his routines and activities. In 1979, his base of operations, as it had been for seven years, was a small apartment on 3411 Race Street in the Powelton Village section of Philadelphia. It rented for $135 a month. It was not far from the University of Pennsylvania, and recent expansion of Drexel University had almost engulfed the block on which the white stone, three-story apartment house stood. Einhorn's apartment was on the second floor of the building, called Lerner Court. A flight of stairs headed toward the rear of the building, going north, toward his door. Visitors to the apartment would find a narrow hallway with a small kitchen on the left. In addition to the expected kitchen paraphernalia, there were rows of books, and a squat computer terminal, quite unknown as a home appliance in 1979. Proceeding north, one passed a bathroom with a prominent claw-foot tub. Over the toilet was an enlarged photograph of an enchanting little blond girl: a baby picture of Einhorn's former girlfriend, Holly Maddux, who had curiously dropped out of sight in the early fall of 1977.

Still walking north, one entered the main room of the apartment, a cozy twelve-by-twelve or so square that Einhorn used as both living room and bedroom. The bed was a mattress on the floor. There was a small desk covered with letters and papers. The room was furnished with plants—most of them remnants of the days when Holly had tended them—and especially books. Hundreds of books, filling the cinder-block shelves on all the walls, and placed in towering stacks at various points in the room. Otherwise, the furnishings were minimal. There was no television, not even a radio. The room had a spartan, almost oriental, feel.

On the north wall a long maroon blanket was hung over a French door that led to a screened-in, unheated porch.

From the main room, Ira Einhorn kept his watch on the planet and stage-managed his efforts to save it. His normal schedule was to wake around nine, take a bath, and hit the telephone. During the mornings he would talk to business contacts, scientists, editors, anyone who ventured into his orbit and seemed susceptible to the latest on what Einhorn considered the transformation to a New Age. Between calls, he might work on correspondence or do some reading; Ira Einhorn devoured books more efficiently than a shredding machine. Lunch would invariably be on the Penn campus at La Terrasse, an airy French restaurant that Einhorn had helped to popularize. During the course of the midday meal, Ira would mesmerize the corporate executive, journalist, or institutional leader who was footing the tab. Then perhaps a walk on the campus, or a visit to a bookstore, or a subway to cover the twenty-block distance to Center City Philadelphia, where he might have a meeting or two. Back to 3411 for more calls and correspondence. Time spent deciding which papers should be circulated on his network, and to which network members they should be addressed. Then dinner, movie, and home. Up until late—maybe as late as dawn—reading. Einhorn required only a few hours' sleep.

In the days after he returned from England that March, Ira resumed this routine with vigor. The telephone got a workout. He spoke to a Lockheed executive about unexplainable psychic events in Texas. To a local business leader about city politics. To a well-known economist about her theories on matriarchy. To a British reporter about CIA activities in covert psychic warfare. To a television producer about the possibility of Einhorn's doing regular appearances on a youth-oriented television show to appear opposite "Saturday Night Live."

He sorted through papers for possible network distribution. He maintained his regimen of a book a day, and often more. He saw movies. Delighted by *The China Syndrome* (as a solar energy activist how could he not be?), he wrote a friend, "Jack Lemmon should get an Academy Award . . . the nuclear issue is going to heat up."

He traveled. On March 19, after a busy morning on the phone and a lunch at La Terrasse with a woman who recently awarded him a $5,000 foundation grant to continue his work, Ira hopped a train to New York City. He met with two close friends, one of them the managing director of the Lehmann Brothers investment firm, the other an executive vice-president of AT&T. Then, in a crosstown hop that could well stand as definitive of his present existence, Ira rode in the phone company executive's limousine to former radical Jerry Rubin's apartment, where he would stay the night. The two sixties' veterans rapped until two. The next day, Ira saw futurist Alvin Toffler, whom Einhorn was instructing on the hands-on aspects of computer conferencing. Then he was off to Washington, DC, to visit with the Congressional Clearinghouse for the Future.

Hectic. But hectic was routine for Ira. Einhorn did not have a slow day in March until the twenty-seventh. He slept late, ambled downtown for a lunch with phone company friends, and spent time reading. The book of the day was *Barbarism with a Human Face,* by Bernard Henri Lévy. That night his friend Stuart Samuels had invited him to an advance screening of the movie *Hair.*

Ira and Samuels—a gregarious, balding Penn film instructor who had been an Einhorn consort for years—watched the movie from the front rows of the Sameric Theatre on Chestnut Street. Einhorn marveled to Samuels at how millions of dollars of film-studio money were unable to capture the ad hoc energy and risk taking of that resonant era. After the screening, they dined at a West Philadelphia restaurant, and came back to Einhorn's apartment for more talk and a smoke. Most of the conversation centered around Ira's interpretations of Albert Einstein's theories, but Ira did take time out to tell Samuels that he thought his apartment had been tampered with lately. He showed his friend a place on the living-room window, over his bed, where he thought the caulking had been removed. Samuels left at around two o'clock, and Ira read until a few minutes before six. Then the Unicorn lay down for the last night of sleep before his amazing and ambiguous career would be forever shattered.

Wednesday, March 28, 1979, would have been an eventful day for Ira Einhorn in any case. At around four A.M., while Ira was reading, radiation began leaking into the atmosphere near a nuclear plant 100 miles to the west of Philadelphia. The plant was named Three Mile Island. Ira Einhorn's prediction a few days earlier of the nuclear issue heating up had been fulfilled sooner than he had expected. In normal circumstances, Einhorn would have been on top of the crisis. As a figure in the environmentalist movement, he might have even assumed an active role in the media circus that would assemble in Harrisburg over the next few days.

But Ira Einhorn was destined to make headlines of his own.

The Unicorn was still sleeping when Detective Michael Chitwood rang the outside buzzer of 3411 Race Street on the morning of March 28. It was approximately ten minutes before nine. Ira Einhorn grabbed a robe and pressed the button that unlocked the outside door. Chitwood, accompanied by six other police officials, opened the door and began climbing the steps. Before the detective reached the door, Einhorn had opened it. Ira had not bothered to fully cover himself with the robe. It was then that Chitwood identified himself as a homicide detective, and told Ira that he had a search-and-seizure warrant for his house. Michael Chitwood, a tall wiry man in his thirties, was smiling. Einhorn laughed. "Search what?" he asked.

What could the Unicorn have to hide?

Chitwood told him to read the warrant. He handed Einhorn the thirty-five-page document, signed the night before by a Philadelphia municipal court judge, granting permission for the police to search his apartment for any evidence relating to the disappearance of one Helen (Holly) Maddux, age thirty-one.

Holly was the woman Ira had lived with on and off since 1972. A blond Texas-born beauty, she was shy and waiflike—people who described her always seemed to light on words like *delicate* and *ethereal*. Ira had not seen her since September 1977, when, he told his friends, she went out to do some shopping at the nearby food co-op and did not return. Ira said something to this effect to the policemen invading his sanctum.

Chitwood led his crew inside. There were three men from the Philadelphia Mobile Crime Detection Unit, two police chemists, and the captain of the Homicide division. Some of the men were carrying tools—power saws, hacksaws, and crowbars. Others had photo and sketching equipment. It was quite a crowd for the small apartment.

"Can I get dressed?" Ira asked.

"Certainly," said Detective Chitwood.

It only took a few seconds for Einhorn to throw on jeans and a shirt. He was still tired from being suddenly wakened, but he prided himself on his excellent control in stressful situations. A few days later he would explain his behavior to a reporter:

> My reaction was, what is this all about. And of course, I have very good control of myself. I immediately gave myself an autohypnotic command—just ... *cool it.* Cool it and watch this as carefully as possible, which is what I did. Which to them translated into as my being nonchalant, but I was just being totally observant. Because I've been through [tough situations], I've faced guns, I've faced the whole thing. So if you don't act quickly, you can make a mess. I was not about to do anything. So I observed, literally, when they marched to the closet on the back porch.

Almost as if Chitwood had no interest in the apartment itself—though in fact he had never seen a place with so many books, and it held a strange fascination for him—he brushed aside the maroon blanket covering the French door on the north end of the apartment and opened it to the enclosed porch overlooking the backyard of 3411 Race Street. The porch was a narrow space, less than 7 feet wide, extending back 13 feet. The floor was slightly sloped. The floorboards were painted for a striped effect, every other one blue or white. There were windows on the north and west walls. On the east wall was a closet that took up a decent chunk of the porch. Chitwood had walked purposefully to that closet. Now he stopped, contemplating the thick Master padlock on the closet door.

Chitwood asked Einhorn if he had a key to the closet. Einhorn said he didn't know where the key was. "Well, I'm going to have to break it," said the detective.

"Well, you're going to have to break it," Einhorn echoed.

Mike Chitwood planned to follow strict procedure on this case.

He did not want to make a mistake that might invalidate any evidence that might later be presented in court. He also wanted to create documentary proof that his search was being carried out legally. Thus the photographers from the Mobile Crime Detection Unit. Chitwood instructed one of the crime unit men to take a picture of the locked door. *Photograph.* Then, he took a crowbar and broke the lock. Another photograph.

The closet was 4½ feet wide, 8 feet high, and a little less than 3 feet deep. There were two foot-wide shelves that were crammed with cardboard boxes, bags, shoes, and other paraphernalia. Some of the boxes were marked "Maddux." On the floor of the closet was a green suitcase. On the handle was the name "Holly Maddux" and a Texas address.

Behind the suitcase on the closet floor was a large black steamer trunk.

Chitwood began removing items from the closet, first having them photographed, then examining them and handing them back to the others for closer examination and cataloging. The boxes contained items such as kitchenware, clothing, schoolbooks, and papers. The suitcase also had women's clothing in it, and four or five letters. They were addressed to Holly Maddux, and their postmarks indicated they were more than two years old. *Photograph.* Chitwood opened a handbag he found in a box sitting on the trunk. Inside the handbag was a driver's license and social security card; they bore the name "Holly Maddux."

Photograph.

Chitwood began to notice a faint but unpleasant odor. He continued to remove boxes from the closet. Ira Einhorn, who had been shuttling between the main room and the porch while all this was going on, was now standing by the doorway again.

Chitwood thought that he could sense the fear rising in Einhorn at that point. But Ira Einhorn would claim that he was almost in a meditative state. He would say he suspected that this intrusion was somehow connected to his efforts to disseminate crucial information about highly charged subjects like psychotronic weaponry. Perhaps the police were working in concert with intelligence agencies. As a student of the Kennedy assassination, Einhorn understood that anything was possible. At a conference in Harvard last year, Einhorn and his colleagues had discussed the riskiness of their crusade.

"What we are trying to do," Ira had noted, "is change the reality structure that we're living in—*of course* the CIA is going to be after us." They must not be foolhardy, he warned, but they must continue with their work. If Ira was to be killed, so be it—but he was not going to let fear prevent him from doing what he thought was correct.

Was this search now the result? Only a few weeks before, Ira had gotten a letter from a close friend warning that the FBI was spreading rumors that he had murdered Holly. Ira would later say that the letter flashed through his mind as he stood, still groggy from exhaustion, surrounded by these strange and unfriendly men.

Michael Chitwood took off his suit jacket. He was now ready to open the trunk.

The black steamer trunk had been resting on a filthy, old, folded-up carpet that seemed jammed underneath to compensate for the slope of the porch floor. The trunk was 4½ feet long, 2½ feet wide, and 2½ feet deep. Chitwood opened the two side latches, but the hasp-type latch in the middle was locked. He asked Einhorn for the key. Again, Einhorn said he didn't have one. So Chitwood took the crowbar and broke the lock. *Photograph.* He opened the trunk. The foul odor Chitwood noticed was now much stronger. Now Chitwood was sure he knew what that odor was.

"Hey," said Mike Chitwood to one of the Mobile Crime men, "get me a pair of gloves."

Chitwood put on the clear rubber gloves and went back to the open trunk. On top were some newspapers. *Photograph.* Chitwood looked at the papers before he lifted them out. Some were from the *Philadelphia Evening Bulletin* dated September 15, 1977. Others were part of the *New York Times Book Review* of August 7, 1977. Underneath the newspapers was a layer of styrofoam packing material. It looked to Chitwood like stuff you'd find inside a pillow. He could also see some compressed plastic bags with a Sears label.

Photograph.

Chitwood moved back to the trunk. Beginning on the left-hand side of the trunk, he slowly scooped the foam aside. After three scoops, he saw something. At first he could not make out what it was, because it was so wrinkled and tough. But then he saw the shape of it—wrist, palm, and five fingers, curled and frozen in their stillness. It was a human hand, and now there was no doubt in Mike Chitwood's mind about the contents of this trunk. He dug just a little deeper following the shriveled, rawhidelike hand, down the wrist, saw an arm, still clothed in a plaid flannel shirt. And he had seen enough.

Chitwood backed away from the trunk. He removed the rubber gloves. He told one of the men to call the medical examiner. He headed to the kitchen to wash his hands. Then he turned to Ira Einhorn, who was still maintaining his studied nonchalance. "We found the body. It looks like Holly's body," he said.

"You found what you found," said the Unicorn.

In the kitchen, Chitwood noted some keys hanging from hooks on the wall. "What are these for?" he asked Einhorn. Ira said that maybe they fit the locks that Chitwood had just broken. Chitwood took them back to the porch and found that, indeed, one of the keys fit the closet padlock and another fit the trunk in the closet—the trunk where the partially mummified body, dressed in shirt and slacks, retaining its long blond hair, was found.

Detective Chitwood went back to the kitchen. Einhorn had remained there, either in shock or fear or a meditative state. "Do you want to tell me about it?" Chitwood asked.

"No."

Mike Chitwood pulled out a card and read Ira Einhorn his Miranda rights. When he got to the part about the right to remain silent, Ira Einhorn said, "Yes, I want to remain silent."

By now more people were arriving at the third-floor rear apartment of 3411 Race Street. The medical examiner, an assistant district attorney, two more homicide detectives, another technician. A private detective who earlier had been hired by Holly Maddux's family. The rear porch was becoming a beehive of activity; cameras were clicking madly, and men were preparing power tools to cut up the floorboards on the bottom of the closet. More search warrants were arriving that specified additional areas and items the police could search and confiscate. Ira Einhorn remained in a state of almost eerie languor. As police parlance has it, he presented no resistance. Perhaps in deference to his former prominence, he was not handcuffed as the policemen escorted him out into the clear spring day for the ride to the Roundhouse, where he would be booked for murder.

Stuart Samuels' route to the Penn campus took him from his Germantown home, northwest of Center City, past the zoo and through

Powelton Village, and then to Penn. The popular instructor had no classes there that day, but he was teaching an extra course at the Y downtown, and had left his notes in his office at Penn. As he drove on the Schuylkill Expressway, approaching the turnoff that would take him close to Einhorn's apartment in Powelton, his thoughts turned to the friend with whom he had dined the night before. Samuels' vision had been shaped by the sixties, as had Ira's, and he held a post that never would have existed had it not been for the reverberations from that decade's upheaval—he taught courses about movies in an Ivy League college. Both he and Ira were articulate urban Jews who, through mastery of a hip vernacular and the ability to invoke exciting ideas, had established themselves as forces in easygoing Philadelphia. In the few years he and Ira had become friendly, they found much in common; Ira became, in the words that Stuart's wife Julie would soon swear in court, "a member of our family. . . . I have two children, three cats and a dog, and Ira." But despite their common interests, Stuart's and Ira's lives were different, and in many ways, Samuels envied Ira. Samuels' life was pressured, filled with obligations. He had entanglements and hassles of multiple families and multiple jobs. In contrast, Ira Einhorn had gone all the way. No compromises. You had to hand it to Ira, Samuels mused. Other figures from the sixties had burned out, or become jokes. Ira was still growing, and in the eighties he would be even more formidable.

In the midst of these thoughts, Samuels flicked on his car radio and heard that Ira Einhorn had been arrested for murder.

What?

He pulled the car to the side of the road. The announcer shifted to other topics—after all, it was Three Mile Island day. Samuels desperately wanted to make the announcer repeat the incredible news about his friend, but of course the announcer did not do that.

It was one of the most absurd things Stuart Samuels had ever heard. Ira Einhorn? A murderer? Ira killed Holly?

It had to be a railroad job of some sort, thought Samuels. A frame-up. Maybe this Tesla stuff had caught up to him.

Three Mile Island—the biggest story of the year, possibly of the decade—was not so dominating a news event that the arrest of Ira Einhorn for murder could be kept off the front page. In Philadelphia, Ira was a cultural icon. When someone would ask, "Whatever happened to the sixties?" a common response might be, "Check out Ira Einhorn." This new development thus had an ominous resonance. Not to mention lurid details—a woman's body stuffed in a trunk, only a few feet from where the accused killer slept.

So in the *Philadelphia Daily News,* at least, Three Mile Island was squeezed to a box on the lower left-hand side of the front page. The bold headlines read HIPPIE GURU HELD IN TRUNK MURDER. The town's leading paper, the *Inquirer,* had a large story on page one—titled simply IRA EINHORN CHARGED WITH MURDER—and another story on page two. The conservative *Bulletin* had its story on the bottom of the front page.

None of the papers had much of an explanation for why Ira Einhorn had a body in his closet. Nor was there much information about the alleged victim. It was reported that she hailed from Tyler, Texas, a small city about 100 miles east of Dallas. Her father was a draftsman for the Texas Department of Highways, but some thought her independently wealthy. She was "very graceful and very beautiful," "a wanderer." She had attended Bryn Mawr, where she appeared in dance performances. After her graduation in 1971, she began a relationship with Einhorn. By some accounts it was a stormy union.

In September 1977, after the two had returned from a trip to Europe, Holly Maddux had disappeared. Police sources told reporters that Holly's parents hired private detectives to look for their missing daughter. One of the investigators, a former FBI agent, came to suspect Einhorn, especially when he talked to neighbors who complained of a strong and horrible odor coming from Einhorn's apartment. Eventually, the investigator convinced police to search the apartment.

Prominent in all the stories was the shock of those close to the accused. The *Bulletin* said it succinctly: "Those who knew Einhorn and Miss Maddux found the murder charge difficult to understand." The story quoted William G. Whitehead, a senior editor at the E. P. Dutton publishing firm and a friend of Einhorn's: "I find it very hard to believe and I don't believe it for a minute. It doesn't jibe one whit with what I've seen of this person for the last eight years."

Indeed, even the reporters suffered some dissonance in shifting the metaphor from Ira the Guru to Ira the Killer. Consider the glowing description bequeathed on the accused "trunk murderer" in the *Inquirer:*

> He was an original, the man whose mold was his own. He was, through the tumult of America in the sixties, the best-known and first social dropout in the fourth largest city. But clearly, to drop out for Einhorn was to drop in—into a multitude of causes and philosophies, of life-style alternatives and mental explorations. He did, and still does, defy identification by profession or job title. Through the years he has been known as the city's oldest hippie, a rebel, a free spirit, a social philosopher, a guru, a teacher, a counterculture poet, ladies' man extraordinaire, a freeloader, a writer, a lecturer, and none of the above.

But never as a murderer. Of all the people in the City of Brotherly Love, Ira Einhorn had been the one most closely associated with nonviolence, conciliation, pacifism, and the Love Generation. Was it really plausible that he would commit such a brutal act? And compound the deed with the Gothic touch of retaining the corpse? It just didn't jibe.

Ira Einhorn later noted the incongruity himself: Only weeks after he was a guest of the crown prince of Iran, he was now a guest of the Philadelphia Police Department.

On Wednesday, the police had taken him from 3411 Race Street to police headquarters, a building called the Roundhouse. They searched him, and left him in a room, where for the first time he had time to read the long search warrant. Then he was formally booked and fingerprinted. He again exercised his right to remain silent.

Einhorn spent the next few hours in the holding block, while police technicians periodically visited him to take samples of his blood, scalp hair, facial hair, and pubic hair. It was almost eleven at night before he was driven to the City Detention Center, where prisoners spend the limbo between charge and disposition.

He later described the place as a "noisy, black-filled cyclone." His fellow inmates were aware of the publicity his case had aroused, and when they saw him they would shout, "Here comes the trunk man!" But Einhorn did not sulk in this dismal purgatory. After the first day, he was moved to the psychiatric ward, where he was asked by the prison "block captains" if he would teach them some meditation techniques. Soon, he was teaching not only meditation but some grammar and arithmetic to the inmates.

He fasted most of the time he was in the detention center to help him maintain control over his environment.

He did not suffer any physical brutality. At 227 pounds, he was a formidable man. Also, the notoriety provided by the voluminous press coverage bequeathed him status. As Einhorn later said, "The more publicity, the better I seemed to be treated there, among the inmates, too. To be written about in the newspaper means you're important. [The inmates] make you a hero."

Ira Einhorn was not satisfied to sit by silently while he was being discussed and dissected in the papers. He had his own side of the story to tell, and he thought it would help him. Ira Einhorn had enjoyed good luck with the media in the past, and now he turned to it again, in his time of need.

A reporter for the *Inquirer,* Howard Shapiro, had been sitting in the City Room earlier that Friday when an editor, hoping to get more mileage out of the Einhorn story, suggested he go to the detention center to see if Einhorn would talk. Shapiro headed to the prison. Though there usually were no visitors permitted in the detention center, Shapiro told officials that as a reporter he had a right to see an inmate. They agreed that if the prisoner wanted to, it would be all right. Somewhat to Shapiro's surprise, Einhorn said it was all right.

A guard led Shapiro back to a small cubicle, where Einhorn sat on a straightback wooden chair. The reporter was somewhat worried about whether Einhorn had spoken with his lawyer about being interviewed. Ira had not, but he felt enough in control to do the interview. He said that in order to protect himself, there were certain things he could not say—in particular, the identity of those who had "set him up." But he did want one thing on the record.

"I have been outspoken all my life, but never have I been violent," Ira said. "I want to be very direct about this. *I did not kill whoever was supposed to be in there.* I am not a killer. I do not know if a body got in there—if it was a body."

He was apparently unaware that in the previous day, medical examiner Halbert Fillinger had confirmed the partially mummified body found in the trunk to be Holly Maddux's.

Then Ira Einhorn said a few things that demonstrate why defense lawyers advise clients not to speak on the record. He praised the police for conducting an "absolutely meritorious" search. "Everything was done properly," he stated. (Later his lawyer would try to get the search voided due to technicalities.) He described the search, commenting that the trunk in which the body was found "was mine. I bought the trunk a couple of years ago." This was something that the prosecution otherwise might have had to verify itself. It is no wonder that Shapiro felt compelled to remind Einhorn a couple of times that he was speaking on the record. But Ira apparently felt confident that he was clever enough to handle the press without harming his legal status.

He explained that he and Holly were fighting when they returned, separately, from a European trip in the summer of 1977. Holly was in New York for a few weeks, seeing another man. She returned to Philadelphia, to 3411 Race. One day she went out on an errand and did not return. Not long afterward, Einhorn said she phoned him and told him to leave her alone, that she wanted to "live her own life." Ira agreed, vowing to himself that he would "keep my eyes and ears open in case she needs help." But he heard or saw nothing of Holly, ever again.

Since Holly had been planning to move out anyway, Einhorn thought Holly's silence was part of a decision to break away, not only from him but also from all her attachments. Ira described himself as very upset by her decision. When Holly's mother called him asking where her daughter was, Ira said, it was Mrs. Maddux who told him, "Holly's a grown-up, and she can take care of herself." Ira finally decided to respect Holly's wishes not to be contacted. That is why he refused to cooperate with the private detective who was attempting to locate Holly.

To the *Inquirer* reporter, Ira Einhorn professed to still love Holly Maddux.

That same day, Ira entertained another guest in the tiny cubicle: *Bulletin* columnist Claude Lewis. He and Ira were well acquainted. One of the few black voices granted prominence in the conservative newspaper, Lewis had long been an admirer of Einhorn's buoyant joie di vivre. Ira Einhorn, he felt, was not a guy you confined to a cell. The journalist was obviously at a loss to explain his friend's current situation, and his puzzlement was reflected in the subsequent article.

"He had always been a free spirit, a man who loved whole populations and who taught others to appreciate the Sun," wrote Lewis. "Close friends say he never displayed a dark side. He was a graceful, loving, human being who regarded peace as 'the ultimate weapon.' . . . Not one person I spoke with ever dreamed that he might resort to violence, certainly not murder and months of deceit, hiding a woman's body in his closet."

Yet the body of Holly Maddux *had* been found in the closet. In light of that fact, Lewis admitted serious doubts about Ira's claims of innocence. Ira threw these doubts back at him. "*You know me,*" he said. "You know I could not harm anyone."

Einhorn admitted to Lewis that he did hit Holly. Once. On the other hand, Holly hit *him* many more times. "We loved very hard, very deeply," he explained. "We were two intense people."

Ira seemed optimistic about the outcome.

"This is a time of testing," Ira told Claude Lewis. "I try to learn from every situation. Now I'm going to see if my friends believe in me. I think they do. I know that many people will help. I know that many will refuse to believe what's being said. These people know *me*. They'll stand by me. I'm sure of it."

The test of whether people would stand by Ira Einhorn would occur on Tuesday, April 3, at the hearing to determine Einhorn's bail. By then Ira had secured an attorney. Ira originally thought he would use Bernard Segal, an expert criminal lawyer who before moving to California had been one of Philadelphia's best-known attorneys. (Segal was more recently known for his futile defense of the Green Beret doctor Jeffrey McDonald who murdered his family.) Ira had used Segal years before, once to help him beat a bogus drug bust, and later to successfully squelch a challenge to the validity of Einhorn's nominating petition for his mayoral run. But by the time of his bail hearing, he had a different lead counsel, an even more powerful courtroom figure. Arlen Specter.

Specter was in some ways an unusual choice for Ira Einhorn. Specter was a member of the Republican establishment. His political career had temporarily peaked at two terms as Philadelphia's district attorney, followed by ill-fated runs for mayor and governor. Within months, though, he would successfully run for the U.S. Senate. His national profile was enhanced or sullied—depending on where you stood on this matter—by his participation in the Warren Commission. Specter was the strategist who conceived the controversial "single-bullet" theory that used Jesuitical contortions to explain how a single assassin killed John F. Kennedy.

Ira's dealings with Specter had been spotty in the past. For years, Einhorn considered himself in the vanguard of the criticisms of the Warren Commission and held particular contempt for the single-bullet theory. In an article Einhorn wrote for *Philadelphia Magazine* in 1970, when Specter ran to retain the DA's office, Einhorn analyzed the astrological charts of the two opponents, and though he conceded that the stars favored Specter (the stars were right), he thought the Democrat a preferable candidate. The problem with Specter, Ira wrote, was his undeveloped Scorpio.

The stars aside, Ira's problem was immediate. So when a mutual friend of Einhorn's and Specter's suggested that she should bring the two together, Ira discarded concerns of single bullets and astrology. Having the somber, sharp-tongued former district attorney on his side was a very big plus for Einhorn's defense.

Arlen Specter's first objective was to secure a low bail for his client. The procedure in bail hearings was not to present details of the alleged crime but to determine whether the suspect should be freed pending trial. The defense attorney presents witnesses who will attest to the reliability of the accused and the accused's strong bonds to the community. The more prominent the witness, and the closer the witness is to the accused, the more weight his or her testimony will have on the judge who sets or refuses bail. Would the gravity of a first-degree murder charge lead Einhorn's friends to abandon him?

Not according to the list of character witnesses who appeared on April 3, 1979.

Perhaps the encouraging show of support from his friends contributed to what seemed extraordinary composure on Ira Einhorn's part. A reporter noted that Einhorn, led into the courtroom in shackles, "frequently smiled at the audience and showed strong interest in the proceedings but no emotion."

The first witness was Stephen J. Harmelin, a lawyer who was partner in the prestigious Dilworth, Kalish and Paxton firm. Specter elicited the information that Harmelin had known Einhorn since high school, and Harmelin was the first of many who would use the word *excellent* in describing Ira Einhorn's character and reputation.

Cross-examination of the witnesses was handled by Joseph Murray, the assistant district attorney who had monitored the case during the six weeks it had been developed by the police. Joe Murray was a strict by-the-book man who came from a family long involved in law enforcement. His uncle and three brothers were FBI men. He had been with the district attorney's office since his graduation from Notre Dame Law School in 1972 and was the youngest man ever to be appointed chief homicide prosecutor in Philadelphia. Murray's job here was to find indications that Einhorn, faced with the possibility of a long incarceration, might be tempted to skip any bail that was set.

"What does he do for a living?" Murray asked Harmelin of his friend. The complement of reporters in the room in particular were eager to hear the answer to *that* question. For years, just what Ira Einhorn did for a living had been a matter of lively speculation.

"My understanding is that he acts as a consultant for various institutions in Philadelphia."

"Like what?"

"My recollection is that he was doing some consulting work for the Bell Telephone Company. Mr. Einhorn seemed to be able to bring to the attention of corporate executives a kind of broad spectrum of information to which they otherwise wouldn't generally have available to them."

"Like what?"

And so it went. After Stuart Samuels gave his testimonial, Edward Mahler took the stand. A vice-president of personnel relations at Bell Telephone, where he had worked for twenty-nine years, Mahler was a lanky, short-haired executive with a WASP-y look of corporate confidence. Specter had the telephone company executive explain his relationship to the accused murderer.

"We wish to be responsive to the needs of the community. In that context I was introduced by a friend to Ira, and we started our relationship. I became, as it were, the [telephone company] contact with Mr. Einhorn. I think I would dare to say we would meet two to three times a month. . . . We talk fundamentally about things related to the community. . . . I would discuss with him things we were proposing, and he would respond to them. Then we'd talk, of course, about myriad things that had nothing to do with the telephone company."

"And did Mr. Einhorn have contacts with other key executives at Bell Telephone?"

"Yes, he did from time to time."

"Such as?"

"Such as our president and former president."

Joe Murray wanted some more detail on the unusual union between Ira Einhorn and the telephone company. He asked how much Einhorn was paid for his Bell consultancy.

"Nothing in cash," said Mahler.

"What? In check?"

"No, nothing. Nothing like that. No money changes hands."

At that point, the judge could not contain his curiosity. Judge William M. Marutani was a respected jurist whose name often tempted low-level Italian crooks to angle their way into his courtroom: They were always startled to see a gentle man of Japanese extraction who considered himself a hardliner on criminals. After acknowledging the unorthodoxy of what he was about to do and inviting either counsel to object if he wished, Marutani addressed the witness directly.

"Do I understand, Mr. Mahler, that you meet Mr. Einhorn, say, two or three times a month?"

"Yes."

"And what would these be, you would happen to bump into each other?" said the judge. He still didn't get it.

"No, no, no," said Mahler. "Excuse me, Your Honor. . . . Ira represented a group in the community that we did not hear from. Where it seemed to us he could represent their point of view. It was not one we could [otherwise] be aware of. . . . And at least that was the reason for maintaining regular contact."

Judge Marutani *still* didn't get it. "Was this a public relations venture by Bell Telephone?" he wanted to know. By now, the judge felt compelled to confirm to counsel that the line of questioning from the bench had journeyed far afield. "I'm just kind of curious," he explained.

Mahler answered. "Oh, OK, community relations, Judge."

It apparently began to dawn on Marutani that *the telephone company actually took Einhorn seriously.* It had an arrangement with him.

It *learned* from him. "And Bell Telephone," the judge asked, "with all its wealth, never gave him a dime?"

"No sir, no sir. We did do one thing for him. I feel I should mention it to explain in part what went on. It seems that Ira represented the people in the community, like the professor you heard, the lawyer, the physicist, the futurist, and so on. [We] would reproduce articles that Ira would find, or others would find, and mail them to members of the group. . . . It was a service we performed, you could say, for Ira. He was very appreciative of it. But again, it was in line with our communicating with this broader network, Judge."

The judge had one more question. "What would be in it for people such as Ira to go to all this trouble?"

Ed Mahler did not have an easy answer to that question. No, it was not money or any such motive that led Ira to set up his unique operation. Ira operated on a different kind of value system. He worked, without pay, for Planet Earth. That's the kind of guy he was. How do you describe this in court? "This is what seemed to be happening" was all Ed Mahler managed to say, and he was excused.

And the parade of testimonials continued.

Joe Murray seldom had been faced with such an array of character witnesses on behalf of a murder suspect. In his plea for high bond, he chose to emphasize the charge against Einhorn and the possibility of flight. "This is a very serious case," he said. "A case that indicates planning, intention, all the earmarks of a very serious first-degree murder case." He pointed out that Einhorn's extensive travels over the years, and his access to money, might indicate that he might possibly flee before his trial. Then he asked Judge Marutani to set bail at $100,000. Considering that in Pennsylvania only 10 percent of bail need be posted, this did not seem unreasonable in light of the charges.

Specter objected, calling the amount excessive, especially considering that the State had no direct evidence whatsoever that Ira Einhorn had killed Holly Maddux.

Judge Marutani had a little problem with the claim that no evidence existed. "Isn't it a little unusual to have a dead body . . . in a trunk in one's own residence? Doesn't that raise some eyebrows? . . . Remember, I am not determining his guilt—indeed, I want to be candid with you. I think the *Inquirer* quoted him as saying he was framed. He well may have been as far as I am concerned. I mean, he's not in his apartment twenty-four hours a day and somebody . . . who knows, strange things happen in life. . . . [But] you know, I wouldn't want somebody to find *my* wife's body in a trunk in my home, particularly if I lived alone. I think I'd be in hot water."

Specter objected vociferously. He cited a few legal precedents dictating that bail should not be determined by the violence of the crime or the likelihood of conviction. He explained that Einhorn was not rich, and what money he could generate for his defense would have to be divided carefully between bail and investigation and counsel fees. "This is going to be a complicated case to investigate in terms of scientific tests . . . it's going to be a very, very expensive case to investigate." He argued that Ira Einhorn, on the basis of who he was and his extraordinary accomplishments, was entitled to "a great many presumptions." Taking all that into account, a reasonable bail would be, Specter said, $5,000.

Judge Marutani was ready to make his ruling. He said that despite Specter's claims, he was troubled by the possible likelihood of conviction. "It's not a good picture as we all I'm sure can easily recognize," said the judge. "And if it's not a good picture, the possible penalty may very well be life." The judge also noted that Einhorn was a sophisticated traveler who, if tempted to flee, would certainly know how to do so. On the other hand, the judge considered that the crime Einhorn was charged with was, after all, a so-called crime of passion, and this fact (not to mention the glowing testimonials given under oath that day) meant that freeing the accused on bond did not present a threat to the community.

"Balancing all the factors," said the judge, "the court hereby grants forty thousand dollars bail."

The $4,000 cash required to post bond was, according to Ira's friends and family, provided by another prominent Einhorn supporter, Barbara Bronfman, wife of Seagram Liquor heir Charles Bronfman. Ira's parents assumed liability for the remaining $36,000. The Unicorn was free.

What Einhorn himself called "a condition of mystery" was more cloudy than ever. Those who knew Ira Einhorn, and even those who had followed his career from afar and identified him with the pro-Earth causes he promoted, wanted very much to believe that Ira was innocent as claimed. In the months ahead Ira was to look many people in the face and say, "*I did not kill Holly*." His deep blue eyes, intense even in less stressful circumstances, would engage his doubters steadily. And for that moment, at least, they would not be doubters.

But if Ira didn't kill Holly Maddux, who did? How did her body wind up in his apartment? Einhorn had told the *Inquirer* that his work "skirted the edges of national defense." Could this be, as Ira seemed to imply, a scandalous covert act by intelligence agents? As Judge Marutani admitted, "strange things happen in life." Could they be *that* strange?

Any way you looked at the situation, no answer was satisfying. If you concluded that Ira did murder Holly, then you also had to assume that for a full year and a half, Ira Einhorn made no effort to dispose of the evidence that would ultimately indict him. You would also have to assume that Ira Einhorn was nothing like the person he seemed to be.

If Ira Einhorn killed Holly Maddux, how could so many people have been so wrong about him? What had their relationship really been like? Was there another Ira Einhorn that no one really knew?

And why did no one seem to know who Holly Maddux really was?

Since Ira had been so closely identified with the idealistic sixties, and then had done so much in helping to establish what was known as the New Age Movement in the next decade, the stakes were high in asking these questions. To seek their answers would require regurgitating the history of an era, from not one but two perspectives: that of Ira Einhorn, a leader and improviser in those times, and that of Holly Maddux, who seemed to many no more substantial than a tender leaf blown by the wind currents of change.

If there were answers to be found, if mystery were to be dispelled, one would have to start from the beginning.

2

THE MAKING OF THE GURU

"Oh the sheer joy of the mind on the wing as it roams throughout all of knowledge. I'm up in the air on that pure world of intellectual speculation where one calmly surveys the entire realm of human knowledge and slowly fits it together. All seems possible—nothing is too difficult when I occupy this rarefied atmosphere—I exalt in the expectation of my future dreams as I encompass all I touch. In these moments when one reads Chinese like a native, zips through the quantum theory without a pencil, and explains Wittgenstein to his dog, the mind seems to be an entity that is able to digest data faster than an electronic computer."

Or so Ira Einhorn wrote in an October 1963 letter. At age twenty-three, Ira Einhorn was spinning off into a self-imagined world. It was a world based on literature, philosophy, psychology, sex, drugs, and intense personal encounters. He had one foot in graduate school and the well-worn tradition of romantic scholarship implied by that, but his other foot had already stuck itself quite firmly in the door that led to the mind-shattering changes that the sixties would bring.

He was preparing himself for a major role in that era, testing his powers, seeing how far he could stretch from convention. He raced on all his cylinders, high on pot or hashish sometimes, but overall, simply drunk on his own thought.

Ira Einhorn was living then in the Powelton Village section of Philadelphia, already known as one of the characters in the neighborhood. He was matriculating toward a graduate degree in folklore at the University of Pennsylvania, and his load was heavy. He was taking a seminar on the works of Walter Pater, taught by a Penn professor he considered his mentor. He had several courses in language—Old Norse, Middle High German—and a tutorial in Sanskrit. His linguistics course required retention of about two hundred pages a week of dense material. But his very being rebelled against what he considered the sterility of academia. And despite working on a mammoth novel that he hoped would blow the lid off American literature, he was losing interest in creative writing as his main pursuit. He realized even then that his lifelong work would not be so easily summarized as "teacher" or "writer" or "scholar."

"I've been wandering of late along paths that have never felt my footprints before . . . a quiet waiting has pervaded over my entire being. I'm going through a radical change—to and from I know not, but who does," he wrote.

And not long afterward he came to his conclusion. He attributed it to a marijuana-inspired epiphany on Christmas Eve in 1963. He described the experience as completely reordering his world, as aging him years in the space of hours, and deepening his understanding of where he stood in the universe.

"I feel no desire," he proclaimed, "to be anything but Ira—fully realized in whatever manner possible."

Thus was a bright lower-middle-class Jewish kid from Philadelphia transformed to a guru, and the odyssey begun that would end with the opening of a trunk sixteen years later.

"One's life history is only understood in retrospect," said the Unicorn in an interview he gave in London during the summer of 1977. He was trying to impart to his interviewer a sense of where he came from. Toward that end, he made some cursory remarks about his neighborhood. He did not mention his first influence, who would be his earliest, best, and to this day his most loyal supporter.

That would be Beatrice Einhorn. She is a small, shrewd woman with vibrant eyes and a cutting voice that often crows with exuberance when she speaks of her firstborn. As Bea Nissenson, she grew up in North Philadelphia, an area of row homes that is now the city's most notorious ghetto. In the 1920s, however, it was one of Philadelphia's several bustling Jewish neighborhoods, though soon thereafter migration began to the more northerly areas of the city.

. Bea Nissenson's family had been in the United States for two generations. Her mother had been born in Philadelphia; as a young girl, Bea's mother worked at the fancy Wanamaker's store downtown. Her father worked in what people delicately called "the installment business." He would sell a family a piece of furniture, a washing machine, a watch—any item necessary or desirable for people of humble means, but too dear to buy without credit. The cost was a down payment to the installment man and a weekly sum for so many weeks thereafter. Including interest, the total paid would be considerably more than the original price. Installment men earned their money, collecting their fees in person; often they were not welcome visitors. Bea Nissenson's father did very well at his work and was able to support his family handsomely.

Living only a few blocks away in that neighborhood of tenements was Joseph Einhorn. His father had immigrated from Russia as a boy, in the first few years of the young century. Gilbert Einhorn ran a produce store, and young Joseph followed him into the fruit business. Joe Einhorn was a friend of one of Bea Nissenson's cousins, and the two met casually when Bea was only fifteen. Nothing came of the meeting, but a few years later, in the early 1930s, they met again. Bea Nissenson was impressed with the young man's gentleness. Recalling what attracted her to him, she uses a single word: sweet. "It's a terrible thing to say, but that's what he was, he was a nice sweet person," she says. The courtship lasted about a year. They married in 1935.

It was a complementary union. Joe was quiet and sincere; Bea was gregarious and ambitious. And very canny. She worked, in those Depression days, for the staid firm of Dun and Bradstreet, tied closely to the WASP establishment. She suspects that her ethnically neutral maiden name was a factor in her employment. Beginning as a typist, she came to be responsible for reporting and writing the financial "D&B" reports that are the backbone of that company. Eventually, she became head of her department. As for her husband, soon after the marriage she decided that the fruit business would not do. Aware of her own father's success in the installment business, she chose that field for her mate. Dresses, rings, anything that anybody would buy. Many items were from stock—Joe Einhorn may have had 100 boxes of silverware or 50 dresses on hand at a given time—and for bigger-ticket items he would accompany the buyer to the wholesaler and carry his customer. Despite the Depression, the Einhorns never were without a meal, and they had an apartment of their own, in a nicer neighborhood named after the bustling intersection of Broad and Olney, where the subway and trolley lines met.

There were certain things taken for granted in that culture. The Old Country and its anti-Semitism was more than a distant memory; the community was both insular in its Jewishness and proud to be part of the country that had allowed them escape. There was a determination to rise and succeed in this country. For most, this was achieved by two paths. For themselves, they would work hard and earn enough to better their lots. But the ultimate gains would come from the next generation, who would benefit from their efforts. The love and hopes devoted to this new generation were fierce indeed.

On May 15, 1940, after five years of marriage, Bea and Joseph Einhorn began their family. Bea left her job to take care of the infant, whom they named Ira. When the country went to war, Joseph Einhorn, who suffered an ulcer condition, was awarded a deferment. But he lost his business and was assigned to work in the shipyard. The job was too difficult for his fragile health and he managed to get transferred to defense-related work that suited him better—driving a cab. He loved cars and could even diagnose an auto problem by simply listening to the car as he drove. After the war, he would sell used cars, storing them in a lot and selling them from home. Bea would keep the books.

Bea Einhorn was irrevocably smitten with Ira Samuel Einhorn from the instant she laid eyes on him. "Everybody loved him," his mother asserts. "He was the most beloved child." Four years after Ira, the Einhorns bore another son; this second child was not as robust as his older brother. Family friends recall Stephen suffering various ailments throughout his childhood. Whether or not this had anything to do with Stephen's inheritance of a supporting role in the family drama is anyone's guess. It was obvious that the star of the family was young Ira.

It was Bea Einhorn, not her husband, who took charge of the children, not only in the daily duties but in what discipline had to be meted out. "He was too easy with them; if they had to be disciplined it came from me," she says.

But Bea Einhorn was less likely to mete out punishment to her firstborn than to bestow praise. The bond between son and mother was strong, and she imagined the powerful positive impact of that budding genius on the world at large. Even forty years after Ira Einhorn's childhood, Bea Einhorn's amazement of her offspring's brilliance has lost none of its luster. This faith was a significant factor in building the child's ego.

"My mother lavished a tremendous amount of attention on me before I started school," Ira claimed once in an interview. "She fed my curiosity and was teaching me at the third-grade level before I went to kindergarten at five. Aside from giving me a strong ego, this tutoring just made me a freak in my milieu when I entered school."

"He read incessantly," says his mother with pride, making it clear that the habit was acquired with her encouragement. "He'd come to dinner, a book would be in his hand. He'd go on his vacation, he'd take so many books, you wouldn't know what would be up. I don't think he slept more than three, four hours a night, *ever*. Five would be the top. I would get up in the morning to call him, and he would be reading."

It was obvious, to Bea Einhorn at least, that this was no ordinary bright child. For proof, she refers to the bridge incident. Mrs. Einhorn was an expert bridge player and young Ira would often watch her play. One day, when Ira was about ten or eleven years old, he picked up the thick Charles Goren book on bridge and sat down with it, underlining sections carefully. Finally, he made his announcement. "Mom, I'm ready to play bridge."

"You're kidding," said his mother.

"Try me."

She did. It turned out he was skilled enough to hold his own with Mrs. Einhorn's friends. In fact, they found him a desirable partner. They would call up Beatrice and ask, "Is Ira home? We want to play bridge with Ira."

Ira's precociousness, however, had its price. The boy was a behavior problem in school. "I was always bored," said Ira in that same interview. "The school wanted to skip me about three years from the beginning but my father [worried about the social consequences] wouldn't let them. I had to remain in a regular school, held back to my age level, where I could learn absolutely nothing. It was so excruciating that I threw up my breakfast every morning before starting to school."

Once in school, Ira's restlessness would be disruptive. He would yell out in class, get out of his seat, and wander. His report cards reflected the problem quite specifically. For his subject grades, there was a line of O's for outstanding. But his marks for conduct were always P for poor.

The problem was mitigated when the Einhorns moved to a newer neighborhood that required a transfer to a different elementary school. Mrs. Einhorn says she received a call within an hour after Ira's arrival at the new school. Wondering what Ira could have done so soon to cause trouble, she rushed over. The principal had Ira's report card in her hand. In front of Mrs. Einhorn, she admonished the ten-year-old that even if he was as bright as the report card indicated, there would be no outstandings in his record if they were accompanied by poor behavior. It was an indication that this woman understood the problem, and Ira's mother noted with satisfaction that this new school, even if it did not challenge his mind as thoroughly as possible, made an effort to keep him busy. "They realized what they had in his mentality," she explains.

In 1950, the Einhorns moved again, this time to West Oak Lane, in the northwest part of the city. Their house was a two-story stone row home on the edge of the area's previous development from the south and east. It was on the 1700 block of Wynsam Street, a quiet one-way corridor with parking on each curbside and room for one lane of traffic. The house was two streets from a large cemetery and several blocks from shopping on relatively busy Stenton Avenue.

It was a predominantly Jewish neighborhood, populated largely by young families moving out of the more urban areas—the old neighborhoods—which were unsentimentally ceded to black people. The houses were new and the sky was closer to the ground; there were no buildings of four stories or more. If there was a distressing homogenization, no one seemed to regard it as problematic. No lamentations that the corner luncheonette and grocery store had been replaced by the druggist and butcher shop on strip-shopping streets several blocks away, and the supermarket with its vast parking lot. Residents viewed West Oak Lane as a step to the good life. Across the city limits, less than a mile away, the *better* life existed: the suburbs, with their ranch houses, schools of legendary quality, and freedom from the Philadelphia wage tax. But that was for the lawyers and doctors and more successful merchants. West Oak Lane was for the workers, who assumed their progeny would make it to the suburbs.

Toward that end, education was a mania. Though the majority of the new home owners in the neighborhood were not college graduates—the Einhorns among that majority—almost all of their children would be. By the time the last of that generation received its degrees, the neighborhood would have self-destructed, vacated by an exodus of white Jewish families panicking at the first wave of racial integration. A neighborhood legacy or a set of traditions never formed: West Oak Lane was literally a jumping-off spot, a base camp for the upwardly mobile climb. Ira Einhorn grew up in a characterless, temporary neighborhood.

When a West Oak Lane boy reached high school age, he generally had two options. One was Germantown High, a racially mixed coed school with a full range of courses, from academic to vocational. The other, available only to those who achieved top grades in junior high and had high scores in standardized intelligence tests, was Central High. This was a college preparatory, male-only school that drew the city's best students. There was considerable pressure to "make Central," which was seen as the gateway to college. Ira made it without any trouble: His grades were excellent and his IQ, according to his mother, was "genius level." (Einhorn later professed not to know the exact score but said it was "upwards of 140.")

As Ira Einhorn's friends recall him, by the time he entered Central High School, he was already a distinctive figure.

One of his close childhood friends, Ted Fink, recalls Ira as an astonishingly independent thinker for a young teenager in the 1950s. This sometimes emerged in odd ways; for example, Ira was the first one in the neighborhood to wear Bermuda shorts. Nothing startling in itself but impressive when one considers the little tolerance teenage boys have for unique modes of attire. With his scrawny legs, Ira in shorts was a particularly vulnerable target, yet his ego was so strong, he dared dress for his own comfort.

West Oak Lane was not Greenwich Village by any stretch of the imagination. But Ira, seemingly in sync with the Beat Era, had somehow discovered that rambling form of poetics. Fink recalls him even at thirteen involved with incessant wordplay. Rhyming, trying out strange words, seeing how they fit.

"I would say, 'What the hell are you doing?' And he would say, 'I'm practicing.' And he was," recalls Ted Fink. "His flow of language was exquisite. He could mesmerize people through language. He had the most incredible vocabulary that ever came down the pike. Ira could talk constantly, without hesitation, without pause."

In school itself, Ira used his time disruptively, challenging his instructors, breaking up assemblies with loud behavior, and supplying dada responses to standardized test queries. But he got good grades, probably because he was able to apply the fruits of voluminous reading to his course work. His aptitude for science and math was particularly high, and his parents assumed he would eventually make his mark in that field. But he read *everything*.

"Ira was really a force to be reckoned with," says Mel Richter, a classmate who met Einhorn during their first week at Central. "He would attempt to be dominant in conversations, yet when he was in the presence of somebody whom he knew to have more knowledge than he, he would listen intently and respectfully, and find out where it was that they got that information."

Then he would seek it out. To place his own mark on the information, he would annotate the books, or jot down significant points in the journals he kept. "It was part of this image Ira had of himself, as not being a straight, conventional suburban kid of the 1950s, but being a member of the European, intellectual, philosophic movement," says Richter.

Mel Richter recalls visiting Einhorn at home in those days. As often as not, Mrs. Einhorn would direct him to the bathroom. There he would find Ira, sitting in the tub, an open book in front of him, and his notebooks by his side. To Richter, it was bizarre, like that painting *The Death of Marat*. But Ira was oblivious to his visitor's discomfort. He'd want to discuss what he'd been reading, be it Spengler, Thucydides, or the *Principia Mathmaticus*.

According to Richter, Ira responded to book club advertisements in the back pages of *Harper's* and *The Atlantic*, sending away for comprehensive collections of philosophy, history, and mathematics. Richter would ask him how the hell he was going to pay for them. "Don't worry! They're not going to get me—I'm a minor," Ira would reply. "If they're dumb enough to send it to me, they're not going to prosecute me."

"It was like Robin Hood," says Richter. "Everything was for a good cause—to aid and abet the intellectual development of Ira. He saw the world around him as supporting him as he grew, and in return he would feed it back. If he 'took' a little bit, that was really part of his bargain with the universe."

Ira Einhorn's activities were not limited to the mental plane. By virtue of his own determination, he was a striking physical figure. For reasons unclear—perhaps to compensate for his shortness and his being a year younger than his classmates—Ira spent the summer before tenth grade methodically building himself up and solidifying his gains by weight-lifting workouts. Ted Fink explains that "he was kind of a scrawny kid, and then he went away for the summer, and did, like, one hundred pushups every ten minutes. He became almost a *hulk*. An incredible upper body. He became a very powerful guy in the area. And became very macho because of it."

No one recalls Ira Einhorn starting fights, but when fights occurred he would not shy away. There are several tales told by his friends in which Ira was among a group of Jewish boys overmatched by tough gentiles. The common thread running through these stories had Ira emerging as one of the few who stood up to the goys, and if he did not emerge victorious on every occasion, at least he gave it to them good.

This machismo sometimes displayed itself in troubling fashion. Fink remembers one occasion at a hangout called Littleton's Diner. *"Nothing can hurt me,"* Ira Einhorn was boasting. *"If I don't want to feel something I don't have to."*

Ira's friends scoffed at that. "If I put this cigarette on your hand, you'd feel pain," Fink said. Ira insisted that he would not. So Fink took the cigarette and squashed it on the back of Ira Einhorn's hand. Ira held the hand steady. Not a word.

Einhorn even went out for the football team. He first played a year for the junior varsity and eventually made varsity. He was a reliable halfback, known more for his aggressive style than polished gridiron skills. The high point of his career came in a 1956 game against West Philadelphia, won by Central by a score of 6–0. The lone touchdown came on a 65-yard drive, 30 yards of which were gained on a pass reception by Ira. According to the Philadelphia *Bulletin*, "Einhorn bagged the pass while going at full speed on the forty and made the thirty-five before he was overhauled."

He *looked* like a football player: stocky, with ruddy facial features (marred by adolescent acne) and a square-top crewcut. Only his smallish, bony legs belied the image. Yet he was sturdy enough, despite a slight asthma, to run cross country, and lithe enough to become a wizard at Ping-Pong, captain of the Central team.

By his senior year, he embodied many contradictions. Jock and intellectual. Poet and scientist. Rebel and middle-class Jew. But as he later explained it, it was not until that year, at age sixteen, that he began to deeply absorb his voluminous readings and act upon them. It was as if he had taken a decisive step toward being different. He had always been ahead of his peers on certain matters, but now he asserted his forward thinking with more of a sense of panache and risk. He had his first experience with marijuana, a rare substance in Central High School in 1956. By the time he graduated in 1957, he was a strange mix of outsider and achiever. He'd won two letters and a scholarship to the University of Pennsylvania. But he refused to let his picture appear in the high school yearbook, and did not, as almost all his classmates did, buy a class ring. He told his mother it wasn't worth the money. He had a similar indifference to attending the senior prom, an event that in any case conflicted with his brother's bar mitzvah. But as the family reception wound down, Ira told his mother that he and his date for the affair would go to the prom after all. But before he went to his prom, he went home to change out of the tuxedo he'd worn for the bar mitzvah, and into a shirt and jeans. His appearance in that state created such a stir, his mother recalls, that Central threatened not to graduate him. But a sympathetic English teacher intervened, and all was well. Bea Einhorn can still recite the words of the teacher to her, repeating them like a mantra: "I ought to wring that boy's neck," the teacher said, "but I cannot deny the world Ira."

By the time Einhorn entered the University of Pennsylvania in the fall of 1957, he had, according to his friend Mel Richter, "already declared a certain type of open warfare against conventionality." Ira Einhorn's style of combat was indeed public, almost exhibitionistic. Yet it was not a mean-spirited form of war. Then, as later, Einhorn managed to extend a hand to the Establishment even as he railed against it. So while he may well have been one of the most ferociously independent-minded freshmen the university had ever seen, he also pledged one of the most prestigious fraternities. After successfully completing Hell Week, though, Ira concluded that the level of discourse and imagination in the house was beneath his attention, and he left to follow his own path in college.

Ira's university education was almost entirely self-directed. He disdained the idea that one could best learn by dutifully attending classes and regurgitating the instructor's pet theories at test time. Instead, he increased his personal reading. "In order to read tangentially, he wouldn't go to classes and he was not willing to fulfill all the minutiae of a class," says Richter, who entered Penn with Einhorn. "For instance, if you had a reading list for a course, and there were ten books you had to read, along with a hundred suggested supplemental readings, Ira would read the hundred suggested readings before he'd read the ten required books."

Football was forgotten by now. When a friend asked him why he didn't go out for the team, he said he didn't need it any longer. The gridiron battles were replaced by intellectual athletics. Ira would challenge teachers, citing obscure works that contradicted their premises. Did you read *this?* Ira would ask. Did you read *this,* and *this,* and *this?* The same reckless glee that allowed him to break through the line as an undersized halfback now propelled him to classroom destruction.

But his classroom appearances were rare. Ira himself later explained this in a 1977 interview: "I didn't like what was going on in classes, so I went to very few classes. I was pretty determined to get a basis of knowledge before I did anything, so I spent a great deal of my time traveling and seeing people and reading."

There was one teacher, though, who not only compelled his attendance but provided unlimited fuel for the intellectual fires raging inside Ira Einhorn. His name was Morse Peckham.

Peckham was simultaneously the prize and the pariah of Penn's English department. He stood as an embodiment of scholarship, a throwback to the era before specialization, when a professor's breadth of knowledge was expected to extend not only through history but across disciplines.

For Peckham, the life of the mind was the only life. This had been the case since childhood. He has described his parents as imbued in nineteenth-century culture; his mother read Tennyson to him before his naps. At ten, he was using chess pieces to emulate the stage movements of Shakespeare's characters. He was the first University of Rochester student to take graduate English work at Princeton, where he earned a doctorate, but not before serving in World War II, where he spent his European tour writing the official history of the Ninth Bomber Command.

At Penn, Peckham cut an imposing figure—he was a large man, more than six feet tall, with fine features and a beard recently grown during a year spent in Italy (his Roman residence had provided no hot water with which to shave). A lifelong bachelor, Peckham dressed elegantly, and smoked cigarettes in a long white holder.

But his primary impact was intellectual. The thrust of his work was transdisciplinary scholarship. In the 1950s, Peckham had strived to understand romanticism, a task he proclaimed as central to the twentieth century. Through the way he approached the task, the lyric verse, paintings, novels, and musical compositions of the period became vital elements in a heroic struggle over the meaning of values. He saw the culmination of that era in the writings of Friedrich Nietzsche, and his book on romanticism, *Beyond the Tragic Vision,* would be hailed in academic circles as a masterpiece. By the early sixties, Peckham was starting a more ambitious project that would use his cultural knowledge to go beyond criticism of art, music, and literature and probe the essence of humanity itself.

These were deep issues, and Peckham found most of his colleagues insufficiently serious and too compartmentalized to enlist in his quests. The fact that he made no bones about the general insipidity around him did not enhance his popularity among his peers. He has written that in the modern college campus, "almost nobody talks seriously to anybody else. If you want some decent intellectual conversation you have to form a club or group and keep it secret." At the time Ira Einhorn found his way into one of Morse Peckham's classes, Peckham was working in virtual isolation, living alone, sharing his intellectual theories and discoveries on a daily basis with no one.

The course was in world literature. Peckham would begin with Stendhal and go on to Balzac, Carlyle, Flaubert, Whitman, and others—all toward the thematic resolution that Peckham kept clearly in his own vision. It was tough going. Among the student cognoscenti, Peckham had a daunting reputation as an eccentric maverick who by sheer dint of cerebral devotion could jar you out of your intellectual stupor, delving in areas that other professors didn't even dream existed. The trouble was keeping up with the man's omnivorous mind.

By the time Ira Einhorn took world literature with Morse Peckham, he was fed up with being a physics major: His courses were not challenging, and he felt that specializing in sciences was too limiting. As always, he was figuring out how to avoid being, as he later put it, "put in categories that didn't encapsulate what I wanted to be." So he switched to literature in his sophomore year and found a father figure in Peckham, a man with a universal range of interests. Ira connected with him instantly: Here was an infinitely bright man whose reading was as extensive as Ira hoped his would be.

Surprisingly, the hypercritical Peckham was quickly impressed with Ira Einhorn. Even though the students taking the world literature course were among the university's best, Peckham says, "Ira stood out because of his really wide reading and his ability to understand what he read." Peckham also appreciated Ira's ability to express himself verbally, something he considered rare among his students then.

It was soon clear to the other students in the class, as it would be to students in subsequent Peckham classes where Ira attended for credit or just schmoozed, that there was some heavy cerebral bonding between Ira Einhorn and Professor Peckham. While most of the students were gasping for breath at Peckham's hairpin intellectual turns, Ira would ostentatiously be keeping pace with the master, providing verbal footnotes or suggesting esoteric comparisons to the point under discussion. It was no secret that this mental jam session continued outside of class as well. They would sit over coffee at Horn & Hardart's, or meet at Peckham's house in West Philadelphia. Eventually, Peckham gave Ira a key to his house.

Inevitably, some of Ira's peers wondered how close the relationship really was. Peckham insists that the friendship was strictly intellectual, and there is no reason to surmise that the speculation of homosexuality was in any way founded. While working on his book about the problems of human behavior, epistemology, the nature of historical discourse, and social structure—typical Peckham fare—the professor was out on an academic limb. So far out that he had virtually no substantive contacts among his peers. He considered his mental life intense and thrilling, but it precluded any emotional life outside of the pursuit of ideas. "In Ira," he says, "I found someone whom I could try these ideas on. Because I didn't have anybody else." Ira, who still read extensively on science and was trying to apply that knowledge to the study of literature, was useful in providing feedback. He was a good companion, someone whom Peckham could invite over to his house to listen in silence to the entire fifteen hours of Wagner's *Ring* cycle.

Einhorn appreciated the professor's maverick standing within the institution and his indifference to the semiostracism that came from flouting convention. But more important, Peckham provided a blueprint for Ira's prodigious readings as well as a critical touchstone for interpreting what he read. "Ira imbibed the whole Peckham approach," says Carolyn Matalene, a fellow student, "which was to be a cultural historian, so that all of the arts are equally interesting—music, sociology, psychology—and you have to know everything." Peckham's modus operandi of making "intellectual raids" on a discipline, reading so extensively in a field that he soon could think in the way the professionals in that area thought, appealed greatly to Einhorn. He emulated this approach. For the last two years of college, Ira went through libraries of thought in philosophy, medicine, psychology, and other subjects. When he was hot on the trail of a subject, Ira was capable of reading for twenty hours straight.

Morse Peckham urged Ira to stay at Penn and attend graduate school. This was much to the dismay of Ira's parents, who had been disappointed when Einhorn switched majors from physics to literature. But there was no way Ira was going to pursue a conventional career. During one of his summer breaks, he had toiled in a blast furnace and during one semester he had worked in the post office. This experience, he later wrote, convinced him that "earning a living was an old form." Instead he proposed for himself "a lifetime occupation of *learning* a living." Graduate school, or some sort of life centered around the university, seemed at the time the best way to do that.

But a more immediate concern was graduation. He had, by his own estimation, been present for only 5 percent of his classes, the other time being spent in reading, conversation, sex, and drug experimentation. He had spent weeks at a time away from campus, spending six months in California during his junior year and logging time in Vermont the year after. So he was dependent on the goodwill of his instructors to accept his final papers as proof of his successful mastering of the course subject matter. This they generally did. But during his last semester, one instructor displayed considerable pique at Ira's blithe disregard of the class sessions, and gave him a failing grade.

To make up the grade, Ira would have to repeat the course in summer session. But he refused. This caused considerable consternation among the friends and family of Ira Einhorn. His classmates at Penn sat up late in the night, trying to turn him around. Bea Einhorn herself drove down to the campus and talked to the instructor, hoping to change his mind. "Look, Mrs. Einhorn," he told her. "I don't even know what your son looks like—how can I pass him?"

It was Ira Einhorn who had the change of mind. He might have been a rebel, but his own well-being was sufficient cause to bend to the institution. Einhorn attended the summer session. The instructor he drew for that makeup course was the same who had failed him. He complained to his mother about the situation, remarking that he knew so much more than the instructor that *he* should be doing the teaching. But this time, he fulfilled the course requirements and received his A.B. in 1961.

He would duly claim this credential on his subsequent résumés.

For the next few years, Ira Einhorn's life might best be summarized by a line from one of the detailed letters he sent to his friend Michael Hoffman: "I'm trying to resolve my future," he wrote, "but at present all I see is chaos—boy do I love it."

Hoffman had met Einhorn in the fall of 1959. Ira was a junior, and had just moved into an apartment on Locust Street near 37th, on the Penn campus—his first apartment after spending his freshman year at home and his sophomore year in the dorms. Hoffman, a native of Pottstown, an industrial town fifty miles north of Philadelphia, was entering graduate school in English. He, too, had moved into the building, and he became one of many people whom the Unicorn would affect deeply and permanently. Years later, Hoffman lightly fictionalized the introduction in a short story. The character's name is Sam Irwin, but the scene is pure Ira Einhorn:

> I first met Sam Irwin banging open my front door after only the most perfunctory knock. He was wearing khakis and bedroom slippers, his pink-skinned and hairless chest bare, slight rolls of fat hanging from his broad, muscular shoulders and expanded-for-the-occasion chest.
>
> "Do you have a copy of *The Decline of the West?*," his eyes peering out impishly from behind clear-rimmed glasses.
>
> "Spengler?"
>
> "Yes. I'm writing a paper on Thomas Mann and I need a quote."

As did the characters in the story, Hoffman and Einhorn became friends very quickly. They shared a love for literature, and both were in the thrall of Morse Peckham, though Ira's personal relationship with the professor was much closer. The two spent a lot of time together, in late-night bull sessions or just hanging out on campus or at the corner drugstore. A subtext of the friendship was the recognition that they were headed in different directions. Hoffman's future was well mapped out—he was soon married with a small child, and he knew that after his doctorate he would go into teaching, whereas Ira's plans were amorphous but daring, decidedly unconventional. Hoffman lived somewhat vicariously from observing Ira's excesses, and Ira constantly proselytized a riskier life-style to Hoffman, urging him to ditch his wife and job and *live*. Einhorn had already made the mental jump, vaulting over the gap that separated the outsider from the crowd; from the other side, he kept urging his friend to take the leap, too.

"Ira would want to manipulate you so you would lead the life he wanted you to lead," says Hoffman. "He would tell people the books that they needed to read, the thinkers they needed to think about, the ideas they had to come in contact with. He was sort of a cultural Bolshevik in that way. It was wonderful to be around him, because he had all this free time and he'd read the book that came out yesterday."

In 1962, Michael Hoffman took a teaching job in Maryland and moved there with his wife and baby. Ira would shoot off letters every couple of weeks or so. There was a lot of posturing in those missives, and more than a little melodrama, but they stand as a record of Einhorn's mind at a crucial stage in his life.

For much of 1962, Einhorn was traveling. He was not yet a full-time graduate student, but in the midst of what he later simply described as "two years of continuous reading." He spent much of his time in Bennington, Vermont, with a girlfriend he'd met while an undergraduate. He had friends in Greenwich Village and often would stay in an apartment near Sixth Avenue and West Fourth Street. He made trips to Chicago and Ohio. Morse Peckham was traveling in Europe, and he wrote a letter that Ira described as so "filled with friendship, love, and trust" that Ira considered joining his professor overseas—a journey Einhorn eventually rejected "until I have some sort of perspective on Ira."

That perspective was slow in coming. He was constantly reevaluating the wisdom of pursuing life in academia. He was working on a novel about his intense relationship with the Bennington girl and worried that the "sterility" of scholarship would ruin him for creative writing. He felt he had a gift for teaching but wondered if it was too soon for that.

> At present I can't even dream of teaching before thirty. The more I read about the background of great scholars in various fields the more I realize the great importance of long years of careful preparation. . . . I must learn to wait and be patient—the moment will arrive and then I will be able to bring to bear all I have read on the problem that confronts me. Americans just don't know how to ripen—they all want to produce, produce, etc. We must learn to wait and be silent.

Silence was a tough order for Einhorn to fill. After his intense communions with the great minds of literature and philosophy— "Blake, Nietzsche, etc., are just as alive to me as my closest friends," he wrote—he would spring like an unwound coil, showering his knowledge and ideas hurly-burly on unsuspecting listeners. This could have disconcerting effects on his audience, particularly young women confronted with what amounted to a tidal wave of intellectual intensity. "I've talked a blue streak of late," he wrote typically. "All have listened—few understand." Ira related one tale to Hoffman where a woman was so shaken by his outburst that she returned to her dormitory "hysterical and on the verge of a breakdown."

His moods swung wildly, sometimes even within the space of a single letter. One day he could write of "the unimaginable hell of my esoteric inner life" and describe himself standing "on the peak of a cold abyss drawing circles about myself." But not long after he could crow that:

> My mind has become ten times as strong and agile as it was in the past and I find myself on a level of maturity and strength which I never dreamed of reaching so early. I travel in the circle of best minds with comparative ease and find myself able to think and question right alongside of them. I feel the deep beauty of self-realization quite often and know I'm becoming what I am at a bewildering rate of speed.

Listening one day to Bach's B Minor Mass, Ira decided that he wanted "to teach not English or history, but the deepest involvement with that which is ever present—life." A few weeks later, he claimed that "my intellectual grasp of my novel has reached august proportions . . . literature both critical and creative is my life—to this I give myself."

In early 1963, in the midst of this mental volleyball match, Morse Peckham returned from Europe and convinced Ira to give graduate school a serious effort. The professor even volunteered to pay Einhorn's tuition, an offer made unnecessary when Ira received a one-year Ashton fellowship. Ira moved into Peckham's house while waiting to move into a new apartment he had rented, and the two renewed their friendship. "We are closer than ever and a deep understanding has developed between the two of us," Ira wrote. "He needs the companionship, understanding, and constant stimulation (he has told me this a number of times quite recently) that I provide."

Among the books that fired Ira's imagination in this period were Alan Watts's *Psychotherapy East and West* and Thomas Kuhn's *The Structure of Scientific Revolutions*. The latter, introducing the concept of paradigm shifts—those earth-shattering changes in the way we view the world, generated by new discoveries—particularly entranced Ira. He believed that when the next paradigm shift came, he would be among the few who perceived it right away, squaring off against the old guard defending obsolete truth. He would eventually meet and befriend the authors of both those books, a habit that he was increasingly cultivating. It was symbolic of his willing-ness to take that extra step, to refuse to recognize boundaries. So when Ira completed a book that impressed him, he was compelled, if the author were living, to seek out that person and begin a correspondence, perhaps a friendship. With Peckham around once more to discuss ideas with (they would not only analyze weighty tomes, but cluck at the sad state of the civilization as portrayed in the *New York Times*), Ira flung himself into cognition with renewed fury.

"The only thing of worth which I still treasure is the joy of self-cultivation," he wrote in May 1963. "All else has become ephemeral and illusory. . . . My response to art has been emotionally violent, much more than normal, and I'm constantly being ripped apart. At times I become so sensitive, listening to music becomes too dan-gerous for my nervous system. I feel like a fine receptor attuned to all that goes on around me."

To read these outbursts one may get the impression that Einhorn was an esthete, a brooding sort, clutching wilted flowers as he thrashed helplessly in the throes of his overheated cogitations. This was not the case. The letters might well have been accurate dis-patches of Einhorn's internal reality, but to those who knew him, Ira was the embodiment of the positive life force, the Falstaff of Penn's English department. He was having a great time. He met dozens of girls, zeroing in on their souls and cheerfully settling for their bodies. He would buoyantly strike up conversations with strangers or delight in reacquainting himself with old Central High friends returning to Philadelphia after spending their college years out of town. With no provocation he would share his opinions on techno-logical revolution, classical literature, the civil rights movement, and the plight of the American novelist. He was always ready for a party.

Ira also was reaping the benefits of a grand new apartment. It was a more-than-ample space in a century-old building called the Pow-elton Apartments, known in the neighborhood as the Rockpile, or simply the Piles. This moniker was earned by its stone edifice and perpetual disrepair; the building was entering a state of intentional neglect that would worsen over the years until the city ultimately condemned it. But the dilapidated condition of the Piles did not prevent it from being a desirable building—to many Powelton Vil-lagers, it was prime.

This anomaly has more to do with Powelton Village than any feature of the Piles itself. Powelton was Philadelphia's Bohemia— the place that housed its outcasts, fringe characters, mavericks, counterculturists, and lunatics, along with a number of people— possibly the majority in 1963—who were just plain poor. Located only a few blocks north of the University of Pennsylvania and virtually abutting the growing campus of the Drexel Institute of Technology, the Powelton was an amiable enclave of declining Victorian houses on quiet tree-lined streets, with a dash of ghetto tenements mixed in.

Powelton had always been different. The tone had been set by the private rebellion of William Powel in the late 1600s; dissatisfied with the inefficiency of the English-licensed ferry across the Schuylkill, he established his own service. When the state demanded he shut down, Powel marshaled such public support that William Penn himself had to grant a dispensation. Powel built a house on the river's west bank to start the settlement, but it was not until after 1775, when his descendant Samuel purchased 96 acres of land, that the area assumed its name. Sam Powel, incidentally, established an academic standard for the neighborhood—a graduate of nearby College of Philadelphia (which would become the University of Pennsylvania), he and a friend visited Voltaire who described them as "amiable young men who love investigation and truth." As bridges made the west Schuylkill easily accessible, there was a mid-nineteenth-century building boom, first in Italianate houses, and later in roomy Victorians with mansard roofs, front porches, and high-ceilinged rooms. Among the more affluent residents were a Quaker colony unperturbed by the upper-crust convention that "nobody lives north of Market Street."

In the twentieth century, many of the wealthy home owners moved out. The Depression hit the area hard, and the fancy homes became subdivided and run down. After World War II, though, a cooperative housing venture was begun with the help of the Quakers, luring adventuresome residents, many of whom had ties to the political left or the universities. The area became a magnet for students and professors who were willing to put up with a few extra deadbolts and a continual plague of cockroaches in exchange for great location, cheap rents, and the most tolerant neighborhood in the city. Aware of the constant threat of encroachment on its housing stock by Penn, Drexel, or various city agencies, and anxious to preserve Powelton's lively urban gumbo, activists set about forging a sense of community in the underdog region.

The Piles was almost a cross section of the neighborhood. Like many of Powelton's homes, it was originally built as a no-compromise luxury project, but now was feeling the pain of physical neglect. The building spread over the entire south side of a city block, a series of stone-and-concrete structures fronting on Powelton Avenue, with wings extending around the corners. An alley ran behind it, accessed by arches that opened to Thirty-fifth and Thirty-sixth streets. Ira's apartment was in the eastern wing of the Piles, on the first floor, with an entrance on Thirty-fifth Street. The living room was perfect for holding court—it was two steps lower than the rest of the apartment, and had window seats on the big bay windows overlooking Thirty-fifth Street; typically one would find people spread out on a bunch of cushions spread in an oval, with Ira sitting on the window seat, at the oval's crown, expounding on consciousness, Marshall McLuhan, or LSD. ("Ira was almost a medium in the way that when a television is on, everybody in the room will pay attention to it," recalls one Einhorn friend.) There was also a spacious kitchen, a huge bathroom—its substantial tub pleased Ira, who took at least one bath a day—and a hallway that led to two bedrooms. Ira's bedroom overlooked the alley, and the other bedroom, occupied by a succession of roommates who had a front-row seat to the circus run by Philadelphia's ringmaster of the sixties, overlooked Thirty-fifth Street.

The apartment—surprising to those who considered Ira's appearance unkempt at best and at worst an offense to hygiene—was almost always clean and orderly. Ira would explain to visitors that his mind was so active, so wrapped up in preparadigmatic issues and rich insights into cellular consciousness, that if he did not structure his environment almost obsessively, the delicate house of cards would crumble.

Ira was the first and most noticeable of the tenants who would dominate the Piles over the next few years: counterculturists in the vanguard of Philadelphia's version of the sixties rebellion. He came to regard the entire complex as an extended version of his living quarters. He would feel comfortable entering any number of apartments in the Piles and launching into one of his patented raps while ravishing the refrigerator. Or he'd bang on a friend's door to announce to her, "We're going to make chocolate chip cookies" and supervise the process.

Ira's monetary requirements were modest. His rent was $72 a month, which he shared with a roommate. He almost never bought clothes, and he mooched most of his food. Books were perhaps his biggest expense. The furnishings of the apartment reflected this: cushions to sit on, mattresses to sleep on, but every wall filled with books, everything from well-worn Anchor paperbacks to a sixty-volume set of Jung's writings. What money Ira did require, though, had to come from *somewhere*. For short-term shortages, he borrowed from friends and family, sometimes keeping detailed accounts of the sums he borrowed, a practice that he and his creditors understood as a joke. And he dealt marijuana.

It is difficult to say how critical Ira's dope dealings were to his financial situation. In his letters, he makes it clear that the money helped. At one point he wrote that "a 'head' has been over to buy my last bit and we celebrated with a quick reefer. . . . I've been pushing a little lately to make some extra bread. The heat's on, so if you don't hear from me for a while, I'm in jail."

Some contemporaries of his conclude that he was a big-time dealer, and there are suspicions that for years he financed his activities from dope profits. One fellow resident of the Piles believes that Ira had a friend act as his "mule," bringing home solid bricks of pot from California.

Others think the dealing was almost incidental. "Ira did some dealing, but I don't know if you could call him a dealer," says Michael Hoffman. "He never had a roll of money in his pocket. He could get you [pot] and he'd sometimes make a profit but would sell it to his friends for cost if they didn't have the money. He would give it to me. He was never in anything for the bucks. He was in it to pay his rent."

While smoking some potent weed on Christmas Eve, 1963, Ira experienced a state of calmness that he saw as signaling the end of his period of turmoil. He claimed that the experience "completely transformed my way of looking at the world and acting in relation to it. . . . I have become calmer and learned to transform my discontent into positive energy which allows me to glow with a deep beauty quite frequently and even provides me with a greater access to states that can only be called mystical. I feel no desire to be anything but Ira."

Ultimately, that experience was less of a turning point than a clarifying episode in a steady path toward a decision to drop out and go his own way. As Ira gained more confidence in his own powers, he became more comfortable with the idea that whatever he was going to become, he did not need the artificial scaffolding of the university to prop himself up.

"I see our profession as more of a fraud every day," he wrote. "I will leave the field of literature if the opportunity presents itself, for my ideas are developing in a manner completely antithetical to the intrenched system of ideas. I could stay and fight the battle, but the prospects of getting anyplace are rather dim."

Einhorn felt it was his task to lay bare the phoniness of the institution and often created a spectacle in the process. Michael Hoffman, who returned from Maryland in 1964 to accept a position on Penn's faculty, recalls one incident when Kenneth Rexroth came to campus to address the graduate students. The venerable poet and critic, riding high on his reputation as an elder presence in the Beat Movement, read his poetry and gave a talk. The audience was generally put off by Rexroth's overbearing pompousness and apparent drunkenness. But it was Ira who burst the bubble. "Mr. Rexroth," he asked, when the seminar was thrown open for questions, "how old were you when you discovered the secret of life?"

The inflammatory behavior marked Ira as a troublemaker and jeopardized the renewal of his one-year fellowship. Hoffman: "A lot of us kept trying to talk to Ira, saying 'All you need to do is play the game this way, play the game that way.' But the lesson Ira was learning from his life, the way he thought about things, the way he came to understand the world, was that you *don't* play the game. That is selling out. Ira was a very high-voltage Holden Caulfield—he really believed there were certain ways you just destroyed your vital fluids. Ira did it pretty much the way he wanted to do it. When he got tired, that was it."

Ultimately, Ira could not abide the increasing dissonance between the dry, well-trod approaches in the institution and the wild, subversive ideas he was discovering in his readings and travels. There was too much going on outside, and Ira was so infused with these possibilities he got a physical thrill from them. After displaying the breadth of his knowledge at a breakfast with friends one morning, he crowed "The outlandish is my possession—*c'est moi.* I'm on the firing line, quickly reached for but always softly evasive—as they reach for me I quickly elude them and hover inches above their grasping fingers—all I am is a quiet smile."

Without looking back, he quit the graduate program. If Ira were to gain a doctorate it would be in the real world.

Morse Peckham professes that it came as a surprise to him when Ira dropped out of graduate school. The departure apparently had its effect on the professor. Peckham believed that graduate school, despite its absurdities, filled the function of preparing someone for a profession, and toward that end one had to shoulder a lot of hard work, some of it studying texts that are less interesting than what one would read by choice. He suspected that Ira, by continually seeking ideas that excited him, lacked a certain rigor. As the years went on, Peckham began to see Ira in a more critical light. "He was primarily interested not in the validity of ideas, but in their excitement," he says. "If you examine the trajectory of his life, I think you will find that he simply was swept along in what was the advanced fashion of the moment." Peckham also began to suspect that Ira was parroting his own words back at him. "I was still very interested in him and very friendly with him but I began to feel that talking to him was like being in an echo chamber, just my own ideas being fed back to me without any modification or any thought on his part."

From all appearances, though, the two remained close. Ira still was a frequent visitor to Peckham's house, still had the key. He was a regular at the long-running, informal Wallace Stevens seminar that Peckham led at the house, in which the group would tackle a Stevens poem strophe by strophe, not leaving discussion of a line of poetry until everyone in the group was agreed on its meanings and implications. When Peckham finally completed his work on human behavior, *Man's Rage for Chaos,* Ira was prominently mentioned in the acknowledgments.

But Morse Peckham harbored deep doubts about his protégé. In particular, Ira's unabashed support of drugs made Morse Peckham uncomfortable. Ira tried to explain to his professor the significance of mind-altering drugs—he even got Peckham to try marijuana once, with disappointing results. Things got worse when, at one of the Wallace Stevens meetings, Ira went on a tirade about the virtues of pot; the academics found it a very tiring digression.

The final straw came when people warned Peckham that Ira might be hiding some marijuana in Peckham's cellar, and the professor himself could potentially be implicated in a drug scandal. They suggested that Morse would be wise to replace the locks on the house.

So Peckham changed the locks.

It must have been a shock to the Unicorn that first time he tried to open Morse Peckham's door and found that the lock would not accept the key. Later, Ira would tell at least one of his cohorts—his roommate Dave Peterson—that he and Peckham had stopped seeing each other because, as Peterson recalls Einhorn claiming, "Morse wanted to make it into a more sexual relationship than Ira wanted." (Those who know Peckham well doubt this claim, saying that the professor is "nonsexual.") Peckham, for his part, had this reply when Mike Hoffman asked him what had happened between the two: "I dismissed him."

Hoffman saw the split as revealing the essence of both players. "I think that Ira just got too extreme, and Peckham—who obviously had fallen in love with Ira, but loved him in the ways he could love him, like a father—had to reject him."

Morse Peckham sums up their sundering in a sentence. "I was his guru," he says. "And then he decided to become a guru himself."

3

DOODLEBUG

Holly Maddux was definitely a dark-horse candidate in the election for cheerleader for the 1964–1965 school year at John Tyler High. She had not been a member of the Blue Brigade, the marching squad from which most of the cheerleaders hailed. She had not intertwined her life with any of the popular cliques typical of life in an East Texas high school in the early 1960s. Though people respected her, she was considered a loner. Quiet, always polite, and mannered. Clean. Shy, with a reticence that some took to be imperiousness. Not a party girl at all—no daughter of Fred Maddux's would dare maintain a reputation anything less than spotless. Holly Maddux would also have been considered something of an egghead—acing all her subjects and winning scholastic awards—had she not been so pretty and seemed so sophisticated. So much so that she seemed almost not a part of Tyler, Texas, a town of 50,000 built on oil and roses, a community that blended the xenophobia of the Deep South with ingenuous Texas Babbitry. Even though she was Tyler-born, Tyler-raised, she had managed to avoid that distinctive, jerky Texas drawl with which her neighbors spoke. Almost as if she had been living in a world of her own, one where people spoke in broadcast-quality accentless diction, and by residing in that world so long, she had shaken her native dialect. It was assumed in Tyler that Holly Maddux would go far, both in achievement and geography. But it was a surprise that she would challenge the whole school to compete for cheerleader.

"Let's go out for cheerleader," she'd said one day to her friend Toni Erwin, just like that.

It was almost an absurd premise. Of all the honors Holly had won, and the activities she had mastered—Merit Scholar, National Council of Teachers of English Award, brown belt in judo, and solo dancer—none presented more of a challenge than winning election to the John Tyler High cheerleading squad. It was the ultimate status for female students, and the competition for that role was held with the utmost seriousness. Though it was the dream of almost every girl to be a cheerleader—inculcated in an East Texas girl almost from birth—only six could hold the post. Those six seniors would represent the John Tyler Lions in every athletic contest, be it basketball or football. They would lead each pep rally before the game, they would perform on the sidelines during the game, and they would celebrate the victories after the game. They would be on call to represent the town of Tyler itself for civic events. They would constantly be reminded of the responsibility of their posts, for they were role models for the entire school. Below-average grades, or setting a poor moral standard, were grounds for suspension from the cheerleader squad.

Therefore, the election process was rigorous and public.

It was not a spectacle that one would have expected Holly Maddux to put herself through. As Toni Erwin remembers her best friend, "Holly was a social misfit. She was noticed as being different because she dressed differently, she carried herself differently, she spoke differently. She wore her hair long and straight when the rest of us were ratting and spraying and messing with ours. She didn't wear makeup. She had an almost European air about her— in this little podunk community. It was just awesome that Holly could be elected cheerleader. In my case, I thought it was absurd, too—but at least I was a little bubbly friendly person and I was in the Blue Brigade. But for Holly it was even more amazing because she wasn't the joiner type that I was. She was discriminating, even then."

The two girls had met only the past summer, when Toni's family had moved to Tyler from San Antonio. Toni Erwin considered it mortifying, coming from a Lone Star metropolis to this plain East Texas community. When the family arrived, they went to the main square in the center of town. "There was Tyler Square with grass and trees and squirrels and the activity of the town," she remembers. "The shopping area was still downtown and there were little men sitting on concrete benches. And there was the courthouse and the post office and it was all just right there within a block. I was only fifteen but I could figure out that it was small. There were only two high schools and no tall buildings."

It was Toni's mother who found Holly. She had noticed the Maddux girl's elegant profile in church. Mrs. Erwin collared Holly in the church parking lot and asked her if the church had a youth group. It did, said Holly, in a drawlless voice that astonished the Erwins, but the group did not meet in summer. When the two girls found themselves in English class together that autumn, they fell together. "I don't really know why we were such good friends because we were more different than we were alike," says Toni. "Except that I didn't grow up in Tyler so I wasn't caught up in all the social crap that goes on here. And Holly had grown up here but her parents had not allowed her to be influenced by that."

It was around Christmastime when the two girls decided to risk going out for cheerleader. This allowed barely enough time for the requisite preparation. Every day they would meet at Holly's house. They would work together by the swimming pool, refining cheers, practicing on flips, jumps, and cartwheels. Evaluating the other's performance, suggesting where this could be done sharper, that should be yelled with a different cadence.

The nation at large was reeling in the wake of the Kennedy assassination, which had occurred less than one hundred miles from the Maddux home on Shady Lane. But the sounds of the shots had not penetrated the two high school juniors yet. They worked and they worked, and both performed well during the initial screening, when the field was narrowed to ten finalists.

March 12, 1964, was a sunny day. Holly consulted her horoscope in the *Tyler Courier Times*. It read: "Gemini: Your conservatism can make a fine impression on high-placed persons at this time. . . . Don't be elusive." At 8:30 A.M., with the entire school massed in the large gym building on the John Tyler campus in the center of town, the tryouts began. Ten would compete; only six would survive. After each girl was introduced, she would begin the routine, alone in a pair of shorts and a sleeveless sweater, in front of more than a thousand critical classmates, connoisseurs of cheerleading by virtue of Texas breeding. First she would prance in front of the packed gym bleachers that extended from three of the room's four walls, letting everyone see her, doing gymnastics, trying to build excitement. Then she would perform the particular yell she had chosen, encouraging the school to yell along. Everybody would bay in response, rising in tribute as the girl executed a triumphant final circle around the gym. Toni Erwin's yell was the one beginning, "We're the Champs," and it is her recollection that Holly's was the same.

Without a base of popularity, Holly's chances of winning were dicey. Some girls with drill team pedigrees could brazen it out on dimpled smile and reputation, but Holly, whose only assured supporters would have been secret admirers struck by her beauty and carriage, would succeed only by virtue of bravura performance.

This she did deliver.

After all the girls performed their routines, the incumbent cheerleaders led the school in a final yell, and the students joined together to sing the Tyler Alma Mater.

At the end of the sixth period, last of the day, everybody gathered again in the gym. To quote Mary Morphis, who reported on the event for *The Lions' Tale,* the school paper:

> Prolonging the final moment until the last possible time, this year's cheerleaders announced the new ones. The student body waited with bated breath, many with prayers on their lips, and hope in their hearts for the names.
>
> Amidst screams, resounded applause, and streams of tears, the cheerleaders made their way to the front of the gym to receive the football necklaces worn by the present cheerleaders.

One of those new cheerleaders was Holly Maddux. Both she and Toni had made it. The incumbent cheerleader who handed Holly her necklace also slipped a personal letter to the junior, another tradition. "Holly," she wrote, "you have acquired a tremendous responsibility as well as a title. . . . To be always joyous and cheery is so important. . . . Holly, never be afraid to love. Remember we're all God's children and He loves everyone with the same infinite love. And I love you, Holly. I wish you the best year ever."

Unlike the other girls, Holly did not receive her necklace and letters in, as Mary Morphis put it, "a stream of tears." Her composure was so unshakable that even the school paper noted in the caption of her picture that "Holly refuses to cry."

*   *   *

Fred Maddux's pappy was a railroad man, a West Texas roustabout born late in the nineteenth century, who married a Louisiana girl named Estelle—a generation out of Paris via Canada—ten years his junior. It was 1913. Fred Maddux recalls that "My father was quite an old rascal. My mother was a hard-working, bridge-playing old lady." In 1916, baby Joe came along and ten years and a day after the wedding, Fred Lanham Maddux was born.

Fred Maddux describes his hardscrabble life in Natchitoches, Louisiana, as a good upbringing. But there was a component of toughness. Though his father, Fred Senior, worked in the business for over fifty years, on and off, he never stuck with one railroad, never built up seniority. As his son puts it, "He built up a propensity for saying, 'Well, I'm going to do something else.' " His son's son, John Maddux, adds that "My grandfather was the most contrary man you'd ever met. My grandma said he was so contrary that if his head itched, he'd scratch his butt." In the late 1920s, for instance, he quit the railroad and went to work for Standard Oil, working the "bug" (the telegraph wire) near a pumping station. Young Fred recalls going down to the pump station and hanging around the tanks; it planted a deep respect for the oil business in the boy. But then the Depression came, and Maddux, Sr., took on what jobs he could. "Pappy got a bread route with Cotton Brothers Bakery in Alexandria and he became the distributor for the *Shreveport Times*," says Maddux. "So he had two jobs, and he would get up at two in the morning and get the papers, and roll them up, go deliver the papers, and after he got finished with the papers got the bread, and took it through the grocery store, and then he went on home and went to sleep."

As the country prepared for the next war, the elder Maddux took a job as railroad telegrapher in New Mexico. About then, a family tragedy occurred—young Joe Maddux, an avid hunter, died while cleaning his gun. Not long after, Estelle Maddux, who had learned to work the bug in a women's training program during World War I, took on full-time work on the railroad, too.

The younger Fred Maddux, meanwhile, was itching to go to the war brewing overseas, a struggle between good and evil that would not only distinguish its participants but, by its deep mark in history, would elevate them beyond their mundane origins. More immediately, he sensed the romance of battle. He had admired his high school classmates who had gotten some flight training and went into the Army Air Force as flying cadets. "Oh boy, you talk about glamour," he says, painting vivid pictures, as he often does, in his reminiscences. "Every one of 'em who came out a second lieutenant bought a convertible, and they were all making $125 a month, and they were the real flyboys." Fred Maddux's gambit was to go North, enlist in the Canadian Air Force, and wear a uniform to glory in the European fray. But at the end of the three-month training, he washed out.

He had his chance to serve, of course, as an American soldier. He trained in New Jersey. Before he shipped out, he got as much of a taste for the East Coast as he cared to—the night before his division went to Europe, he went to New York City on a last-chance pass, and got rolled in Grand Central Station. "They were kind enough to leave me with thirty-five cents and a return ticket back to camp," says Fred Maddux. It was Christmas Eve, 1943.

The War was important to Fred Maddux. Though his early family life had been, as he describes it, "casual," the Army provided a structure he seemed comfortable with. He was, and remains, a respecter of authority. Whenever he speaks of the War, and the G.I. tales of woe he suffered in the 508 Parachute Infantry Regiment, there is an unmistakable nostalgia for a time when everyone knew the rules, and understood rules existed for a reason. If you bent them a little, well, fun was fun. But when the bullets came, that was not a time for fun. It was a time for courage, a time for men to act like men. Afterward, this firm standard slipped. It was not as if the rules did not apply; people just respected them less, or—just as bad—people failed to see the disastrous implications of letting transgressions slide. On the issue of rules, Fred Maddux has never left the War.

After victory in Europe, his regiment stayed on as part of General Eisenhower's bodyguard. ("I've seen General Eisenhower and General Patton in full dress uniform, both at the same time," Fred Maddux would often say afterward, "and I ain't been impressed with anybody ever since.") It was easy duty, staying in Frankfort, Germany, taking parachute runs every so often to get jump-pay bonuses. Fred Maddux—barely twenty, slim, dark-haired, and handsome in a sly, almost wolfish way—had almost accumulated enough time to be sent home when he became interested in a pretty WAC. With that incentive to stay, after his discharge in October 1945, he got a job with the Red Cross in nearby Wiesbaden, working in a locator unit. He had a little office with teletype machines and messages from the States would come in to find this soldier or that, and Fred Maddux would try to locate the man's unit. One day he noticed a new young lady in the office and immediately offered to take her across the street for some ice cream. She captivated him. After trying to juggle his time between the WAC in Frankfort and the Red Cross lady in Wiesbaden, he realized that he was running himself ragged when he only wanted one woman: the Red Cross lady. By then, the office was getting ready to disband, and so Fred Maddux said to her, "I think it's time to get married."

And Elizabeth King said, "I guess it is."

Her background could not have been more different than Fred Maddux's. She was from Minneapolis. Scandinavian stock. The family business was the Northrup King Seed Company, one of the state's largest corporations. While Fred Maddux's pappy was driving a bread truck and delivering newspapers, Liz King's family was being served by maids and butlers. Four years older than Fred Maddux, Liz found herself in Europe in a spirit of patrician do-gooding, an act of mercy to our boys overseas from a recent graduate of prestigious Wells College. Then she found herself in love with Fred Maddux.

They married in Wiesbaden and returned to the States in 1946, to Longview, Texas, where Fred would go to school on the G.I. bill. Perhaps recalling those days with his pappy at the pump station, he had the idea of becoming a petroleum engineer. But, as he puts it in typical good-natured self-deprecation, "between inadequate preparation in the schools of Louisiana, and inadequate applications of the brains in the time I'd been in the Army, I was pretty damn rusty and couldn't do it." He transferred to Texas A&M, hoping to get the credits to go into the school of veterinary medicine. But he wasted a year in that track, not having been informed that his out-of-state status meant he had no hope of getting into that school. He promptly switched majors to engineering. "Sure enough," he recalls, "the next damned year out of the clear blue sky comes an invitation to attend the school of veterinary medicine. And of course I told them then they could go straight to hell. I sure did show 'em." The last sentence is spoken without bitterness, but an irony long accepted of his prideful mistake. Fred Maddux realizes that a stand on principle sometimes has ill consequences. But whether by stubbornness or idealism, he'd rather suffer than be wrong. He graduated A&M as an engineer, and that was it for veterinary medicine.

By the time Fred Maddux moved to Tyler, Texas, in 1951, Liz had borne him two children. The first was Helen, born May 25, 1947, a perfect little girl whom they called Holly. Her brother John came a year later. Those years were tough on Liz Maddux; after her privileged upbringing in Minnesota society and the classy women's college in upstate New York, East Texas must have seemed more a foreign country than Germany. The heat in particular enervated her; for much of the year the outdoors is like a vast bread oven, reaching unbearable hundred-plus temperatures about ten or eleven in the morning and maintaining that spirit-breaking intensity until early evening. She doubts she would have made it had not air conditioning been introduced in the early 1950s. But even that could not have much mitigated the difficulties of being a northern-born bride raising children in the town of Tyler, Texas.

Tyler is the heart of Smith County, 934 square miles of the pine trees and sandy soil that are characteristic of East Texas. The country was first surveyed in 1828, and was named after an Indian fighter, General James Smith. In 1847, the county commissioners, asked "to locate the county site at the most pleasant place available having elevation and good water," condemned 100 acres from a farmer and named the town after President John Tyler, under whom Texas was annexed to the United States. Streets were laid out and a town square placed directly in its center. From the start, Tyler had many of the characteristics of the Deep South (Louisiana, after all, was as close as Dallas, 100 miles away), and as a history of the area puts it, "the arrival of the news of the outbreak of [Civil] war found no lack of enthusiasm on the part of Smith Countians to form military companies with which to repel the abolitionists." As the War Between the States continued, Tyler became an industrial power, its largest manufacturer changing its name to the Confederate Ordinance Works, which turned out 2,225 rifles and over 6 million rounds of ammunition for rebel troops. Despite the Union victory, the town would actively maintain identification with the Confederacy a century later, both in symbol and spirit.

In the twentieth century, Tyler first became known as a center for flowers, particularly roses; the climate and soil were ideal for them, and at one point almost three hundred nurseries thrived. But the more significant economic breakthrough came in 1927 when the Boggy Creek Oil Field was discovered to the southwest of town. This set off a series of strikes around Tyler. Workers flocked to man the thousands of wells in the region, and oil companies rented office space in town. The boom helped Tyler thrive while the country suffered in Depression, and in 1937 the city directory boasted that Tyler was "The Oil Capital of the World."

By the time Fred Maddux and his family moved to Tyler, the boom town had ossified somewhat. Tyler had its caste system, its prides and its prejudices. Also its hypocrisy. As one civic leader puts it, "There is a cultural religion here: There is a prayer before everything—the football game, the council meeting, the Rose Festival. The county votes dry every year and then celebrates its victory with a drink." The town also boasted of its fine schools. John Tyler High School, on a 63-acre plot. Robert E. Lee High School, on 69 acres. And Emmett Scott High School, the blacks-only public school, on 6.6 acres. (It would remain so until the courts forced integration— in 1970.) Though there were no racial problems in Tyler, there was a race "situation." Journalist Sam Blair once wrote of it. Working on the Tyler paper as a beginning newsman in 1954, he submitted a picture of a boxer on the eve of a big fight. He was informed that the picture could not run. "But the guy is the world champion," he protested. "Yep," said his editor, "but he's still a nigger."

Though the people in Tyler are never less than friendly, and fiercely loyal to their own, the social structure is rigid and unforgiving. It forever sticks in Fred Maddux's craw that his first home there was "in the wrong part of town." Not the *worst* part of town by any means, but in the seat of Smith County it is well known that South Tyler harbors the best families, the old money from early oil strikes and even before. The Maddux home was a spacious ranch home in West Tyler, a few blocks west of the fairgrounds and the rose garden. Sitting on a corner of well-named Shady Lane, it had a steep and long driveway and was nothing at all to be ashamed of. Fred Maddux even gained a leg up in status when he installed a new "Cinderella-style" swimming pool in the backyard, an event worthy of a feature article in the *Tyler Courier-News*. But the Madduxes, especially when attending Christ Episcopal Church, where many of the best Tyler families worshiped (Fred Maddux had converted from the Baptist faith to his wife's religion), sensed what they considered snobbery.

They especially worried about the effect of this on their eldest daughter. Holly Maddux was the prettiest little girl you would ever want to see. She was nicknamed "Doodlebug" from childhood. Early pictures of her unfailingly show an adorable, blond-haired waif with a smile that would send Norman Rockwell sprinting to the palette. She was by all accounts a happy child. Like Ira Einhorn, she showed early signs of brightness, but unlike Bea Einhorn, Liz and Fred Maddux thought it best not to jump the gun in teaching Holly to read at age three or four. Inveterate respecters of authority, they would leave those things to the teachers. They did enroll her in a local dance academy, and she warmed to that form of body expression instantly. When it was time to attend school, she took to it right away. But in middle school—Hogg Junior High, where she came into contact with youngsters from the highfalutin South Tyler crowd—her parents suspected that something happened. They do not know the precise incident, if indeed one event triggered this sorrowful shift in demeanor, but surmise that insensitive classmates hurt her in some deep private place.

"She was the happiest little thing through sixth grade," says Liz Maddux. "We had always taught the children, or tried to, to take people for what they are themselves, and that nobody's better than anyone else. But there's a certain core of society that lives on how rich daddy is, and when she got into seventh grade, she got in with them and the kind of thing they did was, 'Well, we're going to have a secret club, and we'd ask you but you live in the wrong part of town.'"

Events in the Maddux family prevented the issue from being fully aired. Fred and Liz, in effect, had begun a second harvest of children. Meg arrived in 1955, Buffy in 1958, and Mary would come in 1961. Fred, meanwhile, had changed jobs since moving to Tyler. A partnership he started in the feed business ran into bad times, and he managed to get a job at Sohio Petroleum. But about that time Sohio was pulling out of Tyler, and Fred Maddux went through a period of insecurity before finally accepting a job he would maintain until retirement: a draftsman for the state highway department. A proud man, he had continually resisted drawing on the resources he knew existed in Liz's family coffers.

There was no question who headed the household: Fred Maddux. His earthy style and unchallenged leadership set the tone for family interaction. Elizabeth's influence was more subtle. She would transmit her refined Northern culture by reading to the children, exposing them to cultural events. Holly's sister Meg says, "We were brought up real classy. Kind of like, 'You may not *live* in a high class, but you will *behave* high class.' We were always taken to symphonies. We were always in church, *every Sunday*. We sat with our legs together. We were clean. We said, 'Yes, ma'am, no, ma'am.' "

When Holly's Junior High crisis—if that's what it was—occurred, this decorum worked to disadvantage.

"Holly was very reserved," says her mother. "You could ask, but you weren't going to get an answer. You know, you get hurt a few times and you lower the curtain, you're not going to let anyone see when they hurt you."

One outlet she might have used to express her feelings could have been her schoolwork, routinely given top grades by her instructors. A flurry of papers written for an eighth-grade language arts class in 1961 shows some unusual preferences for a chronically shy and well-behaved young lady. There was a 12-page paper on the origins of witchcraft, a book review of something called "The Monsters Are Due on Maple Street," and a study of Bram Stoker's demonic writings. Oddest of all is a short story Holly wrote called "The Model Mother." It begins:

> Mother and daddy never could get along. Mummy would nag him suspiciously if he got home the least bit late from the lab. His opening words were something like this: "At least I came home, did I not?" And mom would mutter something in this line: "We wish you hadn't"—which wasn't true, at least on our part. Speaking of us, I sometimes wonder (in fact, I often wonder) why the rest of the family, us kids, never grew up as warped personalities—or didn't [we]?

The punch line of this precocious Gothic tale is that after disappearing, "a strangely transformed mama" comes home, apparently the product of daddy's lab experiments.

Perhaps Holly's low point came when she unsuccessfully tried out for the cheerleading squad at Hogg Junior High. She later relayed this mortification to her friend Toni. According to this version, her father, perhaps to protect her, refused to let her compete until the last minute. She did not have the proper outfit and had to do her routine in gym clothes and socks. She took her rejection hard. In addition to that calamity, she also ran into trouble at the Christ Episcopal Church; her sister Meg recalls that Holly quit the choir because someone criticized her singing.

From her troubles came a sort of defiant determination, the sort that Fred Maddux could understand well: "She was gonna shoot the bird to them, boy, and that's what she did." Holly always had shown a stubborn streak: One day on a boating trip, she'd had a shouting match with Fred and she jumped out of the boat and started to swim home—seven miles from shore. (She allowed herself to be coaxed back into the boat for the trip home.) Now she used her obstinacy to her advantage, working diligently at her studies and participating in activities with equal fervor. It was as if a gauntlet had been thrown down, and Holly Maddux accepted the challenge. It was Holly against the nameless forces who would belittle her. In the process of succeeding, she attained an eerie maturation.

She was one of two valedictorians who spoke at the 1962 Hogg Junior High graduation. Inspired no doubt by the soaring optimism of the Kennedy era, her speech was entitled "Their World Today; Ours Tomorrow." She could not have imagined what her generation's world would become before the decade was over.

Holly Maddux's high school career embodied her contradictions. She was a member of the Class of '65, a landmark aggregation in the history of John Tyler High. Holly and her classmates marked an ending: After they graduated, the school would move from the downtown location at which it stood for a century, to a new campus on the fringe of town. It was known that at some time, this new campus would not be able to stave off the inevitable surrender to integration. That was only one of the many ways that the Class of '65 represented the end of the cloistered, "Archie-and-Veronica" life that Tyler students had enjoyed for decades. The class theme was "Our Legend Is Not Ended," but the truth was that the closing of John Tyler did mark the end of an era. It was the last class that would graduate in innocence. To the Class of '65, marijuana was unheard of; the wilder crowd would "drag Broadway," which consisted of cruising down Tyler's main street, and sneaking gulps out of forbidden beer cans. The real tough guys puffed cigarettes behind the gym. Vietnam was only beginning to arise as a topic in current-events class. Sex was *not* unheard of, but news of it seldom rose above the volume of clandestine whispers, except when an accidental pregnancy resulted in a hasty marriage. It is poignant to ponder the concerns documented in *The Alcalde,* the Tyler yearbook—the proms, pep rallies, and home economics classes—and note the absence of any connection to the simmering caldron of the sixties, the world of Ira Einhorn, a time bomb about to explode with such fury that the fallout would reach even so remote a location as Tyler, Texas.

Holly took her place in what seemed a frenzy of apple-pie activities. Indeed, any casual reader of the "Youthful Living" page of the *Tyler Courier Times* would assume that Holly Maddux was among the most well-adjusted, outgoing students in town history. The school year at John Tyler was marked by innumerable elections, contests, and competitions, and Holly did well at any she cared to participate in. Here was Holly, elected Class Favorite of the Junior Class. Winner of an award sponsored by the National Council of Teachers of English. One of three "Ideal Girls," selected on "their all-around personalities." Member of the National Honor Society. Merit Finalist. One of the court of princesses to the annual Basketball Queen. And, of course, elected for a coveted post in the cheerleading squad, for which she cartwheeled and leapt at football games and a political rally for Barry Goldwater, Jr., who visited Tyler while stumping for his father's presidential campaign. Meanwhile, she participated in a slew of outside activities. She taught judo at the Tyler YMCA. She pursued her interest in drawing, filling sketchpads with wistful representations of objects of nature. She kept up at the Marye Frances Dance Academy, starring in performances of "Adventures in the Sea," and "Hansel and Gretel." She also performed in a synchronized swimming exhibition at the Tyler Y, taking her place in the aquatic ballet choreographed to the tune, "I Enjoy Being a Girl."

But despite the accomplishments, Holly Maddux stood apart. Her "differentness," as Toni Erwin put it, was never far away. If her full plate of activities and honors was indeed a studied revenge on a town she despised, it was a private matter. To most, she was a cipher, an almost ethereal presence in the halls of John Tyler. She had developed into one of the most beautiful girls Tyler had ever seen— her limbs were long and strong, her blond hair flowing on her shoulders; her face was proud and elegant, with soft blue eyes blazing. Yet few of the boys dared approach her.

Max Clark, one of Tyler's football heroes that year, recalls her as "proper. Always very neat, clean. Hair combed, made up. Never would you hear of her being at a party where there was booze. Didn't date that much, I recall. Very few boyfriends. Kind of shy. She was a free spirit, a free thinker, and very meticulous in her manner, her demeanor, her ethics about opening doors for people—a man should open a door for a woman. I can recall when I was running track senior year, and I had pulled a muscle during that track meet. She was walking home, and I offered to give her a ride, and I can't hardly walk. And she said, 'If you'll come around and open the door for me, you can give me a ride.' "

One had to look no further than her parents for the cause of her conservatism. Fred Maddux had many strong ideas about the rules of human behavior, and he had no bones about making them clear. He was protective of his first-born daughter, and could be an intimidating presence to any who asked out his Doodlebug. For one thing, his reputation preceded him—his gruff exterior was renowned. (Those who knew him, though, realized that one-to-one he was more often than not an outright softie.) A case in point was his driving around in a Mercedes—he was one of the first in Tyler to drive that make of auto—with a custom license plate that read FUHRER. He had little tolerance for those who criticized the message as insensitive; to him, it was a laugh, partially a spoof borne of the irony of his driving a car made by those he fought in the World War, and partially a joke told on himself, a man sometimes kidded as the führer within the walls of his home. The more people talked about the license plate, the more dogged he became about keeping it. In any case, imagine the consternation of young men coming to drive virginal Holly away in their car for a few hours—at age sixteen she was granted permission to date—when they confronted this talked-about figure, hair cropped close to his head in military style, sitting in a chair on the front porch ... cleaning a big old 10-gauge shotgun. Around him would be the cluttered cacophony of the Maddux living room, surrounded by the stuffed heads of huge game animals Fred Maddux had felled with his gun. When Fred set the curfew at midnight, the boys listened.

Bill Ferrell was one who did ask her out. His few dates with her were uneventful. They saw *The Sound of Music,* ate at El Chico Mexican Restaurant, one of the two eateries where Tyler kids dated. (The other was Nick Doyle's Steak House.) They talked, and he appreciated that unlike the other girls, Holly carried on serious conversations. He recalls they talked about the church, he contending that their parents' generation attended more out of duty than devotion. "Well, if you're serious about it," said Holly, "let's go to church at seven-thirty next Sunday," instead of waiting until the more social eleven o'clock service. And that's what they did.

But despite her almost unbearable attractiveness—or perhaps because of it—he could not bring himself to make a sexual advance. "There was an awe about her, from her beauty," he says. "Like a figurine you can place on a pedestal. I know I kind of put her on a pedestal."

Holly was also incredibly naive about sex. At one point she tearfully spilled the news to her parents that a local boy wanted to make love to her before his incumbent demise from terminal cancer. "Mommy and Daddy thought that was hilarious," says Holly's sister Meg. "Here was a junior or senior in high school saying this line to one of the prettiest girls in school. And she's falling for it! But Holly didn't think it was funny at all. Because she cared for this person, he was going to die of cancer, and she's going to lose her virginity over him. That's the kind of person she was, very gullible."

Her first kiss came late in high school, and Toni Erwin remembers her almost swooning because the boy snuck his tongue in. "Her father would have just died if he'd known," she says. "Holly was not turned on, I'm certain. But she was a little excited because she had done it and her father didn't give her permission to do it. She was just astounded that she had gotten past that landmark occasion in life. She was real, real naive and inexperienced."

A boy two years older, Lawrence Wells, took her out a few times during her senior year, and began what turned out to be a long friendship. It was her beauty that first drew her to him. "You could look at her and tell she was a queen," he says. "There wasn't any doubt about it. The way she carried herself, the way she acted, the way she related. But she wasn't stuck up, she wasn't arrogant. She really wasn't. She was quiet, introspective, studious, a lot more serious than other kids her age—even though she did the same things. She was cheerleader and all that, but she didn't have anything to do with that, really. I think a lot of it was defensive. I think it was hard on her—to look perfect, to act perfect. She never did anything wrong, made straight A's, won everything she entered, did everything well, never lost her cool, never became emotionally involved in anything, and I think it had a hell of an effect on her."

Wells says that at first she was intimidated by his being in college. "She was sheltered," he says. "She finally loosened up when she realized I wasn't going to hurt her. I think that was a real thing with her, of being hurt. Physically, emotionally." Wells recalls one evening when he and Holly were taking a stroll in Tyler's famed rose garden, where rows and rows of voluptuous blooms had been planted to substantiate the town's claim to prominence. They left the premises around eleven o'clock and headed back toward the Maddux house. Suddenly a pack of Tyler rednecks rattled by in a pickup truck, apparently juiced. One shouted an obscenity; another tossed a beer bottle. Even by Tyler standards, no atrocity. But Holly, says Wells, "was just horrified. It was just totally out of her frame of reference. She just couldn't handle it."

There was no one special boy for Holly. She attended the major dances in her senior year with different dates. Sometimes her lack of a steady embarrassed her. There was a custom, for instance, of the cheerleaders going out on the field before the game wearing outrageous corsages given to them by boyfriends, family members, "little sisters" in Blue Brigade, and so on. Toni Erwin tells the story:

> Holly didn't have a boyfriend, and she wasn't in the Blue Brigade so she wouldn't have gotten one from a little sister. It was a real deal to have one, especially for the Robert E. Lee game, because that was our big rivalry. So I bought Holly a mum for that game. I wasn't even sure she would wear it. She was real sensitive about it, real hesitant to take this mum, right up there in the stands, and I was so excited about surprising her and so excited because she hadn't gotten another one

and it was really going to be special. But she was afraid that it was one someone had given to me, and I was just passing it on to her. So I made a big point of showing her where it had her name, on the ribbon they put your name in glitter.

Later, she wrote a short story about it. It was called "The Friendship of the Flower." 'Cause it was really great, she had to read it in the class. I didn't know she was going to write it, and I wasn't named in it.

To outward appearances, Holly Maddux's high school career exceeded Ira Einhorn's. She received perfect marks for her courses, and performed excellently on the SATs: 722 verbal, 624 math. She also scored highly on the English and French achievement tests. Her teachers thought her among the brightest students they had encountered. Yet her accomplishments were compiled from a sense of duty. She may have felt defiant toward her surroundings, but she did not dare to reject the rules imposed on her; instead she transcended them by her success. Certainly, there was not the fiery intellectual passion that characterized the way Ira Einhorn devoured texts. There was not the depth of reading; there was not the curiosity to absorb the vanguards of current thought.

Generally, Holly Maddux hid her passions. Some thought her reticence was snobbery, but since she was always careful to be nice to everybody, she never really alienated people. It was just accepted that Holly Maddux was going to go on to something else, probably not in Tyler. No surprise that among the honors she received in senior year—including being named salutatorian out of a baby boom–inflated class of 426, biggest in Tyler's history—was the traditional laurel: Most Likely to Succeed.

Just where she would begin to fulfill this prophecy was a matter of contention within the Maddux household. Fred Maddux exercised considerable pressure for Holly to stay in Texas. He drew support from a source no less than Texas governor John Connally, whose signature appeared underneath a letter congratulating Holly for the English award. "It is my hope," he wrote, "that you will select one of the fine public or private colleges or universities in Texas for advanced study. The future of Texas will be charted by you, or those like you, who have demonstrated a capacity for outstanding performance." If Fred Maddux had his way, Holly would attend Texas A&M as one of its first women students. If not that, Rice University in Houston would have been preferable to the odious East Coast.

But this was one case where Fred Maddux did not get his way. Holly had her own ideas. She applied at schools out of state, including Bryn Mawr, the revered women's college on Philadelphia's Main Line. Her grandmother, Elizabeth King Maddux's stepmother, sat on the board of directors, but Holly's high school record was sufficiently outstanding that she could have been accepted anywhere she chose. And in January 1965, she received notice that she had been placed in the "A" category of applicants to Bryn Mawr, guaranteeing admission if she kept her grades up. The "Youthful Living" reporter of the *Tyler Courier Times* dutifully reported this, tripping on the spelling and location of this unfamiliar institution. "After graduation from high school," she wrote, "[Holly] hopes to attend Bryn Mawer [sic] in Tennessee, where she will study languages, English, or psychology." Apparently, few of Holly's peers were acquainted with the school; in a subsequent *Courier Times* feature entitled "Top Tyler Graduates Fit Well in Space Age," we hear of Holly that "the tall, striking-looking blond young woman plans to enter Bryn Mawr, which she emphasizes is not in Virginia."

The point, of course, was that Bryn Mawr was not in Texas. It was as if Texas came to represent everything that held her in, reined her passions, told her what to think and do. Her only recourse in high school was to excel in her classes and activities, to wrestle to the ground the labels of "popularity" and "success." And rub her victory in everyone's face by not giving back, withholding the person she really was. It is reasonable to assume that Holly Maddux, willowy and vulnerable at eighteen, believed that the clouds casting shadows on her life thus far would lift when she escaped her home state. It was a bitter pill for Fred Maddux to swallow. He doesn't remember exactly when she told him point blank that she would never live in Texas, but he recalls his reply. *"Don't you ever say anything about Texas,"* he said. "Texas put the clothes on your back and rode you right, up and down. It gave you a home and gave you hellacious damn opportunities, so don't you ever kick Texas in the ass, 'cause Texas is *great*."

But Holly Maddux had left long ago. Somewhere behind the demure smile in her graduation picture, a posed cordial smile brought off with the expertise of a Grace Kelly or Jackie Kennedy, was a mind already dreaming of the new life she was destined to live. Come autumn 1965, she was going to college on the East Coast. She knew things would be different there. But she had no idea how different they would be.

4

THE MAYOR OF POWELTON

Ira Einhorn had been preparing for the sixties long before the coalescing forces of rebellion, drugs, liberation, and baby-boom power reached critical mass. An experienced seeker of mental excitement and a natural iconoclast, Ira bopped to a sixties' beat even before the Jefferson Airplane plugged in their first amplifiers. He was grokking Ginsberg, toking weed, and establishing a local crash pad; he goofed on the Establishment, boasted dropout status, and presented a no-apologies scruffy appearance. Most of all, he thrived on chaos, and sensed how his talents could best be used as traditions and rules crumbled under their own weight. In the dust of those fallen edifices, he would make his presence known.

It was a chronological masterwork, this temporal match of Ira Einhorn and the sixties. They grew in tandem, swapped symbols with each other, and shared the contradictions that came from embracing both the raised fist and the flower. A seemingly perfect fit.

Ira first glimpsed what was to become a sea change in cultural history when he visited California in the summer of 1964. It was only weeks before the Berkeley Free Speech Movement would throw down the campus gauntlet. Ira drove cross-country in seventy-two hours to find that something was happening, and if Mr. Jones didn't know what it was, Ira Einhorn figured it out with instant cognition.

He split his time between Berkeley and Palo Alto, twin epicenters of the movement. Within days of arrival, he met the paisley surge head-on—a party at La Honda, Ken Kesey's place, where the "acid tests" would launch the counterculture on its long, strange trip. This was one of the few times that even Ira Einhorn's mind got too boggled to assimilate a happening: "I was so high and the experience was so strange that I must have more distance," he wrote in a self-described "pot missive." It did not take long for the distance to resolve itself. Not long after, he wrote, "I lay under the stars and watched a procession of unbelievable visions for hours. . . . I feel, at almost every moment, like the last movement of Mahler's Ninth."

It is not clear whether these visions were impelled by one of Ira's roiling love affairs—common occasions in that period—or mind-bending chemicals. But certainly, the coast was awash with talk of LSD. Ira later claimed that he first tried the psychedelic in 1959 and eventually dropped acid twice a month for two years. He considered it a tool to heighten one's personal explorations, a skeleton key to self-understanding. He believed its impact on civilization would be profound.

Still, when he returned to Philadelphia in the fall of 1964, it was not yet time to go public. Despite his phobia of categories and pigeonholes, he could not yet imagine a life for himself totally free of institutions. Einhorn had managed to secure an instructorship at Temple University for the 1964–1965 school year, teaching English 31, a literature course for sophomores. The students were shocked—though some delighted—to find at the front of their classroom a chunky, cheerful, bearded man who carried a green Harvard book bag to class and wore a rumpled tweed jacket and a sawed-off tie, clothes that winked at you, "I'm really not a tie-and-jacket person." He would do strange things such as beginning a class by writing the word *sexuality* on one side of the blackboard and *eroticism* on the other side, and then spent the whole hour getting his students to ponder the difference. Borrowing from Morse Peckham's techniques, he led discussions of poetry in which the second line could not be discussed until the first was fully understood. From his rambling classroom monologues, it was apparent that his life-style was different, even daring—he was living a Bohemian existence in Powelton Village. The rumor spread that his apartment held nothing but books and a bed. Romantic stuff to middle-class students in 1964.

By the spring semester, Einhorn was more relaxed. "Call me Ira," he urged students and was generally less cautious. "I don't wear a shirt and tie to class," Einhorn explained to an interviewer. "I dress like the students. If they ask about marijuana and LSD I give them straight answers about the delights and the dangers. I make no bones about my contempt for the academic world. I'm very popular with the kids. I wouldn't say I was with the administration."

He was right. Temple did not renew his post.

Ira spent the next year reimmersed in reading, still struggling to come to terms with his strong convictions on the future, and the seeming impossibility of making them real. He continually vowed to clear away the garbage and get to serious work on his novel, which in his aspirations was beginning to take on white-whale aspects. But the fact was that Ira Einhorn was never much of a writer.

"He was a *terrible* writer," says Bernie McCormick, a *Philadelphia Magazine* writer who profiled Ira. "It was Ira's frustration." Einhorn's poetry, reams of which he wrote in block capital letters, was strong on Whitmanesque yawp, but lyrically awkward. As for his novelistic talents, suffice it to say that the following passage is typical:

> Like a fallen warrior I had lain on the bed of our misery awaiting her return from work and brooding over the emptiness we had become. Her arrival, as always, created a new stage and a new game. Our parts allotted and the tension pulling us together and apart, we began act one.

Even Ira had to realize that sentences such as "December 29 floated by, I softly grabbed it and began to peel it like a grape" did not stack up to those in the fiction that he was excitedly reading— Gaddis's *The Recognitions,* or David Storey's *Radcliffe.* On the other hand, he was aware of his personal charisma, the power he could generate by his intensity, his intellect, and his gleanings from millions and millions of words written by the best minds civilization had produced.

That power would be the force behind his career.

He saw that power in his one-on-one dealings with people; the power was also unmistakable in his class sessions at Temple. He commented repeatedly on the profound effect he had on people: Sometimes he opened their minds to the amazements of the world, and other times he opened their minds to the amazements of Ira Einhorn. An example of the latter case is the woman who, according to Ira, told him that "it seems unfair that one person can be so beautiful."

This was proffered to Ira during his California trip of 1966, at a time when Ira Einhorn's participatory researches on the counterculture were in full blast. Ira was blown away by what he saw: "California is definitely a product of the twentieth century in a way that New York or Philadelphia will not possibly be for years to come," he wrote. "Things are moving at a rate that even frightens this once very intrepid explorer."

Far from frightened, Ira was delighted. For a person terrified of being hemmed in by convention, the stirrings of a mass movement of irreverent freedom were sweet manna. The so-called Hippie Movement in California was propelled by a trippy anagram of factors, among them Berkeley protest, Beatles and acid-rock music, baby-boom anomie, Eastern religions, hedonism, good drugs, and an intoxicating hit of idealism intensified by the previous factors. It did not have the rigor of academic thought, and one was unlikely to meet people in Haight-Ashbury crash pads with the scope of Ira's readings, but Einhorn would have been quick to sense that literary values were not as important in this rebellion as they were in the Beat Movement that had so captivated him as a youngster. This was a sensual revolution, as seen in the pages of Ira's favorite San Francisco newspaper, the *Oracle*, which ran little text but plenty of stunningly detailed graphics that glowed simmeringly under ultraviolet blacklight. People were bound not by ideas but by feelings: When Ira basked in the afterglow of a Grateful Dead performance at the Avalon Ballroom—the entire room linking hands and swaying to a thirty-minute encore of "Stomp"—he conjured up visions of community, bound in a primal sense not seen since early Christianity. Connections in this movement were forged not so much by logical concatenation but by intuition. A well-reasoned argument was not as effective as a long stare in someone's eyes. An outrageous statement—far from discrediting its speaker—was an invitation to contemplation and perhaps a Zen-like illumination. Though Ira had the training (if not the patience) to compete in academia, this new world was much more to his liking; here, his energy, his intensity, his protean vision, were powerful tools.

In the sixties, Jim Sorrels was a psychologist working in a Palo Alto mental health clinic who saw how Ira Einhorn's verbal presentation drew maximum impact in that intense era. "Usual social convention has people sitting at slightly oblique angles to each other," says Sorrels. "With Ira, most likely, he would take a position seated directly in front of you in a lotus posture. And the eyes would just lock in, and it didn't matter whether you were talking about Marshall McLuhan or your own life, but the contact, the engagement, was complete. You almost never made small talk with Ira. He came with the parentheses: This man is not made for small talk."

Author William Irwin Thompson agrees with that assessment, though not with the same enthusiasm as Sorrels. He met Einhorn at a seminar at Esalen, and was simultaneously fascinated and repelled by the Unicorn. In his book *At the Edge of History*, he memorably described Ira Einhorn in full sixties regalia:

> Ira came all over you like the weather in Cuernavaca: rain and sunlight at the same time. He had the plump, affectionate envelopment of a Jewish mother, but it made me slightly uneasy to realize that he was going to love everybody whether he liked it or not and that, in many ways, love was his newly discovered instrument of aggression.

Speaking of Einhorn's LSD consumption, Sorrels says that "he had done that to his own sense of self-satisfaction—he was worlds ahead of most of us who were just beginning to experiment with acid. He acted as our babysitter, or guide, for a lot of us on those trips." Sorrels recalls one trip to Big Sur, where a group of people went to the beach and took LSD. "Ira took three times as much as we did. I remember I sat knee to knee with him on the beach, both of us nude, staring into each other's eyes, which I could tolerate only briefly, and then my mind would go into the cosmos and my eyes would close. And each time—it must have happened fifty times during three hours—the very moment I would open my eyes, Ira would be opening his eyes, with this incredible beatific expression on his face. And it was absolutely clear to me that he had been with me wherever he was. It was just phenomenal!"

Ira moved from the peninsula to the Haight to Santa Cruz to

Berkeley, a wandering seminarian. To those he visited he must have seemed a wandering Buddha. He carried almost no luggage, and the first thing he would do upon entering a private residence was shed his clothes. Even if others demurred at following his lead, he would be perfectly comfortable nude among the clothed. As William Irwin Thompson noted, despite Einhorn's do-your-own-thing looseness, Ira's very presence carried with it a measure of aggression. He could not be ignored, he had opinions about everything, and he often engendered emotional tumult within minutes after entering a room. His energy never flagged, and he infused even simple things with his patented intensity.

In California, Ira partook of all the revolution's pleasures, instantly assuming the posture as one of the wise men of the movement. Long a fan of Bob Dylan, he now picked up on the acid-rock groups in the Bay Area, noting Plato's maxim that "When the style of music in a culture changes, the political style of life will soon follow." He visited communes, and briefly considered saying to hell with things, and joining one. He began to assemble his own little network of revolutionary seers, people like Alan Watts and the Berkeley education radical Michael Rossman. He scanned the newspapers with interest—it seemed to him that with Vietnam, racial strife, pollution, and consumerism, the country, maybe the world, had gone mad. He began to sharpen his personal vision, a curious mixture of dire apocalypse (The structure is collapsing! Behold the destruction of America!) and spiritual transformation (People like us will usher in the millennium!). While perusing the San Francisco *Chronicle* one day, Ira was impressed by the cacophony of resonant articles about random events, and began to formulate what would be his major essay, a rambling pastiche called "The Sociology of the Now." As with most of his nonfiction it was more digestible than his poetry or fiction, liberally peppered with passages from classical or contemporary sages, and depending on one's outlook, either deeply evocative, semi-incomprehensible, or both.

By the time Ira Einhorn returned to Powelton in late August of 1966, he was ready to introduce the excitement of Berkeley and the Haight to Philadelphia, as yet untouched by the psychedelic revolution. This was a pattern that would be repeated throughout his career—his visits to the vanguard would never end with his signing on full-time, but instead see him leaving the front lines to impart the new wisdom to his hometown. "A lot of people during that time discovered this new life-style and rushed to New York or California to devour the young hippies and generally use them," says Victor Bockris, then a Penn student. "Ira was cleverer than that. He basically realized that being a big star in a little pond like Philadelphia was a more profitable way to go. And indeed Philadelphia was culturally starved in the sixties, so consequently it was a venue for him to operate in."

He was now in touch with his powers. His public persona was formed. His career would be linked to his charisma, along with his uncanny ability to hook up to new and visceral concepts. He was coming home to claim his audience.

The Unicorn found his first public forum at University of Pennsylvania's Free University. Free U was an experiment in alternative education. "There was something lacking in the academic sector," explains Bob Brand, one of the founders of Penn's version of Free U (other campuses around the country had their own counteruniversities). "There was a certain lack of rigor, and there was a minimum of Left critique. We wanted a more participatory form of education, a more democratic substance, and we were interested in Marx, in socialism, in civil rights, in peace stuff."

In Free U anyone could declare him or herself as teacher—the students would decide whether or not that appellation was deserved. The SDS-affiliated students who founded the Penn version of Free U (FUP) thought this a serious exercise and expected perhaps a hundred or so to enroll for the first term. But when registration started, 750 students clamored to get in and new courses had to be opened on the spot.

Ira Einhorn quickly became, according to an article by Ralph Keyes in *The Nation,* "the new hero in today's Free University." Keyes saw Einhorn as a long-haired, bearded, education crusader with a daffodil behind one ear. His first course was called "The World of Marshall McLuhan," but the three-page syllabus covered the full range of his interests; Bob Brand referred to it as "Introduction to Hippiedom." Keyes wrote that "Einhorn's courses are easily the most popular in the Free University. His teaching tools range from candles and incense to rock 'n roll and free-word association. . . . [His 'McLuhan' course] actually *rose* in participation from 60 to 75, more people attending the last class than the room would hold."

While Einhorn's McLuhan course was undoubtedly popular, it was not the most controversial FUP course in the first semester of 1966. That honor went to the offering by Curt Kubiak and Grant Schaefer, respectively, an architect and the owner of Powelton's first head shop. The course was on psychedelics, and both instructors were officials in the Timothy Leary–inspired Neo-American Church. (In the loony hierarchy of this Church, Kubiak was "Primate" of Pennsylvania, Schaefer was a "Boo Hoo.") According to the *Daily Pennsylvanian,* 100 students, some hostile to the premise, showed up at the first class, where the two teachers promised discussion of the laws, history, personalities, and religious significance of the LSD experience.

In other words, the heart of Ira Einhorn territory. And sure enough, before the students were dismissed, Einhorn himself appeared, sharing the drug pulpit with the Primate and the Boo Hoo, calling for open forums, "where people will listen, instead of shoving drugs under the rug." Einhorn became a third instructor for the course.

It was a strange triumvirate. Schaefer was interested in dispassionately disseminating information; he and Ira got along only casually. Kubiak and Einhorn, though, took to each other right away. Curt Kubiak was slightly older, a family man partly rooted in the traditional middle class. Another part of him was somewhere else. "He was an architect who got a little discombobulated along the line," an acquaintance described him. He was short, a bit rotund, resembling a Mandarin with a little beard and his hair slicked back. Sandy White, a friend who witnessed the first meeting between Ira and Curt, says that Kubiak "was very serious about his LSD church . . . he would have ceremonies on mattresses in his den, and candles, and he'd go through his LSD trips. Ira had been passing out DMT and hash and stuff to selected people for a long period in Powelton Village. So he was very glad to meet Curt. Here we had two self-styled gurus, shaking hands and complimenting each other on their work."

The next semester, in addition to his McLuhan course, Ira had his *own* psychedelics course, called "Analogues to the LSD Experience." The turnout was splendid.

The LSD class, as expected, was controversial and instrumental in creating a reputation for its instructor. Even though the psychedelic experience was on the lips, if not within the mouths, of any mildly hip Penn student in the year 1967, very few in the conservative burg of Philadelphia dared to publicly address the drug's virtues, let alone advocate its use. Ira Einhorn was the most notable exception, presenting himself as a visible and gleeful target to those who sputtered objections. When a group of conservative students decided to monitor the LSD course and document the instructor's blasphemies by tape recording, Einhorn didn't bat an eyelid, even when a young woman with fundamentalist beliefs almost invoked the wrath of the heavens when the Unicorn urged discussion of the religious aspect of LSD. When Ralph Keyes asked Einhorn if any of this bothered him, he replied, "No, my policy is maximum jeopardy at all times."

Einhorn wrote to his friend Michael Hoffman that the only problem with his FUP courses was "too much worship of me."

By 1967, the Unicorn was also holding classes in two locations. "Evenings with Ira Einhorn" were held on Wednesday evenings in Logan Hall, a lecture room on the Penn campus. The curriculum was to cover "McLuhan, Brown, Marcuse, air pollution, population problems, automation, guaranteed annual income, drugs, Third World revolution, Wilhelm Reich, cancer, and California."

Other classes were held in his huge apartment in the Piles. In these sessions, Ira planned to lead his students "from the revolution of the body to the revolution of the mind." As explained by one Penn freshman in attendance, these were heady gatherings, especially when considering the revolution of the body: "After four or five sessions," she says, "he proposed turning the evening into a party. Out came the joints. Suddenly, he wanted us to get rid of all inhibitions, and he took off all his clothes. He began to dance . . . he sort of wiggled around."

The sight of this, of this massive naked body shaking, the big head half covered by the dark beard bobbing, and those blue eyes blazing, was too much for this young woman, who lunged for the door, escaping only after extricating herself from a playful Ira bear hug—the Powelton guru obviously showing her that it was *all right,* she *could* freak out if she wanted, and in fact people *often* were not evolved enough to contend with the psychic paradigm shift that Ira Einhorn could usher into their consciousness.

* * *

By 1967, it seemed that Ira Einhorn had enrolled the entire population of Philadelphia as students in his ongoing Free University course. "My classroom is just an extension of myself," he proclaimed, and when the guru spoke, people listened. Those people increasingly were reporters for the city's major newspapers, who had aggregately crowned him as Philadelphia's leading hippie.

Ira's career as a news source began with a *Philadelphia Magazine* article about marijuana. During the course of investigating whether the sons and daughters of the upper-middle-class readers of his magazine had fallen prey to the odious blight of marijuana, a skilled investigative reporter named Gaeton Fonzi attended a meeting at Penn and approached a woman who seemed, as far as Fonzi could determine, stoned. She directed him to the obvious source for information about the dope scene in Philadelphia: Ira Einhorn.

Fonzi expected some degree of paranoia. After all, here he was, in a tie and jacket, writing for a straight magazine, asking this bearded fellow who lived in a crash pad for a glimpse into his illegal activities. But Ira Einhorn was open, shockingly so. "He trusted me totally, like it was an almost instinctive thing on his part," says Fonzi. Einhorn invited the reporter to the Piles, and sitting on the living room floor, Ira spoke for hours into Fonzi's tape recorder. He wasn't hung up on attribution, or protection. He seemed happy to hear himself talk, but was also a good listener. And he had an endearing attitude that none of the stuff he was saying was really that important. "I remember Ira mostly laughing at the seriousness of everything," says Fonzi. "He had a perspective in terms of the world that 'in the long run, we're all dead,' that type of thing."

Gaeton Fonzi, being a thorough reporter, wanted to experience the substance he was writing about. So Ira helped him set up a "pot party." Ira arrived with two young women in tow, shed shoes and socks, and pulled out the pipe. And the threat of violence dissipated. "Do what you want," Einhorn instructed. "There are very few basic rules. One of the main functions of the situation is to just enjoy yourself."

Fonzi wrote a widely circulated article, and for Einhorn the experience of being singled out as a man with the power to turn people on was not only delightful but addictive.

For the next five years, when the word *hippie* cropped up in a Philadelphia news story, there would inevitably be a cross-reference to the Unicorn, most often with a memorable, if cosmically cryptic, quote from the bearded one himself.

The clincher was Ira Einhorn's personal Be-In.

In January of 1967, San Francisco had celebrated the first event of that sort, the Human Be-In, a truly cosmic gathering of 25,000 in Golden Gate Park with Allen Ginsberg and Alan Watts, and innumerable rock bands. Not long after, New York City had the East Coast equivalent in Central Park, again with reports that the heavens beamed a blessing on these illuminated beings. It would not necessarily follow that Philadelphia, certainly a backwater in the Age of Aquarius, would have its own Be-In. But Ira Einhorn, who followed the events in California and New York closely, asked "Why not?" Stating his position as "lecturer in psychedelics at the Free University," he wrote the commissioners of Philadelphia's Fairmount Park asking for a permit to use an area near the Schuylkill River on April 16, 1967.

The commissioners worried that such an ill-defined event might endanger the park's Japanese cherry trees. But the newspapers, enjoying the novelty of the situation, took the side of the hippie underdogs, and eventually the park director's meek "maybe" changed to a reluctant "go ahead." As is the wont of newspapers, they focused in on the personality behind the event. Ira, with a cool grasp on the needs of reporters, was only too happy to provide them with quotes and color.

"If it rains, it rains," he told them. "I'll show up. If other people show up, it's their business." Somewhat more seriously, he predicted that a thousand would attend, "more people than hippies." At the time, of course, there were nowhere near one thousand people in Philadelphia who would vaguely qualify as "hippies."

The actual event was sedate. The Be-In crowd shakily emulated the behavior they'd read about at previous Be-Ins—body painting, exchanges of daffodils, wearing of floppy hats. If there was much open pot smoking, the half dozen narcotics policemen in attendance missed it. The kinkiest extreme was a group who briefly burned dollar bills, yelling "Down with Capitalists!" People began arriving at noon and stayed until sunset. The *Inquirer* estimated 1,500 Be-ers; the *Bulletin*'s headline claimed 2,000 came "to promote flower power." The pioneer Philadelphia acid-rock bands plugged in their instruments and played for free (one group, Woody's Truck Stop, featured a guitarist named Tod Rundgren, later a top musician). In retrospect, it was a coming-out party—the sixties had arrived in Philadelphia.

Ira Einhorn was ecstatic. Though he proclaimed the event "totally unorganized," *somebody* had done things to make sure things were there when needed. It is not clear just whom. Ira stood above scut work, preferring a sociological, or perhaps Olympian, distance. "This is just a gathering of the people in the community, to give everyone an opportunity to look at each other," he told the *Inquirer.* "The split in the younger generation is widening all the time. Maybe this will help close the gap."

It certainly closed whatever gap remained between Ira and the media. A *Bulletin* columnist rhapsodized about Ira, "an agent for the turned-on generation." She claimed that by throwing a bash for thousands of people for $50 out-of-pocket expenses ($40 of which he made back from profits of button sales), Ira was a party giver in the league of Truman Capote and Perle Mesta.

A full month after the Be-In, the newspapers were still talking about it, and the remarkable twenty-seven-year-old who was behind the event. It was much easier to discuss the youth revolution in terms of Ira Einhorn and his ilk than it was to examine the other side of the movement, the SDS and the civil rights activists with their work shirts, their earnestness, and their pinko cant. The *Inquirer* even ran a story about Ira's relationship with his mother, who had been spotted at the Be-In handing out homemade chocolate chip cookies. The headline read "Parents Back Son's Goal," but the picture of Ira Einhorn provided the context: his face surrounded by a bushy circle of hair and beard, his eyes blocked by dark sunglasses, a button (probably with some down-the-Establishment message) festooned on his dark shirt—in short, something out of an updated *Wild One,* a parent's nightmare. Claiming that the Einhorns were "a typical Jewish family," Bea Einhorn admitted confusion about what the reporter called Ira's "quest for understanding, peace and love."

"Who knows what motivates young people in the direction they take?" she asked. But she insisted that "We have a wonderful relationship with our sons and we love Ira dearly."

Actually, the appearance of the elder Einhorns at their Ira's Be-In cemented a rapprochement after years of on-and-off stress considering their son's behavior. Whatever Ira had set out to become in the years after his graduation, it was drastically at odds with what Bea and Joseph Einhorn quite had in mind. Somehow the Jewish-American immigrant dream of upward mobility and ascension into the respectable mainstream had gone awry. Their son, with his talents and the advantages of superb education, had been given the keys to the kingdom. Yet he had spurned the castle, preferring to set up camp outside its walls, posting notices of the kingdom's corruption. Bea Einhorn—always loathe to pin the blame on her beloved firstborn—suspected that the trouble began with Professor Peckham's intellectual seduction. Before Peckham, she thought, Ira had been headed for a career in science. Now, he seemed determined to invent his own career. Not a project for a nice Jewish boy.

Ira's life-style only made things worse. The beard, the hair, the run-down apartment in Powelton. Mrs. Einhorn "is a meticulous woman," says Bea Clegg, a family friend sometimes called on to mediate the Einhorn family disputes in those days. "The way Ira branched off . . . was hard for her to accept. And there were times when she was not too happy about introducing him [to her friends]."

There were periods in the early sixties when Ira avoided visiting his parents. Once, when he was penniless, he did return home—to the new home the Einhorns had purchased in the suburbs—and was delighted to find himself treated like a conquering hero. Bea Einhorn was the architect of this reception. "I was on the brink of starvation," Ira wrote in a letter, "and my mother calmly fed me, gave me money, filled up my car with gas and packed me a care package."

For a while, though, the rift over Ira's life-style continued. It seems that the schism was deepest between Ira and Joe Einhorn. "My father hardly exists for me at all," Ira wrote in 1965. He mused that his "hatred for labor of any type" might be seen as a rebellion against Joe Einhorn, whom he considered overly concerned with the trivialities of breadwinning. Ira also attributed his "abhorrence for . . . any religious thinking which places a strong emphasis on God" to his nonrelationship with Einhorn *père*.

However, it appears that through the will of Bea Einhorn a healing was effected. An intelligent woman, she came to realize that a parent's powers were limited in influencing her son's behavior. And she apparently convinced her husband of this wisdom. "Ira was good, he was a good person, really," she says. "So we eventually accepted the hair. You get used to anything, I guess. And everybody else was accepting him . . . so we thought, Well, he's our son, we're gonna accept him."

Bea Einhorn became a huge supporter of Ira's career—whatever *that* was—and she even attended some of the lectures that Ira gave. Many of these were delivered to audiences of older people who wanted to see a hippie in the flesh. Ira would be provocative but not offensive. Everyone would go home happy. Ira once explained this to a friend who asked where he got his money. "I do speeches here and there," he said. "Little old ladies invite me over to their teas to have me gross them out. They pay me." The friend asked how it was he grossed them out.

"Very gently," Ira replied.

Judging from the considerable volume of news clippings generated from these appearances, Ira's lectures were newsworthy occasions. By reporting the twists and turns of Ira Einhorn's public pronouncements, the newspapers felt they were conveying the thoughts and feelings of the vanguard of a new, complicated generation. If Ira's exclamations were sometimes extreme, the reporters almost always tempered their fury with a bit of whimsy, an air of entertainment. Ira came to learn how to add just the proper amount of preposterousness to his talks so that the papers could give the straights something to chuckle over.

It could even be argued that in the great morality play of the sixties that was taking shape, the city was crying out for a nemesis to its dominant figure, Police Commissioner Frank Rizzo. The "Big Bambino" was a working-class Italian-American whose education stopped at eighth grade, but was consistently cunning in winning a bedrock constituency of blue-collar law-and-order advocates. His style was embodied by a classic photograph—Rizzo in a tuxedo, a nightstick stuffed into his cummerbund, facing down angry black protesters. In an age where blacks, long-haired freaks, and pointy-headed liberals seemed to approve of eroding standards, Frank Rizzo dared say no. The civil rights of his foes did not seem foremost in Rizzo's mind, as the time he attempted to close Philadelphia's rock-music palace, a converted tire warehouse called the Electric Factory, apparently because he despised the generation it catered to. Ira Einhorn—a hippie, drug-taking, Jewish intellectual with cheek and charisma equal to Rizzo's—was the city's most prominent member of that generation, and as such he became Rizzo's mirror-image *Doppelgänger*.

"If there was a sixties game, and you had various pieces representing the important characters, you'd have to have an Ira piece," says William Wolf, a Philadelphia assistant district attorney then. Wolf would often appear on panels with Einhorn. "I'd be the resident fascist, and he'd be the free spirit." Actually, Wolf was impressed with Ira's persona. "He was forceful . . . we're talking about body language—he used his bulk in the same way that Frank Rizzo did. He gave off a sense of solidness, a sureness bordering on cockiness. He had a little bit of the prophet in him."

In the newspaper articles written about his speeches, Ira was described variously as "Writer-lecturer," "Local Guru," "Pot Smoker," "Be-In Organizer," "Hippie Philosopher." A sampling:

MAY 1967: Ira tells the Philadelphia Peace Convocation that "America is dead for me. It does not exist." He says that he and others in the "psychedelic community" are trying to create a "sense of joy" in life, and though they despise war, they eschew demonstrations, preferring not to "celebrate our hate by carrying signs."

NOVEMBER 1967: At a panel to discuss drugs at the Moore College of Art, Ira promised, according to the *Inquirer*, that the hippies, in order to "break the back" of law enforcement, would flood the jails with arrests for drug use.

DECEMBER 1967: As "hippie representative" on a panel discussion, Ira said that the Movement consists not only of visible hippies, but millions of teenagers who were virtual "undercover agents" in their parents' homes, conducting "guerrilla warfare" for the cause. "Remember, it only takes 3 percent of the population to start a revolution," he tells the astonished Philadelphia Chapter of the American Jewish Committee Agency.

FEBRUARY 1968: The Unicorn tells a YMCA luncheon forum that "What the country needs is two months of silence."

Ira Einhorn spread his message not only by lectures but by the printed word as well. In August 1967, he had returned from the disastrous California "Summer of Love" appalled at the exploitation and ruin of the hippie dreams in Haight-Ashbury, burning with rage over the state of the country, convinced that violence seemed inevitable. An indicator of this decline was the proliferation of Methedrine—the destructive drug called "speed"—which was popular at the expense of constructively cerebral chemicals like acid or pot. Ira himself, upon his first taste of intravenous speed, judged the substance as "a ticket to nights of dark paranoia," and a symbol of the fire to come. Between nuclear holocaust, race relations, the surge of angry young protesters, and bubonic plague epidemics overseas, he surmised, the caldron was about to overflow; he warned people to consider emigrating to Canada if the thought of a bloodbath made them squeamish. When his friends noted that his message was sounding somewhat shrill, he replied that "My program isn't apocalyptic--just my awareness."

He scribbled missives in the night in hopes of making this awareness more widely known. His mode was now a free-form essay writing that varied his own proclamations, musings, and quasi-Ginsberg lyrics with snippets of salient writing from sources he respected.

Fortunately for Einhorn, the phenomenon of the underground press had finally reached Philadelphia. A former Penn State journalism student named Don DeMaio began the *Distant Drummer* in October 1967. Started on a shoestring, the *Drummer* was able to plug into the city's slowly awakening counterculture. A small enclave of "hippie capitalism" had emerged, not far from Rittenhouse Square, the formerly tony urban garden that had become the promenade of Philadelphia's freak community. The new head shops, concert promoters, progressive rock radio stations, and other counterculture-oriented businesses welcomed a target-market advertising outlet, as did the national record companies, who used the *Drummer* and underground papers like it to place ads like the remarkable "The Man can't bust our music" campaign, implying that Columbia Records, like the *Drummer's* readers, raised its fist in defiance to the Establishment.

It was inevitable that before long, Ira Einhorn would march into the tiny, cluttered Pine Street *Drummer* office and announce his availability for stories, both as contributor and subject.

"The whole relationship between Ira and our newspaper was Ira seeking exposure, either personal or for his ideas as a writer," says DeMaio. "I felt intimidated by him. He was very aggressive, but at the same time he was a nice Jewish boy.

Ira's *Drummer* writing was usually signed by the pseudonym "The Unicorn," sometimes accompanied by a handwritten symbol of his astrological sign, Taurus. Since someone had pointed out how his name (Einhorn = One Horn) relates to the mythical horselike creature with a single horn between the eyes, Ira had fancied himself as kin to that mythological creature, representing purity, uniqueness, gentleness, and sexual power. The Unicorn was a rare being that bloomed when it ran free. Its only weakness was a propensity for young virgins.

DeMaio finally agreed to print a column by Einhorn called "The Unicorn Speaks." DeMaio was ambivalent about its quality. "I remember the first column we got in, we had just gotten new typesetting equipment and I set the piece up real nice in type. He called to complain afterwards that I had done so—he wanted the stuff printed up just the way it was. Which was sloppy, everything uppercase, no punctuation. The staff really rebelled against that. They said that made it even more incoherent. I thought that was kind of his smoke screen. The more incoherent it was, the more people would say, 'Wow! If he can understand this and write this, he must be really bright!' "

Finally, DeMaio recalls, "the staff pressure really built up to dump the Unicorn. So I terminated the column but kept the relationship open so he could send in stuff on an irregular basis." Ira maintained his visibility there; DeMaio accepted his writings with full knowledge that it was part of a campaign. "Ira just knew how to get publicity, and what things were best for him. That's why the Establishment used him so much—he was safe that way. He was rebutting the Establishment in a way they could relate to, for the most part. Even though his writings for the *Drummer* were full of blood and violence and everything, he really wasn't as radical, or as violent, as a lot of other people were in Philadelphia at the time, who were such freaks that no TV whatever would put them on the air. They were just so . . . ugly. Their pads were sloppy messes. Their heads were fried from LSD. But Ira was the safe thing. He had the nice TV smile, and he was able to relate to the Establishment in a way they could understand. When you talked to him in person about bloodshed and the apocalypse and all that, he kind of laughed as he talked about it. He was always laughing."

*   *   *

One cannot easily laugh away legal troubles, however, and Ira Einhorn's visibility in promoting the counterculture made him a prime candidate for a drug bust. In 1967, the Philadelphia police would harass the Unicorn, who of course cried foul. His complaints would be echoed much later when in quite different circumstances Einhorn declared he was framed for the murder of Holly Maddux.

The irony was that by the time Frank Rizzo's police department launched its campaign against him, Ira Einhorn was relatively clear of drugs. Not that he disavowed them: He always considered them useful tools for exploring one's consciousness, and marijuana was often good for a relaxing diversion. It's just that, always ahead of the game, Ira was into the next thing. At the moment, it was macrobiotics. An old friend named Craig Samms had recently returned from London, raving about organic foods; Samms had been staying at Ira's apartment in the capacity of macrobiotic cook. Einhorn frequently would entertain groups of four to a dozen, serving them meals totally lacking protein as they previously knew it. Most enjoyed it, though some guests, like Don DeMaio, recalled struggling with muffins that "tasted like sand."

Ira also watched himself by maintaining good relations with some of the authorities. The head of the Civil Disobedience Squad then was an even-tempered fellow named George Fencl. A reporter once said that with his burly, implacable demeanor, Fencl would have been well cast as a cop in a 1930s movie. Fencl took an enlightened view of his job: He believed that by being friendly with the dissidents and potential troublemakers, you could gather information with less trouble and certainly less danger. Fencl developed relationships with counterculture leaders, among them the Unicorn. "I consider Ira Einhorn a friend of mine," he told *Philadelphia Magazine.*

But others in the law-enforcement community were not so friendly. They still bore a quixotic hope that Philadelphia could stave off the drug menace. It galled them that Ira Einhorn was garnering wide attention—some of it positive—by writing and speaking on the virtues of illegal drugs. In 1967, the battle lines were drawn.

The police's first assault occurred during one of the Unicorn's fabled parties at his pad in the Rock Pile. After announcing their presence, the invasion force of officers systematically shuttled the party goers from one room to another and searched them. Ira, though, had been prudent, leaving no contraband where police might find it. One of Einhorn's students, attending the party that night, recalls that the narcs were taunting Ira. Einhorn diffused the scene with nonviolence. "Most people would get uptight at their apartment being busted, three or four narcs running around, searching everybody," says the student. "But not Ira. He's the picture of cool, he's joking with people, and he's telling the narc how many push-ups he can do. And as he engaged the guy, he was giggling, his sort of amphetamine giggle."

Einhorn was still feeling bold when he appeared on a Sunday-afternoon television show called "Generations in Conflict" for a panel discussion on the dangers of taking drugs. After hearing a local judge and other people lecture on the dangers of marijuana, Ira calmly pulled out a doobie and lit up.

The next salvo belonged to the police. At eleven-thirty on a Tuesday morning in December 1967, they banged on Einhorn's door. Ira left his bed (according to one account, he had been in the midst of a love embrace with his girlfriend of the moment) to answer the doorbell. Nude, as usual. In an eerie harbinger of what was to occur twelve years later, Officer Charles McSorley and two others presented Ira Einhorn with a search-and-seizure warrant. They proceeded to tear the place apart looking for drugs. Somehow missing the small amount of marijuana affixed outside the window sill, all they could come up with was two jars full of pills, found in the medicine cabinet.

Ira identified these pills as medicine for a kidney ailment; at one point before going on a long trip, he'd gotten his doctor to prescribe him a thousand pills so he wouldn't have a problem getting more. He had only used a hundred or so, and left the rest in their jars. He suggested the cops call his doctor; she was on vacation. So the cops arrested not only Ira but also his girlfriend—a descendant of a former president of the United States. Craig Samms was taken into custody as well.

Samms remembers that the police drove them to a distant precinct house. Again, in the face of violence, Ira kept cool. "One cop there really wanted to provoke a violent outburst," says Samms. "He came in where we were standing, and he called her the whore, me the faggot [due to Samms' slight English accent], and Ira the scumbag. And Ira held off and said, 'Look, I'm a black belt in karate. I can be very violent, I can do a lot of damage to you. I don't want to do any damage.' And that cooled the cop down, in fact. It was scary, because I thought they were gonna kill him, right there in custody."

The lab analysis of the pills taken from Ira's apartment proved that, indeed, they were Reserpine, prescribed by his doctor for hypertension due to a kidney inflammation. But also confiscated were other pills, most found to be vitamins, but two of which were identified as Librium, a tranquilizer for which Einhorn had no prescription. For this—two pills of a mild tranquilizer—Magistrate Samuel Clark, Jr., after a preliminary hearing, refused to dismiss the charge of possession of dangerous drugs. Ira was released on $300 bail.

Ira's attorney was Bernard Segal. "It was a nonsense prosecution," he says. "They arrested because Ira was Ira." Segal was shocked not so much at the police behavior—in Rizzo's police department this was no anomaly—but at the prosecutor, a young assistant DA whom he had previously respected. Holding a man for two Libriums! But Ira took it in stride. "I remember being there with him. Ira then was like Ira at every place. This warm, wonderful, loving person, generally with a beatific smile about him—not one of those smiles of those who are intoxicated on religion, not one of those smiles of those who are intoxicated on drugs. Ira was happy being Ira."

Months later, the case was dismissed. Lesson: The Man could bust Ira Einhorn, but he could not make it stick.

Powelton Village was the center of hippie activity in Philadelphia. Its Victorian houses sheltered any number of communal families, with names like "The Family of Peace." The vibrations were terrific—you could walk outside your door, as the Unicorn did one day, and see a freak in a tuxedo playing an upright bass for delighted black kids. In the eyes of the police, "Powelton Village was like a commune with traffic lights," recalls prosecutor Billy Wolf. And Ira Einhorn? "He was the village chief," says Wolf. But someone else put it more succinctly: "The Mayor of Powelton."

You could make a case for it. Ira was a cosmic politician, working the streets, promoting his platform, projecting a carefully constructed image that obliterated whoever might really be lurking behind the ponytail and beard, the trademark flannel shirt, the

beat-up sandals—which he wore even in winter—and the characteristic body odor. He was aware of his role as the city's titular
counterculture leader, and conscientiously built on it.

Perhaps in a gesture to become closer to his constituency, he had
disposed of his most serious tie to a staid, conventional life of the
mind: the famous Einhorn book collection. "He had come to feel
like the books were really a millstone around his neck," says Craig
Samms. "It was just too much knowledge there on the shelves, and
his conversation was interspersed with so many literary references
that unless you had the same reference points culturally or literally,
you couldn't really communicate with him. And selling the books
was just symbolic of throwing away all that stuff."

Another acquisition that would eventually be jettisoned was a fine
stereo system that Ira had obtained by bartering 300 capsules of
LSD. It played rock music for parties and classical music for the acid
trips where Ira acted as guide. Naturally, Einhorn's apartment
became known as a community gathering place. "It was sort of a
hippie version of a salon," says Bob Brand, a political activist at
Penn. "You would drop by and as likely as not there would be people
hanging around, chatting, eating, whatever. It was an eclectic group
of local Philadelphians, campus people, out-of-towners drifting
through." Another friend describes it as the Grand Central Station
of Philadelphia's underground.

The Mayor of Powelton's program of community improvement
emphasized the best values of the sixties: resistance to the Establishment for the benefit of humanity. He was active in the continuing
struggle against the expansionist tactics of Penn and Drexel. As
social leader, he made himself available to his constituency. "The
phone calls are becoming maddening," he wrote during that
period, "even though I would probably be unhappy without them—
pot, LSD, abortion, poetry, advice—I feel as if I'm running a
strange kind of general store."

Ira often put himself in the position of a peacemaker, a sort of
one-man Supreme Court of the counterculture. For instance, in late
1968, a dispute erupted between The Warlocks, Philadelphia's
equivalent to the Hell's Angels motorcycle gang, and some members
of Resistance, a group that ran an antiwar print shop and counseled
young people in avoiding the draft. It seems that someone put sand
in the gas tanks of the Warlock Harleys while the bikers were

attending a George Wallace rally; the outraged victims blamed the antiwar group, and, according to the *Inquirer,* "stated their grievances, which they emphasized by punching a Resistance member in the jaw." Father David Gracie, an Episcopal priest affiliated with Resistance, asked Ira Einhorn to step in, explaining that "he communicates better than anybody in Philadelphia." Ira forthwith convened a press conference to announce a benefit "happening" at the YMHA to raise money to fix the motorcycles and, in the process, heal the rift.

More seriously, he pondered the problem of young people unprepared for the license of the counterculture he helped form— the burnt-out druggies and the young runaways. One day he went to the psychiatric unit of the Pennsylvania Hospital and urged the young residents to get out of their sheltered environment and "help the people downtown." The force of Einhorn's lecture deeply affected Charles Holland, a newly minted doctor of clinical psychology and to that date a clean-cut young man.

Holland says that Ira Einhorn's philosophy "is something that I have carried with me for a long, long time. I talk about it to my kids. What he said to the psychiatric residents was, 'You had everything handed to you on a silver platter. You have to go out and exercise your brain, but that brain was born to you. There are folks who aren't that fortunate; if you've got something, it's up to you to share it.' He didn't cut you any slack on that. A lot of us heard that and really responded."

From that initiative, Holland, with Einhorn's help, started the Powelton Trouble Center. It was located in space Ira liberated in the basement of the Piles. A dump. But from six in the evening until midnight, it was a place where young vagrants or runaways could drop in, get something to eat. Speed freaks could cool out, attending the group sessions Holland ran for them. "Food would appear someplace," says Holland. "A bunch of mattresses. Really sick people would be taken care of."

The Mayor of Powelton made himself available to any in the city who cared to avail themselves of his wisdom. Many reporters took advantage of this—for instance, Gaeton Fonzi benefited from Einhorn's close study of the Kennedy assassination—but also some unexpected officials. For instance, Robert DeWitt, the bishop of the Philadelphia diocese of the Episcopal Church, not only met periodically with Ira but actually put him on a small monthly retainer. The bishop would quiz Einhorn on various aspects of youth culture; often he relied on Ira to "overcome my deficiencies" in certain areas of thought. As in the time he confessed to Ira that he knew little about Marxism. "A week or so later, Ira came back with about five or six carefully selected volumes, which I read," says the bishop. "Kind of a quick course."

Ira was also Powelton's chief diplomatic officer. He was able to boast kinship with the superstars of the movement. He often visited New York City, hanging out at activist Jerry Rubin's East Village apartment with the founding fathers of Yippiedom. It was a movement Ira liked; as Rubin wrote in his 1970 tome, *Do It*, "Yippies are leaders without followers. Yippies do whatever we want whenever we want to do it." This was displayed in famous acts like dropping money onto the floor of the New York Stock Exchange and watching the straights go crazy. Though some of the more militant protesters thought Ira's devotion to the cause was not sufficiently single-minded, Rubin liked the Unicorn. "Ira represented Utopian thinking, which I wanted to bring into the left-wing perspective," he says. "I welcomed Ira's mind—he was very smart."

Ira was included on Yippie raids. On one excursion, a weekend blitz of a college newspaper conference in Washington, Ira documented his participation in the *Drummer*. He called himself one of the five Marx Brothers, "arriving via train from New York and Philadelphia, armed with chalk, smiles, pot, hash, acid, and the sense that America is quickly dying." The other brothers were Jerry Rubin, Abbie Hoffman, *Realist* editor Paul Krassner, and psychedelic artist Marty Carey. Einhorn helped disrupt a Eugene McCarthy press conference. To those at the conference wondering who was this fifth Marx Brother, Ira provided the following explanation: "a unicorn here as a guerrilla."

To Einhorn, theater was the best form of protest. He had little taste for hard-core demonstrating, for being a face in a crowd. "He avoided the national demonstrations," says Stew Albert, part of the Yippie brain trust. Albert recalls Ira sitting in on the planning sessions for the grand 1968 Yippie invasion of Chicago, designed to disrupt the Democratic National Convention. "Scenarios, that was his big word. He'd give scenarios. He used to like to lay out complicated structures. It wasn't simply, 'we'll do this.' It was 'We can do this to get them to do that, and we'll respond with this.' . . . And then of course he didn't go."

To some movement people, this trait, combined with his interminable speechifying, branded him as arrogant and self-involved. To those who saw the split between hippie and lefty as contentious, Ira was an insidious danger, draining the energies of would-be protesters into navel-contemplating dead ends of sloth, bad poetry, quasiacademic babble, and chemical fantasias. One woman recalls seeing Ira outside a Penn antiwar teach-in, warning off onlookers with the admonition that "bad vibes" were inside.

On the other hand, as even his lefty critics admitted, he was always clever, always interesting. His whirlwind charm had its effect. He also had other things to offer besides talk: In *Mug Shots*, a 1972 book on the counterculture, Ira identifies himself as the person who gave Jerry Rubin his first hit of acid. (Rubin's recollection is otherwise.) Ira once claimed that the SDS called him to task for "turning on all the politicals"; he defended himself by insisting that "we can know a little bit more, when we travel a little bit further."

When celebrity Yippies came to town, Ira acted as unofficial advance man. At Abbie Hoffman's whistle-stop tour of Philadelphia, Ira hosted a news conference, then introduced him at a lecture hall. A *Drummer* reporter noted of Ira's short speech, "Einhorn's heart may or may not be in the right place, but his prose runs to cliché, and the light in his eye seems to have less to do with the fire next time than with the desire to blaze a path across the Philadelphia firmament." Nonetheless, when Abbie's speech was degenerating into warmed-over Lenny Bruce schtick, it was Ira who perked things up by suggesting that Abbie lead a street demonstration in nearby Rittenhouse Square. Within minutes, almost 500 people were massed in the square, crowded around the visiting radical; almost immediately the police appeared. An ugly confrontation loomed. Again, it was Ira who took control of the event, putting the brakes to a potential disaster. "C'mon Abbie," said Ira, the peacemaker, "I've got two soft pretzels waiting for you back there. No sense you getting busted."

Jerry Rubin's visit was less successful. After an afternoon rally, the feisty Yippie, in his trademark polo shirt and jeans, went to Einhorn's apartment in the Piles to reconnoiter before a speech scheduled for that evening. Ira and Jerry had an argument over exactly who was supposed to be the featured performer in the visit. As Rubin recollects, "He was using me. I realized that I was going to be some pawn in an Ira production." Though Rubin had never before walked out on a commitment, he did it then, to emphasize his disgust with Einhorn. "I'm just leaving," he said to Ira. "You deal with it." That night at the Ethical Society, Ira and his friend Curt Kubiak unsuccessfully attempted to soothe a crowd of 700 who showed up that night to hear Rubin speak.

Ira's guests were not limited to political figures; they ran the gamut from spiritual to intellectual to literary. Ira's roommate Dave Peterson recalls that when Ira hosted these well-known figures he would often invite twenty or so friends over to absorb his guest's wisdom. The visitors included Richard Alpert (Timothy Leary's cohort who later called himself Baba Ram Dass), Jean and Julian Beck of the Living Theater, Allen Ginsberg, avant garde musician John Cage, and, for a macrobiotic New Year's Day dinner in 1968, the Mothers of Invention rock group.

Powelton etiquette required that someone attending a party bring either a bottle of wine or some grass. Or perhaps some record albums to play on the stereo. "But when I had a party," says one Powelton Village resident in the sixties, "Ira brought the Fugs." Not the album. The band members.

By the time the decade was ending, Ira Einhorn had finally perfected the role he had carefully built for himself. For many in Powelton, indeed in all of Philadelphia, he was a touchstone. When he stopped to chat, you would get not only local gossip but the benefit of his connections in New York, California, and the communes of Arizona. He presented himself as the consummately plugged-in person, the ultimate citizen of his time and place.

True, some people regarded him as a buffoon, a caricature, the type of all-knowing guru satirized in Al Capp's cartoons. At a party of graduate students and English faculty at Penn where Ira held court for those still imprisoned in the academic world he had liberated himself from, an emboldened Ph.D. candidate approached him and said, caustically, "Ira, will you be our guru?" Einhorn took these affronts in stride. He laughed—his flighty, uplifting giggle— as if he, too, were in on the joke.

He *was* in on the joke.

He had his rivals, even his enemies. Many seriously involved in left-wing politics considered him frivolous, possibly even an informer. Even some of his friends in the Piles regarded him with resentment—after all, no one had *asked* Ira to be a guru, he had just become one. And it was impossible to challenge him—after all, your average Philadelphia hippie would never be able to cite fourteen obscure texts on a given topic, along with a supporting remark that Alan Watts had uttered personally to him while meditating at Esalen. When Ira rolled out this sort of verbal artillery in casual conversation, he could be overbearing. What an ego! Who did he think he was?

But others found him consistently fascinating, even wise. Outside of Philadelphia, he might not have been a household word, but some felt he outshined his counterparts on the national scene. His lawyer, Bernard Segal, recalls attending a great protest rally at the University of Pennsylvania. "All the great gurus were there," he says. "Rubin, Hoffman, Charles Garry who represented Bobby Seale. . . . And I thought to myself that Ira was the best of all of them. He was humorous without being a fool; he was bright without being over-bearing; he was a true believer without being an ideologue or zealot. And that's a remarkable combination."

Einhorn did have his effect on the sixties. He often took his act to other colleges, collecting lecture fees for being Ira Einhorn. He would pitch his tent on campus, stay for a week or so, and blow the minds of those who creeped into the tent for enlightenment or other activities. Some of his listeners still swear by the ideas he espoused back then. He even had the ear of people he had long admired: for instance, Humphrey Osmond, the pioneer of mind-altering drugs, included an essay by Ira in his book *Psychedelics*. He was on a first-name basis with Allen Ginsberg, buddies with Jerry Rubin. Locally, he was the man called on by the city's premier newspaper to summarize the view of his generation (Einhorn's article was entitled "Money Stinks of War, Slavery").

In a sense, Ira Einhorn exemplified that giddy, contentious, tumultuous era. He may have worked it like a con man, but he also strived to embody its positive aspects—the sharing, the empathy, the call for benevolent apocalypse, and the antic irrelevance. The latter characteristic was no mere joke, but an essential deterrent to the ineluctable evil that seemed to have taken over America—a happy antidote to the Establishment's pesticides and genocides. His message was proferred by theater, and the actor may have been a somewhat egomaniacal self-promoter, but that did not dilute the message of the performance—*come on people now, smile on your brother, everybody get together, try to love one another right now.* Ira's personal rendering of this anthem was on a headier intellectual plane and certainly used a more challenging vocabulary, but it still ran neatly into that American Ganges that was the rich flow of the sixties. "My generation is tired of defining man in terms of its differences," he wrote in an essay. "It wishes to look at another in terms of common factors: that which we can share, that which brings us together, rather than that which isolates." Thus Ira Einhorn became at one with the message of the times—a precociously wise plea for nonviolence—and remained so, at least until the morning that Holly Maddux's body was discovered in his closet.

5

FALLEN ANGEL

Each year, pictures of all incoming freshman women at Bryn Mawr College are printed in a plain pamphlet. Its informal appellation is the "Pig Book." In autumn of 1965, Richard Olver, a freshman at Haverford College—Bryn Mawr's "brother" institution, just a few miles south on the Main Line—was looking over this book with a few of his friends. Olver, a tall, lanky son of a United Nations executive, had been schooled in Switzerland and Italy; despite spending his final year of high school at Andover Academy, he did not feel in sync with American life. In fact, his intense perusal of the Pig Book was a conscious effort to get into the swing of things and plan a social life for himself in college. It seemed logical for him to choose the three prettiest girls and then, after meeting them at one of the inevitable Haverford–Bryn Mawr mixers, romance the one who was available and willing.

Holly Maddux was one of the three girls on Richard Olver's short list of would-be girlfriends. At one of the earliest mixers, he recognized her instantly and was impressed at her carriage, her dignity, and her beauty, which had only been hinted at in her picture. They began dating soon after, seeing quite a lot of each other. Richard Olver quickly came to understand that Holly Maddux had been eager to get out of Tyler, Texas. "She had constructed a world for herself in Tyler that had very little to do with the kind of redneck patina that people affect down there in East Texas and all over the South," he says. "She was very much into dance, she avoided any trace of regional accent, and so on." But now, in 1965, she was very far from Tyler, with peers who were intimate with the sophisticated

97

styles she had only been able to dream of at home. And to Holly Maddux's alarm and dismay, things were just not working out. What bearings she had been able to count on in the past seemed kicked out from under her.

Richard Olver sums up Holly's problem: "She didn't fit in Bryn Mawr any more than she fit in East Texas."

Bryn Mawr College was founded in 1885, endowed by the estate of a Quaker physician named Joseph Wright Taylor, to fill "the need of such a place for the advanced education of our young female Friends, and to have all the advantages of a College education which are so freely offered to young men." The campus was sited on slightly rolling hills eleven miles outside of Philadelphia, in the Main Line town with which it shares a name. The architecture was collegiate Gothic, in the mold of the classic English educational institutions. Early on, it gained a reputation for serious education, being the first women's college to offer a Ph.D. program. The young women who attended were known not only to be serious about their studies but serious in general, independent of men and the frills of courting rituals. They formed a sort of sorority of genteel defiance. Long after it was fashionable, Bryn Mawr girls would clutch to outmoded rites of celebration: maypole dancing on May Day; and Lantern Night, when the sophomores, in full academic gown, would pass lanterns to the freshmen outside the ivy-covered Cloisters building. The Bryn Mawr student would be known as very bright, plainly dressed, practical, independent, and perhaps a little flaky. She would often hail from a wealthy family, or at least a venerated family. It was a school where Emily Dickinson would have felt at home, and though it was founded too late for the Amherst laureate, it did provide foundation for Marianne Moore, Hilda Doolittle, and Katharine Hepburn.

When Holly Maddux arrived in September 1965, the school had not really budged much from its long-held position as the matriculation point of the blue bloods' more studious daughters. "Bryn Mawr is a very intense place, a very scholarly place," says a woman in Holly's class. "The atmosphere is intense and academic in a classical sense. People who are self-motivating and self-driven go there. It's very full of good little girls—who worked very hard and did all their homework."

Since the 1890s, Bryn Mawr had supposedly allowed the students to regulate their own conduct. But the reality in 1965 was that, like most colleges then, parietals restricted an underclasswoman's activities, especially first-year students. Jane Friedman, a classmate of Holly's, recalls, with only slight hyperbole, that "when you went out at night, you had to sign out on an index card, giving something like ten pieces of information—everything from the hubcap size on the car of the person, to where you were going and when you were coming back. And if you weren't back by a certain time, the so-called 'Lantern Man' would call the number you left to find out where you were." But the period in which Holly Maddux attended Bryn Mawr saw more change in regulations than in the school's previous eighty years. By the time Holly graduated, not only had the Lantern Man's light gone out but overnight visitations from male students were common practice, and there was even a coed Bryn Mawr–Haverford dormitory. As far as peer groups were concerned, not an eyebrow was raised at formerly uncommon chemicals such as marijuana and birth control pills. And the class that saw the biggest changes was the one that entered in 1965.

From Tyler to a hotbed of avant garde youth culture. It would have been a difficult transition for Holly to make even if she had felt comfortable in her new surroundings. But she failed to make close connections. Her lodgings were a single room in Rhoads Hall. "It was the largest hall then," says Fern Hunt, whose room was next to Holly's. "A very urban kind of hall, with over a hundred people." The bustle of self-assured classmates was undoubtedly intimidating to Holly, whose sophistication—considerable by Tyler standards, dicey when measured with an East Coast yardstick—was put to a wilting test. "There's a Bryn Mawr 'style' which is hard to identify with," says Richard Olver. "If you're not from the Connecticut horsey set or something like that, you don't naturally fit that style, and you think you're the odd woman out. She had that feeling. Other women I knew there had that feeling, too; but they each felt very much alone."

Compounding the problem was Holly Maddux's well-constructed personal armor. Her grace and bearing could seem pretentious, almost royal, and that prevented her from getting close to her classmates. "She was very striking, but it was not a face that betrayed emotion," says Fern Hunt. "A cool, condescending demeanor. A lot of people got the idea that she was patronizing. A cold fish. But [when you got to know her] she was basically a warm person—an insecure person."

"Holly was distant and quiet," says Julia Kagan, a classmate of Holly's. "She had a moon-child quality . . . a waif quality."

One way she did express herself was through dance. In the freshman show, dubbed "Persecute Us Tomorrow, We're Busy," Holly danced the role of a harlequin. As the first performer on stage, with a song to herself, she cut a striking figure. The years at the Marye Frances School of Dance in Tyler had paid off. "Her dancing was absolutely spectacular," says classmate Pam Anderson. "Even though sometimes she didn't have the biggest parts, she riveted your attention."

Holly's Bryn Mawr dance teacher, Paula Mason, agrees. "You get a bunch of dancers on stage, they're going to see *her*. You would love watching Holly. She was a lovely girl to look at. She had a very beautiful leg, high extension. Moved very well. She had maturity in the face . . . she didn't have these eighteen-year-old expressions and ways of being that the other girls had. So in a way she was set apart."

Holly Maddux worked hard at dancing and did turns at all the school performances, working with some dancers who would eventually make careers of it. Reviews of the dances in the school paper would invariably note her beauty and skill. But she never really considered dancing professionally. Though Paula Mason says that Holly's size did not disqualify her from professional dancing, Holly believed that she was too big for serious dancing. (In any case, she never asked her instructor.) When one dormmate asked Holly what she might like to do in life, Holly answered, "landscape architecture," the profession she had spurned when refusing Texas A&M. But she never missed dance classes or rehearsals, striking an intense, solitary pose at all times.

"She was a very private person," recalls Paula Mason. "I never really saw her socialize with the other girls. She was given to a kind of introversion. I could see her all the time in the corner, with her head down, kind of thinking, dwelling on something."

Things were going awry for Holly. Her parents link the troubles to one course required of Bryn Mawr students, The Bible as Literature. (Ironic, since Bea Einhorn also faults a single course, Morse Peckham's, for diverting Ira from a career in science.) "It shook her up," says Fred Maddux. "They don't do things like that down here. Every woman that went in there, regardless of what her faith was, [the professor] did his best to absolutely destroy it. Down here, you accept a few things on faith, then you build it up from there, and then when you got something to *stand* on, you can start jumping up and down to see if it's going to hold up." The Madduxes' worst fears about how her faith was affected at Bryn Mawr were realized after her graduation, when they presented all four of their girls with crucifixes like that one at Christ Episcopal Church in Tyler. Holly refused hers. The rejection "flabbergasted" Fred Maddux.

Liz Maddux was later philosophical about it: "It was just as though she belonged to *their* world instead, now, you know?"

Richard Olver, by then close to Holly, confirms that the Bible as Literature course had an impact on her. In his recollection, though, her shock at this blasphemous presentation was mixed with a clandestine excitement. Even though Holly was rocked by revelations not hinted at in Tyler, she daringly courted them. Presumably, the opportunity to engage in heretical discourse was one reason she'd left Texas. Olver believes part of her attraction to him was due to his being a skeptic. "Her boyfriends tended to be agnostic types, people who questioned," he says.

In a sense, Holly would use her men to ask the blasphemous questions *for* her.

Richard Olver played right into this conundrum when he explained to Holly something she had not heard discussed at Christ Episcopal Church in Tyler: the political origins of the Episcopal Church. "I told her about Henry VIII's wives and his problems with the Pope," he says. "She had no knowledge of that. As soon as I did that, her whole faith structure began to crumble."

Another challenge to the world view she had grown up with concerned current politics. The Quaker-founded schools Haverford and Bryn Mawr were early hotbeds of protest against racism, the Vietnam War, and the greedy oppressiveness of the Establishment. It was Holly's first contact with the youth movement that, several miles away, was enthralling the imagination of Philadelphia's first hippie, Ira Einhorn. The overwhelming sympathy for the civil rights movement must have created some dissonance in the young woman from Tyler, where oppressive segregation was still in force. But as someone who had grown up in a cocoon of military discipline—the Maddux children were even raised on a serviceman jargon wherein the toilet was referred to as "the head"—the antiwar sentiments provided a dramatic clash with her family beliefs. "Within a month of my arrival at Haverford, an upperclassman sat me down and spent two and a half hours with me, convincing me of the wrongness of the war," says Olver. "I did the same thing with Holly. It spread like wildfire." For Holly, this was to present a particularly distressing revelation: Not only was it horrifyingly at odds with her father's deepest beliefs but her brother John had joined the Marines and was about to serve in Vietnam. Olver had to reassure her that being intellectually opposed to the war did not mean that she was a traitor, or abandoning her brother.

Bryn Mawr wasn't all bad for Holly. She enjoyed being around girls who were as bright or brighter than she was. And she had little trouble adopting some aspects of the less circumscribed collegiate, East Coast life-style. She went to movies, concerts, took the train to Princeton, where she dated some underclassmen and, according to one report, was voted by its students "the most desirable freshman woman in the East." But in a sense, the difficulty of adjustment had given her a slap from which she still was stunned. Here, the rules were not only different, but at times there seemed a premium on defying them. This was not only true in the political realm but in the standards of personal behavior. "It changed her mental outlook," says Lawrence Wells. "Being intimate, which she always felt was forbidden to do until you were married . . . that with all the drug culture and the political stuff. In the early sixties, you just weren't exposed to that at Tyler. You just weren't. And all of a sudden, wham! She was thrown in the center of it all. It was a tremendous culture shock."

When she had thought that leaving Texas would obliterate her past, she'd underestimated how much of Texas was still in her.

Holly began to shrink from the Bryn Mawr community. People came to realize that her quiet demeanor was either shyness or self-containment, and not snobbery; she became known as a sweet, somewhat airy girl who was sort of a mystery. She spent a lot of time in her room, fondling "Furze," the beloved possum ("a repulsive little pet," says Richard Olver) she'd brought with her from Tyler. She even began to yearn for some of the accoutrements of Texas. She asked her family to send a certain kind of corn tortilla to her, a Lone Star State delicacy unavailable in Philadelphia's Main Line.

Fern Hunt, living next to her in Rhoads Hall, noticed Holly's silent withdrawal toward the end of their freshman year. "That's about when things began to deteriorate," she says. "She began to dress exclusively in black. She would come back from dates in tights and a jacket and look worn out. She became afraid to go to meals and took to eating in her room—she said she smelled old food, and that upset her. It was kind of the whole scene that was difficult."

Her relationship to Richard Olver was deepening, but was not without its tensions. Both of them were virgins, but it was Holly who seemed more eager to end that status; Olver, besides being young, was still intimidated by her awesome beauty. He explains that "I had this whole mythology in my head that she fitted into as the Botticelli Venus type." Holly, meanwhile, had absorbed enough of the liberal atmosphere of Bryn Mawr to look at things more matter-of-factly. The issue of intimacy would have to wait, though, as Holly told Olver that she needed to have her unusually strong hymen surgically pierced, a procedure she promised to undergo in Tyler that summer. It is unclear how she determined that the operation was necessary.

When she returned to Bryn Mawr for her sophomore year, she and Olver had trouble resuming the relationship at its previous pitch. They both dated others, and by the time they got back together late in 1966, Holly was no longer a virgin. She'd written to her brother John in Vietnam that it had been a difficult initiation. "I think it was [due to] the guilt, and the idea that wasn't the way a nice girl from Tyler was supposed to act," says Lawrence Wells, to whom she also corresponded. "I think she was bitter about it—bitter about the fact that she had been so sheltered, so Pollyanna-ish and everything." But Richard Olver contends that Holly had no problem with her sexuality when they finally slept together that year. Quite the contrary, she seemed confident and experienced about those matters. The relationship got back on track and soon, he says, "we basically considered ourselves engaged."

But Holly was still uncomfortable at Bryn Mawr. During spring semester she began telling people that she would not return for her junior year. She was not at all sure that her new life was right at all.

She yearned to regress to the more orderly world she had discarded. She was thinking of becoming an airline stewardess.

Richard Olver was unhappy at her decision to leave school but agreed that it need not end their relationship. Fred Maddux had driven up from Texas to pick Holly up after the term ended, and they all went to Nantucket together. Richard liked Fred Maddux, though he was uncomfortable with Fred's right-wing tirades and his German Army field cap. Fred Maddux thought Richard a nice boy, but got the impression from Olver's antiwar sentiments that Richard was the leader of antigovernment protesters at Haverford. (Olver insists he was but foot soldier.) Opposing the Vietnam War was not the way to Fred Maddux's heart. Before the visit was over, Holly got word that Delta Airlines was ready to grant her an interview for the stewardess job. In preparation, she cut her hair, which had flowed halfway down her back in the best Bryn Mawr folksinger tradition, to a perky pageboy. But the interview was sabotaged by her lack of emotional equilibrium. "She just froze up hard as a rock, boy," says Fred Maddux. Delta rejected her.

Holly remained in Tyler that next year. She was back home, in the structured world she knew she could handle. The Madduxes had moved since she'd left Texas; they finally had their house in South Tyler, the "right" side of town. It was a sprawling ranch home, which filled instantly with the flotsam of magazines, hunting trophies, clothes, and knickknacks that a large family accumulates. The clutter came to be as much a part of the house as the windows or walls. Holly had moved into the far bedroom, three rooms from the living area.

The one most likely to succeed in John Tyler's class of 1965 was thus humbled. "She thought of [taking a year off] as something she needed to do," says Toni Erwin, with whom Holly resumed a friendship. "It was like a change, changing tracks for a different train. She had done all these things that she had expected to do in college, and she was bottoming out there. She came home to get her stuff together again."

Holly attended classes at Tyler Junior College, a cakewalk compared to the rigorous academics at Bryn Mawr. But she seemed to enjoy her regimen of language classes and especially her art classes. She filled page after page of large sketchpads, drawing figures, trees, flowers, animals. She did not apply herself to classes and activities with the same spiteful vengeance that she had in high school; she drifted. In a move that surprised most of her friends, she even entered a school beauty contest. She did not win, as most observers had assumed she would, but was named Miss Congeniality. This dubious honor—a consolation prize in a third-rate beauty contest—brought her tears of joy.

"She was thrilled with that," Toni Erwin explains. "It was just a message to the world that all these people liked her."

Richard Olver came down to visit her in early winter. The reunion was unsuccessful. A sour note was struck even before he arrived, as Fred Maddux, not wishing to share space with someone opposing a war fought by our country, suddenly found it essential to drive to Indiana to peruse an antique automobile someone was selling. But the real trouble came when Holly dispassionately announced that she wanted to break up. In retrospect, Richard Olver realizes that she had always insisted on freedom, on seeing other men. That there always had been something distant about her. "I don't think that she was ever madly in love with anybody," he says now. "At one point I was protesting undying love for her and she, in a very serious way—so serious as to be almost comic— replied that her feelings for me were like a cool gem. That's the way she was."

While her Bryn Mawr classmates were going clean for Gene McCarthy, and then mourning the deaths of Kennedy and King, Holly was spending time that year with a Texas boy, a simple fellow totally unlike the sharp, skeptical intellectuals she'd dated at Haverford and Princeton. He fell for her totally, and she liked him, though she cared very little for his friends, whom she considered endemic of the redneck strain she had always despised in Tyler. Since her room was distant from the rest of the house, she could safely sneak out early in the morning and spend some hours away before the house woke up. But the relationship was doomed. Holly was marking time, and the young man came to know it.

He also had a temper. One day Toni saw Holly with bruises, and when she asked for an explanation, Holly told her that her young man had beat her. She spoke not in anger at him but almost in awe at what her father would do to her friend if he found out. "She still saw him after that, but there was a period of time where she wouldn't see him intimately," says Toni. "But Holly was incredibly softhearted. He could hurt her, and then cry about it, and she probably would try to embrace him and comfort him, that kind of thing."

It was not the last time that Holly Maddux would forgive abuse.

With a new pet—a flying squirrel—in tow, Holly returned to Bryn Mawr in the fall semester of 1968. This time she was more conscious of what she was leaving behind—there would be no more beauty contests or Texas boyfriends. She had briefly flirted with the idea of staying in the state and had traveled to the Texas A&M campus with her father. Fred Maddux recalls that the head of the department asked her, "How would you like to be the first woman graduated in landscape architecture at Texas A&M College?" But Holly resisted. The freedom of the East beckoned once more. Bryn Mawr was a heady outpost of the counterculture—now exploding in the wake of the summer protests at the Democratic Convention in Chicago. (Ira Einhorn, in fact, made several lecture appearances at Bryn Mawr during the period.) She would cast her fate therein.

But while approving of the free-spiritedness of the era, she held herself back from it. The same melancholia took over. She led an active social life and kept up in her classes, but as one boyfriend of hers put it, she was simultaneously out of the closed loop of Haverford–Bryn Mawr society—and above it. Among her courses was a Spanish class that required her to write papers describing her life at the time. In translation, some are revealing:

> I believe at times that the winter is my favorite season of the year. . . . Everyone probably feels sad at the arrival of winter. Do they believe that it is the season of death? That nothing exists except dead trees and heavy, gray clouds? That the special colors of the winter give us nothing to admire? It seems to me that it is a marvel how they reveal to us the bones of our world. We shouldn't cover our eyes when we put on our cloaks, hats, and boots.

For much of the year she dated a svelte reddish-blond-haired drama student at Haverford. Acquaintances remember them as being inseparable that year, even dressing in similar dramatic fashion, in black turtlenecks and jeans. (Holly, in keeping with the casual Bryn Mawr acceptance of the Women's Movement, had dispensed with her bras.) Besides the standard college activities—seeing Bergman's *Persona,* going to a Buddy Guy concert—they would drive through the countryside, stopping at an isolated little church, exploring the grounds and the adjoining cemetery. It was an idealized relationship: After the young man's appearances in Haverford drama productions, Holly would create a drawing of him in costume.

Years later, though, the drama student would realize that despite the time they spent together, he never really *knew* this stunning young woman. Though both were juniors, Holly was more than a year older, more experienced sexually—but he always thought it seemed out of place when she, much in keeping with common habit, would emit the random expletive. He would later admit that he saw her as walking six inches off the ground. In truth, she had always been a mystery to him. "I thought I knew her inasmuch as you think you know someone you're with five or six days a week—but looking back, I haven't a clue as to what made her click," he says. "I have this vision of her being kind of aloof—not in a snotty way, but just not cut out for where she was at the time."

By the time Holly returned from Christmas break in 1969, things once again were becoming intolerable. In a paper for her Spanish class she told of getting a C in a midterm for one of her courses. "Let me tell you the reason," she wrote, in Spanish. "During a pause between the first and second hour I sat in the window seat and stared at the library. Always, whether I know it or not, I feel trapped. I began to cry; I had to leave. I'm not crying anymore, but I don't know how I'm going to pass the five months before the end of the year."

She planned to leave Bryn Mawr again, this time to attend the renowned Rhode Island School of Design. Perhaps she would make a career out of her skill in drawing and the visual arts. She traveled to Providence in February and took the qualifying exam, which she felt was not difficult. She was accepted for the fall term. Presumably, she would not return to Bryn Mawr, or the Philadelphia area again.

But in Rhode Island, she ran into trouble immediately. No one is really sure what happened, but in the version her parents heard, one of the teachers told her that her work simply wasn't good enough to cut it. This cruel assessment apparently had such an effect on her fragile sense of self-esteem that she assumed it correct, and did not return to Providence for the following semester.

There is another possible explanation for her departure. Sometime in 1969, perhaps during her time at Rhode Island, Holly Maddux became pregnant. A lover of all life-forms—possums, flying squirrels, flowers, even bugs—it must have been an absolute nightmare for her to contemplate snuffing out a human life within herself. The weight of her background undoubtedly filled her with guilt at the prospect. Also, this being some years before the legalization of abortion, termination of pregnancy was no simple thing to arrange. On the other hand, the rising consciousness of feminism, pervasive at Bryn Mawr, had also struck a note with Holly. Above all, the Holly Maddux of 1969 had been through a lot: There had been many unthinkable experiences for the determined girl who had "showed 'em" in Tyler, but was, for all that, a naive and frightened young woman.

Holly Maddux had an abortion.

She returned to Philadelphia's Main Line. For a while she worked as a proofreader at *TV Guide* in Radnor. Finally she found a job more to her liking, doing odd jobs at the Philadelphia Zoo. The year before, she had met Alan Torledsky, a curly-haired native of Johnstown, Pennsylvania, who looked a lot like the actor Paul Sand. Alan Torledsky was different than Holly's previous boyfriends. Though he was her age, he seemed more adult. He did not have a college degree and was a Navy reservist, fulfilling his active duties as a seaman in a program affiliated with the Merchant Marines. But he was a familiar figure around Bryn Mawr, where he found more than one of his girlfriends. "He was a nice person, but a very defensive kind of person," says Pam Anderson, a classmate of Holly's who later became involved with Torledsky. "He was strong; he could have been dominant to someone who allowed herself to be dominated."

When Torledsky first met Holly at a mixer, he "bird-dogged" her for a month, struck by her exceptional beauty. Though she had showed little positive response, she suddenly called him one day at the small house he then occupied in Devon, a few miles up Route 30 from Bryn Mawr, and asked him to pick her up. He had the impression of some urgency, that he was a means of escape for this strange and lovely blond woman. They had stayed in contact through her interlude at Rhode Island (though Torledsky was not involved in the painful abortion episode), and upon Holly's return she moved into the well-lit carriage house Alan was renting in Cheney, on an estate that once belonged to the actor Claude Rains. Alan had landed a job as a mortgage banker.

They lived together for a year and a half, troubles coming only when Holly felt constricted; in those cases she would suddenly take another lover. Generally, it was a peaceful domestic relationship. "She found a comfort level in me," explains Torledsky. Alan and Holly spent time in outdoor pursuits, riding horses and bicycling. They kept an extensive garden. Though he was deeply involved with her and constantly in awe of her beauty, Torledsky found Holly a "private, close-mouthed" person who seemed to have little interest in pragmatic concerns such as what she might do after college. "She wasn't what one would call on a day-to-day basis with the real world," he remembers. She read copiously, favoring fantasy and science fiction.

Cohabitation without marriage was, of course, a scandalous matter in Tyler terms, but Holly, now a modern woman, seemed casual about the arrangement. Certainly it was no anomaly among her peers. She had her sister Meg up for a visit and made no apology for the situation to the thirteen-year-old, who was shocked. Meg did not tell her parents about it, and they did not learn of Holly's living arrangement with Alan until some years after Holly's body was discovered in a trunk in the closet porch of Ira Einhorn's apartment.

Holly and Alan Torledsky even ventured to Tyler to visit the Madduxes. Fred Maddux was impressed at Alan's ambitiousness; if he was bothered that the boy was Jewish, he did not mention it. Since maintaining their sexual relationship in the Maddux house was out of the question for the young couple, Holly took Alan to her friend Toni's house so they could be alone. Toni by now was married with a child; oddly, Holly felt it necessary to boast of her sex life. "It was almost like a status symbol," recalls Toni. "I don't know if she tried to shock me, or she was telling me these things to validate it for herself, or why." Holly also told Toni that she preferred Jewish men, even had a fascination for them. "I would suspect that it came out of some sort of rebelliousness toward her father," says Toni, "but I don't think she would have done that consciously."

The relationship continued as Holly returned to Bryn Mawr for her final year. (She had given up on the idea of transferring to yet another college and figured she would simply complete her senior year at her original school.) Though she had maintained her interest in dance and visual arts—musing occasionally on the thought that she might make a living illustrating children's books—her eventual major was noncommittal: languages. Many of her colleagues in the Class of '71—two years after her original class graduated—never got a chance to know her well. Many who did know her hardly saw her during senior year, when she spent her time off-campus with Alan. Compared to the 1965 *Alcalde,* the John Tyler High School yearbook, where Holly Maddux was a triumphant, dominant presence, the 1971 Bryn Mawr *Akoué* barely acknowledges her existence. None of the candid photos of the miniskirted young women trudging to classes are of Holly. The graduation pictures in this yearbook were informal shots, most often with the students posing outdoors with a tree in the background (in many cases the girl would wrap herself around the tree). Holly supplied no picture. Only her formal name, Helen Maddux, and address—actually, a post office box on the Main Line—is given.

Her graduation was a bittersweet event. Holly felt compelled to apologize to her parents for not graduating with honors. Liz Maddux came up from Texas. Fred Maddux, after Holly commented that she might want to accept her diploma barefooted, decided to stay behind, and not risk witnessing such a disrespectful spectacle. The ceremony was brief and stately, followed by the definitive Bryn Mawr celebration: a "tea." A garden reception with finger foods and raspberry sherbet streaked with coffee ice cream served in a little glass cup with a handle. Holly wore a white antique dress, her hair tied behind her neck. She looked slightly bedraggled. Fellow graduate Jane Friedman asked her what she planned to do. Friedman says, "I remember her expressing some kind of trepidation about it—'What next?' "

Holly Maddux really didn't know.

The matter of what Holly Maddux would do with her life was put on hold for a year or so when she decided to use her graduation money to take the grand tour of Europe so popular then. It required only a plane ticket, a backpack, a sleeping bag, a youth hostel pass, and a wallet full of travelers' checks. Leaving Alan Torledsky behind, she flew off that summer to see England, Scotland, Scandinavia, Germany, Italy, and Greece. By autumn, she found herself in Israel.

This choice undoubtedly resulted in part from her rebellious fascination with the exotic Jewish male. But just as likely, Israel, and the promise of living a sheltered existence for a while on a kibbutz, meant some relief from the strain of traveling as a single woman. She had almost experienced a violent calamity when on a boat cruising the Rhine; apparently she had to disembark suddenly, under threat of sexual assault. This was only part of a constant barrage of come-ons ranging from annoying to terrifyingly physical. In any case, she wound up at the youth hostel in Tel Aviv in September, where she made arrangements to work on the Ashdot Ya'akov kibbutz, on the Jordan River.

Life in the kibbutz was hard, but Holly did not seem to mind the regimen. In exchange for room and board, along with a nominal per diem, she worked full-time. She picked lemons in the fields, or cooked and cleaned in the kitchen. She also ran some dance classes. During off-hours, she would pick flowers, draw, and read. She was particularly captivated by *The Tin Drum*. After her recent experiences, she apparently did not want a threatening relationship. So she initiated something with a person who had little potential to dominate her. He was Jesse Reese, a recent high school graduate from Long Island who was taking a year off before entering college. "She seduced me, if you want to get down to it," admits Reese. The kibbutz allowed them to move into a room together. Reese quite understandably was stunned at his good fortune—at age seventeen, he was blissfully involved with a beautiful, gentle, blond, twenty-four-year-old *shiksa* from Texas.

"I think she really liked intelligent men, and I guess she thought I was intelligent," he says. "Like, I said I was going to India and she thought that was an interesting thing to do. She didn't have a lot of career ambitions . . . she was just experiencing. Israel was a whole new adventure for her. She had a fascination for Jews—sort of an infatuation with Jewish people."

Most of the times were good. They worked in the fields together, and even joked about a "Museum of Mutant Fruit" they would form with all the misshapen lemons and bananas they found. A couple of times, they drank themselves silly, but Holly didn't really enjoy that. "She was not really comfortable with that—with the mainstream of the drugs-and-rock-and-roll generation," says Reese. "But she still wanted to find a place in that. A place where activity had real purpose and meaning. Which she couldn't find within herself. She couldn't find her own life important enough. Because of insecurity, or rebelling against her parents, or whatever, she never really had a chance to grow as an individual."

For a while, Jesse was troubled when he went away one weekend and Holly slept with someone else. "That kind of blew me away," he says. "But that's kind of how she was. She was just really sexual. I took it personally, but it wasn't like betraying me. She just had a very open attitude towards sex."

As months passed, Holly came to care for Jesse very much. Ultimately, the intensity of the relationship was too much for Reese. "If I wasn't as young and inexperienced, I probably would have been more inclined to stay with it. But it seemed to me at the time she was so much older than me and I needed to explore my own shit." In mid-February, Jesse left the kibbutz and went to India.

Not long after, Holly packed up and returned to the Tel Aviv youth hostel. Again, she felt sexually threatened by advances from some of the men there. When she saw a familiar face from the States—a young man she'd seen a few times at Haverford—she struck up a conversation. His name was Dennis Berman, and at first he was struck by how reluctant she was to respond to his innocent invitation to tour the streets on the eve of the Purim holiday. She told him she was distrustful of men and related her harrowing travel experiences. Finally she agreed to go out with him, and began a platonic relationship, though Berman would have preferred something less lofty.

Not long after, she moved to Berman's place in Jerusalem. The visit began with an air of crisis: Holly was worried that she was pregnant. The last thing she wanted was to have to deal with that situation again. Berman took her to the hospital, garnering some strange looks—a nice boy like him, sporting *peyes* and a *yarmulke*, escorting this unmistakably gentile woman for a pregnancy test. The results were negative.

Holly lived on the porch of the apartment Berman shared with a friend for perhaps two months. She had run low on money; he staked her. They would sometimes go to the villages nearby and talk to the people. She introduced him to *Dune*, and he got her interested in vegetarianism. At one point Berman got her together with a friend named Ann, who had met Holly when attending Haverford College. "It was the height of the Women's Liberation Movement and the two of them were really excited to meet each other," he recalls. "Ann showed the hair on her underarm, and Holly lifted up her arm and showed the hair on her armpit, and they sort of embraced and hugged."

Berman's relationship with Holly never became physical. Holly warned Dennis that "she already had enough experience breaking in young virgins, and she'd gotten tired of it." Berman, then twenty-one, accepted this. "Holly had an ability to become, without hardly doing anything, very much loved by the men she was with, and then she would leave them for another," he says. "Which would provoke an incredible anger as to why she would do that."

It did seem to be a pattern with her. In almost all of her affairs, Holly had been the one to break it off: Richard Olver, the drama student, the Texas boy, Alan Torledsky. During the course of the relationship, she would not be particularly assertive, though; as Richard Olver put it, she would "quietly and unobtrusively insist upon having a private side to her life." And then, all at once, as if she were a wild horse who suddenly realized she was in danger of being broken, she would bolt. *You can't have me.* But she did not have the confidence for true independence: She would always go straight into the arms of another. In this case, she took off with an older man, a restaurateur in his forties, and moved in with him. She also washed dishes in his restaurant. Berman would see them sometimes in Jerusalem. He was sad, and not only for himself. Something was missing in this young woman, rudderless in the prime of her life.

"Holly never seemed really *happy* happy," he explains. "Every once in a while—walking around looking at the flowers on the hillside—she seemed more happy than she normally would be. She walked around in neutral. I don't know how to describe it. I don't think she had a clear sense of what she was going to do with her life."

Holly Maddux returned to America in mid-1972, and settled in temporary quarters in Philadelphia. The tidal wave of the sixties was over; some had been exhilarated by it, some washed to sea. Holly herself had barely avoided being swept away in the undertow. She was not the same person she had been in Tyler, but neither was she quite in touch with the identity of this new person. There were countless of her generation in similar situations, and many would find the confidence and positive experiences to build their lives from that point on. Holly Maddux's experience would be different.

She would become involved with Ira Einhorn.

6

TURNING THE CORNER

It would be almost three years into the 1970s before Ira Einhorn met the former Texas cheerleader who would change his life in a way he never imagined. During those years, the Unicorn executed a dazzling transition from his sixties persona into a more subtle, and more durable, figure: a Renaissance man whose tendrils extended from the fringes of society to its central core. The key event in turning the corner from the sixties to the New Age that lay beyond was an April 1970 celebration called "Earth Day." It was simultaneously the peak of his public visibility and a shift in paradigm that provided him the means for thriving in a postsixties world that demanded more of its gurus.

In the waning days of 1969, he announced to a *Bulletin* reporter that he was now focusing on "an international conspiracy to make the planet livable." He sensed that those wary of the potential explosiveness of political differences might rally to this movement "because it's safe." He noted that while the Black Panthers might evoke differing sentiments among reasonable people, "everyone's got to be interested in oxygen—you need oxygen to breathe."

Actually, environmentalism was only part of the surprisingly coherent philosophy Ira had formed during the cacophonous years of the sixties. While he had physically discarded his texts, along with the pretext of competing in the academic circles that revered them, he had continued pursuing his own brand of thought. "I have

114

a mind that reaches all over the cosmos," he once explained. "I read everything effortlessly. Math, physics, biology, chemistry, poetry, history." Out of these various disciplines came the alloy of Einhorn's ethic: an eccentric blend of science, cybernetics, and Yippie rap, usually expressed in free verse or concrete poetry.

(If his poetry, as well as some of his public pose, owed a lot to Allen Ginsberg, Ginsberg himself—while not regarding the work very highly—was not bothered. "There were several hundred fat Jews with beards that I got confused with constantly," Ginsberg says of those times.)

In a sense, Einhorn was venturing far beyond the anarchist Yippie Movement; he was applying educated analysis of the world in terms of systems. Kiyoshi Kurimaya, a founder of Penn's Free University and later an editor of Buckminster Fuller's writings, claims that Ira was a master teacher for that very reason: "Ira seemed to have a complete system. He had a unique analysis of world events and contemporary culture that was not available in any other source that I had come in contact with. And they were ideas that were later confirmed through study, sometimes a year later, and sometimes ten years later."

With those ideas, Ira Einhorn was ready to broaden his constituency, from a counterculture leader who was covered by media to a bridge between the counterculture and the Establishment, working toward a cause everyone shared in common. To make this personal transformation, though, would require a vehicle. And that is why it was so fortuitous that Austan Librach came to Ira Einhorn's door almost literally on the day when the 1960s ended.

Austan Librach was a twenty-year-old grad student in city and regional planning. He was part of a small group of students and faculty who were aware that Senator Gaylord Nelson had declared a national Earth Week for late April 1970. Some localities were planning seminars, lectures, and celebrations, but as of December 1969, nothing was happening in Philadelphia. So some Penn students and their professors, chief among them the environmentalist Ian McHarg, began organizing. Librach became the student leader, working with a small fund from the university.

"From the very beginning, we realized that whether we wanted to or not, we really had to work with Ira Einhorn," says Librach. "He was the counterculture leader in Philadelphia, and at that time you couldn't afford to ignore a guy like that. You had to deal with him, or you had to make some sort of accommodation with him."

So Librach contacted Einhorn, who invited the Penn student to his apartment in the Piles. When Librach appeared, he was thrown immediately off balance. For one thing, the apartment seemed to be some sort of weird communal arrangement where an unclear number of adults came and went at will. For another thing, the walls of the place were filled with bookshelves—but the shelves were empty except for one book. Its author was Buckminster Fuller, and Ira held up the book and told Librach that "Everything is in here. This is philosophy, this is history, this is art, this one book has it all." When Ira Einhorn offered Librach some banana bread, he accepted it with dread, hoping that some hallucinogenic drug was not among the ingredients. Finally—and this bothered the fairly straitlaced Austin Librach most of all—Ira Einhorn had answered the door naked and remained so throughout the visit.

"After we had been together for a couple of hours," says Librach, "he asked me if the nakedness bothered me, and at that point I said, 'No,' it was fine. Of course I was totally undone about it."

Thus discombobulated, the younger man attempted to reach an accommodation with Ira Einhorn concerning the Unicorn's role in Earth Week. An agreement was forged: Ira would deliver what constituency he had, and work with the Earth Week committee behind the scenes. On the main celebration, Earth Day itself, he would act as the public master of ceremonies. "He would get exposure," says Librach, "and to the world it would look like he was MC, the guy in charge."

As a broad-based celebration, Earth Week's success would be to some degree dependent on the cooperation and funding of Philadelphia's business community. This assistance was by no means assured. Certain corporations represented in the Greater Philadelphia Chamber of Commerce viewed Earth Day as an annoyance at best, and possibly a threat. Those companies were sensitive to the charges that they themselves might be fingered as polluters, exploiters of the environment, abusers of the very Earth that people were to honor. "This was the stormy sixties," notes Thacher Longstreth, a long-time Republican city councilman who was then head of the Chamber of Commerce. "And there was a feeling that Earth

Week was another sort of preparation by students and radicals to create a ferment in the community."

Longstreth, a gangly patrician known by his trademark argyle socks, did not share that feeling. Affected by a reading of Rachel Carson's *A Silent Spring,* he was open to the alternative view offered by the young people who came to his office to present Earth Week's case. Among them was Ira Einhorn, who was turning out to be quite an asset for Earth Week in terms of winning Establishment support. "He was somebody whom I'd known and regarded as a slightly eccentric wacko, but as I got to see more of him, I learned that he was highly intelligent and had a very valuable thrust on this whole action," says Longstreth. "He really was quite good fun—a personable, entertaining person to have around. And we got to be friends."

Longstreth argued the Earth Week case to the Chamber, and got them to listen to the organizers. Austan Librach made a strong pitch for business support, but the more memorable presentation was made by Ira Einhorn. "He made a personal request for cooperation before a fairly large group, and he did a perfectly beautiful job," Longstreth recalls. "The major thing about Ira was that in areas of disagreement between the Establishment and the flower children, Ira was a pretty good bridge. He wasn't antibusiness at all. He was quite business-oriented himself, and had he chosen to go in that direction, he would have probably been a very successful businessman."

With the business community donating money and resources, and the local media drumming up support and enthusiasm, Earth Week was shaping up to be a much bigger festival than anyone had dreamed. Librach and the other organizers had felt it necessary to hire an experienced administrator to manage the event full-time. His name was Edward Furia, and when he arrived, the situation was chaos. "For reasons that were not entirely clear," he recalls, "Earth Week galvanized all sorts of people. At one end of the spectrum were extremely conservative WASP, Main Line, Teddy Roosevelt, garden club people. On the other end, the Rachel Carson, no-fluoride-in-the-water, they're-going-to-kill-us paranoids. It was a careening merry-go-round going down a mountainside." The program itself had ballooned dramatically: Earth Week was now a series of rallies, speeches, teach-ins, and demonstrations, culminating in two mammoth gatherings, one near Independence Hall, and the second on Earth Day itself, April 22, an environmental Wood-stock with noted luminaries and rock musicians. The latter would be televised by CBS. Walter Cronkite would be the host. And in addition to all of Furia's problems of managing the calendar of events, the thousands of dollars of corporate support, the publications, the printing of buttons, the publicity, and the millions of other details, there was Ira Einhorn.

Whether Ira Einhorn's heart was in the right place or not was irrelevant to Furia; he was among those who considered the Unicorn as someone who had mastered the posture, the clothing, and accoutrements of a counterculture leader, but had no laudable goals except self-aggrandizement. But he needed Ira—the Mayor of Powelton's presence helped diffuse those in the radical community who were accusing Earth Week of draining the energy from the more righteous antiwar and civil rights movements. In one meeting between the committee and some local interest groups, a black politician, Charles Bowser, accused the organizers of being "co-opted" by the Nixon administration, and stormed out of the session, leaving the stomachs of the mostly left-wing Earth Week people churning with liberal guilt. Einhorn leapt to his feet and explained that they had just witnessed a performance, a thespian tactic that Ira had himself used a million times before. "If what you are doing has any meaning for those people, they'll be back," he said. "If not, they won't. But don't get upset about what you heard just because it was theater."

Furia also appreciated it when "Ira got on the phone and started calling gurus and famous people in the counterculture. All of whom he knew." Ira got commitments from Allen Ginsberg, Alan Watts, *Dune* author Frank Herbert, and Nobel laureate George Wald.

On the other hand, Ira was totally unpredictable, and, at least through the eyes of Furia and Librach, potentially destructive. "He had a habit of popping up out of nowhere," says Austan Librach. "He would disappear for a couple of weeks and all of a sudden he'd come in and he'd want to have a say. He felt like he was part of the inner circle, and that was mostly Ed and myself."

By the time Earth Week arrived, Ira Einhorn was in his glory. As he later put it, "the city vibrated to the call of ecology." The distinctive Earth Day logo, a circle with yellow on top and blue underneath, a sort of ecological yin-yang, was distributed in button form by the thousands. When one called the telephone service's weather report, he or she got an Earth Day message along with the forecast. "For once," Ira Einhorn proclaimed, "this much-fractured city was united around a common cause."

Meanwhile, Austan Librach's "accommodation" proved significant: As the week headed to a climax, Ira Einhorn came to be the personality most associated with the event. On Tuesday, April 21, a convoy of electrically powered hay wagons—provided by General Electric—left West Philadelphia in a parade down Chestnut Street toward Independence Hall. In the back of one of those hay wagons was Ira Einhorn, mingling with the fully costumed cast of the Broadway show *Hair*. By the time the caravan reached the birthplace of the United States, there were thousands of people crowding the Independence Mall north of the Liberty Bell, listening to Alan Watts, Ralph Nader, and Senator Hugh Scott. Ira took the stage with the *Hair* contingent, and when the singers broke into an impassioned, extended rendition of "Let the Sun Shine," the Unicorn leaned into the microphone and bleated out the words with them.

Earth Day itself, April 22, was cold but clear. The Belmont Plateau area in Fairmount Park, overlooking the Philadelphia skyline two miles away, began filling with people.

Ira Einhorn, resplendent in a purple football jersey, began the program at noon with a benediction peppered with his own unique philosophy. The program cheerily proceeded, with alternating musical groups and speakers. George Wald. Ian and Sylvia. Allen Ginsberg, playing harmonium, reading a poem called "Kiss Ass," and leading the crowd in Blakean chants.

Meanwhile, Ira Einhorn, ponytail flowing down his back, paced the wooden runway extending into the maw of the crowd, his reedy voice booming bad poetry into the microphone. Ed Furia marveled at how Einhorn seemed to soak up the energy of thousands of human beings, transforming himself into quite another creature. But as the afternoon progressed, Furia became worried about whether Ed Muskie's speech was going to go off smoothly—or at all. To Furia's astonishment, Einhorn had unilaterally shuffled the schedule of events. At 3:30, when the live CBS feed was scheduled to kick in, the Unicorn failed to present the celebrated speaker; instead, he introduced a rock-and-roll band consisting of American Indians. Ominously, Ira Einhorn did not retreat to the backstage area while the band played, but remained out front, a sort of grotesque go-go dancer, shaking his hairy head to the beat of the music.

"What the hell is going on?" Ed Muskie asked Ed Furia.

Furia apologized to the senator. Then he ventured out to the stage to confront Einhorn. As he remembers it, he said to Ira, "Senator Muskie is here."

Ira Einhorn's reply betrayed something quite distinct from the upbeat hippie poet-activist. To Furia, it was chilling. "I am not going to leave this stage," said the Unicorn. "If you want to physically remove me from this stage, you can do it. These kids are *mine* now."

Furia reeled at the thought. "We were totally organized for this twenty minutes, televised live. Out of this, we wanted legislation, action, to involve the middle class. But now, America would think Earth Day was a rock band and a guru in beads."

Finally, Furia could stand it no longer. Risking total disaster, he led Muskie directly onto the stage, to the end of the runway where Ira had set up camp with the microphone. To his eternal relief, Einhorn yielded the mike. But not without incident. First, he said a few words to his minions to the effect that even though a politician is going to speak, everybody should hear him out. But if he speaks bullshit, they should let this politician know about it. And then, perhaps to indicate no hard feelings, he kissed Edmund S. Muskie square on the lips.

Casual observers assumed that the Earth Day was largely an Ira Einhorn show, and in future utterances, Einhorn fostered that impression himself. By 1979, he was claiming that "I planned, directed, and emceed the entire event."

Ira was now more well known in Philadelphia than ever: *Philadelphia Magazine* ran a long feature article profiling him as he turned thirty in May 1970. "Ira has become one of Philadelphia's unusual success stories of the decade," wrote Bernard McCormick. "By rejecting it all he has become better known than the rest of his generation who did what they were supposed to. He is the town guru."

But the lasting consequence of Earth Day as far as Ira Einhorn was concerned was that the event provided him with a well-paved entrée into the business and civic life of the city.

It was John Brennan, a General Electric PR executive, who brought Ira into the city's power structure. Brennan had sat on the Earth Day committee, and during the meetings he and Ira developed a rapport. The two began to have lunch together. The site of these lunches was a restaurant on the Penn campus called La Terrasse, in honor of the broad terrace in the back. It was a sunny place, with plants and large windows, serving omelettes, salads, and light French fare. Ira had gotten to know its owner, a former Penn architecture student named Eliot Cook, and actively supported the restaurant, both as a customer and as an activist in La Terrasse's epic struggle against condemnation by the University of Pennsylvania, which wanted the land for its own purposes. In these lunches, Ira seemed deeply curious about corporations. How did they operate? What were the management dynamics? Could the pressure points in the big-business system be easily identified? Could one then apply targeted pressure to move the system in a way that could benefit society? Brennan agreed to help get Einhorn in contact with people involved in these issues, thinking that not only would Ira get a better understanding but that the executives might themselves benefit from receiving Ira Einhorn's perspective on the world.

The first executive whom Brennan introduced to Ira was Moses Hallett. He was a burly, gray-haired man with an unaffected air and a surprisingly open-minded attitude for someone who had toiled for thirty-plus years for the biggest corporation in the world: the telephone company. He was then an assistant vice-president in organization planning at Pennsylvania Bell, then one of the twenty-two operating companies owned by American Telephone and Telegraph (AT&T). While his employer was known for turning out executives in a certain single-minded mold, he was the exception: a person who held a vision. By the time Ira Einhorn met him, he had sufficient seniority at Bell so that he had no pretense of hiding that vision. The sixties had affected Hallett deeply, and it alarmed him that many of his peers seemed to have their heads in the sand. He believed that the telephone company should be more responsive to the community at large—*needed* to be more responsive—and he directed a large share of his energies to communicating that need to certain top executives, among them Bell of Pennsylvania's president, William Cashel.

The chemistry between Einhorn and Hallett was potent. They

both shared an excitement about communications, and both believed that the phone company could be instrumental in improving the lives of the entire population. Others in the phone company were wary of this scruffy, bearded fellow who would visit Hallett's office, but Moses Hallett liked to point out that Alexander Graham Bell wore a beard, too. Beard or no, the Unicorn became a valuable resource for the phone company.

A case in point was the switching center that Pennsylvania Bell planned to build on the Schuylkill River. The South Philadelphia neighborhood bordering the property was up in arms about possibly losing access to the waterfront. Moses Hallett asked Einhorn if he might help out. Ira approached the leaders of the groups opposing the project and suggested that all sides meet; he negotiated the terms of the meeting. A dinner was arranged at La Terrasse, and with tensions eased—and Einhorn assisting—a series of talks was initiated. Ultimately, Bell compromised on its design of the switching center, and the settlement was acceptable on all quarters.

Ira took no payment for his role as arbitrator; his stance was that he was out to change corporations, make them responsive to people. Business was power, and Ira's tactic for the seventies was to get as close to that power as possible, to leverage it in a positive direction. Not being paid allowed him autonomy. Moses Hallett would never presume to say, "Ira, do something for me." Instead, he always asked. "It was strictly a friendship, a labor of love; we both enjoyed doing it," says Hallett.

Frequently, Ira, who had access to all sorts of unusual information, would provide Hallett with a view of the world other than the one available in the newspapers. Hallett would often pass the fruits of his interactions with Ira to others working for the telephone company. Besides local lowdown, those fruits included recommendations of various books that Ira felt would be enlightening to progressive corporate executives. Books on game theory, new ideas in physics, sociology. Ira began to accumulate a following among telephone company leaders. He would later boast that "within a year of my first meeting with Moses, I had a flourishing network of friends within the Bell System: a small, invisible organism buried within the bowels of the world's largest corporation."

Einhorn's greatest conquest was Bell of Pennsylvania's president, William S. Cashel, Jr. Cashel was a company man, a fifty-year-old former Marine who had come up the ranks of the Bell System to his present lofty post. But he, too, was sensitive to how his company was viewed by the community. (Indeed, he would soon ascend to the chairmanship on the board of the Greater Philadelphia Chamber of Commerce.) Eventually Cashel became curious about the source of the information Hallett was blitzing him with. Hallett urged he meet Ira Einhorn. Cashel agreed, but insisted that the setting be private.

According to Hallett, the meeting occurred at a room in the nearby Sheraton Hotel, a room-service lunch. Here was the corporate president, overseer of more than 35,000 employees, a payroll exceeding $280 million, in charge of the communications system on which every Pennsylvanian depended. And there was the long-haired guru. At first, the conversation was stilted. Finally, Hallett, struck by the absurdity of the scene, broke out laughing. A few seconds later, Ira burst out laughing as well. Finally, Cashel himself joined in. From then on, it was easy, and soon Cashel had a rapport with Ira Einhorn that would last for years. They would meet at La Terrasse, where Ira now could be seen almost every day, lunching with a different man in a business suit who would charge the food on a corporate tab.

It became almost a secret club, the powerful executives and officials who broke bread with Ira Einhorn. Membership ranged from Russell Byers, then the Philadelphia regional director of the U.S. Housing and Urban Development department, to John Haas, president of the Rohm and Haas chemical conglomerate. Their experiences were similar—initial wariness broken down by the disarming charm of the Unicorn. "Because Ira was so much bigger than life, he was too much to swallow at first meeting," says Don Kenley, the vice-president in charge of public relations at the Philadelphia Gasworks. "He seemed to be a walking encyclopedia—who's who in Philadelphia, the movers and shakers in the area. It turned out that he did have an entrée into some of the most innermost places of power in the city, and was genuinely respected for that."

"His appearance, his dress ... were not what was formally accepted in the executive suite," says Jim Bodine, then the president of the First Pennsylvania Bank. "But he got there, by being very articulate. By being on the 'in' thing. Environment at the right time. Energy at the right time. Perhaps even ahead of the right time. For those with minds a little broader than the typical corporate executive, he had appeal. He stretched their minds. He was convincing."

Surely, one factor involved in these executives accepting Ira was, as Don Kenley puts it, "the excitement and glamour attached to him because of his notoriety." Some scoffed that a peculiarly Philadelphia form of "radical chic" was in effect here: Instead of the overheated New York version, where wealthy artists embraced Black Panthers, the patrician civic leaders of the City of Brotherly Love were rallying around someone who looked unusual and had unorthodox ideas. But unlike the hostile Panthers, Ira was willing to accept them. It was befitting a city founded on Quaker tolerance. As Bernard McCormick put it in his *Philadelphia* profile:

> There are lots of nervous people in the straight world and when they meet somebody like Ira they half expect to be spat upon. But Ira comes on with all his friendliness and good nature and exudes interest and after a few minutes the straight is thinking, almost in alarm, "Jesus, I think this son of a bitch really *likes* me." There is a built-in temptation to reciprocity in such an approach and people who have met Ira a few times generally find that they like the man.

Inevitably, some claimed that Ira was conning these executives. For certain people, it was true that no matter how many times they sat across from Ira at a table for two at La Terrasse, listening to Ira talk of local politics and cybernetic management structures while munching salad, they would never shake the nagging feeling that this character was setting them up for some sort of hit. On the other hand, *everybody* one met in the corporate realm was supporting some sort of self-interest. "I don't think in his way Ira was any more of a con man than I am," says Thacher Longstreth, now a city councilman. "*I'm* a con man. As president of the Chamber of Commerce, I tried to get my members to do things that I thought were good for them." Likewise, Ira's interest really seemed to be the betterment of the world at large. If that was a con, it was one a person could support wholeheartedly.

Ira himself was open about his goals. "I realized when I started [networking with businessmen] I was involved in a long-range process," he once explained. "I wanted to understand what it was about the structure of some of these personality types. Because they are the people who really run America. There's no doubt about it, they are primarily overcompensating, male-dominated . . . it's a particular type that Western society has generated. Now my concern was that they were human beings and how can I reach these people, how can I humanize them in some way. . . . The chairman of the board of AT&T has a million workers under him. And if he's a little more human, a million people live a little better. Simple as that, nothing grandiose, in the sense of what can be done. I also knew that they could be very helpful to me."

In the midst of his push into the business world, Ira took a step backward, into the kind of Yippie theater that he so enjoyed in the sixties. The Philadelphia mayoral election of 1971 was promising to be a particularly divisive one in the city's history, and the issues were sufficiently crucial to move the mayor of Powelton to throw his own hat into the ring.

The idea first came up in January when *Evening Bulletin* columnist Sandy Grady wrote a piece entitled "Phila's Guru Decides Not to Run for Mayor." Ira claimed that he was too busy. "Not that I wouldn't make a groovy mayor," he said from his perch at La Terrasse. Grady seemed to agree, airing some of Ira's opinions on ecology, LSD, and politics. "I'd like to see Rizzo and Nixon smoke a little pot, listen to kids talk," said Ira. Grady was impressed. "Too bad Ira Einhorn's schedule doesn't allow him to run for mayor," he wrote. "If this city needs anything, it is a first-class guru in charge."

Two months later, Ira exercised the politician's prerogative to change his mind, and decided to make a run at it. Not a serious run, but a sideshow, which might inject some ideas into the arena. Meanwhile, the ringleader would have a lot of fun, and not a little publicity. The latter was no small factor in Ira Einhorn's campaign to lose—he never pretended otherwise—the Democratic nomination for mayor. "Publicity helps me to create a myth about me and I have to use that myth to do what I have to get done," he explained to *Philadelphia Magazine*.

At the time, Ira was hanging out with an informal aggregation that called itself The Synergy Group, in honor of Buckminster Fuller's philosophies. The idea was to generate energies to strengthen community, particularly an undeveloped area on South Street, just below the city's historic area. Synergy's dominant personalities were Curt Kubiak, whom Ira had been close with since the Free University, and Tom Bissinger, a bean pole–slim playwright who had recently been in charge of the avant garde Philadelphia Theater of the Living Arts. George Keegan, another member of the group, explains that "We began using the ideas of synergy applied to South Street. We were going to take it—young and arrogant, and unknowing—and lift it up out of the ashes, get it going again." (The group's efforts were so successful that the neighborhood became an active arts mecca; ironically, this set into motion a gentrification process that eventually drove out the original community that Synergy set out to aid.) Ira became a frequent visitor to the frequent parties in Bissinger's small townhouse on American Street, participated in the Synergy street fairs, and afterward was involved when the Synergy people bought an old paint factory and converted it to a theater and community center named WPCP, an acronym that meant either Where Planets Coexist Peacefully, or Work Peacefully Communicate Patiently, depending on who explained it. Others said the name was a tribute to PCP, the drug known as "angel dust." Einhorn's participation in these projects was usually spiritual rather than physical—the joke was that Ira would not be part of a performance, but would gladly come on stage to accept the bows. In any case, one of Synergy's 1971 projects became Ira Einhorn's candidacy, and Bissinger became the campaign manager.

On March 8, Ira Einhorn held a press conference in the back room of La Terrasse to formally announce his candidacy, joining a field that included Frank Rizzo, Thacher Longstreth, a liberal city councilman, a black state legislator, a U.S. congressman, a soft pretzel vendor, a former Miss Universe contestant, an elderly gentleman with no apparent credentials, and a Samoan prince. The Unicorn wore a blue wool cap, green corduroy pants, heavy leather boots, and a gravy-stained work shirt with an upside-down George Wallace button affixed.

"Press people, are you ready?" Ira began. "Let's play games. That's what we're here to do—play games!"

The announcement speech was later characterized by one reporter as using "the old political trick: If you can't convince them, confuse them." It was a pastiche of LSD philosophy, guerilla advocacy, and pro-Earth slogans. The real fun in the press conference came when reporters had their chance to question the candidate. Listening to Ira's answers gives a taste of his rhetoric at the time:

QUESTION: Can you explain your philosophy of not running to win? Why if you thought you could win you wouldn't run?

IRA: Because I don't think the mayor's job is a very important job right now. It's a kind of old, fading symbol. And those of us who live to a certain extent on the frontier—those of us who are trying to bring the new models to the planet—are attempting to generate those models before they crystallize in the minds of other people. That's what I am specifically doing. If I could win, I wouldn't have to run. Somebody else who would do a better job and be more interested in the job who thinks the way I do would get the job.

QUESTION: You talked about national issues and international issues, but you're running for mayor. What can you do for the city?

IRA: Turn it on!

QUESTION: What are you doing now?

IRA: I keep myself busy twenty-four hours a day as part of the international conspiracy to make the planet livable.

QUESTION: So how would you describe yourself then?

IRA: I'm an Earthling living at the edge of evolution at the edge of the mind here on planet Earth, right before the great war of transformation.

If quantity of media attention, and not votes, were the currency of election, Ira Einhorn would have been mayor the day after his press conference. Not only the newspapers but the local television stations covered the announcement. "Can Einhorn Be Stopped?" asked Sandy Grady in his column. An *Inquirer* columnist declared that "Ira has my vote. I feel that a political candidate who doesn't want to be elected can't be all bad."

The only campaign appearance of note was on a television show that featured the whole slate of candidates, not only the ones considered "serious" contenders. It was a fiasco: A light bulb broke and the pretzel vendor, fearing an assassination attempt, dove to the floor. When Ira spoke of fiscal problems, the elderly candidate testily asked, "What physical problems?" Ira, in the chaos, stuck his Super 8 camera into another candidate's ear and, according to the *Inquirer,* "the TV newsman who was running the show almost bit his tongue in half."

A week before the primary, Einhorn withdrew, yielding his support to Congressman Bill Green. On primary night, when other candidates met in hotel ballrooms, Ira and his campaign staff partied at Bissinger's house. "We don't want to spend an inordinate amount of time watching the returns," Bissinger told the *Inquirer.* Frank Rizzo won the primary, defeating Thacher Longstreth in the general election later that year.

Einhorn's run for mayor was a sidelight. He concluded that his goals would not be attained by large events like Earth Day or guerilla theater presentations like his mayoral campaign but by a more private struggle. He would learn the pressure points of the power structure and manipulate them to bring about his cherished transformation. His contacts with the business community were certainly a part of this. But at the center of his efforts was a close affinity with a movement shaping itself out of the embers of the sixties' fire— what would later be referred to as the New Age.

Much as he had anticipated the sixties, Ira Einhorn prepared for this era years in advance. He had been devouring the texts that would be central to the New Age long before *human potential* or *transformation* or *getting in touch with yourself* became household terms. He was astonishingly well informed in the latest developments of "fringe" physics—the post-Einsteinian discoveries that New Agers would later metaphorically link to the rhythms of Eastern religion. He had been a visitor to Esalen (the California capital of the self-realization movement) in the mid-sixties, cozying up to Alan Watts and such, and himself wound up leading seminars in consciousness at Esalen's San Francisco annex. And in the early seventies, he became deeply involved in the study of the paranormal.

His mentor in much of this was a wispy yet charismatic former medical inventor named Andrija Puharich. Puharich is a central figure in the history of contemporary esoteria, as well as a world-class enigma. Ira once called him "the great psychic circus manager of this century." He is of medium form and gentle visage, his hair stringy in the Einsteinian mode, and his voice soothing and calm, even as he utters outrageous claims. He will, for instance, speak with nonchalance befitting a description of a trip to the supermarket as he describes communication from extraterrestrials urging him to stop a war in the Middle East (directions that he claims to have followed successfully). Born in 1918, he received a medical degree from Northwestern University in 1947, about the same time he became interested in unexplained psychic phenomena, specifically interested in ways he could document them, and perhaps enhance them, by electronic means.

Puharich served in the army in the early 1950s: The details of his assignment, like much of his life, are clouded in a murkiness he has come to wear like some exquisite garment. In any case, his activities have raised the perception among many that under the auspices of the U.S. government, Puharich had been involved in actual experiments in parapsychology and psychedelic drugs. Those with a conspiratorial bent have often assumed Puharich has dark Intelligence connections; Ira himself claimed that Puharich "was doing LSD work for the CIA in 1954."

Immediately after leaving government service, Puharich set up a lab to further study subjects like ESP, faith healing, mental telepathy, and other psychic phenomena, attempting to examine these peculiar events in a scientific setting. He also set up a medical electronics business called Intelectron Corporation, for which he designed hearing aids. (Puharich holds fifty-six patents for his various inventions.) Intelectron was apparently quite profitable, for Puharich was able to conduct his psychic experiments at a country estate at 87 Hawkes Avenue in Ossining, New York, about thirty miles outside of New York City. In addition, he ventured to Mexico to view hallucinogenic drug rites with the Chatina Indians, and to Hawaii where sacred mushroom cults inducted the good doctor as a tribal "kahuna." In the sixties, he spent much time documenting the healing powers of Arigo, a Brazilian civil servant by day who ran evening clinics wherein he routinely cured severe medical problems by unceremoniously hacking away at the problem, *sans* anesthetic, with an uncleaned blade (earning Arigo the appellation "Surgeon of the Rusty Knife"). Puharich himself eventually allowed Arigo to remove a lipoma from his right arm under those conditions, with favorable results.

Despite these startling interests, Puharich became fairly respected as a researcher in an area fraught with unreliability. An indication of his status is his appearance on an episode of the "Perry Mason" television show, on which he played himself, appearing at

Mason's request as an expert witness on parapsychology. At his first meeting with Ira Einhorn, in 1968, Puharich felt by far the more conventional of the two. "I was doing research in connection with the Atomic Energy Commission, working with the head of bio-physics," he says. "One day he shows up in my lab in New York with a pink-cheeked, wild-looking guy he introduced as Ira Einhorn. This [AEC scientist] was a conservative-looking guy, more like a banker. I thought, What the hell's he doing with this guy off the street?"

Ira had read Puharich's book *Beyond Telepathy* and expressed his excitement about it. "I thought it was *the* book," he later explained. It embodied a lot of Ira's new interests—his doodlings with the premise that there was a relationship between information and energy that had extended to a consideration of the boundaries of the definition of "human" being. He later tried to explain this evolution of his interests to a crowd gathered at a "Physics and Consciousness" conclave he organized in early 1977: "My quest in the last seven or eight years [is] to try to understand the laws that govern the nonphysical."

But by 1970 *Beyond Telepathy* had gone out of print. With his characteristic activism, Ira did something about this situation. His partner in this was a young editor at Doubleday named Bill White-head. Hired to edit psychology books at the division called Anchor Books, Whitehead was not as interested in the world of traditional psychoanalysis or Skinner boxes as in the less conventional fields that had suddenly been thrown into focus by the great social changes occurring in the aftermath of the youth revolution. The Hippie Movement had created an interest for alternative philoso-phies, particularly the meditative paths of the East. In the wake of this was a hunger for knowledge about human consciousness, self-realization, and global thought that acknowledged both the Bucky Fuller systems sensibility and the strange worlds unlocked by psy-chedelic drugs. Perhaps no one in the United States of America was more in touch with this mode of thought in 1970 than Ira Einhorn, and the two developed not only a warm friendship but a mutual respect that led to a highly unconventional arrangement, as far as the publishing world went.

Ira became a de facto consulting editor to Anchor Books. White-head would solicit names of potential authors from Einhorn and often Einhorn would provide the initial contact. Or if a promising proposal came in, Whitehead would send a copy to Ira for his comments. Sometimes, Ira would even act as agent for the author, but mostly his financial compensation would be in the form of small checks sent on a job-by-job basis for his help. The larger compensation, of course, was an elevation to a power center in New Age publishing. Through Ira's help, Whitehead signed books by Michael Rossman, Bob Toben, Itzhak Bentov, and many others. As well as Andrija Puharich. Whitehead republished *Beyond Telepathy*, with a new six-page introduction, written in a rambling free-verse burst of effusion. The introduction, of course, was penned by Ira Einhorn.

Around the time of the book's publication, Puharich was in Israel. Andrija Puharich had found Uri Geller. A brash twenty-five-year-old Cyprus-born Israeli citizen, Geller was doing stage shows that displayed his apparent talent for metal bending, making objects materialize and disappear, and reading people's minds. Puharich not only thought Geller was for real but hoped that by exposing his new protégé to scientific scrutiny, in respected institutions, he could finally prove beyond question the existence of paranormal phenomena.

According to Ira's later account, Puharich and he sat up an entire night talking about Geller—Ira divined immediately that the proof of Geller's powers would jar conventional physics and create the "paradigm shift" that Thomas Kuhn described in his book—and the meeting concluded with Ira's vowing to aid Puharich in "making Uri Geller a worldwide phenomenon." The latter indeed occurred, as Geller became an international celebrity, partially due to the notoriety created in the scientific community when two researchers at the Stanford Research Institute studied Geller under laboratory conditions and wrote up their positive findings in the respected journal *Nature*.

Much of the respectability, though, was called into question when Puharich wrote his own account of Geller's powers in a book called *Uri*, midwifed to Anchor Books by Ira Einhorn. Puharich lost much ground among Establishment figures by asserting that Uri Geller's powers derived from an outer-space force called the Hoovians, agents of an interstellar council called "The Nine," who left odd messages on Puharich's tape recorder and occasionally appeared in person in the form of flying saucers. Geller, while not denying any of Puharich's claims, began to distance himself from his mentor, and eventually the two, joined by now in a business designed to market Uri in movies and licensing ventures, parted amiably. By that time, Geller was permanently part of the celebrity establishment.

How much Ira Einhorn had to do with all that is a matter of dispute. Certainly his one-time claim that he spent all his waking hours for six years promoting the Geller cause is an exaggeration. Geller himself denies that Einhorn had much to do with the effort—he told journalist Al Robbins in 1979 that he only met Ira a few times and though he considered Ira a sincere, peace-loving person, he never liked him much. By 1987, Geller's memory of Einhorn was foggier, and he couldn't even recall meeting him. Puharich describes Ira's efforts in the Geller circus as "peripheral— he wasn't in on any of the planning, or the orchestration, or the travel to the extent that Geller and I bopped around the world." Ira's efforts instead were behind the scenes—he was a frequent visitor to Puharich's home in Ossining and spoke often to Andrija during those years. More important, he worked the edges of the scientific community and exploited his media and business contacts to spread the Geller gospel. So while Uri might not have known Ira too closely, writers Colin Wilson and Charles Panati, working on book projects about Geller, found Einhorn an invaluable resource. The one time Ira's contribution moved to center stage was during his intervention to get Geller admitted to the telephone company's prestigious research facility, Bell Labs. Through his Pennsylvania Bell contacts, Ira arranged for Geller to meet some of Bell Labs' top scientists. Geller went to the New Jersey headquarters, did some metal bending, and intrigued some of the researchers, but nothing much else came of it.

In a sense, how much Ira did or did not have to do with Geller is irrelevant. By 1972, Einhorn was neck-deep in the hot field of psychic research, one of the several pillars of the New Age. He had ties to the futurist wing of the movement, as an unofficial cofounder of the Committee for the Future, which held periodic "Syncon" conferences. Ira also was one of the key organizers of the Comet Kahoutek Festival in 1973, a gathering of New Age minds that made a more lasting impression than the overhyped comet itself. He began corresponding with physicists testing the edges of quantum theory, and insinuated himself with top theoreticians in that field. Meanwhile, he merged these interests with his recent enthusiasm for changing the world through enlightening corporate executives. It was a complex life plan, most satisfying to Einhorn because it was unique. It was probably a safe assumption that if he kept up with it, others would recognize its shrewd effectiveness, and the celebrity he had attained locally would accrue nationally, perhaps internationally, for this more serious style of politicking. After all, Ira Einhorn's life was a public one, played in the spotlight, even if he often had to provide his own scrim. The very openness of his activities—he considered himself the embodiment of a citizen of Planet Earth, and toward that end he was willing to make his public life a breathing museum piece—was central to his efforts in bringing positive change to the world.

All of this was explained, more or less, in the one published book authored by Ira Einhorn. Naturally, it was edited by Bill Whitehead and published by Anchor Books. This was in keeping with Anchor's growing reputation as a counterculture island in Doubleday's sea of conservatism. Years in the making, Ira had envisioned his book as a touchstone for New Age, an ultrahip yet scientifically sophisticated Baedeker to the planetary transformation. Greatly impressed by the style of Marshall McLuhan's *The Media Is the Message,* Ira planned a similar graphic cacophony; unable to get his friend Quentin Fiori (who had done McLuhan's book) to design it, he relied on a graphic artist named Marshall Henrichs to shoot the copious photographs, choose the intricate illustrations, and lay out the complexly ordered text, generated by an IBM Selectric typewriter to emulate the concrete verse handwritten in Einhorn's block lettering. Ira's old Yippie friend Martin Carey did the liner illustrations, baroque drawings of a unicorn pulling a plow, directed by a burly Einhornesque figure on whose bib overalls were written esoteric scientific equations.

It is a book that defies description; accordingly, Ira at first suggested that it bear no title. "That worked very neatly," recalls Bill Strachan, then Whitehead's assistant, "until it came to printing order forms. The people in the order department insisted on *something.*" So Ira, still refusing to have his book categorized by any title that suggested its content, compromised by naming his book after its Library of Congress identification number. So it came to be that Ira Einhorn's book was entitled *78-187880.*

The first page sets the tone. A photo of the Unicorn himself—a human gargoyle mask enshrouded in shadow, with Ira's thick beard, graying mustache, heavy features, and, above all, his wide, piercing, Phantom-of-the-Opera blue eyes—dominates the page, while white letters declare that "I AM THE PRODUCT OF ALL THE IMPRESSIONS RECEIVED SINCE I BEGAN RE/CORDING." Those impressions are subsequently thrown back on us, but reprogrammed, as if someone had stuffed the thousands of great books in Ira Einhorn's library into a food processor jointly owned by Walt Whitman, Bucky Fuller, and Lord Buckley. It is a romp through history, biology, religion, psychoanalysis, economics, drug theory, and Yippie. At times, one cannot read the text, as the cryptic photographs on which the type is set do not allow sufficient contrast. Other times, one can read the text but cannot hope to make any sense of it. Overall, though, one gets a clear flavor of the Einhorn theory of global transformation—with the Unicorn in the center of things, the archetype of the next stage of evolution.

There was some hope at Anchor that *78-187880* would be a popular cult book. This was certainly not to be. There were some favorable reactions: Ira's friend Barbara Hubbard wrote a four-page rave in *The Futurist,* and the *Atlanta Constitution* effused that the "Counter Culture Has New Guru." Other reviews, though, bore unfortunate kinship to the one in the *Augusta Chronicle* that began, "This is a meaningless piece of inscrutable sophomoric drivel, pretentiously packaged to be passed off as visionary madness by a supposedly hip young member of the counterculture."

Bill Strachan, assistant to Ira's editor at Doubleday, guesses that of about the 10,000 paperback copies printed, perhaps 2,000 were sold.

As reviews and sales reports came in, it was clear that Ira was destined not to become a best-selling author. Yet the book was a forceful expression of who he was, or at least whom he wanted to be known as, as well as an opportunity to extend his public persona a little more. For the *Drummer,* long his local publishing base, he arranged to be interviewed by the person who understood him best—himself. Interviewed by others, he was candid and entertaining. For instance, the *Daily News* reporter who spoke to him at a book-signing event on the Penn campus, a journalist who once excoriated Ira as "a thirty-year-old adolescent," now found him delightful.

"He is disarmingly open," wrote the reporter about the newly minted author, "a man of affirmative humility who does not find it necessary to hoist his intellect up a pole, or play the emerging genius, or shell-game the come-on, the put-on, or put-down."

The public persona of Ira Einhorn, to a T. A guru destined to work behind the scenes, monitoring the fault lines of the culture, omnisciently aware of changes to come—and at peace with his role. A man at ease not only with a chaotic world but with himself, so much so that he could blithely intermingle his philosophical musings with shocking details about his own sexual explorations in the *Drummer*. Out front, always. The one and only Ira.

But this was not the only Ira. There was also a private side to the Unicorn, one at odds with the cosmic citizen Philadelphians knew and had come to appreciate. There were no articles, no published writings, no boardroom gossip or chatting at La Terrasse about this other side of Ira Einhorn. Those who knew something of this other side of Ira Einhorn considered it a quirkiness, an anomaly, a blip on an otherwise stable radar screen. Almost no one suspected that it would be his downfall.

That downfall began on October 7, 1972. He was still basking in the glory of his book, thrilled by the prospect of promoting Geller, excited by his success in penetrating the business world, and overall satisfied by his turning the corner from the sixties to the New Age. He was brunching at La Terrasse. And his eye was struck by what he described later that day as a "lovely shy blonde," a beauty with blue eyes, with whom he struck up a conversation, and jotted her birth-date so he could divine its astrological significance. She was a frail young woman, a leaf shaken from the tree of the sixties, recently returned from a trip abroad and fluttering aimlessly in a town 2,000 miles from the home she had rejected.

She was Holly Maddux. She and Ira would hit it off instantly, beginning a passionate and tumultuous relationship that would last five years. And end with her death.

7

WHERE FEAR COMES FROM

Ira Einhorn once told an interviewer the circumstances of his meeting Holly Maddux.

"She moved in with me about ten days after I first laid eyes on her and that was either in late September or early October of 1972," he recalled. "I was having breakfast on a Saturday morning, In fact I remember very clearly . . . I looked over to a table, I saw an attractive lady."

"This was in La Terrasse?" the interviewer asked.

"La Terrasse," confirmed Ira. "I went over, I was introduced, and we talked for a while, and there was an obvious attraction between the two of us. And I gave her my phone number and she took my phone number. And I don't remember what the next contact was, but it was within a very short span of time. And within that span of time, either before she called me or after she called me, she went off . . . because she really was not feeling very good psychically and had to get away. When she did come back, I know I called her, and chided her, about making a date and not keeping it, or not calling me. And she came over and she saw me and I think it was an hour later that we were making love and that was, I think, either a Thursday morning or a Friday morning. Monday morning she moved into my apartment . . . at 3411 Race Street, second floor rear. And we've been living together, off and on, until her disappearance. So for five years we spent most of our time together. It was a stormy relationship, so that she was away from me and I was away from her—we were separated for the summer for a month or so. But we always came back together."

A "stormy relationship" is an accurate, though not complete, epithet to explain the half-decade of attraction, repulsion, affection, jealousies, squalor, revelation, oppression, and frustration that characterized the union of Ira Einhorn and Holly Maddux. Both lovers were ripe for something momentous. Ira had much to celebrate, but no special person to celebrate with. Holly was just plain needy, but she had learned enough hard lessons about the world to know that a long-term commitment could not be with just anyone.

Ira Einhorn was certainly not just anyone. The very first time he and Holly got together he was fielding phone calls and handling matters of book publicity from the tiny apartment he had moved into after being forced to abandon the Piles in 1971. The Powelton Apartments' once-militant tenant organization, led in part by Einhorn, had petered out as people got fed up with the lack of maintenance and the hassle of living on condemned property, as well as the drug-addicted poachers who'd moved into vacant apartments. Fires were set in the halls, and most disturbingly, a young woman living in the building was found dead in the basement. That mystery was never resolved; she was simply declared a victim of the times. The Piles, which once stood for the glorious spirit of the sixties, barely survived the decade. (It did avoid the wrecker's ball, and now, renovated and restored, is a gentrified, upscale apartment house.) Ira was one of the last to go. Periodically, he had to call up Don Kenley, the vice-president of the Philadelphia Gas Works he had befriended, to get the gas turned back on. And then one day Ira scanned a Penn bulletin board and spotted a notice of a nearby apartment for rent at around $100 a month. Though it was small, the living area only about twelve by twelve, Ira liked it. After only a brief once-over, he told the architecture student living there to take down the notice.

Thus was Ira's base camp established at 3411 Race, and Holly Maddux, on their first date, must have been impressed to see this teddy-bearish man fielding what seemed like very important calls. In the apartment was the latest copy of the *Drummer,* with an article called "Ira Einhorn Speaks: A Rare Interview with Phila's Elusive

Seer of Cosmic Consciousness." In that self-interview Ira asked himself whether his modest fame had affected his life, his answer being

> To the extent that people respond to the
> ### IMAGE
> rather than
> the reality I've affected, particularly if I allow this response to disturb me. I've had my cock sucked a few times recently without any real contact occurring—it really made me aware of the horror that most women go through—"tits," "breasts," "cunt," "ass," "good lay," "good blow job."

In very little time, Holly was conquered. How could she not be? When Ira Einhorn focused his attention on a woman, it was overwhelming. Those blue eyes would fix in on her, and she'd feel almost drunk with attention. This man, who seemed to know everything and everybody, was easily the most dynamic person Holly Maddux ever had a chance to be involved with, and Holly was thrilled that he was interested in her. Ira, on his part, apparently deemed that a sexual experience was worth the risk he had articulated, of no "real contact occurring," and his generosity paid off. They spent, as Ira wrote that day, "hours of lovemaking," with a "great desire to produce mutual satisfaction."

For the next ten days, they carried on what, for Ira, was a courtship. This meant that he fit Holly into his overstuffed schedule. As usual, he had dozens of projects going, and was busy monitoring events ranging from neighborhood to global. Also as per routine, he was seeing other women then. But almost immediately upon meeting Holly Maddux, he intuited that she could be something different. Within days of meeting her he reported, in one of a series of private writings that documents the relationship, that "Holly [is] returning me to the deep pleasures of a woman." Others had made it known to Ira that they would be willing to chance a serious relationship; one of the very first times Ira had seen Holly he'd opened some mail in front of her and discovered a marriage proposal from a smitten lover. But Holly, in an instant, seemed right for him.

Some of Ira's friends were not terribly surprised. Ted Fink, for instance. Einhorn had used his graces to help get his old high school chum the manager's job at La Terrasse. So Fink was one of the first of Ira's friends to view the new woman. "I don't know where Holly came from," he says. "You wouldn't ask—Holly was there to listen. She offered things, but she was not quite sure of herself. She would take off at the drop of a hat." Still, Fink saw why Ira would pursue Holly. "She was the kind of girl you could look at and fall in love with instantly," he says. "Ira seemed to have a lot of women, but he wanted a woman he could really love. They looked good together, it was obvious they were in love. He loved her sense of beauty; she had a mystical quality about her that was almost oriental. . . . In the beginning, you never heard Ira putting her down."

"She was everything he'd always dreamed of in terms of a woman," says Judy Wicks, who was also working at La Terrasse at the time. Ira had befriended Judy when she arrived in Philadelphia in 1971; they shared a relationship that Wicks describes as nonromantic. "He liked blondes, he liked thin blondes, he loved dance and motion," she says. "And she was very open—just a very lovely person."

For Ira Einhorn, opening up personally was not easy. He was accustomed to being a public figure, willing to throw himself body and soul into the struggle for planetary transformation. But most who knew him considered him less progressive in one-to-one relationships. His last long-term romance, with another willowy blond WASP of retiring aspect, had ended in spring of 1970, after two years of storms. For a while, he'd been considering marrying her, and then suddenly it was over. He'd resumed his social life, one in which women were consumed as voraciously as books. Many observers of these affairs thought that Ira's behavior with women was rather scandalous. Certainly not liberated, as the Women's Movement used the term. At times, he would bully a woman through his superior intellect, or even by insults. Other times, those watching Ira turning his charms on susceptible young females were offended at what they considered a manipulative streak. In circles Ira traveled, free love was perfectly acceptable. But Ira seemed to press an unfair advantage, through his brainpower, his intensity, his celebrity, and sometimes even his size. Though Ira Einhorn was capable of leaps into the realm of the "leptoid"—the superevolved human of the future he rhapsodized about in his book—most of his friends thought that he was curiously lacking when it came to understanding the opposite sex, despite his penchant for paying lip service to feminism. "I remember once he was interviewed in the *Inquirer*, and he said that the most important issues today are women's issues," recalls his friend Tom Bissinger. "We just sort of looked at each other—people who knew Ira—and said, 'What is *this?*'"

Einhorn's friends considered this failing a peccadillo: immature, perhaps, but not damnable. The assumption was that the right woman would do the trick for Ira. But not many thought it would be Holly Maddux. On first glance, at least, she seemed too ethereal, lacking the substance and grit it would require to domesticate the Unicorn.

On October 20, less than two weeks after their meeting at La Terrasse, Holly was ready to move to 3411 Race Street. Ira asked his friend Don Matskin, an architect living in Powelton, to help transport Holly's things in his station wagon. Matskin got the impression that Holly was leaving a tense situation in her current apartment, perhaps something nasty with a male roommate. She didn't have much in the way of clothes and possessions. Still, Matskin was impressed with his friend's new woman. "She was really sweet, very beautiful, hard to communicate with. She certainly wasn't unfriendly—I guess she was shy, unsure of herself. One way of describing her would be *drift-y*. As a manifestation perhaps of her inability to give direction to her own life."

Ira went out immediately after Matskin left Holly and her things at the apartment, and when he returned, found it remarkable that Holly was sitting at the kitchen table. Waiting for him, as if she were a frightened, yet defensively independent, cat. The first days of their living situation were tense. Lots of discussions and second-guessing. Ira read his notebooks and his poetry to Holly, perhaps to give her an indication of his breadth. Holly was feeling, in Ira's words, "a bit shell-shocked" at the suddenness and intensity of things. When possible, they made love to preserve their best feelings, but that did not go smoothly. Holly was suffering a bout of vaginitis, a periodic and chronic condition. Ira for some reason felt pain in his penis, and as always with him in the winter months, he was trying to fight off colds and flu with massive doses of vitamin C. However, the times when things did go right on that sole mattress on the floor of the living area, the air between them would clear. Ira was moved to write a poem entitled, simply, "Holly Maddux," which reads, in entirety:

Her asshole has been occupied by the prick of a Chinese lion.

For a while, though, it looked like the relationship would not last the remaining weeks of 1972. Holly and Ira would battle. Apparently much of the cause was Ira's dominance. Ira was used to having his own way, accustomed from childhood to a role at the center of attention. The small apartment was more than filled by Ira's ego. Holly, worried about maintaining her individuality in the face of a shrunken self-esteem, must have worried about disappearing entirely. While she retained gumption, she could not muster up the energy or confidence to follow up on her natural stubbornness. Back in her school days at Tyler, she could absorb a blow and vow to "show 'em." But now, twenty-five years old and uncertain of her abilities, she was unable to make good her vows. There was also the concern that after having grown up under the influence of a dominant father, she now found herself ruled by a dominant lover—a surrogate Fred Maddux. Ira recognized this problem right away, and noted in an interview after his arrest that it was possible that Holly shifted aspects of her paternal relationship to her situation with Ira. "In fact," Ira explained, "I said to her often, 'I'm not your father.' I had to keep reminding her."

When Holly and Ira fought, when she suspected that the relationship was just not going to work, when she would storm out and find somewhere else to sleep that night, her defiance would ultimately wither. Typically, as Ira turned the light out to go to sleep, Holly would be at the door. Instant reconciliation. But often, within hours, they would again find grounds for disagreement.

"Battle again," wrote Ira in late 1972. "She wants to be alone. I hurt her so. Makes me want to end it. The pain of the other is often too much to take. . . . What is this pain that we always cause to those that we love?"

At some point in this fitful beginning, Holly went back to Tyler for a visit. Her old friend Lawrence Wells was also in town, having just graduated from law school. They saw each other every night, and Wells was recaptivated by her. "She had just met Ira, but she was having a lot of conflict with him," he says. "I remember talking about Ira. She had this incredible fantasy view about him. It was like, 'Oh how could he be interested in 'lil ol' me?' That's the kind of attitude she had. . . . She felt richer [being with important people] because she had such a poverty attitude about herself. She had this incredible world built up [within herself] . . . And she protected this world."

Wells yearned for Holly to come back to Earth. He felt deeply for her and wanted her with him. "I asked her to leave him, and come with me," he says. "I don't remember what her answer was. It wasn't much of one, or she didn't have one."

"I don't know," Lawrence Wells recalls Holly telling him. "I'm real confused now. I'm kind of with Ira, but I don't know what's going to happen."

By the end of 1973, the pattern of the relationship was well formed, perhaps indelibly. Ira spent his time being Ira. Holly was his support structure. Of course, no self-respecting couple in the postsixties mode could dare admit a truism like that—certainly Holly hated to come face-to-face with that admission—so Holly sought satisfying work. (This came after an extremely brief and contentious fling at being Ira's private secretary.) But not with ambition or hopes of earning money. The student most likely to succeed was focusing more on crafts, cooking, and other "whole Earth" womanly chores that somehow snuck under the counterculture umbrella past the eyes of vigilant feminists.

This work would, of course, be in addition to her everyday routine of sewing, seeking out old clothes in Salvation Army thrift shops and other secondhand outlets, and tending the virtual indoor garden of houseplants she had created at 3411 Race. "Holly had a relationship with those plants," says Fran Harriman, a friend of the couple. "The plants in that apartment were vibrant, beautiful—it looked like they could get up and talk to you." Holly also did the cooking for Ira, a person used to having tasks performed for him. (Fran Harriman says that even at that late date, Ira still was taking his laundry to Bea Einhorn for cleaning— "Here he was, world-famous New Age guru, still taking his laundry home to his poor mother," says Harriman. "The fact that Ira was still a pampered child was something Holly and I both laughed at.") Holly attacked her cooking chores with diligence, making her own tofu, brewing soups of lentil and split pea, making Jewish specialties like knishes, even learning some tricks from Bea Einhorn, who came to love Holly like a daughter, despite her *shiksa* pedigree.

Holly finally landed a job in a Sufi bakery run by Vakil and Reza Kuner, who were friends of Ira when they went by their pre-Sufi names of Peter and Sue. They met Holly when she'd accompanied Ira to their wedding in late 1972. The bakery, on the corner of Baring Street and Powelton Avenue, was to be a center in the Sufi community of Powelton Village—"Our model was the Zen bakery in San Francisco where it is required that employees be Zen disciples," says Vakil Kuner. Holly was the lone non-Sufi.

"She was a wonderful person and certainly a match for Ira," he says. "Not intellectually, but in terms of her character. She was very independent and a very, very strong being."

Holly was a hard worker. She and the other bakers would report at five in the morning, so that fresh bread would be ready by nine. At first, Vakil Kuner had to realize that Holly's manner, slow and steady, was not sloth but a productive pace that could be maintained for an entire shift. The bakery had an electric mixer for kneading the dough, but everything else was done by hand, hard physical work, sometimes lifting 80-pound batches of dough. The heat generated by the ovens would raise the room temperature well above ninety degrees. Holly did what was required of her, in good humor.

Vakil had liked Ira from the time they were neighbors in the Piles, and even afterward, as Ira maintained ties—he once brought over Baba Ram Dass for a vegetarian meal. But Kuner had his doubts about the Unicorn. He'd always felt intimidated by Einhorn. "I think because he was interested in pushing things, he was interested in pushing the limits of whatever through drugs or through everybody taking off their clothes, or [defying] conventions, and so forth." More than that, Kuner thought Ira, though always friendly, was not *personal*. "He always presented himself as being a very strong person, so his role would be the person that other people would confide in." As Kuner got to know Holly, he began to wonder why she had thrown in her lot with him.

Reza Kuner also worried about Holly. "There's no doubt from knowing her, even in the beginning of that relationship, that he was dominating her in an unhealthy way, and she was relating to him in an unhealthy way," she says. "She was like a planet revolving around Ira."

Vakil Kuner recalls seeing Ira lose his temper around Holly and yelling at her. Once he visited the apartment on Race Street and saw the two of them in the middle of a fight. Who knows what the cause was? It could have been an inane domestic quarrel. Or it could have been yet another battle centered around Ira's insistence that he be free to make love to as many other women as he cared to. This was a privilege that in theory was available to Holly, but actually was difficult for Ira to accept—he literally had nightmares about strange men picking up Holly.

Compared to Ira's concerns and responsibilities, troubles of this nature were absurd. It shouldn't happen. After all, in his own view, he was a brilliant human being working full-time on behalf of the planet. He considered himself a person of measure and discipline. While the sixties might have been characterized by drug use and political craziness, Ira's latest passion seemed perfect for a man of vision and discipline: the oriental game of Go. This Eastern pursuit, where two competitors arrange stones on a gridded board in a struggle for territory, makes chess look as childish as tic-tac-toe. Immersed in the study of this game, Ira believed he saw the very forces of history play themselves before his eyes. It was through the study of Go, he contended, that he understood why the United States could never have won in Vietnam. His participation in the game was scholarly and methodical, emblematic of the seriousness with which he comported himself in this perilous age. Compared to the Geller controversy, the advances in physics he was helping document, and the merger of new consciousness with the business world, his clashes with Holly Maddux seemed trivial, almost beneath his attention. His normal response to a battle ended was to sadly write, "How silly we be," as if one's proper position was above it all.

But though he frequently wrote off the relationship with bittersweet words, he never totally let it go. This, despite his occasional realization that his dominance might be destructive to this troubled young woman, eight years younger, and—as mutually agreed— many measures less wise. At one point after snapping at Holly, he wrote that he needed to "send her away so she can be with someone who will appreciate her love. Something in me is threatened by her independence which I want so badly. Time for others!"

But Ira and Holly would not split up for good. Things went on as before. Ira, if not daddy to Holly as daughter, was at the least the teacher to Holly as student. And Ira was not the most tolerant of instructors. The prime example was their difficulties in reaching a mutually satisfying sex life: Holly had difficulties reaching orgasm with Ira. To Ira, this was Holly's problem, something that *she* must fix, in a learning process that would presumably allow her access to the higher plane that Ira had already attained. Ira was not above making Holly feel terrible about her deficiency in these matters.

"I'm at loose ends again," wrote Holly in spring of 1973. "I'm getting awfully cranky these days and can't really tell whether or not it's a sign of darkness before the dawn, or worse perpetual darkness. Ain't crazy, just screwy."

"Holly was never really very happy with Ira," contends Pamela DeMaigret, who knew Einhorn from the psychic-phenomena circuit. It was obvious that in some ways he viewed Holly as inferior, and in DeMaigret's eyes Ira treated her badly. "Holly was very needful of emotional support. Ira would almost deliberately withhold it so she would always be off balance." She thought Ira's behavior was a tactic of control.

DeMaigret remembers that she and Ira were once among the participants in a séance, not an unusual circumstance for a paranormal explorer like Ira. Holly was there as well, and quite uncharacteristically, she felt confident to contribute to the psychic doings. She described a strange scenario she was receiving. As she spoke, the listeners felt that she was gaining strength, a child trying a two-wheeler for the first time and just finding balance. Suddenly, Ira snapped out at her, calling her a fool and snorting that she ought to know the difference between her own imagination and what was real. Holly was devastated. "I took Ira to task," says DeMaigret. "What Holly had to say was as valuable as the great Ira Einhorn. I said, 'You don't have to put up with this, Holly. Don't let him bully you.' [But] she was an adoring acolyte."

Tom Bissinger and others in the Synergy Group would be exposed to Ira and Holly's spats, too. "You had two willful people," he says. "Holly had her own attitudes. But you wondered, 'Geez, why is [she] bothering to get him into a fight when he could outargue her until the end of time.'" Ira was overpowering, and he would overwhelm Holly with logic and scorn. "There was no way Holly was going to win a match like that."

Ira and Holly spent the summer of 1973 apart. The separation set the pattern for future episodes. Ira, usually the one urging an open relationship, found himself most possessive of Holly when she would spend their "vacations" with other lovers. He brooded on her, cast the I Ching for positive signs of their reunion in September, envisioned holding her once again. He vowed not to upset her by his power. "We will have to go slowly," he wrote. "[She is] afraid of the physical, I sense. No push, easy. One goal: to be together with her."

The reconciliation in California, conducted in the midst of Ira's participation in a consciousness seminar, went well enough for the couple to take the next step in understanding each other: On their way back East, Holly would bring Ira Einhorn to Tyler, Texas, to meet the Maddux family.

Under the best of circumstances, Holly Maddux's bringing this boyfriend home had slim chance of success. Though Holly had always maintained warm contact with her family, relations between her and the clan's dominant figure had been tense ever since she'd left for Bryn Mawr. Fred Maddux had regretted his daughter's move to the East Coast ever since he'd visited her at college in her sophomore year and cast his eyes upward to the windows of the ivy-covered dorms. To his astonishment, there were Scotch bottles visible in almost all the windows. "Down there at A&M, if they find you with a jug of booze in your room, your ass went out the door," he says. "And I drive up [to Bryn Mawr] and there's booze all over the place! It was a social shock to me."

Now, the Madduxes had to face up to the fact that their daughter was living with a person to whom she was not married. There was no way for Fred Maddux to think of that arrangement without the words *in sin* cropping up.

"I didn't approve of the way she lived, but whether you approve or disapprove, you never stop loving your child," says Fred Maddux. The Maddux household was in a quandary familiar to thousands of families in that era. They disapproved of Holly's life-style but did not want to alienate her so much that she would end the contact that both sides wanted to maintain. So both parties, without overt negotiation, honored an uneasy truce.

This visit, though, would put the unspoken agreement to the test. The Madduxes were determined not to provoke a scene. Considering what they already knew about Ira—Holly had sent them *78-187880,* a book Fred Maddux judged as "a bunch of crap," so they were not totally unprepared—this required considerable stamina. If one imagined the Madduxes constructing a nightmare boyfriend for Holly, he might well be the person they first laid eyes on when they picked up Holly and Ira in Dallas. A Jewish hippie, known to advocate illegal drugs and opposition to the policies of the U.S. government. Eight years older than their daughter, and looking fifteen years older, with his thickening midriff, ruddy features, and graying hair. With thick long hair tied back in a ponytail, a beard that befitted a Russian revolutionary, sawed-off jeans that exposed spindly legs, and wire-rim glasses with purple lenses. His crusty clothes wafted a stale odor—or was it *him* that smelled so bad? To boot, he was suffering from a bad case of poison oak, a condition that seemed to command much of his attention—to the point of neglecting the pleasantries one would naturally expect when greeting the parents of one's sweetheart for the first time.

According to the Madduxes, his first words upon entering the house were, "Well, I can see why Holly's a casual housekeeper." Then he asked to use the phone to call his mother. After chatting with Bea Einhorn, he took to bed to nurse his poison oak. He arose in time for the dinner hour. Fred Maddux, at the head of the table, carved the roast and began passing plates around the table. As the Madduxes recall it, before the whole family had been served, Ira had not only gobbled his portion but was reaching toward the roast with his fork to stab more of it for himself.

All this, even before Fred Maddux had intoned grace! Holly's sister Buffy, around thirteen years old then, was shocked "We serve our guests first," she says, "but we didn't have our plates yet, and he's eating. And I go, 'Mom, Dad, are we going to say the blessing?' And that didn't even penetrate—he ate through the blessing." After he had sated himself, Ira got up, went over to the television, pulled a chair very close so he could view the screen without requiring his glasses, and put his feet up on either side of the television, assuring no one else could see the screen.

One courtesy Ira did extend was his acceptance of the sleeping arrangements. He slept in John's room while Holly slept on the floor of her sister Meg's room.

Only Ira knows why he behaved the way he did. As someone who could overcome the suspicions of high-powered corporate executives, he certainly was capable of sufficient diplomacy to make, at the least, a sizable dent in the Madduxes' distrust of him. Yet he did not. Perhaps he turned off instantly upon seeing the FUHRER license plate, or another of Fred Maddux's war remembrances: the large, red Nazi flag that hung in the den. It is also possible that the poison oak so overwhelmed him that he was incapable of mustering the civility required to endear himself to the Madduxes. Holly herself seemed to have accepted that explanation: She later wrote Ira of her father's criticism of his behavior, noting that Fred Maddux was "forgetting . . . to mention that you were in misery from poison oak."

The Madduxes' suspicion was that Ira was deliberately trying to provoke them into booting him out of their house, thus forcing Holly to side with him against her parents. "I think he resented the fact that he couldn't get Holly completely away from her family," says Liz Maddux.

Though Ira did not care to explore many of the sites of Holly's triumphant girlhood, he did accompany Holly when she visited Toni Erwin. Holly's old friend found him offensive. They went to Hernando's restaurant and somehow found themselves in a conversation about what Holly would do if she ever found herself pregnant. Toni got the impression that the subject had never come up between Ira and Holly before. "I think Holly might even have been thinking that it might be nice [to have a child]," says Toni. "And I know that she was probably thinking that it would be nice if she and Ira were married. And he was real cold, and it was absolutely clear that if she got pregnant, it would be her problem and it was his opinion that she would have an abortion. He never asked her what she wanted. I took an instant dislike to him. It was clear he didn't care about Holly. She was fascinated by him, dominated by him, very anxious to please him. It wasn't her nature to be anxious to please people. Holly didn't try to win approval in ways that most people do. She never compromised herself—but with Ira she didn't exude that kind of confidence. It was as if she was just a nothing that he let be with him."

What bothered the Maddux family most during the visit was what they considered Ira's cavalier treatment of Holly. He spoke to her brusquely, and bossed her around in a manner that her parents had never previously seen her accept. "*We* couldn't have talked to her that way!" says Liz Maddux. At one point while watching television, the Unicorn called her over, and commanded her to brush his hair. Holly asked if he would like to look through her old scrapbooks, and Ira cut her off, saying, "I want you to brush my hair first." Holly obeyed.

Ira did make an attempt to ingratiate himself to Holly's sisters. The youngest Maddux, Mary, was struggling with her math homework, and Ira sat down at the table with her and enlightened her on the particulars of the new math. Even Fred and Liz Maddux would later admit that watching Ira Einhorn teach was a revelation: He had a talent for it. "He explained it to her in the most clear, concise, patient manner," says Fred Maddux.

Perhaps the worst part of the visit for the Madduxes was Holly's exit. "They weren't here more than two or three days and then suddenly he said, 'We gotta go,'" says Liz Maddux. The elder Madduxes asked Holly if she wanted to stay longer, but she would not. "They stood by the back door," Liz Maddux says, "and he put everything heavy on her shoulders to march her out to the car and then he picked up one little bag. He had the Injun sign somehow on her. He had her so convinced she was nothing, she was just stupid, and she really didn't have sense enough to go around the block unless he was nice enough to lead the way. And I just don't *understand* how someone can get that way, the way she was."

There was one mitigating instant in that premature departure. Just as Holly and Ira were about to leave, Holly called in Buffy and told her that Ira had written a poem for her. "And he hugged me," recalls Buffy, "and gave me a kiss and all of this, and I just went 'Can I go now?'" But she felt honored to a degree, that Holly's special person would write a poem just for her. She accepted the poem, read it over, and kept it, not throwing it out until five years later when her sister was discovered dead in Ira Einhorn's closet.

Ira's poison oak had hardly faded when an opportunity arose for another sojourn with Holly—this one even more ill-fated. The site was a cabin in Surf City, New Jersey, shared with another couple who would witness the dynamics between Ira and Holly more closely than they cared to.

Ralph Blum, an experienced researcher of fringe phenomena,

had met Ira through Andrija Puharich, and while impressed with Einhorn's energy, was a bit wary of him. He wondered how much of Ira was brilliance and how much was posturing. One thing was certain, though. Ira was totally immersed in the workings of the New Age, and had thrown himself into that world with contagious verve. At the time, Blum needed some of that spirit: He was plagued by writer's block at a most inopportune time. In a few months, he and his wife, Judy, owed Bantam Books a volume about unidentified flying objects. UFOs were, of course, one of thousands of subjects on which Ira Einhorn spoke with authority.

"I was kind of stuck," Blum says. Just as one must occasionally prime the dry pump, he needed priming on this book. "Ira was nothing if not a good primer," he says. "But sometimes he tended to become the pump when he was priming." In any case, the Blums asked Ira to work on the project with them. Since nothing short of a total blitz would get the book done on time, the Blums rented a cottage on Long Beach Island, New Jersey, a seaside resort thoroughly abandoned in winter. There would be four of them: Ralph the writer, Judy the editor, Ira the creative force, and Holly, whose role was undefined except perhaps in the unspoken expectation that she would handle domestic tasks. Years later, Blum would say Ira was with "nobody real—just Holly."

For the Blums, the November 1973 book offensive began awkwardly. Ira had arrived first, but didn't have a key. So he put his fist through a window to gain entrance to the cottage. "That hole in the glass gave me a momentary blip of concern," admits Blum. "And then the four of us moved into this small seaside cottage. Where they proceeded to be sick the whole time."

"Holly's role seemed to be just doing the cooking and keeping quiet," says Judy Blum. "I felt very sorry for her. She seemed like a very timid person. I have this mental image of Ralph and me and Ira sitting around the table, a sort of round kitchen table with a checkered cloth on it, and Holly's back was always to us. She was always at the stove. She was left to her devices a great deal. Ira was not nice to her. He bullied. He picked on her. He criticized her a lot. He made her cry."

Ralph Blum, given to understatement, asserts that "Ira was not nourishing to Holly. He didn't whip her, but there was a cowed quality in her reverence toward Ira. I remember walking one day with Holly and her feeling quite down in the mouth at the way the relationship was going. But she held it in. I suppose Ira is what would be called a charismatic or magnetic personality, as seen through a woman's eye."

The one bathroom in the cottage separated the two bedrooms, and there was little privacy. "They had fights, but it was mostly Ira doing the shouting," says Judy Blum. "And Holly, I couldn't hear her, she had a quiet voice. I had a feeling that he hit her once or twice; I remember thinking he was being, quote, 'physically unkind.' I did not see it. I'm not sure—Holly didn't tell me. I remember asking her what on Earth she was doing with him, and why she didn't get away. I felt it was terribly important for Holly to get away from him. It was just damaging as a person for her to be this way around him."

As Judy Blum recalls, Holly's response was inarticulate, ultimately pathetic.

"She felt kind of caught, almost as if she couldn't get away. Basically, she felt she should [leave him] too, but she didn't have the strength."

The idyll at the Jersey Shore ended badly for almost everyone. Ira and the Blums had been working on two tracks, having divided the subject of UFOs into pieces; Ira handled the so-called cosmology of UFOs and produced three chapters that synthesized a New Age consciousness view of flying saucers, spiced heavily with the theories of Wilhelm Reich. Ralph Blum, without comment, submitted Ira's chapters to the Bantam editor, who proclaimed them unpublishable. The Blums continued to do the book, without Einhorn. But, as the authors recall it, the Unicorn noted that they had contracted to do the book together, and was willing to bow out only if they yielded the $7,500 advance to him. Feeling against the wall, and desperate to make their deadline, they acceded to his demands. The only contribution of Ira's in the finished book, besides possibly the energy that Ralph Blum admits got him past his writer's block, is one sentence. On page 209 of *Beyond Earth: Man's Contact with UFOs,* Ira Einhorn is quoted as saying, "The problem of space is the problem of time."

Holly's legacy of the trip was even more painful. A month later, her period was late. This recalled the horrors of her 1969 abortion, which had not only forced her to confront the irrevocable steps she'd taken from her pristine girlhood but further punished her by physical pain. The "mass," she later wrote of that first experience, "did not want to go *out*," and Holly had to remain in the hospital. She was tormented by the very thought of facing another abortion. But as the recent conversation in Tyler indicated, she could not count on Ira's support for any other course of action.

This was only one of Holly's discomforts in the early days of 1974. She complained of having cold, stiff hands, and nauseous reactions—hangovers, she called them—from certain foods. She was working with a local dance group, and in rehearsal, she sometimes forgot her combinations. Occasionally she felt faint. Ira's suggestion was that she see Beatrice Clegg, a family friend of the Einhorns who was a certified hypnosis consultant and therapist. Ira had known Clegg, a gentle woman who resembles a suburban Gertrude Stein, since he was a child, and she had helped Ira and his mother get over their difficult period in the early sixties. In recent years she had become Ira's friend as well; they shared an interest in the human mind and its uncharted powers. Several times Ira had visited Bea Clegg for "prenatal regression," an attempt to explore his previous life incarnations. This was done, Bea Clegg takes care to note, in a serious way—not in parlor-game frivolity. When under hypnosis for this purpose, Ira had strange sensations—usually the feeling of being at sea. "He had a couple of darks, one or two times he cried," says Clegg. "But that is not unusual. I just remember this one time at sea, and he would see it was blue, blue all around him."

Betsy Hoffman, a friend of Ira's who witnessed the session, says that "Ira went back in time a long time. . . . He was undergoing what he thought was physical torture. We stopped it."

Bea Clegg's professional work, though, had little to do with regression or other experimental matters—she helped people with self-hypnosis. An optimistic woman, she calls hypnosis "a doorway to better living," and that is why Ira Einhorn sent Holly Maddux to the neat little ranch house in Philadelphia's northern suburbs for treatment. The late period aside, Holly wasn't feeling well at all, mentally or physically.

Holly appeared for her first session on January 4, 1974. In addition to resolving her physical problems, she told Bea Clegg she wanted some direction in her life. Wanted to get beyond her patterns and live. To loosen fears and become more open. And to be able to better handle Ira's "busy busy life." Clegg handed her a 5-by-7-inch card and told her to fill out her interests and activities. Holly wrote down her interests: modern dance, ballet, plants, sex. Healing and other body work. Personality and recognitions of differences leading to dealing with people as people. Animals and the out-of-doors. Making terraria. Languages. The final interest Holly Maddux noted was "where fear comes from."

She also told Clegg of her family background—how Fred Maddux dominated the family, and how she had difficulty dealing with him after she left Texas and she shed his views. She described her father as a "chauvinist führer," certainly aware of the irony of the word's appearance on the Maddux Mercedes.

Part of Clegg's approach to treatment is giving the patient post-hypnotic "cues" to work on, key words to ponder. One word Bea Clegg thought important for Holly Maddux was *acceptance*. "My main thrust," says Clegg, "was to get her to know herself, appreciate herself more."

Clegg's methodology was to hypnotize a patient in her office—a nondescript, wood-paneled den with a yellow shag rug and plaques of certification from various professional associations and the Eastern Pennsylvania Better Business Bureau. The patient would then, using Clegg's techniques, practice self-hypnosis during the week, keeping a journal of experiences and insights to bring to the next session. Holly's first week of self-hypnosis was promising. She reported a relaxed, oceanic feeling, increased access to her own thoughts, fewer self-doubts. "Had occasion to be jealous, and worked that through by myself as it came up. With frequency [of incidents that give rise to jealousy] becoming more and more of a physical possibility, the situation calls for tension, etc. But I function well with Ira," she wrote. However, she did admit that she was less at ease in company, and at times even more "freaked out" than before.

She also knew now that she was pregnant. She scheduled an abortion for January 23.

The second week of Holly's self-hypnosis sessions, probably because she worried about the impending abortion, did not go as smoothly. On January 14, she reported "no trouble relaxing but did stray off in a level of daydreaming. Many violent thoughts, blood and killing." On January 17, the day before her third and final session with Bea Clegg, she wrote of "trying to come to terms with sex, Ira, and abortion. . . . I am picturing my emotional response to next Wednesday. Picturing Ira there with me. Seeing how we will look at each other and what we will know and admit as we look at what will be going on." She confessed that she was still uneasy about the cue of "Trust myself." "Still give up and lose faith," she admitted. "Don't completely accept."

But she ended the sessions on a higher note: "Life with Ira during this particular crisis has been better than ever. I don't mean beautiful because several things that I want someday to happen between us don't yet. But I seem not to get so hung up on the little stuff anymore. It feels like we will be able to get through this thing without disfigurement."

The abortion took seven minutes, during which Ira sat in the clinic's waiting room and read newspapers and *Time* magazine.

Within weeks after the abortion, the old patterns reasserted themselves. Ira and Holly were again discussing a breakup, with Holly getting a place of her own. "Let us hope she is gathering the strength to go," Einhorn wrote in March 1974. "She deserves something better." Ira dedicated a poem to Holly entitled "It's Over," which talked of "bringing to a close an era of my life." That era indeed almost ended that spring as Holly discovered that Ira had continued sleeping with other women; upon hearing it from him directly, she burst into tears and fled the apartment into a rainstorm. In Ira's view—as Holly's lover-teacher—this was a learning experience, part of the cosmic curriculum he had drawn for her benefit. "She doesn't understand the impossibility of continuing unless I get what I need from others," he wrote. "It certainly is not coming from her. It has taken eighteen months for her to realize a bit about the 'real' nature of her difficulties—now will come the much more difficult task of doing something about it. It was necessary to make love to someone else in order to know that." Holly retreated to a friend's house down the street, but soon returned.

Bea Clegg, besides helping Holly through the period before the abortion, had suggested she see a medical doctor at Hanneman Hospital. The doctor concluded that she was hypoglycemic, and possibly diabetic. Holly was at first relieved at this news, grateful that a cause had been found for some of her problems. But controlling her condition was not to be easy. In true New Age fashion, she began a series of diets that ranged from medically conservative to outright flaky. At the bakery, Vakil Kuner would think her behavior somewhat eccentric, stopping at predetermined periods to nibble on packets of fruit or nuts.

In the summer of 1974, Ira and Holly summered in Englishtown, on Cape Breton Island, Nova Scotia. It was a craggy, seaside area, isolated and stunning in natural landscape. They rented a roomy two-story farmhouse with a back door that led directly to the beach. The small, conservative fishing community considered Ira Einhorn an oddity, but no one seemed much perturbed by his eccentricity, even when he went into town wearing little else but a beach towel draped over his lower body like a loincloth. Ira liked to boast he was becoming "brown as a berry," and indeed the sun agreed with him.

Despite frequent bickering, it was one of the better times for Ira and Holly. For a good part of the summer, they had company: Ira's friend Tom Bissinger and his girlfriend Kristen, and later Ted and Ruth Fink. Photos from that time show Ira sitting on a rock in the ocean, naked, the sun glistening off him as if he were a seal. Holly avoided the beach in high afternoon—in the late stages of the day it got too cold for her—and spent much of her time in the copious berry patches near the cabin. She picked raspberries, blueberries, wild strawberries, and then would bake cakes and bread. Since she had difficulty using the ancient oil stove in the farmhouse for baking, she'd go to nearby farmhouses to use their more manageable ovens. The closest neighbors were the Macleans, and Holly became friendly with Charlotte Maclean, a woman also in her twenties. She would spend time at their farm, enjoying the animals, the goat herd and the cows. Charlotte thought Holly angelic and sweet. But she couldn't figure out the man Holly was involved with—he was so *odd*, wearing almost nothing, and always with books spread all over the table. Once she asked Holly just what it was that Ira did professionally. "She said he was a good manipulator," Charlotte Maclean recalls. "That was the only thing she said as to what he did for a living."

Ruth Fink says that Ira and Holly were both "laid back and carefree" at Cape Breton Island that summer. A letter of Holly's sent to Bea Einhorn describes life in Nova Scotia for her and "The

Big I" in glowing terms. "A fine breakfast of daylily buds, tempura, and chopped liver . . . hitched to our favorite post office, walked back in the sun, and harvested late raspberries . . . look at beached whale from whom Ira has harvested eleven teeth . . . we read a lot in the evening, late into the night . . . stroll a lot after dark to check out the Milky Way."

She finished the letter by saying that "Neither of us look forward to the city air. The pollution is going to lie heavy on our heads after this vacation." She might have been talking about the atmosphere of the relationship. The next year proved just as difficult as before.

By that period, Ira was well along in establishing what many would consider the crown jewel of his public career: the network. The enterprise was almost an inevitable consequence of Ira's self-assigned role as a guardian of the global community.

In any case, Ira certainly must have realized that fame was not forthcoming as a writer. The final sales of *78-187880* were dismal; "I just don't know what went wrong on the book," his editor Bill Whitehead wrote him. "We put a lot into it and I still believe in it, but it just hasn't gone over in the marketplace." Meanwhile, the Einhorn proposals Bill Whitehead was circulating garnered little support at Doubleday. Nothing came of Ira's would-be biography of Frank Rizzo, to be entitled *I Never Saw My Mother Naked*. Nor was there enthusiastic response to the proposed $E = MC^2$, a book about Ira's beloved "white-haired medusa," Albert Einstein. "There certainly is a need for a book that would explain to the interested but uninformed lay reader the consequences, side realities, etc. of Einstein's theory," one Doubleday editor noted, but added that "I doubt very much however that Einhorn can [fill that need]."

So, while continuing to write for publications willing to print his unorthodox proclamations, Ira Einhorn—with typical protean vision—focused his energies more clearly. If he was not to be known as a brilliant commentator in his own right, he would make his mark as an intermediary. His energetic schmoozing in the worlds of the New Age, psychic research, fringe science, and progressive corporate management put him in contact with the vanguard of idea makers and conceptualizers in those fields. Many of these people were virtually unknown; in any case, there were few media by which they could get their ideas circulated. Einhorn, with his usual headiness, stepped into this vacuum. By sending the most exciting new ideas to the people who could best put them to use, Ira would be a cosmic catalyst, altruistically promulgating synergy throughout the world. The Unicorn came up for a term to describe his role: "planetary enzyme."

Constructing a network that fulfilled those significant goals required logistics and funding. Fortunately, Ira had a benefactor to support his network, a rich uncle who not only provided elbow grease and cash but a measure of prestige that would propel the network deeper into the Establishment than was otherwise possible. This sugar daddy was none other than the telephone company, AT&T, in the person of its subsidiary Pennsylvania Bell.

The network's beginnings were tentative. It arose from Ira's casual habit of sending information to his friends when he saw something that he thought would interest them. One day when Ira had a particularly large load to send out to a group of people, he mentioned this to Bell VP Moses Hallett, who offered to have the material mimeographed. Ira explained it wasn't merely the copying that was the problem but the mailing as well. Hallett told him to write down the addresses and he'd take care of it. The Bell executive took the papers from company headquarters at 1 Parkway, near City Hall, to a nearby duplicating office, and mailed them off at the post office at Suburban Station a block away.

Hallett paid for this out of his own pocket, as well as buying books that Ira would send along to a list of friends, with an admonition for them to send the books, when they finished, to the next name on the list. Moses considered it money well spent; he was a self-admitted information freak and he considered Ira one of the world's best sources of news of the mind.

Soon Hallett cleared the way for Bell to pay the duplication costs of the network. As the project evolved, he and Ira arrived at a protocol. The names of the members of the network were kept in a card file maintained by Hallett's secretary. The list eventually grew to more than 350 names in more than twenty countries. Each time Ira came with a mailing, usually once or twice a week, he would specify which people would receive this particular set of materials. His list was usually written on a yellow, lined cover page, the names scrawled in Ira's unmistakable block lettering. Depending on how esoteric the material was, Ira might request that it go to four names or seventy. Moses or his secretary would send the stuff down for copying, address the envelopes, and mail them off.

According to Michael Rossman, a Berkeley veteran of the Free Speech Movement and a commentator on the New Age, "[The network helped] Ira move up a step, from local activity to national networking. He advertised himself as an information nexus, and within limits he did a damn good job. He was dealing with a very important coin for that cultural historical time, which was edge information."

When Moses Hallett retired at the end of 1973, another vice-president took over responsibility for the network. Ira's new contact was Ed Mahler, who says it was Bill Cashel, president of Pennsylvania Bell, who directed the switch. At this point Bell began paying for all network expenses—duplication and postage. Mahler was somewhat wary of the arrangement at first. "Coming from a middle-class family, it took me a while to get used to Ira's dress and manner," he says. "My secretary said, 'How can you talk to him? He smells bad!' " But Mahler quickly got past appearances and found Einhorn fascinating. They arranged to have lunch almost every Friday at La Terrasse, where Ira would excite Mahler with tales of Uri Geller and other amazing things. Ed Mahler soon found himself an honored guest in the coterie of business-suited men who vicariously suited up in the space stations of the New Age, courtesy of tour guide Ira Einhorn.

The network covered a remarkable range of subjects, but as Ira explained to one questioner, much of the material dealt with parapsychology and the possibility of creating a new paradigm. "I circulate material in many fields directed toward this particular end and the larger goal of eventual planetary transformation," Ira said. He would sometimes add that just as he once was a political activist, he was now a "psychic organizer." Such a mandate accommodated a broad range of topics. "You'd be amazed at the range of information I circulate," Ira told an interviewer. "It's all over the edge of science—physiology, brain stuff, body stuff. All sorts of new psychic technologies, all sorts of physics, mathematics, economics. Solar energy. You name it. You'd be hard put to find a topic I haven't circulated something on."

A survey of even a fraction of the mailings—so voluminous that some recipients have retained several file drawers worth of papers—confirms Einhorn's contention. There were plenty of reports of Geller's exploits, of course, from sources as varied as *Nature* to London's *Sunday People*. UFO reports originated from *National Enquirer* stories as well as recently declassified government documents certifying strange objects viewed by fighter pilots in Iran. There were snippets from *Aviation Week, Solar Age, Brain-Mind Bulletin,* and *Interdisciplinary Science Reviews*. Here was a paper on ball lightning, there a report on cybernetic management, followed by a study of design and engineering required of spider webs. Papers circulated on topics like hypernumbers, thermodynamic systems of economics, zero-point energy, and Russian experiments in planting hallucinations in one's mind.

Recipients were grateful. "One day we started getting clippings from a man we'd never known, knew nothing about, and they came in envelopes from the telephone company! The clips were wonderful," says *Future Shock* author Alvin Toffler. Heidi Toffler, who works closely with her husband, was particularly impressed with information Einhorn circulated on Ilya Prigogine. It was the first the Tofflers heard of the Belgian physicist who was later to win the Nobel Prize. They followed up on it, and Alvin Toffler eventually wrote the preface to Prigogine's classic, *Order Out of Chaos*.

Einhorn would send out these papers without much comment. Sometimes he would scribble a line or two about the importance of a given document, mentioning perhaps that it dealt with an issue that would attain mind-boggling significance in the months ahead. And while reading the paper, the recipient would often find Ira's underlinings or marginalia: occasionally a large question mark next to a dubious passage, more frequently one or two exclamation points beside a concept that Ira considered crucial. When a communicant, in Einhorn's opinion, hit something directly on the head, Ira would write in boldface letters, "YES!" But Ira did not perform more detailed glossing. Nor did he circulate much of his own work through the network. His art was that of the collage constructor, not the original painter.

"I found the network to be wonderful food," says writer George Leonard. "It was just a bonanza that came to me. It entertained me, filled me with delight. There's nothing more important than ideas, especially ideas that are on the leading edge. *That's gold.*" Leonard claims that a few of the mailings he received—a John Wheeler interview and a piece by Brunowski on paradox and Gödel's theorem—helped him with his own work.

As the network continued, it began to generate its own sources: Recipients of material would forward to Einhorn things that *they* thought might be interesting for others to see. Like a cosmic bug light, the Unicorn drew the world's leading explorers of edge science and futuristic thought. On a given day he might get a letter from a French physicist studying the paranormal, a Welsh cyberneticist who was advising the Allende government in Chile, or a famous science-fiction writer who complained of objects in his apartment spontaneously exploding, and "stunning colored graphics, followed by modern Soviet music" implanted in his mind. Ira would sift through this material, great gobs of it tumbling into 3411 Race Street, weed out the best, and send it to the names on the list he thought would benefit. Word spread throughout New Age circles and the fringe-science community, and people wrote to Ira asking, sometimes begging, to receive goodies from the network.

By the mid-1970s Ira Einhorn's network was a certified phenomenon in and of itself. Names appearing on the cover letters of recipients of a given piece might include economist Hazel Henderson; Lehmann Brothers managing director Shel Gordon; Seagram heir Charles Bronfman; futurist Alvin Toffler; science adviser to the British Commonwealth Christian de Lait; corporate presidents John Haas and George Bartol; Whole Earth Catalog publisher Stewart Brand; physicists Freeman Dyson, David Bohm, Frijtof Capra, and Heinz Pagels; Esalen cofounder Mike Murphy; journalists Alex Cockburn and Jack Anderson; authors Colin Wilson, Robert Theobold, and Thomas Kuhn. "Adam Smith" (himself a recipient of certain network mailings under his real name Gerry Goodman) wrote a column about it in *New York* magazine, calling it the "Far-Out Physics Underground"; Smith described an afternoon discussing various mailings with fellow network recipient Arthur Koestler.

Einhorn's network came under study in a 1978 Diebold Corporation study entitled "The Emergence of Personal Communication Networks Among People Sharing the New Values and Their

Possible Use in Sensitizing Operating Management." It compared the network to the committees of correspondence during the American Revolution, and to the invisible colleges of science in Britain that thrived before scientific discussion was legalized in 1663. It claimed that "much of our future" resides in networks like Einhorn's.

For Ira, the network was a foundation through which he would not only raise the planetary consciousness about the coming transformation but also raise the planetary consciousness about Ira Einhorn. Still, Ira never claimed that his own contribution should overshadow the ideas he freely circulated by the network. It was in many ways a Utopian enterprise, brought off impeccably. Despite the benefits of receiving the mailings, no member of this "invisible college" paid a penny for the priceless information. Bell of Pennsylvania was happy to bear the expense, considering it a fair price for Ira Einhorn's unspecified contributions, mainly in his futuristic gleanings in weekly lunches with Mahler and monthly sessions with Cashel. (There was also an unwritten agreement that Einhorn would not circulate classified documents through Bell, or anything else that could evoke negative repercussions. Einhorn followed that limitation carefully.) Ira Einhorn himself asked for no remuneration.

"Like all my life," said Ira Einhorn of his network, "the arrangements are very strange."

In the spring of 1975, Ira and Holly again decided to summer separately, a trial separation. Ira was about to embark for a four-month trip to Europe. Holly would travel to California. In theory, they would both be free for sexual explorations. Depending on how things went, they would or would not reunite in August.

On the eve of Ira's departure, a *Bulletin* reporter visited Ira at 3411 Race Street for an update on what "Philadelphia's community Renaissance person" had been doing "since the word counterculture dropped out of vogue." She found Ira surrounded by books, sitting in front of his Go board. Holly was perched on a cadet-blue sleeping bag, performing a yoga neck exercise. They seemed the model New Age couple: Ira talking about his network, Uri Geller, and the brilliance of Nikola Tesla, while Holly brewed Lipton tea, apologizing because it wasn't herbal. The apartment, aside from the book collection—rebuilt since Einhorn discarded his library in 1967—was a study in sparseness. As he told a previous *Bulletin* interviewer some months before, "I have one pair of pants, a few shirts, a cheap apartment. I gave up my car a long time ago. I have no TV, no record player, no radio. I don't need them."

Ira revealed his European itinerary. He would first stop in Iceland for a transpersonal psychology conference. From there he would visit Arthur Koestler in London, cyberneticist Stafford Beer in Surrey, Colin Wilson in Cornwall, and Tolstoy's grandson in Scotland. Perhaps then Paris, to see Sartre. Or Belgrade, to view the Tesla papers. The reporter, obviously impressed, concluded that Ira Einhorn might well be a peer of geniuses such as Tesla, da Vinci, and Einstein.

The time apart turned out to be pivotal for both parties, and probably a turning point in the Einhorn-Maddux relationship. Almost three years after meeting Holly, Ira finally seemed to discover that he was deeply involved with her. As he traveled in Europe—even as he wooed and bedded other women—his thoughts kept turning to Holly, even more intensely than they had during the previous separation. This, despite the fact that among the put-downs he delivered to her before leaving was the admonition that he was looking for someone more mature than Holly, a "real woman" to share his life with. Now, he wrote that Holly was "constantly on my mind," and the thought of her with other men made him queasy. At one point, he called her, "stomach churning," only to find out the number he had for her in California had been disconnected. He made attempts to psychically contact her—to make her "feel" him from 7,000 miles away. He was off balance, not in control of his emotions about her. This was a new feeling for him. By the end of the summer he was wondering, "How will Holly respond to my awareness? A question but yet not one as I have a deep sense that we are both closer to US—ready to live out a deep personal intertwined harmony."

Holly, meanwhile, set out to enjoy herself in California. She headed out west with a friend in a car lent for purposes of cross-country delivery. With Ira removed from the scene, the only obstacle to carefree pleasure was her own conscience. Tentative and self-critical, Holly would analyze and reanalyze the situations in which she found herself. She sought companionship, to assuage her loneliness and provide joyful experience to free her from her gloom. At one point, she slept with a Berkeley radical with a family of his own. Later, she spent time in a bucolic, posthippie commune in Albion, California, temporarily cohabiting with a gentle young dropout.

From abroad, Ira received only intimations of her doings but did not like what he heard. After one phone conversation where she revealed that she'd slept with others, he called her liaisons "disastrous sexual things." Disastrous for Ira, perhaps, but Holly did not consider them so. In her sexual explorations, she was learning more about herself. With one of her partners, lovemaking was followed by an analysis worthy of an Esalen encounter session—this was, after all, California in the heart of the seventies—with Holly receiving advice about how to transfer her masturbation skills to coital activities. Letting go was a problem for Holly. She wrote of "constantly being forced to function when my romantic feelings were being crushed by thoughts, words, attitudes, vibes. . . . I have so much to learn." But she was optimistic, hoping "such fine teachers" as Ira would guide her to self-realization. Later in the month, after sleeping with the final of the four lovers she would take during that trip, she mused that "Listening is the key. I dance so well when I hear the music, knowing the little surprises as though I knew the piece, even moving to it the first time. There is no reason why making love shouldn't be the same for me, if I keep listening as I'm learning to. There is no reason why the art of listening to others should not become an act of love, a high conversing, being with others."

It was a season of confronting her fears of inferiority. For years, she had been stuck in a ditch of self-punishment. Now, she consciously fought to extricate herself from that ditch. It was hard work. "How often do I have to analyze my character before something *useful* happens?" she asked herself. Watching her diet closely, she hoped to control her diabetic condition, and eliminate the "ODs" she would get from eating too much of a given food group. She monitored her interactions with others, even rating herself on the quality of her casual conversation. Uncertain in her travel decisions (should she go back to Berkeley? Or proceed north?), she would not just pick a trail and go, but cast the I Ching and ponder the hexagram it chose.

But as the summer continued, Holly gained strength, felt more confident. Her obsessive self-examination eased somewhat as the weeks went by. She began to emanate less of what she called "need vibes," and realized that she, as an individual, had much to give. She won friends. People saw her as warm and willing to extend herself. She performed massages, did horoscopes, played with children and animals, cooked, and above all conversed, about mystic things and close feelings. "I can see my gift," she wrote, "I can make people feel better. Laying on of hands and vibes. Resonating on their wavelength such that they do not feel alone, they don't exactly know why, but they sense a beneficence. They relax. It's good. I will be learning, this summer, what I can do."

Things came into sharp focus in late June, when Holly received startling news in a letter from Ira: The Unicorn, by chance visiting a woman he'd had a fling with the summer before he met Holly, discovered that he was a father. After seeing the child he called "Mr. Blue Eyes," he wrote to Holly that it made him "want to have a child with you." He claimed to better understand the "violation" of her abortions. Holly was bowled over by the irony. His saying *that*, after their own abortion, and after his hurtful contention that he was looking for a "real, full woman to have a child with"—but not Holly! "He needed a heavy turnaround, the cocky bastard, and he got one," Holly wrote to herself. Then she penned Ira a letter explaining her feelings:

> I spent about two seconds, shocked and hurt, myself damaged by your news. Then . . . I found I really didn't take all this personally. . . . In fact, it really is *your* baby, isn't it?
>
> I'm just trying to say I hope she brought a lot of love into the world with that child because I love you and I would be very goddamn mad if she doesn't take both him and you very seriously, as a trust. At least, him.
>
> I realized . . . that for me the procreative aspect of sex has almost always, in my personal sexual history, been present—I got pregnant 1½ years after starting to fuck around, and that's six years ago. And it had been this aspect of sex that I did know about and you did not— that you denied and even shared in the "violation" of. . . . Sex and children have been part of what love has come to mean to me. You fought that.

Meanwhile, the experience of hearing that news, Holly claimed, "shocked my system the rest of the way back into balance." She felt that her sexual attitude toward Ira was different: "He is for sure more accessible, probably humbler, less cruel, more in touch with love in making love for me. . . . I'm sure he will have been much changed. I feel tenderness for him, a loosening of much tightness. And the love he makes makes me recognize that he feels equal. I needed to know it, for not knowing has contributed so much to the emptiness and fear of this vacation project. I feel more capable now. I can be a woman."

A few days later, they spoke on the phone. Holly spoke of her high feelings and Ira told Holly that his energy was up as well—after not reading many books in the last month, he'd read five the previous day. He told Holly he loved her and she belonged with him. He said that their sex problems were not important enough to keep them apart. He had made plans for the end of July, to go to Andrija Puharich's psychic research complex in Ossining, New York, where Dr. Puharich was arranging experiments with "wunderkinder"—a group of children with psychic powers similar to Uri Geller's. He needed Holly with him. Holly agreed, and said she loved him, too. "At last!" she declared afterward. "He [wants] to share our planet with my spirit."

The night of their phone conversation, when Holly went to bed, she tried to leave herself open to "feel" Ira. And she *felt* him, flowing in waves. Then she tried the more difficult task of "opening herself" to what she felt. She was rewarded with a wonderful sensation, and for that instant she did not feel lonely. Even though she made love to her Albion friend that next day—and fairly steadily for the remainder of her trip—she did not consider it a violation of what she felt for Ira: It was as if she was able to transcend the limitations of monogamy without diminishing her partnership, just as Ira always claimed was the case with *his* extracurricular liaisons. Her thoughts were already racing to her reunion with the Unicorn in just a few weeks. It had been a summer of growth, for both of them, and Holly could not help but imagine that things from now on would be different, even though she knew that Ira was "a man whose life-style is entrenched in the rhythms of his own sounding."

When Holly Maddux arrived at La Guardia Airport on the morning of July 23, 1975, Ira Einhorn was there to greet her. They embraced, drove to the Puharich complex called the Turkey Farm in Ossining, and immediately retreated to their room to make, as Holly put it, "magical timeless love." Ira seemed more solicitous of her. "He wants to keep physical check on my presence, touches more often than ever before, smiles and laughs without that horrific edge of before," she wrote. "I feel much more of an 'equal'—i.e., less afraid of his image. We are more the 'same size' now. It will take a long time before I will be able to experience love orgasmically . . . but to be free of that fear is such a relief."

When the mail arrived that day, Holly received four letters from Ira, late arrivals sent from Europe. Ira insisted that Holly read them while he sat in the room. In the first letter was a proposal of marriage, in a "public and legal ceremony." In other letters, he promised patience—he would wait for her "to feel the love he feels in the same way."

The couple began to settle into the unusual rhythms of life on the Turkey Farm. Andrija Puharich's complex in Ossining had been the site of many unexplained occurrences—at one point he wrote of Uri Geller being "transported" there from New York City, the Israeli psychic making the thirty-one-mile journey in a fraction of a second, tumbling through a screen door. But this summer was the weirdest yet. Puharich had assembled a group of around twenty youngsters from seven countries. He called them "Gellerlings," or "Space Kids." They ranged in age from nine to the late teens. Supposedly, they had the psychic powers of Uri Geller. The idea was to train the kids, educate them on their powers and how to use them. Puharich also initiated trance sessions where he attempted to find out where these powers came from. In an unpublished book he wrote about this psychic summer camp; he prints substantial portions of these interviews, which, if they are to be believed, seem to indicate that the Space Kids indeed hail from unearthly locations. The Kids describe strange cities with science-fiction trappings and claim to be messengers from these distant civilizations. Puharich marshals his evidence that they bear messages to save Earth from nuclear destruction.

Many of the sessions were rather benign. For instance, Holly Maddux spent a lot of time with a young woman simply doing ESP exercises. Other times, though, the Space Kids were asked to do things that upset them. One who was fourteen that summer says that he began to feel suspicious about the whole experience when his trainers asked him to do remote viewing at specific locations—to leave his body and report what he saw and heard. What disconcerted him was that the locations included politically sensitive areas, like the Kremlin.

In the midst of this bizarre experimentation, which Puharich claimed was one of the turning points of the entire human experience, the familiar troubles of Ira Einhorn and Holly Maddux reappeared. Even as Holly delighted in Ira's proposal, she was worried that there would be an equal and opposite reaction to his warmth, perhaps when Ira found out the extent of her sexual explorations earlier in the summer. "I realize I keep secrets out of fear for my safety," she wrote. Those secrets were exposed when Ira demanded that Holly let him read her journal. In the spirit of openness—not keeping secrets, facing possible embarrassment—she bravely allowed him. It wasn't a good idea.

"You'll pay for that," he said after reading what she wrote of her love life apart from him. "I have no faith in you!"

The cycle of recrimination, reconciliation, and more recrimination continued. The "public and legal ceremony" was not to be. By the time the two returned to Philadelphia in September, things were virtually the same as before. If Holly had learned something about strength in herself during her time away from Ira, the benefits of that lesson would be delayed. As for now, she was miserable. Reimmersed in life at 3411, she potted spider plants, cooked spaghetti-and-clam-sauce dinners for Ira, and suffered.

Her body obsession returned, and she now practiced bulimia to try to control her diet. After one difficult session trying to vomit after a big meal, she noted wryly how good she was at "keeping things in." Their sexual problems were continuing; she wondered whether she would lose Ira. She wished that it had happened already, so she didn't have to suffer through the rejection of it all.

In the midst of Holly's bleak thoughts, Ira returned home after an evening of Go. The conversation turned to the relationship. Ira told her that, though he loved her, she was getting worse in most aspects. The sex was a problem, and Ira did not know what to do about it.

Holly told him to go ahead, start sleeping with other women again. Maybe they would not be able to live together.

Ira told her to stop torturing herself over the things he had to do.

"Aren't I at fault?" Holly asked.

"Maybe," said Ira. He told her she had a "life problem," a "tremendous psychic block." That she was not doing her share to work on herself psychically.

And Ira Einhorn—the teacher—would help her. "Masturbate in front of me," he said.

Holly could not bring herself to do it. It was part of herself she still kept secret. Ira undoubtedly saw this as a failure on her part, a lesson for her to work on. Holly seemed to agree with this assessment—that she should try to achieve the high state of being that Ira had already attained. On the other hand, something was holding Holly back from giving everything to Ira. Perhaps it was not a failing, but a wise intuition.

The evening depressed Holly tremendously. She wrote:

> What is courage but to go ahead to do what I know I cannot. I saw last night, I live in constant terror and guilt. Somewhere I obtained the idea that there's a bottom to every pit, so all I have to do is wait until I hit and then gather myself back up again. Occasionally I realize that this is not true. It is entirely possible for me to kill myself, choose my weapon. From this time on, I'm in the process, all I have to do is continue as I am. There is no magic bottom.

Ira, meanwhile, had his questions to ponder. "Why does she hold back?" he wrote during that stormy season. "What is the fear?"

8

A PRISONER ON THE PLANET OF PATIENCE

Penny Jeannechild recognized Holly Maddux when she enrolled in Jeannechild's peer counseling class in the spring of 1976. She'd seen Holly at the Ecology Food Co-op, where Holly often handled the cash register. Perhaps—she isn't sure—she even saw Holly and Ira Einhorn together at the Theater of the Living Arts on South Street, where they would often go to see the low-priced double features of classic or second-run films. She certainly knew who Ira Einhorn was. "You couldn't be involved in the Peace Movement or the Save the Earth Movement and not come across Ira's name," she says.

Holly Maddux struck Jeannechild as fragile and shy. Despite Holly's identification with the Women's Movement—the class was run under the auspices of the Free Women's School, a feminist version of the Free U that Ira Einhorn had helped popularize a decade before—she did not seem comfortable around women. In addition, there was also a hard-to-explain charisma about this woman. Not an outgoing charisma but a silent one. She could just sit in a room and her presence would draw attention.

The class was held in a comfortable second-floor lounge at the Christian Association on the Penn campus. Jeannechild's classes accommodated between six and twelve women. Sessions were conducted with the funky intimacy that characterized interaction within the boundaries of still-radical Powelton Village. The women would pull their chairs in a circle, and each would state their goals for this "cycle" of the course. Holly Maddux said that hers were to learn how to be strong inside, and to leave her boyfriend Ira.

Peer counseling, or cocounseling, is a movement begun in 1952 by a Seattle man named Harvey Jackins. The theory behind it is that one need not be a certified therapist to aid people—any two people sensitized to feelings and grounded in Jackins' theories could help each other. Jeannechild's class was designed to be supplemented by two-person peer counseling sessions. These have two parts: one person counseling another, and then a switch in roles. The actual therapy encourages one to relive feelings from one's past, and "discharge" those feelings by experiencing the emotions that should have been released the first time around.

Penny remembers the subjects during the private sessions she had with Holly. "The material was always about Ira, and it always had to do with Ira pushing her to be and do what she wasn't. Sometimes that had to do with sex and sexuality—I got the impression that he in particular wanted to watch her making love with other women, and that wasn't something she felt comfortable doing, but she [did it because she] might lose him. I got the impression very early on that they had a very S&M relationship. Not chains and bondage—much more psychological. That he was very powerful and charismatic, and she had a waiflike, fairylike, ephemeral quality to her."

According to both Jeannechild and John Himmelein, another peer counselor who worked with Holly, Holly was explicit that the sessions not be held at 3411 Race. Apparently, Ira Einhorn would not allow it.

In class, Penny Jeannechild was very careful with Holly. Though the class was designed to accommodate outbursts of emotion, Holly did not participate in that way. She hardly talked. It was obvious that she did not feel competent. Once she came in with bread that she baked. Everybody thought it was a splendid gesture, but Holly's attitude was, "Here's my measly gift to the class. I know any stupid fool can do this but . . ." Later Holly told the class that Ira said to her that she could never make it without him. That all she was really good for was baking bread.

Penny Jeannechild began to get a gut feeling that Ira Einhorn might be physically abusing Holly Maddux. "It makes sense in those situations to wait until the client offers you a little bit more to go on, because making a leap like that in terms of questions can frighten off the client. She was so damned frail. And he was a bulldozer. He'd been a bulldozer in the community, and was much admired for being a bulldozer. And she was like a crushed flower—he had bulldozed over her emotionally. She looked like one of the walking wounded all the time. I knew I was dealing with somebody who was really trapped by her psyche in a relationship that was potentially dangerous to her."

During the ninth week or so of class, Penny Jeannechild's fears were confirmed. Holly Maddux came to class with a bruise on her face. "He had hit her," says Jeannechild.

That is what Holly Maddux told the class. She did not "discharge" as she spoke. As Jeannechild recalls it, she talked without emotion. She did not cry.

"It wasn't her style," says Penny Jeannechild.

Holly Maddux spent a good part of the spring of 1976 living away from Ira Einhorn. For a while, she stayed in a commune on Baring Street, only a few blocks away from Ira's apartment. (Powelton Village was one of the few areas in America where communal living was still thriving.) The commune—called Job Chillaway, after a Quaker missionary—consisted of eleven people in a twenty-room Victorian built in the 1840s. "Holly came here as a refugee because she was having these terrible fights with Ira," says Linda White, living in Job Chillaway then. "He was physically abusing her. She had bruises. One time she had a black eye. She would stay here two or three days and go back. One time she stayed here for a week. She was under some compulsion to be with him. I remember her talking about how awful he made her feel. He made her feel that she was nothing, that she had no value. And she was fighting. She had to prove to him somehow that she was worth something. But of course she *was*."

Linda White believes that Holly's manner might in some way have contributed to Ira's response. "She was afraid of him, and she was also defiant. This is going to sound really cruel, but I could see how she could get herself into that situation. There was almost a kind of provocativeness in the way she would deal with people. Have you ever seen someone invite it? Ask for it? Have you ever met anyone who was a victim? It doesn't mean she found Ira, wanting to be beat up, but that the way she was then came out of what happened to her, her manner."

Linda White saw something in Holly Maddux, twenty-nine years old in 1976, that she thought was provocative and seductive. But these may well have been stirrings of a woman awakening. The defiant streak was something always present in Holly—Richard Olver, her first boyfriend, had noted it. The seductiveness could be attributed not only to her beauty and warmth but to a need to confirm her self-worth by brief affairs, during which she could dazzle an unsuspecting male. Still, something had changed in Holly. She was realizing that her problems would be more difficult to solve if she stayed with Ira Einhorn, a man who obviously was not going to raise her self-esteem. Going to Penny Jeannechild's class was part of that, and leaving Ira Einhorn whenever things got too dicey at 3411 Race Street was another part of that.

"I've been busy being 'separated' for a few weeks," she wrote Toni Erwin in April 1976. "It has really thrown me back on myself, being alone—Ira was always such a cushion. I mean, I let him do that for me. Am beginning to learn by experience that I will have to take charge. That's hard for me, with so many daddies in my life. So far, I don't even want to get out much; feel like I'm in retreat. But that's where I am and I can even accept that better, now."

Holly was so long grounded in her flower-child existence, though, that when she left Ira she had little to distract her from the tedious exercise of hashing over her own dilemma. She no longer worked at the bakery—the Kuners and other Powelton Sufis had moved to an abode in New York State. Holly now worked at the Ecology Food Co-op, at 36th and Race, slightly more than a block away from 3411 Race Street. Founded by Quakers in 1969, the height of Powelton's flower-child era, the cooperative had thrived, its membership ballooning to four figures, and the store itself filling two floors of a brownstone building formerly housing a drugstore. Its philosophy was rigid: Nothing with white sugar, caffeine, or bleached white flour has ever darkened an Ecology Co-op shelf. This was in keeping with the whole-Earth spirit that many Powelton Villagers maintained, and the co-op, besides fulfilling corporeal needs, also served as one of the centers of the community. Though Holly spent many hours there and became one of the trusted workers capable of operating the cash register during busy hours, she did not get paid for her efforts, except in credits that went toward the number of working hours required of each member household. "She was a tremendous asset," says Nicole Hackel, the co-op manager. Holly had long surpassed her quota and had stockpiled enough extra hours of work to qualify as a member for years to come. But still she dutifully signed up for shifts, and the co-op came to depend on her calming presence at the late-afternoon rush times.

During the previous fall, she began baking items that the co-op would sell on consignment. "I've entered the realm of private enterprise, via the backdoor," she wrote to Toni Erwin. "Have begun baking small amounts of goodies for the co-op on a day-to-day basis. Tomorrow I will bring in my first batch, a kind of turnover with poppyseed-honey filling. Why, it could mean the big time! Fifty dollars a week. That makes me eligible for welfare. Enterprise to continue until the Health Department tries to dip a finger in my bowls."

She needn't have worried about the latter her organic muffins and cookies were meticulously baked and carefully cocooned in Saran Wrap. She would display them in large glass jars with hand-drawn labels, depicting flowers and frogs, done in her ornate, whimsical style. Nicole Hackel guesses that Holly's estimate of $50 a week was optimistic by a factor of two. To supplement her income, she applied for food stamps. She never panicked about her finances, though, because she lived frugally paying the low rents of Powelton Village and buying clothes secondhand—and was also aware of generous funds from her mother's family, the King estate, that would eventually come her way.

So Holly had plenty of time to work on herself, to think about her relationship with Ira, to construct rationalizations for his behavior, to envision scenarios where they could live together in peace. And to forgive him for abusing her.

Steve Waterman, a friend of Ira's from the Synergy crowd on South Street, was working in the neighborhood at the time, and around sunset, he would often take a break and visit Holly. She would make tea and serve fresh bread. Waterman knew that Ira was on her mind, so he tried to draw her out. Especially after he saw her with a black eye that he assumed was given to her by Einhorn.

"She was trying to stay away from him but I got the sense it was like gravity or something. She could stay away from him, but then she couldn't. She kept coming back. And I said, 'Why do you go see him?' And she would just . . . you know that look of somebody, like 'I'm in love. What can I do?' "

The Unicorn, meanwhile, was busier than ever. He tended his thriving network, traveled around the country giving lectures, ran seminars in physics and consciousness, and began to accumulate credentials as a management consultant. "Corporations usually have a near-watcher and a far-watcher—that comes from Babylonian times," he explained to an *Inquirer* interviewer. "I'm a far-watcher. I see things before they become visible. I'm the advance man for almost anything I think will be popular." A breakthrough on the consultant front came when George Bartol, the chairman of the Hunt manufacturing company, arranged to have lunch with Ira at Philadelphia's posh Racquet Club. The chief executive of the $30 million firm asked Ira if he would be interested in studying Hunt, and then writing a report to assist the company in preparing for that looming uncertainty, the future. Ira eventually produced a nineteen-page document, written out in longhand and periodically couched in free verse, called "Probes for a Time of Crisis."

One can only imagine the reaction of Hunt's executives when Ira presented his findings at an all-day seminar on May 8, 1976. "*Das Kapital* is not enough," Ira wrote in the report. "We know how to feed the body but we neglect the mind of the worker. Our economic system is transforming. A corporation that wishes to survive must unstick the rigid walls that separate worker and manager." Read over a decade later, Einhorn's observations seem prescient in predicting the business struggles of the eighties: The report was a blueprint for redefining a corporation, making use of Japanese-style management, in-house entrepreneurial efforts, and a sensitivity toward workers that looked beyond standard management-worker conflicts. In that respect, the study was probably worth the $10,000 Einhorn was paid—a sum that would boost Ira's income past the threshold where he would have to pay income taxes for the first time. (Ira bought a new car later that spring, a $3,200 Toyota Corolla.) The Unicorn did go somewhat beyond the pale, though, in recommending that this machine-tool manufacturer establish venture capital projects to invest in "psychic technologies."

Among Ira's other important new business contacts were Canadians Charles and Barbara Bronfman, the former an heir of Samuel Bronfman, founder of the Seagram liquor empire. Besides his management post in Seagram and a visible presence in philanthropy, Charles was later known as the owner of the Montreal Expos baseball team. Barbara Bronfman had a strong interest in the psychic fields that Ira was plugged into, and not only did the Bronfmans become key names in Ira's network but Ira became a familiar visitor to their home in Montreal.

With Ira's work going so well, and Holly trying to restore her equilibrium outside of the relationship, things were perilously close to a final breakup. Holly had found another apartment, responding to a "roommate wanted" notice on the co-op bulletin board. She pointedly moved her belongings out of 3411 Race and into the new place, on the second floor of a Victorian at 3409 Baring Street, several blocks away. Ira, meanwhile, made no secret of his seeing other women. In late April, he consciously tried to "phase her out," as he put it, by mentioning that he and Holly would probably not be spending the summer together.

But the two could not stay apart. Typically, Ira would seek her out during the day, share a meal with her, make love, go to a movie with her. Rarely would a few hours go by before one or the other would aggravate the still-raw edges of their interaction. Holly, in Ira's terms, would "freak," and walk out, determined to protect her space, to assert herself. Sometimes Ira would let her stew for a while. Other times, he would call her to reconcile. After one outburst at 3411, he chased after her as she retreated to the apartment at Baring Street. On the way, Holly said hello to one of Ira's friends while passing him on the street, and Einhorn wanted to know if she was sleeping with the man. This provoked Holly even more. When Ira tried to follow her into the apartment, Holly prevented him, hitting him with her keys. Ira slapped her. He said he didn't trust her and demanded that she show him her journal. Holly sent him away. Ira left, but almost immediately began calling her, persisting until she agreed to spend the night back at his apartment. Which she did.

Earlier that year, Ira had made arrangements to summer again in Nova Scotia. The upcoming bicentennial summer in Philadelphia—which despite Ira's participation in some progressive efforts for the

event was clearly doomed as a misorganized Frank Rizzo extrava-
ganza—was no reason for Ira to remain in town. When it came time
for Ira to sublet his apartment and go to Nova Scotia, Holly went
with him. They were off to the farmhouse in Englishtown where
they had enjoyed such fine times two years before. Ira had the
highest hopes for the vacation. He planned to study the relationship
between Marxism and parapsychology, finish up his work for Hunt,
and spend a lot of time working the vegetable garden—to virtually
become rooted in the land. Perhaps he and Holly would benefit
from the pastoral surroundings and become rooted in each other
once again.

In mid-June, the two drove up to Cape Breton Island in Ira's new
Toyota. Almost immediately trouble flared. The same old story:
Holly's jealousy of Ira's sexual exploring. Ira's fury at Holly's ego-
building love affairs. Holly's demand that Ira not bully her, now
reinforced by her growing desire to take a role as an equal partner
in the relationship. Ira's frustration at Holly's sex problems—in his
view, the dropped anchor preventing smooth sailing in the relationship.

Holly was the chief instigator of these flare-ups. Ira had squan-
dered his capital of trust. Even when he tried to avoid riling Holly,
she found nettling little proofs of his hurtful attitude toward her.
When Ira would leave the bed to sleep in the other room—thinking
Holly could use the extra space—Holly took it as an abandonment.
When Holly dropped something and Ira asked, "What did you do?"
Holly would explode: The question too closely reminded her of
Ira's past criticism and put-downs, the lingering thorns of which
still stung.

The worst came on June 24, when all of Holly's pent-up rage
ignited. She attacked Ira for his miserable behavior toward her. He
left the farmhouse, returning hours later to find glum Holly binge-
ing on food. The fight resumed until Holly overturned the table. By
the light of the Nova Scotia sunset, Ira cleaned up the mess, then
climbed the steps to talk to Holly of what he called their "mutual
misunderstanding." A stray remark about what she should do while
traveling set Holly off once more—further proof to her of Ira's
domination. Too many daddies. As Ira later described the scene,
Holly freaked, screaming that she hated him. Ira tried to placate
her with poems, even making up songs, but Holly was gone, scoop-

ing up the sleeping bag and heading out the door even as lightning flashed in the sky.

Ira Einhorn was frustrated. "I need her ESSENCE," he wrote, "but have much difficulty with her personality. Would love to see her glow, but always make her cry." Ira listened to the "gentle rain as [my] heart fills with sadness and I sense a death within."

Holly fled Canada. For shelter she sought Texas; the world she had once escaped now became her refuge. She would spend most of the summer in Tyler, join her mother and sisters for a cross-country trip, and perhaps even go to Africa with her parents in early autumn, when Fred Maddux would once again stalk the cape buffalo and perhaps even shoot an elephant.

Begun in rancor, this separation was a time for both to reassess the wisdom of continuing.

As during their previous separation, Ira found himself missing Holly. But in the isolation of Nova Scotia, without access to many women and distant from the wealth of conversation he normally could scare up in an instant, his pining for Holly became more intense than ever. He worried about how deeply he felt toward her, vowing to himself that she was a "habit" he could only dare indulge in once he "kicked it." But that was a difficult task. Through July, he kept meditating on Holly. When she would call or send a letter, refusing to accede to his pleas for her to return, he would first want to lash out. After all it was *Holly* who was ruining his summer. He would trek to the post office in the morning and rage when he saw mail arrive for her. "I don't dig sexual abstinence," he complained. "Find myself masturbating a lot. Don't like being in a place where I do not have adequate access to woman [sic]. Would never put myself in a situation like this by choice. For that reason alone, I'm P.O.'ed at Holly." He spoke of "the voice that wants to reject Holly rearing its ugly head."

But then he would distance himself, waxing philosophical. "Holly just too fucked up to return," he wrote after a letter from her. "I understand and probably agree. Feel so sad about her situation. Nothing to do except hope, pray, and send her energy."

Finally Ira unburdened himself in a letter.

Thinking about you today—ruminating on the feelings that I have for you, and exploring a deep sadness about the way that we parted.

I'm totally settled in here and deeply feel the lack of your presence . . .

So much I want to say to you, but it all comes down to a few
sentences:

> I miss you.
> I love you.

I want to love and grow with you. It's possible if I remember not to
power trip and constantly feel the depth of my wanting to be close to
you. The hurts I give, pain me, for you are so soft and lovely in my
eyes. Often when I sense you doubt my love, I feel so stupid for it
ought to be simple. I want you—alone—the rest are distractions that
do not allow the constant focus I need. If you want to just be with me,
come back and live in this land that I know you love. Share my work
on the poetry and feed my being with your presence.

Holly could not help but be moved at this declaration. But her
heart had not sufficiently melted to cause her to change her new
summer plans and rush to Nova Scotia. She went west with her
mother and sisters Buffy and Mary. It was a pleasant trip, driving by
day in Liz Maddux's blue Mercedes, and stopping at motels by late
afternoon, for a quick dip in the pool. At night they would watch the
Olympics. It was the summer of Olga Korbut.

By early August, she was back in Tyler, breathing easier, and
thinking of seeing Ira Einhorn again. "She was on the threshold,"
says Toni Erwin, who spent time with her old friend that summer.
"It was as if she was on the end of a diving board. Like when the
crowd gets quiet before something climactic happens."

Holly told Toni that Ira would hit her, that he encouraged her to
have sex with other women. Things that shocked Toni. But Holly
did not seem to hold these things against Ira. She strained to invent
excuses for him. She reasoned that the sexual experiments he urged
on her were designed to improve her sensuality. And if he hit her,
well, Ira was human. She made arrangements to return to Nova
Scotia in late August.

"I understand a bit more fully why we may be returning to try
each other on again, in whatever way we can," Holly wrote Ira. "It
isn't easy, but I am about to let go the illusion that it should be easy,
and consequently let go much resentment and bitterness toward you
for so long, and so mistakenly."

Holly tried to explain to Ira that she was making progress in dealing with her fears. She felt that for the first time she was able to muster up the courage *not* to make love to men when she intuited that they expected it from her. "From that point on," she wrote, "[I finally knew] that I didn't have to do what I didn't want to do, because I admitted I didn't want to. And nobody died right there on the spot, and I didn't suffer any ill effects either. . . . In fact, the courage to go against my pattern and say no to it, is a newfound friend."

She responded to Ira's plaintive letters by noting that "Being alone, or at least being alone without my presence, I see you are able to gather many quiet lovely moments into your soul and enjoy them deeply. Initially I prescribed this solitude for you over my shoulder, screaming, thinking, That will teach the bastard, let *him* suffer in some loneliness and missing, let him *stew* in those goddamn juices. Kinder now, I am lulled by time and distance and some experience by myself into felicitous feelings that you are growing poems like these out of your garden."

In a written postscript to that typed letter, Holly explained how she lay down one night, closed her eyes, and began to concentrate. She began saying, "I'm angry at Ira," over and over until her body began to burn. Suddenly she felt she was *with* Ira, his soulmate, purged of jealousy. "More!" she wrote. "More of this closeness! If I can have it and trust in it, that it is real and as terribly personal and meant for me, then I cannot feel left out, when you spend time and sperm with others. They will be recognized as people and all, but of no consequence to me and what we are."

This was a brave vow, and not the first time Holly voiced it. "Ira's relationship to Holly was a 'New Age' relationship—that's in quotes," says Kathy Keegan, a friend of both. "He was teaching her how to 'be free,' and how to go beyond jealousy and all these traits that are [supposedly] keeping us from evolving. And she bought that one. She always held it that she was not living up to her potential if she got jealous or had these negative defects in her character. They were defects. It was a double standard, but Ira would play on that."

In practice, though, Holly could not admit that Ira's affairs were "of no consequence to me and what we are." This despite her guilt over her sexual "failings." Ira's dalliances were legendary: space-cadet groupies attracted by his writings and reputation, fellow New Age avatars accosted on the lecture trail, wives and girlfriends of his friends and acquaintances in Philadelphia, and even lonely women advertising their availability in the classified ads of the *Drummer.* Had Holly been otherwise treated as an equal in the relationship, she might have been able to cope with that polygamy. But as it was, she was largely viewed as an adjunct to Ira, an appliance, an attractive accessory. She was the *shiksa* princess from the heartland, a highly regarded prize in Jewish intellectual circles. In addition to all this, Ira's open womanizing was too much for Holly to bear.

When she discovered Ira would be seeing another woman, she would often blow up. One morning when Ira was expecting one of his starry-eyed concubines later in the day, Holly stormed out of the apartment. "Have a good *fuck,*" she snarled.

It is an open question how Holly would have reacted had Ira eschewed all others and settled into a monogamous relationship. Holly's history was also one of asserting her independence by seeing others. But, only twenty-five when she met Ira, Holly may well have acted differently had she been presented with the opportunity to make a mutual commitment. Ira's own mother sensed this. After getting a letter from Holly during that summer of 1976, she wrote her son, saying Holly felt she wasn't getting any younger. Now approaching thirty, she wanted security. Ira had better get on the stick unless he wanted to lose her.

But Ira stuck to his free-love guns. If Holly were to build her self-esteem, he brashly proposed, she too should continue seeking others. If the relationship between Holly and Ira were really "open" this would have been no problem. But Holly saw Ira's other women as a personal rejection. And while Ira Einhorn encouraged Holly to "be free" and see others, his actions showed otherwise—he saw Holly's other men as a personal threat.

Case in point is Holly Maddux's friendship with a man named Larry Liss. He and his wife were fringe figures in the later iteration of the Synergy Group, several of whom had moved to rural Chester County, near the tiny town of Bertramville. Liss, lithe and boyishly handsome, had a different background than most in that circle: He had served in Vietnam, then went into business. He first met Holly at a friend's wedding in the spring of 1976, that most troubled time

a Einhorn, guru, at La Terrasse, the french restaurant on the Penn mpus that was his hangout in the 1970s. He would lunch there with rporate executives, scientists, paranormal explorers, and friends and zzle them with his intellect and energy.

An independent filmmaker in the mid-1960s used Einhorn as an actor in a surrealistic short subject. Throughout the film, Ira wanders through Philadelphia carrying a female-shaped mannequin.

(Photographer: Mary Pat Kane)

Ira Einhorn in 1957—he graduated from high school as a strange combination of intellectual, jock, and bohemian.

Ira Einhorn in his glory, hosting the huge Earth Day celebration in April 1970. Ira was the most visible figure in the massive, nationally televised festival. In the process of working with the Chamber of Commerce to present the event, Einhorn developed contacts that led to his becoming a guru of the business community; eventually Bell Telephone financed his networking efforts.

Holly Maddux, salutatorian and "most likely to succeed" in John Tyler High School's class of 1965.

The Maddux family circa 1967: parents, four siblings, and Holly (age twenty). She had retreated to Tyler, after experiencing culture shock from the loose life-style, political activism, and intimidating sophistication of the East Coast. She resumed her studies at Bryn Mawr in 1968 and never lived in Texas again.

Holly Maddux as a Tyler cheerleader. Competition to win that post was
fierce, and her election was a triumph for the talented yet introspective
Holly. Classmates regarded her with respect and awe, seeing her as
"different," destined to achieve great things in the world outside Texas.

Einhorn at a 1975 poetry reading with his friend, former LSD priest Curt
Kubiak *(center)*. Kubiak and his wife were the last people other than
Einhorn to see Holly Maddux alive.

Ira's companion in New Age pursuits, Andrija Puharich (*right*), with his protégé Uri Geller. Einhorn aided Puharich in publicizing Geller's paranormal powers. According to Ira, he, Puharich, and a few others comprised a "psychic mafia" attempting to educate America about the wonders and dangers of psychic phenomena.

In the sixties, Einhorn hobnobbed with the counterculture superstars: Jerry Rubin, Allen Ginsberg, and, shown here, Abbie Hoffman.

Ira Einhorn and Holly Maddux together at Cape Breton Island during the summer of 1974. The idyll was frequently interrupted by quarrels, but as the photos show there were periods of warm affection between the two.

PHILADELPHIA DAILY
NEWS
The People Paper
THURSDAY, MARCH 29, 1979

15¢
4★ Sports

'Hippie Guru' Held In Trunk Slaying

Page 3

Nuclear Accident: Radiation Spreads

Page 5

Pentagon Marks Ft. Dix for Doom

Page 8

Murder suspect Einhorn in April 1978. Sun Week organizer

The arrest, for murder, of the city's best-known proponent of nonviolence knocked Three-Mile Island off the front page of the Thursday, March 29, 1979 edition of the *Philadelphia Daily News*.

(Photographer: Neil Benson)

A rear view of 3411 Race Street, where Ira Einhorn lived with Holly Maddux during their stormy five-year relationship. On the right is the second-floor porch where police discovered Holly Maddux's body.

The mystery of Holly Maddux, who had been missing since September 1977 took a macabre turn on April 28, 1979, when her remains were found in a steamer trunk in Ira Einhorn's apartment. Here, Philadelphia officials carry off the steamer trunk found in Einhorn's closet.

After his arrest in 1979, Einhorn retained former District Attorney Arlen Specter to defend him. Despite the evidence of Holly Maddux's body discovered in Einhorn's apartment, Specter won a bail of only $40,000 for Einhorn. Specter is now a U.S. senator representing Pennsylvania.

(Courtesy the *Phila. Inquirer*)

between Ira and Holly. While a dashikied Ira delivered the invocation, chanting OM to cement the new union, Larry Liss noticed Holly Maddux, hauntingly attractive in a simple, flowing silk outfit she most likely had obtained secondhand and resewn herself. He later realized that the outfit was a perfect expression of how Holly Maddux presented herself to the world. "It was sort of plain and beautiful," he says, "like vanilla ice cream."

Liss later spotted Holly while she was conversing with Ira Einhorn. And Larry Liss saw something he did not like. "They were talking, and she said something—and he grabbed her by the arm," Liss recalls. "He almost pulled it out of the socket. He pulled her behind the tent. . . . I didn't see anything past that, but really—there was no way she was going to get out of his clutches." Not long afterward, he approached Holly. Her arm was still red from the confrontation. He told her he'd seen what had happened. "She didn't make a big deal of it," he says. But as they talked, Liss was amazed at how Holly opened up. Apparently a deep conversation with Holly was a rare thing among Ira's friends, something Holly welcomed like a famished person imbibes water.

Liss's own relationship was "open," and he arranged to see Holly. "I would never tell her, 'It's you,'" he explains. "What I would tell her is, 'Right now, it's you—and I'm going home to [my wife].' It was very comfortable for Holly to know that the relationship was structured . . . there were no gray areas." Liss was never aware of the painfully deep emotions Holly came to feel for him. The times they saw each other were relaxed. Once Holly took him on a tour of the food co-op, and he was impressed with her quiet pride at her workplace. They would drive to the river and spend time together, spending long periods of comfortable silence. "Just hang out, for six goddamned hours," he says. "And not do anything, which I appreciated. Not *having* to do anything." For both, it was a respite from other troubles. "I never questioned about her life and what she was up to," says Liss. "And neither did she."

Larry Liss came to think that Holly was a powerful person who for some reason chose to cloak her strengths. He saw her magnetism, though, "by the way she reached in to me. It was like, 'I like you, I want you, let's play.'" She was very sensitive about being known as "Ira's girl." Her contrariness would show, then. She would playfully ask, when she was with Larry Liss, "What would Ira think

about this?" Then she would answer her own question: "Fuck him."
Yet her defiance had the pathos of transparent bravado. She obviously was not through with Ira Einhorn.

Liss considered Einhorn a Svengali who dominated Holly. Liss
himself was intimidated by the Unicorn; Ira's self-confidence, he
feared, was so strong that Einhorn was capable of anything. One
day Liss came down to Powelton Village to bring Holly a book for
her birthday. He looked for her in the Ecology Co-op, but she wasn't
there. He came across Ira Einhorn on the street, though, and asked
where Holly was.

"What do you want her for?" Ira asked.

Liss said he had a book to give to Holly. Ira said he'd take the book
and pass it on to her.

"I went a little nuts at that one," says Liss. "I had written her a little
note telling her I loved her, and blah blah blah. Nothing deep, but
affectionate. For a moment I was reluctant to give him the book.
Then I said to myself—they're not together anyway. And he doesn't
run her life. And I'm not going to suppress my affection for my
friend because of him. So I gave him the book. And he walked away,
and the light changed, and I drove away. And I looked in my rear-
view mirror. The fucker threw it in the trash can."

Liss drove around the block, pulled the car over, and retrieved the
book from the trash can. That's when he noticed Ira Einhorn. "He
was standing there, about thirty feet away, just *standing there* looking
at me. So I looked at him, he looked at me. I drove away."

When Holly returned to the East Coast from Texas that summer,
she spent a few days with the Lisses before finally returning to Nova
Scotia for the final days of her vacation. Holly came bearing Texas
cactus along with a gift she made herself: a tiny papier-mâché frog.
It hung in the Liss kitchen for over a year, until sometime late in
1977 one of the legs fell out, just by itself. Larry Liss wondered if
that was some sort of sign, whether it meant he would never see
Holly again. He didn't.

That autumn, Holly moved back to 3411 Race. One more time, she
and Ira would try to live together. After weeks of vacillation about
whether or not to go with her parents to Africa—Ira speaking
loudly against the idea, Fred Maddux dismissing Einhorn's contention that Holly would be laid to waste by terrorists—she'd decided

against it. But she did agree to return to Tyler to babysit her sisters while her parents were away. Even though she had only been with Ira for a month or so after coming back east, she already could use a breather. She enjoyed it.

"I hear my wheels turning, turning," Holly wrote Ira. "I particularly love working/laboring in the briars in the early morning, and remembered in a flash that it carried the same new feelings that working in the kibbutz did, early at sunup; a walking stick; small cuts to render me flesh and blood; a hoe, a tool; new sun; even the distant threat of snakes and rabbits. My body needs work like this."

She also reported a growing self-sufficiency. "Everything I dreaded has happened to the sewing machine, so I've 'had to' learn to thread it . . . next, I'll 'have to' learn to fill a gas tank at the self-serve, and fill tires with air. The old take-care-of-me dies hard."

When Holly returned to Philadelphia, she entered therapy sessions with Marian Coopersmith, a sensitive woman living in the northwest suburbs. Coopersmith suggested that Holly and Einhorn might need "relationship counseling." At first Ira seemed open to the idea, but then changed his mind. Finally, he would not even consent to chat with Coopersmith if she came to 3411 for tea.

The questions Holly had to confront in therapy sessions could not have come as a surprise to the self-analytical young woman. She spoke of Ira not emotionally supporting her, tearing her down. Coopersmith wondered what Ira got out of the relationship, and Holly, mimicking what Einhorn had said the previous week, said, "An education in frustration."

Holly Maddux began a flurry of changes, as if superficial adjustments could effect inner truths. She cut her hair (Ira was not charmed by the new, pixieish coiffure). She took tai chi classes and felt herself gaining strength by that oriental pursuit: a combination of powerful dancelike movement and the relaxation of yoga. She tried another new diet in an attempt to control her diabetes (she continued taking medication as well), and the possible effect it might have on her emotions. Holly also gained financial independence—in November she received a check for $19,400 as her share of a tender offer for family stock in the Northrup King Seed Company. In addition, due to a change in tax laws, her uncle Preston informed Holly she would receive another part of her inheritance early, in the form of an $18,000 gift. Upon depositing the first sum, she wrote to her welfare caseworker and canceled her food stamps allotment. "I received money in the mail today," she wrote him, "which will allow me to live comfortably and at my own speed (self-employed and diabetic), without the stipend." In a typically sweet gesture, she added that she appreciated the "humane, compassionate" treatment she received.

Holly consciously attempted to be more assertive, especially with Ira. Whenever he made a comment she considered "chauvinistic," she would try to freeze him with what she called "a long steady straight look." She pointed out to him quite forcefully that her tolerance was decreasing for his little tricks to maintain his power over her, like forcing her to ask *him* for the keys to the Toyota whenever she wanted to drive somewhere. She would tell him, after lovemaking, that it was marvelous, but she had no "orgasmic energy." No apologies. "Frank," she wrote, "but direct and no big deal."

One day, while taking a walk around Powelton with a friend, she uttered a statement that seemed to sum up her recent awakening. The friend pointed out a tree in a neighbor's yard—a holly tree. He told her that a tree of that species is a slow grower. "Yes," she said, "but it gets stronger as it matures."

"Up to that time, she was almost like a shadow," says Einhorn's friend Stuart Samuels. "Whenever she was in Ira's situation she was like a ghost physically; her energy was very low. And then she started to develop this [new] philosophy and attitude. She seemed to be a lot more alive, she seemed to be more talkative."

Holly began learning to deal with the occasions where she was conscious of being seen solely as Ira's woman. For instance, in late 1976, Einhorn and Holly attended an informal gathering at the home of Hazel and Carter Henderson. Hazel in particular was one of Ira's key network contacts, a tall, forceful economist with whom Ira felt a warm ideological kinship. Without benefit of a college education, the British-born Henderson had become a Nader-style activist and then a New Age economist, the only female member of President Jimmy Carter's Economics Task Force. The Henderson house, a rambling Victorian on Princeton's prestigious Hodge Road, would come alive on weekends, as the Hendersons ran what they described as a "mom-and-pop think tank" formally known as the Princeton Center for Alternative Futures. "People would come from all over the world to exchange ideas," says Ann Medlock, a foundation director who met Einhorn there. "The house had a huge number of rooms—people bought sleeping bags and took part in housekeeping. You'd be washing dishes with E. F. Schumacher [author of *Small Is Beautiful*]."

On that particular weekend, Holly felt her familiar self-consciousness at fading into the background of Ira's garrulous cosmological gossip, but this time decided to do something about it. Holly screwed up her courage and approached the formidable Hazel Henderson, asking if she wanted a foot rub. This personal, one-on-one contact was something at which Holly excelled, and the two women had a long, warm conversation. It was a breakthrough for Holly.

At times, things looked bright for Holly, even when thinking of her life with Ira. "We're liking each other lots these days," she wrote in early December. "Our arguments haven't trod too far into uptight out-of-sight rage for this while."

On the other hand, she would frequently lapse into old, bad habits. One night she and Ira dined at the home of one of Einhorn's friends since high school, Mel Richter, now a doctor living in the suburbs. It was obvious that Mel and his wife, Linda, saw Holly as a cipher, a china-doll appendage to their brilliant, unorthodox friend. The Richters tried their best to be nice to her, but the conversation did not go well. Afterward, Holly saw the exchange as proof that she did not get along with members of her gender. "Why do I turn women off?" she asked herself. "How is it I don't seem to be able to treat them as interesting people and not talk about myself?" Ironically, Linda Richter did not think Holly was uninterested in her, but lacking confidence in herself. "She wasn't a participant in the conversation when the four of us would get together," says Linda Richter. "She wouldn't venture ideas or opinions, she just waited for you to ask her."

Still, Holly was making some progress. She wrote of a small voice within her that said *live alone,* and *wait for the precious few who do not specialize in the negative-feedback theory of showing love.* Viewing a film made from the sadomasochism masterpiece *Story of O,* she wrote Lawrence Wells that "I have finally begun to understand the religious aspect of master/slave relating. As in any good metaphor: a good map of the reality. But *not* the reality itself." After one silly argument, she wrote that "Yes, I'm pissed and it hurts that he feels he can walk on me. But that game is drawing to a close, buddy." She determined to visit the Lisses when Ira was scheduled to visit Canada again. She was, as she called it, "defiant and secret to the point of deciding whether or not to use a phone booth to call . . . so Ira won't know that, and when, I called them." Then she decided *not* to cower—to call from the apartment if she felt like it. "It and I will fall where we may," she wrote, "and lie down or stand up in consequence."

So she did visit the Lisses when Ira was in Canada in December 1976—and seeing other women. When Ira called, she even told him about her visit and was infuriated when he gave what Holly saw as "his short laugh of 'how silly' and ridicule." During the visit she offered to lend Larry—who had suffered a business setback—some money: an act she knew Ira would object to, if he knew. And at a party during Ira's absence, she met a man and went to his home and made love. But she punished herself for her acts and soon was in a funk about her behavior. She tried to get to the bottom of her situation:

> You feel like a babe in the woods, among giants who step on you and/ or condescend, and like you, which makes you feel really confused because you're an ass . . . why—how—can they like you and want to spend time with you? On top of that, you're afraid you're going to hurt everybody, as well as be hurt by everybody (ridiculed, tickled indulgently, etc.). So you withdraw from the fray.
>
> Your body is feeling better now. . . . Nobody's coming out and provoking you cross-eyed. You got $$ in the bank, time on your hands. Consecrate it all to the task . . . to get better.

Nothing seemed to go right with Ira and Holly that winter. Even so simple a thing as Holly's cooking pancakes for Ira wound up in an argument. Ira didn't like the food, and to Holly it was "just another in the long string of rejections." Holly began looking for another apartment, and when she returned to 3411, they had a long talk as Holly soaked in the tub. To Holly, Ira's rap was "the read-out, once more, of everything he's done for me, and how I can't have it every way—in short, he talks as though he just doesn't understand why I am behaving unsatisfied at all—it's all my fault if I am dissatisfied here, he's done all he can. . . . I just listened to him and saw it as a harmless wave crashing over my head and rolling off my back." They retreated to their corners, Ira to the living area and Holly to the kitchen table.

The inevitable reconciliation followed, and for a brief period, hostilities ceased. Holly began to think she might be able to live with her jealousies, Ira spoke of Holly's "healing," and Holly considered cutting back on her sessions with Marian Coopersmith. The therapist disagreed, noting that Holly would need support while she worked on her assertiveness. The question lingered as the new year turned, and, as promised, Holly received the check for $18,000 from her uncle. "We do not want to stipulate definitely how to use these funds," wrote Uncle Pres and Aunt Pat, "but simply suggest that since they are part of your ultimate inheritance, they be used to your own, individual best advantage." As she waited in line at the bank on January 2, 1977, preparing to deposit the check, which would raise her personal fortune to almost $40,000, she felt giddy. She had had a good morning with Ira. "I AM IN COMMAND OF MY SHIP, much more than I let on or behave," she wrote of her feelings at that instant.

But within days, it fell apart again. After another blowup, at Holly calling another man, it was Ira packing Holly's bag. This time, he literally threw her out of the apartment. Since he was about twice her weight, this was not a challenge for Ira. He did not even allow Holly time to retrieve her checkbook; at that point, she wrote, Einhorn "carried me to the door, dumped me . . . using physical strength to fuck me over." Ira's parting words to her: "One of your boyfriends will take you in." Holly went to the food co-op and her friend Nicole Hackel agreed to take her in for a few days.

Though Nicole Hackel had worked with Holly for many hours, she says that was the first sign that there was trouble in the Maddux-Einhorn relationship. "She just said, 'Can I stay here a few days?' And I said, 'Sure,' " recalls Hackel. "It was clear it was in relation to Ira, and she was not sure she wanted to go back. Somehow she was reckoning about that."

In Ira's view, the incident was evidence of Holly's irrationality and mistrust. "Why did Holly fail?" he wrote after the argument. "Fear? So sweet and lovely, yet she be so unable to open and trust . . . putting down my woman friends—stay away yet so fully encouraging her men lovers—could she be aware of this?" Ira finally saw it philosophically. "There has been too much water under the bridge. Too much hurt, too much lack of trust. So we must part."

Of course they didn't. Despite locating an adequate new apartment for herself, Holly was reluctant to hand over the deposit check, which would represent her commitment to leave Ira. She looked into her heart and once again conjured rationalizations for Ira Einhorn's behavior:

> I don't feel that this with Ira is over. He felt ragingly hurt to me—the accusations about other men will take care of me, etc. Why doesn't Holly hold herself for Ira, who has done so much for her, loves her so much, held himself back so much? is the essence of his complaint. The bellow and charge of the bull. I don't feel, and didn't feel, his behavior rational, in the sense it was a peak emotional experience with related behavior. He'd said the day before he wishes I trust him more, and that he loves me.
>
> I will do what I can to talk with him once more—i.e., stay with him . . . and if he slams it in my face, I've done what I could.

Ira did not "slam it" in Holly's face. They had a long, loud back-and-forth. They both agreed they wanted to be together. Finally, Ira cut through it all and asked Holly what she wanted from him. She told him: to be with him, and to have the same privilege that he claimed for himself—to make love to others. "Go!" Ira bellowed. She did but returned instantly. More talk, tender talk this time, and they began making love. Holly was worried that the phone would ring and Larry Liss would be on the other end—the very thought threatened to prevent her from relaxing during sex. So she self-consciously took the phone off the hook. Ira laughed at her. "You're such an asshole, Holly," he said. Holly froze. Ira, even in a joking aside, had struck her in a secret place. She dressed and headed out the apartment. But she could not leave. She remained in the corner of the kitchen, crying, hung in the nowhere land between being with Ira and leaving Ira. A tottering, tortured pendulum.

If there was any suspense over which side the pendulum would rest, Ira Einhorn ended it. He went to his woman and held her, ending what he considered a "silly" disagreement. They made love, and for a while, everything was all right. It was a new year, one Holly had high hopes for, and no suspicions at all that it would be the last year of her life.

* * *

These struggles may have been in the center of Holly Maddux's life that winter, but to Ira they were peripheral distractions to his work, which seemed to him more important than ever. As he delved deeper into the world of the paranormal, he became increasingly convinced that recent psychic revelations could have significant global impact. In some scenarios, these could have alarming consequences. Through his relationship with Andrija Puharich and others, in what he jokingly called a "psychic mafia," the Unicorn assumed a key role in the task of alerting our people about the implications of this revolution. Our old view of the world was a house of cards, set to tumbling by an unexpected breeze: the indisputability of Uri Geller's powers. That breeze would soon turn to a gust, as people understood that a combination of factors was turning our world view upside down. In Einhorn's universe, those factors included the undeniability of UFOs, the startling discoveries in quantum physics, and the inevitability of the new world order—shaken loose by the Aquarian Transformation. Ira saw himself as sort of a New Age Paul Revere, waking the nation to these realities.

Ira always did have his apocalyptic strain, but it was never so strong as when he talked about the implications of the so-called "mind bomb." He said that both the United States and the Soviets have known about the existence of the paranormal for years, and by spreading this information over his network, and his other services as "planetary enzyme," he was bucking a conspiracy of silence. "The ethical situation that I find myself in is that I'm constantly involved with a cosmic Watergate," he said. "And that the information that has been kept from me and that was not provided for me as a child was a lot worse than the Watergate situation."

The occasion at which he spoke the above words was the "Mind Over Matter" conference that Einhorn organized on the Penn campus in late January 1977. It was one of several gatherings of the psychic mafia that Ira midwifed. The key players were all in attendance. Andrija Puharich, the ringmaster of the paranormal, speaking about the Space Kids. Chris Bird, an expert in odd corners of the paranormal with reputed CIA connections, talking about dowsing, as well as the biological implications dealt with in his bestselling book, *The Secret Life of Plants*. Tom Bearden, a retired Air Force colonel whose raucous self-published *The Excaliber Briefing* postulated a grand alternative view of reality, "a theory of biofields which unites mental phenomena with physics." The theory also encompassed UFOs and cattle mutilations.

The conference drew a full crowd despite a snowstorm and energized Ira's interests in the field even more. In the subsequent weeks the focus of his paranormal discussions shifted to another one of Andrija Puharich's pet subjects: mind control and other bizarre effects created by use of extra low frequency (ELF) rays. This was presumably an outgrowth of Nikola Tesla's theories in the early part of the century. (Some of those theories had, over the years, thrust Tesla—universally celebrated as the inventor of alternating current and radio technology—as a cult figure, a mystic Svengali to any number of conspiracy-minded fanatics.) Puharich had thrust himself into a center of controversy, looking into claims that the Russians had beamed ELF rays to Canadian cities and had temporarily scrambled people's minds. Ira burned up the phone lines to his network compatriots, gathering and spreading information on the now-hot Tesla beat. Was it true that Tesla's papers were smuggled out of the United States after the inventor's death? And that those papers, now in Communist hands, held secrets that would bring great power to any country that attempted to exploit them? And that the Russians were actually doing this, in conjunction with their previously documented work in psychic research? And that the United States had its own effort, so supersecret that even Congress was kept in the dark about it?

These questions, along with rumors and speculations, were central to Ira's psychic mafia in the spring of 1977 and ultimately aired at a conference in the Harvard Science Center in Cambridge, Massachusetts, called "Towards a Physics of Consciousness." Though the proposed subject matter was identical to Ira's "Mind Over Matter" gathering, Puharich chose that event to air out the Tesla controversy. All hands agreed that it was a dangerous subject—who knew what the various government intelligence agencies would do to keep this information secret?—and they should be very careful.

The Unicorn's concern over these matters naturally spilled over into his meetings with business leaders. More than one corporate executive or Philadelphia politico, hoping to plug into the mind-set of the baby-boom generation by accessing this fascinating futurist, listened in stunned silence over salad at La Terrasse as Ira spoke earnestly of mind control, UFOs, and cattle mutilations as an expression of a global collective unconsciousness (the latter was an idea of Tom Bearden's and not his weirdest theory). Some of Ira's contacts thought it fascinating; others listened with skeptical amusement. But others, even those who had gone shoulder-to-shoulder with Ira since Earth Day, considered this a bit much.

To John Brennan, the GE public-relations man, for instance, it was indicative of a change in Ira's personality. When Brennan had first met Einhorn, Ira wanted to *learn*, particularly about business. But as Ira became more involved—almost obsessed—with the paranormal, it was as if holding this supposedly essential knowledge put him a notch above everybody else, even incredibly bright people running corporations, or doing world-class science. Though Brennan's complaint was reminiscent of that of Ira's detractors since the sixties, it is significant that Ira was beginning to turn off some of the people he most wanted to retain in the web of his network. Finally, Brennan told Einhorn, "Ira, I don't need a guru. I'm not interested in this kind of bullshit."

By the spring of 1977, Holly Maddux's drive toward independence was well under way. She used bold strokes to distance herself from the confining limitation of "Ira's girlfriend." She had enrolled in assertiveness training, as well as a workshop on the Alexander technique of massage. The latter was only one skill that Holly was developing in her quest for fullness. She had retained her girlhood enthusiasm for drawing, and among her projects had designed posters for Ira's various projects: one for his Mind Over Matter seminar, and one—depicting a peaceful unicorn standing on a rock—promoting a poetry reading entitled "Einhorn on Einstein: The Poetry of Science."

She sensed some progress with the "open relationship" issue, writing Lawrence Wells that "I'm seeing other men now ... am 'allowing' Ira to move in his own space that way, too."

In the most bizarre declaration of independence of all, though, Holly Maddux decided to experiment in something most daring for a woman with a self-esteem problem. She went to the seamy stretch of Center City Philadelphia that housed the porno shops and strip joints and auditioned to become a go-go dancer.

This caused some dismay, not only to Ira, who thought it a miserable idea, but to Holly's other friends. They had trouble imagining this near-angel exposing herself half nude to strange men and wondered what possible motivation could bring her to that point.

Julie Samuels, Stuart Samuels' wife and an expert in dermatology, was stunned when Holly came to her and explained that she wanted to learn to use makeup. Julie told her, "I don't want to put makeup on your face. You're just too beautiful, and you would look just ordinary, and you look extraordinary this way."

"But she insisted," recalls Julie Samuels. "She wanted to be a go-go dancer in a bar. I remember thinking, God, what somebody will do for love in a relationship to get a reaction so the person acts like they're there. That she was just destroying the beauty of who she was—it was so pure. So I put makeup on her. I hated it. I felt like I was ruining a beautiful painting that was just so exquisite all by itself, and making it common. I didn't want to do it, but this was the most assertive I'd ever seen her. She said, 'I want to do this, please do it for me, I want to do this.' So I did."

What Julie Samuels did not understand was that for Holly go-go dancing was a step forward, a confidence-building act of defiance, much in the same way that thirteen years previously she had shucked her restraints and competed for cheerleader at John Tyler High School. The previous year, watching her sister Buffy parade as a majorette, Holly noted cynically "the acres of young firm flesh decked out in red and white," and saw the cheerleaders as burdened with baggage of everyone's fantasies. What difference, really, between the pink shorts Holly wore on her cheerleader tryout and the silver G-string she purchased now? A letter she wrote to Lawrence Wells about her bold initiative leaves no doubt that she attempted it in a spirit of liberation.

"Auditioned for an agent last week," she wrote, "who told me the last person he'd seen dance as well as I wore high black leather boots and boas (boa constrictors, that is); and that was four years ago. . . . I received *applause*, m'boy. I don't think I'll mind being a sex object, because I'll be the one to put myself in the position."

The go-go dancing did not last long, because Holly and Ira were soon to leave for Europe. Ira had changed his mind several times on whether it would be a good idea for Holly to accompany him on the trip, which would be largely dedicated to work on psychic phenomena. His ultimate decision that she would accompany him overcame two reservations, the first being whether they could possibly get along while traveling together for several months. Whenever they argued, he worried how they could ever survive five months in close proximity. The second was that Holly might not be up to the rigors and dangers of the excursion. Einhorn included Eastern Europe on his itinerary, in a quest for information on psychic research behind the Iron Curtain, particularly on the Tesla issue. Ira Einhorn thought he had built sufficient leads through his network to get to the bottom of the story. Though he gravely informed Holly of the danger of this mission, she volunteered to share the peril.

As for the other consideration—Would they get along?—he addressed this in a poem he wrote entitled "Diabetic Woman." He wrote of "a dance of angels upon a unicorn's horn," an ill-coordinated minuet. He asked: "What are we fighting about?/It gets more silly with each passing day/we've done it before/must/we do it again?" He concluded that the answer need not be negative, and thus Ira and Holly would venture abroad together.

Perhaps another reason for his decision was Holly's ability to help fund the trip. It is unclear how much she contributed to the expenses, but in the weeks before leaving, she withdrew around $12,000 from her bank account. This included a $656 check to a travel agency for plane fare, and a $7,300 withdrawal for travelers' checks.

Ira sent a communiqué through his network shortly before leaving, outlining his tentative itinerary for the five-and-a-half month tour. The trip would start in Iceland, briefly jump to the Continent, and move to London. After an extended British stay, there would be eight weeks of Scandinavian travel, then six weeks in Eastern Europe. "If any of you are on my travel route and could provide a night's hospitality, please let me know," he wrote. "I will be with the woman I live with (Holly) and we sleep on the floor at home, so a bed is neither needed or desired."

Holly Maddux had some unfinished business before she left for Europe. She wanted once more to see Jesse Reese, the boy she had so thoroughly bewitched five years previously, on the kibbutz. Since then, she had seen him perhaps once a year. Not long after her abortion in 1974, they had gone to a Bob Dylan concert in New York, and in the late summer of 1985, Holly had left Puharich's farm in Ossining to meet Jesse in the city for a day (he had been disturbed at her tales of the Space Kids). Reese was now at Goddard College in Vermont, studying glass blowing. Holly had written him that winter, in a letter full of her rediscovered selfhood:

> I'm feeling a little bit amused, because I'm becoming fairly transparent to myself and what I see is funny, funny, funny . . . like I never laughed before. In fact, what crossed my mind, who knows where the thought came from, is, where do you come in my life? For whatever cosmic-human reasons it has been my fortune to house, I am only now coming into my life-given inheritance of being able to feel love. Before, years ago, when I first saw you, met you, knew you such as it could be, I called you special to me, honestly and it was as correct as I could say. And for years before knowing you and after, it was a bored, cliff-walking feeling that I walked, talked and breathed, and lived out. But I'm beginning to love. Things are seeming quite a bit different even now. Damn it, I am so inward, it seems so *never* that I'll be able to say/do what I mean, having taken so long to have anything *to* mean. I'm left a prisoner on the planet of patience, again.

Borrowing Ira's car—a deliciously defiant irony—she drove up to spend a few days with Jesse, who was startled at how thin she had gotten since the last time he'd seen her. But she seemed energetic and healthy. The most startling thing was her description of the purpose of the European trip. "She told me she thought she was going to get killed," he recalls. "They were going on this spy mission, she and Ira. Iron Curtain. She told me the Russians had appropriated Tesla's archives as sort of a cultural exchange, because Tesla was a big hero. But once they had gotten it back, they really wanted it for the scientific value of the stuff—that was Ira's theory, or somebody's theory. And Ira and Holly were going to find out what the Russians had made use of, or try to steal them back, or something bizarre. And that it was very dangerous, that there was a good chance she'd get killed. And that she wanted to see me before she got killed."

It seemed a crazy story, and Jesse Reese wondered whether or not Ira Einhorn had Holly going on this trip in order to finance it with the money she said she'd inherited in the beginning of the year. But he tried to give Holly the benefit of the doubt. In other respects she seemed fine, acting warmly toward him, exulting in the country atmosphere, interested in the crafts he was practicing, and letting loose at a college dance. It was a pleasant coda to a long-gone love affair.

When Holly returned to Philadelphia, there were only the last-minute preparations to make before leaving for the first leg of the trip, to Iceland. As usual for summer vacations, Ira had sublet the apartment, this year to a local musician named Rick Iannacone, who had seen the notice on the co-op bulletin board with Holly's hand-drawn picture of the building, and gotten a good vibration from it. Holly and Ira boxed up their belongings and took them to Joe and Bea Einhorn's house in the suburbs. In addition, they handed over an envelope to Bea Einhorn containing the wills they had recently drawn. Just in case something happened to one or both of them.

Ira Einhorn and Holly Maddux arrived in Europe on the day the Unicorn turned thirty-seven. They spent a few days in Iceland and had their first argument of the trip, Holly threatening to go back home right then and there. That crisis averted, they flew to Luxemburg, picked up the car they arranged to buy while in Europe, and drove to London where they would stay in a perfect guest room—with bamboo furniture, a skylight, and a back door leading to a rose garden—at 7 Lansdowne Crescent, the home of Joyce Petschek.

Ira had known Petschek for several years. She was, for a period, the companion of Andrija Puharich, and was a participant in the Space Kids experiment—indeed, two of her own teenage children were among the junior Gellers. American-born, she had married into a wealthy family of Jewish industrialists who had fled the Continent before World War II. Apparently she had retained considerable wealth after her divorce: Besides the London home, she had a villa in Italy and a saltbox on Fire Island. The Lansdowne Crescent house was a large stone structure on a quiet street in the Notting Hill Gate district, not far from the counterculture enclave of Portobello Road. Here, in a drawing room that could accommodate sixty, Joyce Petschek held semiregular gatherings, seminars, and psychic probings. With Puharich as her contact to paranormal circles, Petschek filled Lansdowne Crescent with studies of out-of-body travels, first-person accounts of intimate encounters with extraterrestrials, and grave meetings about the rapidly breaking psychic warfare crisis.

Ira himself was one of the key speakers at one of those summer meetings. "There were about sixty people gathered, a sort of town meeting," recalls Professor John Taylor, a physicist at London University who was in attendance. "He spoke about problems of [ELF] radiation, dangers occurring, all sorts of things." Michael Marten, a British science writer, was impressed at Einhorn's verve: "He carried it all off in a grand manner. He was bubbling with conspiracies and theories. Very impressive—he was a good talker. You could see why he had a whole group of people who looked up to him."

When Puharich arrived in London, he and Ira began organizing a large conference to be held in Iceland that November. They arranged funding from an organization called the Orb Foundation, with additional monies contributed by wealthy patrons. The week before the conference, Einhorn, Puharich, and Tom Bearden would conduct a public seminar at London's Commonwealth Institute.

Besides cementing relations with network contacts like physicist Fritjof Capra and writer Arthur Koestler, Ira had a busy social life in London. He spent time with his old friend Craig Samms, who had converted his 1960s macrobiotic interests into a thriving health-food business on Portobello Road. Among other Londoners, Ira connected with Peter Gabriel, the lead singer of the rock group Genesis. Einhorn also hung out with a group of London survivors of the sixties, many associated with *Oz*, the controversial underground magazine. Some of them were working on an English version of the *Whole Earth Catalog*, and Ira would often be among the visitors who crowded into that small office. He developed a particular friendship with Heathcote Williams, a controversial playwright whose works include *AC/DC*. Richard Adams, an editor in that crowd, recalls that Ira endeared himself by his networking talents, generously pulling out names and numbers from his address book to put people in contact with others who often proved to be valuable contacts. Ira also got involved in some of the local protests: When he heard that American author David Solomon was among those imprisoned in an LSD bust, the biggest in British history, Ira spontaneously visited Solomon in prison and wrote a letter to the officials pleading for mercy.

Ira also was a frequent drop-in at the London Go Center, where he sharpened his Go skills to new heights.

Graham Wilson, who edited a local New Age newspaper called

New Life, heard Einhorn speak that summer and was impressed enough to conduct a long interview with Ira for his publication. Ira came to Wilson's house in typical garb: a bright-colored, patterned dashiki, partially covered in front by his bushy, graying beard and in back by his flowing hair. Approaching forty, he was burlier than ever.

"I am not antiscientific," he told Wilson. "I am anti- what science has made of us." From there, he led his interviewer, a willing straight man, on a tour of his interests, a blithe monologue of near-Biblical self-import. "I am involved in a religious war," he said, "and it's the essential religious war, it is the war about the nature of reality. . . . I feel the whole planet is involved in it."

Geller popped up, of course, with Ira explaining how he and Puharich used the Israeli psychic to transform the world's basic conception of reality. He also spoke of the possibility of a link between UFOs and psychic phenomena like Geller's metal bending, healings produced by the likes of "the surgeon of the rusty knife" Arigo, and other unexplainable acts. In short, "We are dealing with something. The important thing is not what we are dealing with but the fact that we are dealing with something and that something is changing the whole face of human history."

Toward the end of the interview, Ira attempted to sum up his work: "I do basically live a life where my time is my own and more and more I am pondering the incredible mystery of what it means to be a human being. What that means—what it is all about."

While Ira Einhorn was making planetary declarations, Holly Maddux was directed on a more personal quest, making use of the paranormal resources available to her in the Petschek house. "I'm in wonderful company and comfort, surrounded by supportive energy," she wrote. "Have learned more in this two weeks about the world and body I create for myself than in a long time." Working with a visiting "transmedium" named Marshall Lever, she attacked the problem of her diabetes and believed that she had miraculously arrived at a cure. After Lever's "healing," and his suggestion of a week's diet of juice and raw vegetables, supplemented with certain vitamins, Holly felt confident enough to discontinue the DBI medication prescribed by her doctor. She triumphantly removed the Medic Alert bracelet that had previously chastised her with one more charge of inferiority. Sufficiently energized, she now began to pursue her latest idea for self-employment: buying fine fabrics that she would transform, as she wrote in a letter home, into "simply beautiful garments for ladies who will pay for the quality and thought of the design. The clothes will be one-of-a-kind, marketable in Phila-delphia, and New York if I feel like ranging afield."

In July, Holly's sister Buffy visited Holly at Joyce Petschek's house while on a school excursion to London. The first part of the visit was spent with Einhorn, Puharich, and Petschek, with much talk about UFOs and similar phenomena unfamiliar to a sixteen-year-old girl from Tyler. But then Holly showed her sister what she had bought in Europe. "Holly had bought lace and old clothes," says Buffy. "She was really excited. She also had this beautiful embroidered black monk's robe that was exquisite. She was showing me all this stuff, piles of handmade Irish lace, that she was going to make clothes out of. I'd never seen her enthusiastic like that."

Holly's buoyant feelings did not jibe with a parallel upswing in her relationship with Ira. During the invigorating first week in London, Holly and Ira got on well, a harmony signified by a warm Father's Day card Holly sent to Ira, defusing a potentially thorny subject between them—parenthood—by her cheery, even ribald, salutation: "To the popper of corks, greeter of storks, wanger of dorks." Things with Ira quickly deteriorated, though, and soon Holly and Ira had arrived at their familiar impasse. It was even clear to visitors to the Petschek house: Christian De Lait, the science adviser to the British Commonwealth, knew Ira and found him informative as sort of a "spiritual boulevardier," but said the Einhorn-Maddux relationship "was not healthy. It was paternalistic and avuncular and domineering. She wasn't that comfortable. She needed a lot of room and the support of Joyce, without the [nega-tive] attention of Ira."

Soon Holly, practicing her hard-won assertiveness, was lashing out at Ira, and apparently their plan of touring the English country-side was threatened. But when Ira returned from an evening out with Heathcote Williams, he found a note awaiting him:

Dear Ira,

I see I have been a real shit recently, and I'm very sorry for it.

It would please me to continue traveling with you. Would you be up for that?

True enough, there's very little I can do for you . . . but maybe bake some cookies this week, or rub your feet?

love from
H

Ira found something she could do for him immediately: oral sex. Another crisis temporarily averted. They headed out for their motor trip, with, according to Holly, their roles defined: "he meeting people whose names he has been given as people who will have world views, information, etc. to share; me meditating, easing, and transforming the group energy for fuller communications." They first drove down to a paraphysics lab Ira wanted to see in Downton, overnight to Glastonbury, and the next day into Wales. They stayed briefly with George Andrews, a writer they'd met at Joyce Petschek's. Andrews was taken with Holly, impressed with her low-key demeanor and her beauty. He also surmised that in the not-distant future Holly would be on her own. "I got the impression that she wasn't too happy the way things were going. One could see there was a certain degree of dissatisfaction. I wouldn't have been surprised if she had wanted to change, or walked out on Ira."

Also in Wales, Ira and Holly visited a cottage inhabited by Georgie Downes and her boyfriend. Georgie was part of the *Oz* crowd, a bright woman with interests similar to Ira's. "It was a very pleasant visit," she recalls. "We read about a book a day—that seemed to be a sort of joke, really—'Have you read your book today?' And then we'd play Go, take walks, and eat. Holly would eat separately. She had about ten meals a day, odd tiny meals—little bits of carrot. Funny food, she called it." In fact, as Downes recalls it, "Holly didn't really take part in much of anything—she'd just sit in the corner." So much for "transforming the group energy."

When they returned to London, Holly spent much time away from Ira. During bad times in the house on Lansdowne Crescent, she would retreat to the sauna, "to equalize and stabilize 'bad thoughts' and lousy feelings," as she put it. She spent time with Joyce Petschek, off on shopping excursions, and helping Joyce with her book, a "cosmic fairy tale" called *The Silver Bird*. But more and more, she would head off into London on her own, seeing people outside of Ira's circle. She began seeing another man—"a delightful Scot," as she described him—and this riled Ira considerably.

"Strange to be making my own friends now," she wrote to her family. "I realize I actually haven't done so for five years or more . . . laughing a lot and feeling creative with people as well as my hands."

Ira took a countryside excursion without her, visiting Colin Wilson and finding a woman who shared an idyllic sexual encounter with him by a Cornwall waterfall. When he returned, he was not so enthusiastic about Holly's similar revels. "Holly off," he wrote, describing a day in July. "Sex again. UGH!" It affected Ira to the point where his Go game fell off. He and Holly argued: "What a dance we put on," Ira noted. Once again they spoke of living apart when they returned to the States. It was an idea they both endorsed.

Holly made plans to go home alone, early. She booked a flight for July 31. Ira meanwhile arranged to go to Scandinavia in August. Despite all the talk and excitement and bravado about hitting Eastern Europe for the Tesla "mission," that plan fizzled. Ira's later explanation was that when the Soviet correspondent for the *Los Angeles Times,* Robert Toth, was arrested that summer, he was holding documents on subjects that Ira was to investigate in Yugoslavia. But by mid-summer, the situation with Holly was taking precedence in Ira's mind over his battle to expose the psychic Watergate, and it may well have been that Ira did not have the heart to crash the Iron Curtain on his own.

"We're winding down," Ira wrote in late July. "It is obviously over. All that's needed is the ending—to occur when I drift away from here in a few days. I'm out the other side. All that is being run is a series of old habits."

While Ira viewed the end of the relationship in dark hues, Holly was ebullient, as reflected in a letter to her sister Meg, written shortly before leaving for America to spend August at Joyce Petschek's house on Fire Island:

> Ira and I have agreed to split (for now?) (for good?). I'll be at [Fire Island] until Sept. 5 or thereabouts—sewing, sunning, spending much time alone and unattached—Lovely! With the help of some healers and supportive atmosphere around here, I got rid of diabetes in the space of one week. As I become more and more credulous of this new healthy creature I seem to be rapidly becoming, so too does a number of my life assumptions pull a shift. It's been great, realizing I'm capable and ready to live alone. Doesn't mean I will—I may have

to, in order to truly realize that I have choice—but at the present time I am looking very hard at the "us" of Ira and me, as we spend our last days together here in this sunny household. I see so easily too many compromises I've made without realizing their consequences—the loss of any self-motivation and self-esteem. I'm becoming so active you maybe wouldn't recognize me—outgoing and unafraid. It's been quite a radical turnaround for me. And very pleasant.

To settle up some unfinished financial business, the ownership of the car they had purchased during the trip to Europe, they drafted an oddly formal typed IOU: "I, Ira Einhorn, promise to pay Helen Maddux the sum equal to half the sale price of our [car], no later than January 1, 1978." Ira signed it and as witness, Holly signed, using the same formal name used in the body of the promissory note.

The final parting came on July 28, when Ira was to drive to Dover on the first leg of his trip to Denmark, Sweden, and Norway. Ira's sleep the previous night had been fitful: He woke at 5:15, again an hour later, and finally arose at seven. Holly helped him pack. Ira asked Holly if she would put off her decision to find an apartment for herself for the fall. But Holly was adamant. She would live alone. She would maintain her freedom. At age thirty, she had gone too far to let things go back the way they were.

9

PRIVATE INVESTIGATORS

Fred and Elizabeth Maddux did not hear from their daughter Holly in September of 1977. A one-sided silence for that length of time was unusual, but certainly not unprecedented. The only truly unsettling aspect was that the silence had been preceded by a flurry of warm correspondence to several of her siblings and each of her parents individually, welcome communication that ended abruptly. In letters Holly wrote in late August, from the Fire Island home of Joyce Petschek where she had been spending the last few weeks of the summer, she had included the address to which letters should be sent after Labor Day. The address was only a block away from her previous lodging, but the difference—one that pleased the Madduxes considerably—was that she would not be sharing this apartment with Ira Einhorn. It looked like that relationship was finally, thankfully, over.

When nothing came from Holly in October, though, the rambling house in Tyler, Texas, became enveloped in concern. Beginning with Liz Maddux's birthday on October 2, there was a series of three family birthdays that month. Holly had previously been scrupulous about remembering the dates, regularly delighting the honored sibling or parent with a hand-drawn card, a valued item of ephemera to be discussed in the family circle and preserved, good for a chuckle years afterward. When no card or letter arrived, the Madduxes wondered whether something might be wrong. On October fourth, before the family sat down for dinner, Liz Maddux announced, "Well, I'll call him now," and picked up the telephone to ask Ira Einhorn where her daughter might be.

"I was about to call and ask you," said the Unicorn.

Ira Einhorn told Mrs. Maddux that Holly had been in Philadelphia for a few days in early September, and then took off. Liz said that it was her understanding that Holly was to have moved into a new apartment, but the mail they were sending there had generated no reply. Ira told Liz Maddux that he wished she would stop that because he was tired of collecting Holly's mail. Mrs. Maddux, perhaps a bit dazed by Ira's ignorance of Holly's whereabouts, agreed not to send anything. The conversation took four minutes.

Two weeks passed, and another family birthday. Still nothing. From Minnesota, Liz Maddux's stepmother, who usually heard regularly from Holly, called the house in Tyler. "Where is Holly?" she asked. "I haven't heard from her."

"I don't know," said Liz Maddux. "We're concerned."

As she and Fred Maddux discussed the situation, they realized they really had gotten very little information from Ira Einhorn, and on October 20, Liz called Ira again. This time she had a list of questions in hand, so she would be sure to remember to ask him everything. Later, she attempted to reconstruct some of that conversation:

MRS. MADDUX: When did she leave Philadelphia?

EINHORN: Three or four weeks ago. She went to the store and didn't come back. Actually, I was in the bathtub when she left. When she didn't return, I called everyone we knew and checked with the police and the hospitals, but no one knew anything. I talked to a friend of hers . . .

MRS. MADDUX: Joyce Petschek?

EINHORN: Yes. You know, she has houses all over so I had a hard time getting in touch with her, but I finally did. She told me not to worry, that I might not hear from Holly for three or four months. I don't know if she meant Holly might just go off for a while or if she knows where she is and won't tell me. I'm the last one she'd tell.

MRS. MADDUX: Did Holly have any money with her when she left?

EINHORN: Only a few dollars, I think.

MRS. MADDUX: Did she take anything else with her?

EINHORN: Not that I know of.

Throughout the eleven-minute conversation Ira Einhorn had been polite, and he sounded concerned about Holly. This heightened the Madduxes' fears. But there seemed nothing to do but wait. As the holiday season approached, and Holly's absence became more distressing, this strategy became impossible. The Madduxes asked Holly's old friend, Toni Erwin, who worked at the courthouse in Tyler, if she would ask her friends at the Tyler FBI office to look into the matter: Robert J. Stevens, the bureau chief, was sympathetic, but informed them that missing persons cases were not within the FBI's jurisdiction.

They then contacted another of Holly's Tyler friends, Lawrence Wells, who after finishing law school had become an assistant U.S. attorney. Wells had been equally troubled about Holly and, from his office in Tyler, he embarked on a small investigation. He checked Philadelphia hospitals and morgues. He officially reported her to the local authorities as missing. Aware of her recent travel abroad, he alerted Interpol as to her status. He also called Ira Einhorn and heard the same story about Holly going out when Ira was in the bathtub. Not satisfied with Einhorn's replies, Wells called the Philadelphia police and spoke to a Detective Dennis Lane, who promised to look into the case.

To a policeman in the crime-ridden West Philadelphia precinct, the disappearance of an adult flower child like Holly Maddux must have seemed an unalarming missing persons request. Nonetheless, Detective Lane conducted several telephone interviews. He talked to Holly's doctor at Hanneman Hospital, who told him that he had been worried about Holly, ever since she wrote him the previous summer and claimed that her diabetes had improved to the point where she no longer needed the DBI medication he had prescribed. The doctor had not heard from her since. Lane called Holly's therapist, Marian Coopersmith, who told him that Maddux was not suicidal, but Coopersmith had not heard from Holly either. Lane verified that Holly had $21,000 remaining in her bank account at Pennsylvania Federal Savings, untouched since her disappearance.

Finally Detective Dennis Lane paid a visit to 3411 Race Street, second floor rear. Again, Einhorn told the story: After they returned from Europe, separately, Holly came from Fire Island to Philadelphia to visit him around September 9 or 10. Holly was to live in another apartment that fall, but the current tenant had not moved yet. This was fortuitous, according to Einhorn, since he and Holly were planning to get back together, a plan upset around September 12, by Holly's failure to return from an errand. Saying she was going to the store, she vanished. Her clothing and belongings remained at 3411 Race Street until recently, when he moved them to his parents' house. Ira Einhorn then told Lane something that indicated Holly's exit was a conscious escape: Two days after Holly walked out, he received a call from her. *I'm okay*, she said. *Don't look for me. I'll call you once a week.*

When he did not hear from her again, he called her friends to see if they knew where she was. Why did he not report her disappearance to the police department? It was his understanding that since she was an adult, Holly Maddux would not qualify as a missing person under department standards. As Detective Lane told Lawrence Wells, this assumption was correct. In fact, Lane had already done more work on this case than was usual. The police investigation ended.

But the Madduxes' despair only continued. As Christmas and New Year's passed, it was certain that something awful was afoot. In January they learned that R. J. "Bob" Stevens, the chief of the Tyler FBI bureau, had retired on the last day of 1977. Toni Erwin said that Stevens planned to go into private investigation. The Madduxes contacted him, and asked him for help in finding their daughter. Though Bob Stevens was still on vacation, and did not plan on starting his business so soon after retirement, he agreed to look into the case.

R. J. Stevens had been a career FBI man, logging twenty years in the bureau. By the time he reached mandatory retirement at age fifty-five, he was chief of the nine-man Tyler field office, which covers fifteen counties in East Texas. Every FBI matter in those counties goes through the Tyler office: kidnappings, bank robberies, background investigations, organized-crime initiatives, and surveillance of subversives. A confident, solid man, with hair a bold tone of silver-fox gray and thick rings on his fingers, he inspired instant trust, considering even the most gruesome of matters in a soothing, cautious cadence. Like many former FBI men thrown into the civilian work force at a productive age, he felt himself too young to live on his pension, and chose the most logical occupation: an investigator. His contacts in Tyler would assure him a clientele without ever having to place an advertisement.

He found the Madduxes nice folks. Fred in particular was a piece of work: gruff on the outside, almost extravagantly deferential to his guests' needs, but obviously tormented by the disappearance of his daughter. Stevens spent five hours in the trophy *cum* living room of the Maddux residence, then paid a return visit a few weeks later, accumulating as complete a dossier of Helen Maddux as her parents could provide. He had Liz Maddux supplement this by writing an informal biography. She produced six sad pages: the early promise, the puzzling collapse at Bryn Mawr, the drifting thereafter, and the relationship with Ira Einhorn. Stevens noted that the Madduxes "personally blame Einhorn for changing Holly's way of life and turning her against her parents."

Liz Maddux added a bitter postscript to her daughter's biography:

> Ira is our only source of information, although he volunteers nothing. . . . It has occurred to me lately that if she told Ira she would check with him every week or so, perhaps she might have thumbed a ride. It had been done before. I once pointed out to her that any girl is in danger doing that sort of thing, and that an attractive girl is really putting her life on the line. But Holly never thought particularly of her looks, although she must be aware of the fact that she is beautiful because people have been telling her so for many years. Her conscious mind took in the fact that the people she has known since she went to Bryn Mawr have put her down as dumb, in comparison to themselves at least. In spite of the fact that IQ tests showed her eligible for MENSA. These are the same people whom she considers "kind," "aware," "concerned," etc. I think the last letters we had from her showed that she was emerging from her inferiority complex and deciding that she was capable of doing something, after all.

Bob Stevens was, of course, interested in the most recent letters Holly had sent. In mid-August of 1977, while staying at Joyce Petschek's house on Fire Island, Holly had written of her plans. She would return to Philadelphia after Labor Day, whereupon she would move to a lovely apartment at 3310 Race Street, "a block away from where I used to live with Ira." So spacious was this new residence, she wrote her mother, that "if you ever want to visit, there

is *plenty* of room; and we could have a blast—bring the girls."
Speaking of her present circumstances, Holly wrote that "I spend a
lot of time on the beach, by the ocean, in the open air, around
people (but not too much). Gorgeous solitude almost anywhere,
particularly walking the white sand beaches in the early A.M. or
after dark. . . . It's a perfect place to do body work—the constant
security of the waves eliminates subliminal anxieties that one can't
count on anything, and I find that very relaxing. . . . I'm running
now, out of sheer exuberance." Not a letter, Stevens noted, of a
despondent person about to wander off into oblivion.

In February, Stevens rented an office. He would begin his career
in the private sector sooner than he'd planned. Though he had not
conducted missing persons cases per se, he knew that the procedure
was to develop as much background as you could on the missing
girl. He was not wholly convinced that Holly Maddux was in danger,
or had been harmed. From what the Madduxes told him, and
further information he received from Toni Erwin and Lawrence
Wells, it was clear that Holly was a "free spirit," someone whose
behavior patterns had been established in that destructive decade,
the sixties. Witness her choice of boyfriend: a fellow who, as Stevens
wrote in his report, "believes himself to be an intellectual," author of
a book whose title was a number! Indications were that Holly Maddux had been a troubled girl. However, Stevens had to concede that
in light of the fact that Holly had previously been so diligent in
keeping in touch, the Madduxes' fears might be justified.

Stevens had several obvious leads. One was this woman Joyce
Petschek, with whom Holly had stayed in England, and whose Fire
Island home Holly had established as her last address. But Petschek
was not helpful. In a letter addressed to "Fred Maddock," she
claimed not to know where Holly was, suggesting that the Madduxes contact Marshall Lever. "He is the one who helped to stabilize
her physical condition," she wrote. "He is a 'transmedium' and
perhaps could do a transmission for you as to Holly's whereabouts."
Though not eager to search for Holly by paranormal means, the
Madduxes thought perhaps Lever might be able to provide a lead as
to Holly's whereabouts, and they called him. Lever said he was about
to leave on a trip and would contact them later. He did not.

In any case, Petschek was not the most important lead. That
honor was reserved for Ira Einhorn. Stevens thought it crucial to

interview Einhorn in person; furthermore, he knew that the bulk of his leads would not be in Texas, but Philadelphia. So before Bob Stevens flew north in the middle of March 1978, he arranged to work with a local private detective, to whom he would subcontract the investigation upon returning to Tyler. Finding the right operative was a simple matter: Since so many FBI men like Stevens enter private investigation upon retirement, there is a network of former G-men—a silver-haired version of the FBI itself—strung out all over the country. When one PI needs the assistance of another in a distant location, he need only contact a former colleague in the area, who will direct him to a fellow bureau veteran also in business. It was through these means that Robert J. Stevens met J. Robert Pearce.

J. R. Pearce was fifty-four years old, tall and imposing, a pipe smoker, and somewhat more urbane than the relatively earthy Stevens; he'd headed, before retirement, the organized-crime squad of the Philadelphia FBI bureau, where he had developed a smooth working relationship with the police commissioner, and later mayor, Frank Rizzo. He had also gained notoriety for his polygraph work, having conducted lie-detector tests on the major Watergate suspects, as well as witnesses in the cases of Patty Hearst, Spiro Agnew, and Joseph Yablonski. On the latter case, FBI director Henry Peterson had specifically requested that Pearce do the examination. Pearce's office was in Glenside, just outside the northwest section of the city in which Ira Einhorn had grown up, and from that neatly kept suite of three rooms he directed several associates, mostly former G-men like himself. His cases overwhelmingly dealt with white-collar crime. He seldom, if ever, handled missing persons. Had it not been a request from an FBI brother, he would not have taken on the Maddux case.

Stevens arrived in Philadelphia on March 14, 1978, and spent much of the next day in Pearce's office, going over the case. It was evening when they decided to call their chief witness. Stevens got Einhorn on the phone, informed him that he was a former FBI agent now working as a private investigator for the Madduxes. Was it possible to meet the next day so Einhorn could provide information that might help locate Holly?

It was not possible, said Ira Einhorn. He was extremely busy organizing Sun Day, a week-long environmental festival that was taking all his time—he had an office staffed with thirteen people, was trying to raise $50,000, and would have no time whatsoever until March 21.

Stevens, in town for only a few days, persisted.

Einhorn told him that he had no love for Holly's parents—in fact, getting away from her parents was one of Holly's motives for vanishing.

Stevens noted that Holly not only had lost contact with her parents but her friend Toni, and Einhorn himself, according to his own account.

Ira allowed that this was so. But in his view, Holly's silence was due to her wish to totally transform her life, cut all ties, begin anew.

But helping the investigation need not interfere with Holly's wishes, said Stevens. The Madduxes did not hire him to change Holly's life-style, only to assure them that she was all right.

That might be true, said Ira, but he still would not cooperate. Holly didn't want to be found.

By that point, Stevens realized that even when Ira Einhorn's project was completed, the Unicorn would not cooperate. Stevens suspended his efforts to set up a face-to-face interview, and instead tried to glean whatever information he could get right then, on the phone. To Stevens' surprise, Einhorn wound up answering some of the questions. Ira told Stevens about Holly's bank accounts, her diabetes diets, her go-go dancing, the dates of the Europe trip, the name of the woman from whom Holly was going to rent an apartment that fall, and even an account of the last time he had seen Holly. It was the same story as before: Holly had come from Fire Island around September 9, stayed through the weekend, and left for the store around the morning of September 12, leaving her luggage and clothes in the apartment. A few days later, she called and said she was all right, she would call him in a week. That was the last he heard of Holly.

Finally, Ira Einhorn terminated the conversation. Pearce and Stevens decided that Pearce should make every attempt to talk to him again. They could see no reason why someone so close to Holly would be so intransigent about helping an investigation to locate her—when he even admitted that he knew no one who was in touch with her. From that minute on, Ira Einhorn became something besides a key lead in the search for Holly Maddux.

He became a suspect.

* * *

R. J. Stevens was in Philadelphia for only a couple of days, but he managed to contact Marian Coopersmith, who outlined what she knew of the troubled relationship between Ira and Holly. He also visited one of Holly's banks and found a teller named Gwendolyn Coleman who recognized a picture of Holly, and said—to the detective's surprise—that the woman in the photograph had been there only three weeks before. But Stevens was not convinced that the identification was accurate. Stevens returned to Tyler, where he would oversee the investigation, now in the hands of J. R. Pearce.

To Pearce, a missing persons case was to be approached like a fugitive case: Find people who know the subject, look for information, establish who saw her last, and the circumstances. Since Ira Einhorn was not particularly cooperative, Pearce decided that he would begin with Ira's parents. He went to their house, only a few minutes from his office, and they received him more warmly than their son did. As parents, they could understand what Holly's family must be going through. In addition, Joe Einhorn said that he was sure that if Ira knew where Holly was, he would tell the detectives. Ira's reason for not cooperating with Stevens was a good one—he was busy sponsoring Sun Day, and even the Einhorns had not been able to get in touch with Ira recently.

According to Bea Einhorn, when Ira discovered that Holly had gone, he was "hysterical," "at wit's end." He told his parents that in his attempt to find Holly he called all the hospitals, the police, and many friends of Holly's. Neither Joe nor Bea Einhorn had any idea why Holly might take off. She was a smart girl. And why would she leave Ira? She *loves* Ira.

Not long afterward, Pearce called the Einhorns for more information. In the interim, Ira had been home, and his parents asked him about Holly, telling him about the bank teller who thought she saw Holly. Ira found this improbable, and said he had asked people "every day" where Holly was. No one knew. She just disappeared— there was no fight between them, said Joe Einhorn to Stevens. Ira was brokenhearted.

Pearce implored the elder Einhorn to convince his son to assist in the investigation. "Ira has no reason to lie to us," said Joe Einhorn. Then his voice cracked. "I love that little girl," he said. "Even if I told

Ira I would not tell, I would tell if I knew. I have your card—I will call. I will call them in Texas if I find out." Then, as if to himself—or to a son who might not appreciate the remark if it were spoken in his presence—he whispered plaintively, "Her parents only want to know if she's all right."

On March 21, Pearce moved his investigation to Powelton Village, a difficult place to work in the spring of 1978 because several blocks had been barricaded by the police, who had laid siege to a run-down, Charles Addams–esque Victorian house on Thirty-fifth Street. The house was inhabited by the radical group MOVE, and as a result Pearce—who was familiar with the neighborhood since his son had attended Drexel University and had lived in a fraternity down the block from Einhorn—needed clearance to move freely around Powelton. First checking the apartment where Holly had fled Ira in the spring of 1976, Pearce made his way to 3411 Race Street. He interviewed Mr. and Mrs. Harold Johnson, the elderly couple who were superintendents of the building. They lived in an apartment behind the building. Although they had known Einhorn since he moved in six years previously, they were extremely fuzzy on what it was that Einhorn did for a living—some kind of guru, some kind of a consultant, something to do with UFOs. The apartment was strange—no television, almost no furniture! Holly, though, was a favorite of theirs. She had shown great kindness to Mrs. Johnson when her cat was ill. She loved the garden in back of the house. They missed her very much, and had been wondering why they hadn't seen her. Previously, even when Holly and Ira were apart, Holly would check in, look at the flowers in the yard, and joke of her "visitation rights." Not this time. When Pearce asked if they thought that Ira Einhorn was capable of committing violence on Holly Maddux, the Johnsons admitted that they had talked about it. But though they did not like Ira Einhorn, they knew of his reputation for nonviolence.

Pearce walked to the front of the building and perused the mail-boxes, noting that by that standard, Holly Maddux and Ira Einhorn still shared apartment C. He rang the bell for that residence and was buzzed in. Before he climbed the stairs to the second floor, Ira Einhorn poked his head out the door and asked who the caller was. Pearce later described the encounter in his report, with prose honed by decades of summation in government investigation:

He appeared to be dressed in a kind of silk kimono affair. He didn't completely open the door, and I couldn't see how he was attired completely. His eyes are noticeably blue, he has a stocky build, full beard, light brown in color, and rather long hair matching in color. He appeared calm. From what little I could see into the apartment, I didn't think it was heavily furnished, but it did appear orderly. Ira Einhorn was emphatic that he would not "help Holly's parents." He did say he did not know where Holly is but claimed that if he did know, he would tell [me].

Pearce, as Stevens had done earlier, tried to keep the conversation going. He asked, rather futilely considering the circumstances, if Ira would consent to a polygraph test. He inquired about Ira's solar energy project and talked about the MOVE situation, which Ira said he was involved in as an advocate of MOVE. Pearce shifted the topic to his own investigation.

"I tried to appeal to him as a parent, and he said for the fourth or fifth time, he didn't want to talk about it, and finally closed the door."

Pearce continued down the block to the Ecology Food Co-op. Holly was well known there, and co-op manager Nicole Hackel in particular had been concerned when she did not appear for a shift she had signed up for—Holly hadn't even called to cancel. That wasn't like Holly, and when word came that Holly had vanished between the apartment and the co-op, there had been speculation that she might have been harmed on the way over. Pearce asked two co-op employees whether they thought Ira was telling the truth when he said he didn't know where Holly was, and they both said they thought he was. She certainly did seem to be missing—if Holly was in the neighborhood, people in the Ecology Food Co-op would know about it, they insisted.

For the next few weeks J. R. Pearce developed other leads, finding no clear path to Holly's whereabouts. Then, on April 21, Pearce checked in with the bank teller who said Holly had been at Penn Federal in early March. Not only did Gwendolyn Coleman reconfirm from another picture that the person she'd seen was Holly but she also claimed to have seen that woman on the street the previous February. It had been in the vicinity of Ninth and Locust—possibly the area of Holly's short-lived stint as a go-go girl.

Pearce sent his findings to Stevens on April 24, with several suggestions. One was to check out the possibility that Gwen Coleman was correct, and Holly was in Philadelphia, frequenting the gamy Ninth and Locust area. In addition, the Madduxes should attempt to claim her possessions, in hopes of new leads. The letter was not upbeat: "My suggestion would be to discuss with the parents the amount of money expended so far. . . . You could tell the parents that there is no assurance that Gwendolyn Coleman's information is positive, even though I think she is making a positive identification."

When Bob Stevens made his customary evening visit to the Madduxes, their request, as it would be throughout the investigation, was that the effort continue until Holly Maddux was found.

With this mandate, J. R. Pearce continued the investigation. Checking into the possibility that Holly might be living incognito as a go-go dancer or prostitute, he sought assistance from a former Philadelphia vice cop. By chance the policeman's son happened to know Ira and Holly, and the young man opined that the Unicorn was incapable of violence—a "pussycat." The vice veteran checked out his sources and concluded that Holly Maddux had not entered that particular demimonde.

Another Philadelphia police official Pearce spoke to was Inspector George Fencl, who had headed the Civil Disobedience Unit that had been so busy handling protesters in the sixties. Fencl knew Einhorn, of course, and even had been in contact with him recently, in connection with Ira's organizing efforts for Sun Day. At Pearce's request, Fencl paid Ira a visit, and again Einhorn said he had no desire to help J. R. Pearce look for his former girlfriend. Ira observed that this matter was getting an unusual amount of attention for a routine missing persons case—a detective, an ex-FBI man, and now a police inspector had been to 3411. Look, said Fencl, why not ask around to see where Holly is one more time, and maybe I can help straighten things out. Ira agreed, and called back Fencl a couple of weeks later. After talking to his friends, he said, it seemed that Holly was "out of the country." Since Ira was himself headed abroad in the next few weeks, he would check out this possibility himself, as well as put the word out on his network that Holly was missing.

When George Fencl relayed this to Pearce, the private investigator asked the inspector point blank: Would Ira Einhorn harm Holly

Maddux? Fencl said it was true that Ira Einhorn was a funny type of guy—he would write you a letter to set up a meeting and a week later walk in your office unannounced. But everyone knew that Ira Einhorn advocated and practiced nonviolence, and the police inspector had no evidence to the contrary.

On other fronts, Pearce did manage to speak to some people who had seen Holly in the period after she returned from Europe in August 1977 and before her disappearance approximately one month later. He placed a follow-up call to the Johnsons, caretakers of 3411 Race; they recalled seeing Holly in September, on the back porch of Ira's apartment. She looked glum, and did not give her usual enthusiastic greeting, but only waved weakly at the Johnsons. The Johnsons also noted that Ira had not once mentioned Holly in a conversation since she disappeared.

Another person who saw Holly in that period was the man who had sublet the Einhorn apartment during the summer of 1977, a guitarist named Rick Iannacone. Oddly, Iannacone was now living in the apartment building into which Holly Maddux had been scheduled to move after leaving Ira Einhorn. An intense man in his twenties, Rick was thin and dark-haired, and spoke in bebop cadences. At first he was a bit shaken when J. R. Pearce, a serious man in a suit and tie, approached him and identified himself as an ex-FBI man working for Holly's parents. He had a sudden feeling that all of this was an invasion of Holly Maddux's privacy. "Man," he said, "the woman just doesn't want to be found, it's that simple."

Pearce bore down. "We suspect foul play," he told him, laying out the suspicious details of the case. This speech convinced Rick Iannacone to cooperate.

Iannacone explained how he had sublet the apartment. He had previously met Holly Maddux at the Ecology Food Co-op, and liked her. When he saw the leaflet advertising the sublet, with the hand-drawn picture of the apartment, he instantly sensed Holly's "vibe." When he went to the apartment to look it over, he was impressed with the feeling he got from it. He noticed a spider web in a corner and assumed it had survived not by the tenants' carelessness but by a respect for life that permeated the space. He promised Ira that he would maintain that spirit while he lived in the apartment, and believed that it was this vow that won him the subtenancy.

When Holly returned from Europe in August, Rick spotted her

in the co-op and sensed something different about her. She was almost glowing with energy. He invited her back to the apartment and they had a long conversation. Holly told him that she had been cured of diabetes while in London and felt terrific. There was a "new Holly." Rick was much moved by this tale of self-improvement and ceremoniously presented her with a bracelet of abalone to replace her Medic Alert bracelet. She told him she was moving to 3310 Race and mentioned that another building in the apartment might be vacant, a tip he later successfully pursued. The vibrations between them were strong, and Iannacone, apparently sensing a romantic opportunity, asked her about Ira. Holly said, "Ira can stay in Europe if he wants to."

But then he did not hear from Holly again. Ira appeared at Lerner Court in early September to announce his premature return, and Iannacone agreed to vacate early. Once at 3310 Race Street, he saw some mail for Holly in care of Genie Berman, the woman from whom Holly was to rent an apartment, but someone wrote DOES NOT LIVE HERE on the envelope and the mailman took it back. Rick Iannacone simply assumed Holly had taken off, and perhaps developed a medical problem because of her diabetes.

After many attempts to reach Genie Berman, a vivacious, earthy woman in her twenties, Pearce finally had a conversation with her. She confirmed that Holly arranged to rent her apartment, and Berman even gave her the keys so that Holly could take possession in late September, when Berman had planned to travel to Europe. "It really pissed me off," she said, when Holly didn't show up. But things had worked out, since Berman decided not to travel, after all. Then Berman mentioned something that tripped Pearce's investigative guy-wires—Holly had sent her a letter from Fire Island mentioning "some boy" she was seeing there. Could this be a person whom Holly had taken off with? He convinced Berman to hand over the letter, which was dated August 27:

Hi Genie,

I am having a wonderful time here—the ocean has revived me and everything I've brought to it, without fail. It has gotten to the point that I can give some of that back now, as I feel so good. So I spend a lot of time strolling and sitting in companionship with a blank rolling blue gray flat-bodied faceless expressive ocean, often in preference to

spending the time with people. Probably the first time such a relationship has been available to me, with water. Have also met a lovely
man, whom I enjoy so much and he me. So it's all nice here on Fire
Island.

I'm at this mailing address until the day after Labor Day. Would
you please drop me a line, catching me up on your plans and your
schedule, and tell me where you could leave the key and lease for me,
in case I don't get back to Philadelphia before you leave. I will call you
after Labor Day, so we can firm up all the loose ends.

It was now June 1978. Pearce was almost ready to gather his notes
and complete another long report for Stevens and the Madduxes,
but first he paid another visit to Beatrice and Joseph Einhorn, his
closest link to the prime source, and possibly the prime suspect, in
the Maddux case. Pearce showed Bea Einhorn the most recent picture he had of Holly—finally forwarded by Joyce Petschek—a color
shot of her taken on Fire Island. She was smiling in the picture, her
medium-length hair swept back in the wind, one strand falling over
her eyes. She looked content and rested, almost as if she had just
exhaled a breath of cool relief. When Bea Einhorn saw the picture,
she broke down and wept. "I love that girl," she told Pearce. Bea
Einhorn claimed that Holly cared for her, too, that Holly was even
closer to Mrs. Einhorn than to her own parents. She, too, suspected
something terrible had happened to Holly. Pearce turned to Joe
Einhorn and asked him, Was his son capable of foul play? Bea
Einhorn broke in and vigorously defended her son. Ira was not only
a genius—in fact this coming autumn he would be a teaching fellow
at the John F. Kennedy School of Government at Harvard University—but a pacifist who was constitutionally incapable of harm.
Why, he once had even scolded her for stepping on an ant! The fury
of this defense led Pearce to make the conciliatory admission that
he, too, had heard similar support of Einhorn. One person had
even called Ira a "pussycat." Bea Einhorn thought that a splendid
description.

Pearce asked if the Einhorns would forward Holly's possessions to
Tyler, Texas, and they agreed, contingent on the Madduxes' written
request. The emotional visit was over. As J. R. Pearce was leaving,
though, there was an exchange he thought noteworthy. He mentioned that Ira had told people that Holly had called him soon after
she disappeared, assuring Ira she was all right. Bea Einhorn said

that could not be the case. When Ira told *her* about Holly's sudden exit, he was "upset and crying," lamenting that "Holly has been gone for forty-eight hours and I don't know where she is." If Holly called Ira after that, it was news to Mrs. Einhorn.

On June 15, J. R. Pearce sent his report to Bob Stevens. He suggested that "the only logical thing left to do in Philadelphia" would be to get Holly's possessions and examine them for leads. Though Pearce was about to begin work on a different case, and would be unavailable for subsequent investigations for a while, he told Stevens that at the very least, he wanted to hear of any progress on the case. "It has gotten to be a personal interest to me," he wrote, "to locate her and find out what happened."

After conferring with the Madduxes, Stevens wrote Pearce back on July 12, asking for more investigation—to follow up on some previous leads, including the odd circumstance that had Ira's telephone number listed to a mysterious "Wynn Moore"; to help expedite the transfer of Holly's possessions; and to check the morgues outside of Philadelphia. Pearce's assistant, another former G-man named Clyde Olver, contacted fourteen hospitals and morgues in surrounding counties, with negative results.

As to the Wynn Moore puzzle, a few calls yielded the information that Moore was a radio talk show host for local station WWDB. Pearce himself showed up at the station at the end of Moore's morning shift, and got a skittish Moore to agree to a brief interview. Yes, he knew Einhorn, and years ago had made use of Ira's address and phone as a "mail drop," supposedly because Moore had been an investigative reporter and needed an alternative address. He had known Holly, but thought nothing of her disappearance. Certainly not the "foul play" Pearce suggested.

In mid-August, Bob Stevens, who had been trying for months to reach Joyce Petschek for an interview, called the Lansdowne Crescent house once more. Though he still could not reach Petschek, a servant did tell him the address of her house on Fire Island, and he asked Pearce to check out the area. Pearce sent Clyde Olver. Olver's visit to Fire Island was almost a year to the day after Holly Maddux had left Petschek's house for the last time, and almost a year since anyone had seen Holly Maddux (besides possibly the bank teller, whose claim was becoming less and less credible).

One late afternoon in the waning days of summer, Olver took the twenty-minute ferry ride from Bay Shore, Long Island, to Saltaire, one of several small enclaves on the long, thin Fire Island. Motor vehicles, even taxis, are banned on Fire Island, but getting around was no problem: Saltaire was only three blocks wide and eighteen blocks long. Olver marveled at the rows of contemporary homes with sandy lawns, and the fact that they cost "as much as year-round residences in wealthy neighborhoods." Petschek's house, 207 West Walk, an unobtrusive saltbox on the west side of the village, was two blocks from the ocean and a block from the bay. The man who answered the door said he had rented the house from Petschek for the summer and knew nothing of Holly Maddux.

Olver showed Holly's picture to bartenders at the two local restaurants and people in the town general store. Holly had been a customer at the latter and had paid off Petschek's account at the store around Labor Day the previous year. The clerk referred him to a young man named Zebulon Ely, who was not on the island that day. Olver reached him by phone. Ely confirmed that he'd known Holly for about two and a half weeks last summer, speaking to her only occasionally; only twenty years old, he was more friendly with Joyce Petschek's children. Holly *had* told him, though, that she'd broken up with Ira Einhorn, and wanted nothing more to do with him. Apparently taking Ira's place was a man in his late thirties Ely knew only as "Saul." This fellow owned a boat and was a frequent visitor to the Petschek house. He and Holly obviously had been a couple.

Ely also told Olver about Andrija Puharich, the psychic organizer who was well known to Ira and Holly. Puharich had also disappeared recently, under equally mysterious circumstances. When Olver asked Ely who might know where Holly was, he provided four names: Joyce Petschek, Andrija Puharich, Ira Einhorn, and the mysterious "Saul."

The introduction of two new names put new life into the search for Holly Maddux. The private detectives, of course, were unaware of Dr. Puharich's colorful history, but were soon to learn of it, as well as another startling development: Puharich's three-story frame house in Ossining, New York, the headquarters for the mind-blowing experiments of the Space Kids, had burned down. The only fatality was a German shepherd dog who had been felled by smoke. The police had ruled the case arson.

Pearce dispatched Clyde Olver to look into the matter and see if there might be any possible connection to Holly Maddux's disappearance. The house on 87 Hawkes Avenue was empty: Puharich was long gone, rumored to be in Mexico. Talking to neighbors, Olver learned of strange doings at the Turkey Farm—people all over the world coming for unspecified, and possibly unnatural, experiments. Only one neighbor, though, could identify a picture of Holly, and he recalled seeing her two years ago. Finally, Olver tracked down three of the young people who had been living at the house before it burned. Since Puharich had left so suddenly after the fire, they felt abandoned, ill-treated by their mentor. Their ad hoc spokeswoman, Julie Moulden, a woman in her early twenties, said she'd only seen Holly once, about a year ago. She knew Ira Einhorn better, having attended Ira's lecture at the conference at Harvard in May 1977. She had also seen him recently: A day or two after the fire, Ira had appeared out of nowhere. He had been accompanied by an attractive blond woman named Mary. Einhorn had promised to recruit an investigative reporter to look into the cause of the fire.

Olver later contacted the arson investigator who had looked into the case for the Insurance Company of North America. The investigator had concluded that a would-be psychic researcher, spurned by Puharich, was the main suspect. This suspect had once left statements on Puharich's answering machine such as, "I don't know what's happening to me! I'm going crazy!" He had appeared at the Turkey Farm one day and demanded that everyone listen to his personal problems. One of these problems was, as he explained it, harassment by extraterrestrials.

The insurance investigator, of course, had closely examined the role of the house's owner, Dr. Andrija Puharich. His interview with Puharich on August 15 had been unusual, to say the least. Puharich's vitae seemed to check out—a medical doctor who had authored several books, an expert in paranormal phenomena. Puharich also provided information about his income, including a $10,000 grant from one Baron DePauli, a $15,000 advance from Dell for a book on the Tesla situation, $50,000 for movie rights to *Uri*, and between $50,000 and $70,000 for his busy lecture schedule (around a hundred appearances annually).

Despite these credentials, the investigator found Puharich's conversation fantastic. "It is noteworthy to mention," he wrote, "that

Puharich stated he has observed numerous UFOs and has communicated with extraterrestrial beings." Though Puharich confirmed the strange behavior by the rejected would-be researcher—the doctor had been in Los Angeles during the fire—he suggested that the fire might have been started by the Central Intelligence Agency. This would have been a "warning" to him because he had been circulating evidence of Soviet experiments in psychic warfare. Puharich spoke of sending reports to President Carter and Prime Minister Trudeau detailing how the Russians were sending ELF waves that were "softening people's brains." Obviously, if Puharich had actually torched his home, he would offer a more digestible alibi. "Despite the baroque tale spun by Dr. Puharich, we found nothing to implicate him or the occupants of his residence in the cause of the fire," wrote the investigator.

Nowhere in his labors, the investigator told Clyde Olver, did Holly Maddux's name come up.

It was now over a year since Holly Maddux had vanished, and the detectives were unable to provide Fred and Elizabeth Maddux with any solid information about the whereabouts of their daughter. No one had corroborated any of Gwendolyn Coleman's information, and her claim that she had seen Holly in February and March 1978 was therefore unconvincing. By now both Stevens and Pearce were convinced of two things: one, that Holly had met with foul play—their euphemism for indicating that she was dead—and two, that Ira Einhorn was, at the least, withholding key information. At most, he was responsible for the disappearance. But there was no strong evidence to back up this suspicion. As the case had progressed, Stevens and Pearce began feeling very deeply for the young woman they had never met. Conversely, they developed a silent contempt for Ira Einhorn. While working for the FBI during the sixties, both men had been active in bureau activities against subversives, and neither man had much liked the youth rebellion that shook the nation in that period. The fact that Ira Einhorn was now parading around in the war costume of the sixties—long hair, beard, dashiki—and *actually winning the approval of the Establishment* was galling to these career law enforcers. While they were struggling to find Ira Einhorn's former girlfriend, here was this former drug proselytizer not only flaunting his alternative existence but teaching at Harvard University! During Einhorn's Sun Day activities, the same period he had first refused to cooperate with the detectives, he had even been pictured in the newspapers as accepting a congratulations from Pennsylvania governor Milton Shapp!

Einhorn's attitude toward the investigation seemed cavalier. In early September 1978, J. R. Pearce once again requested an interview, solemnly suggesting that Holly might be dead. "Oh, God," said Ira over the telephone, but Pearce could not tell whether his tone conveyed exasperation or amazement. Pearce decided to use veiled threat on Einhorn: Nobody is accusing you of doing away with Holly, he said, but *you* were the last person to see her. Einhorn said that didn't concern him. He said he had no time to talk. Pearce asked about Holly's possessions, and Ira confirmed that he told his parents not to release them unless he "ordered" them to do so.

Pearce tried to extend the conversation, but Ira cut him off, saying he would prefer not to have to hang up on the detective. Pearce began another question. "Good-bye, Mr. Pearce," said Ira Einhorn.

"Can I ask you one question?" asked Pearce, hoping to ask the Unicorn what *his* opinion was of Holly's fate.

But Ira Einhorn had hung up.

It was not long after that the detectives decided to contact the Philadelphia police once more. Fortunately, J. R. Pearce had, in his FBI days, worked not only with Frank Rizzo but Mayor Rizzo's current police commissioner, Joseph O'Neill, and O'Neill's response to Pearce's memo of September 28, 1978, which detailed the case to date, was satisfying. Within ten days, Captain Donald Patterson agreed to immediately issue a missing persons flyer. In addition, he would assign someone to look into the disappearance of Holly Maddux.

Captain Patterson was chief of the Homicide Department.

The police issued the flyer in late October, and on November 8, after Pearce handed over copies of his reports to the police, Patterson assigned Detective Kenneth Curcio to the case. Coincidentally, that was the same day that Bob Stevens, in Tyler, Texas, had a breakthrough in his investigation: He finally reached the elusive Joyce Petschek.

In fact, he had been ready to leave for London that day to interview Mrs. Petschek. As a precaution, though, he had Fred Maddux call Lansdowne Crescent to ascertain whether or not she was in town. A maid told him Petschek was not in London but New York City, staying with a woman named Hilda Brown.

At 7:30 P.M. Stevens called the Brown residence and reached Joyce Petschek. He explained how important it was that he fly to New York to interview her. Joyce Petschek would have none of this. She claimed to have told Fred Maddux everything she already knew. She further stated that her talented friend, the transmedium Marshall Lever, had done a "reading" on Holly and resolved that she had gone to India. Whether this was for religious reasons or not, Joyce Petschek could not say. In any case, she would not submit to a personal interview.

Stevens persisted, but Joyce Petschek stood her ground, contending that Holly simply went off on her own. She saw no reason to worry about Holly's disappearance. Now hoping to at least get some information from the intransigent woman, Stevens asked her if she knew the person named "Saul," and had better luck. This, Petschek explained, was Saul Lapidus. Holly and Saul spent time together that August, and Holly took a trip on Saul's boat before she returned to Einhorn in Philadelphia. Petschek did admit that Saul, at least, had expressed worry when Holly vanished.

Stevens immediately dispatched this news to J. R. Pearce, who called the Philadelphia police to see if Detective Curcio could accompany Pearce to New York City to interview this important new lead. He was told that Curcio would not come with him, nor would the Philadelphia police request any aid from the New York police in attempting to answer the disappearance of Holly Maddux. This demurral was to characterize Detective Curcio's investigation. It turned out that Curcio was on one of the "four" squads, the four units that staffed Homicide on shifts—six days on, two days off. Every newly reported murder in Philadelphia was handled by the four squads, who worked on several cases at once and were not equipped for intense extended investigations; those were handled by an extra unit, called the "five squad." Since the Maddux case still looked, from a police perspective, like a missing persons situation, Curcio felt justified in concentrating on the indisputably dead people who came to his attention. The search for Holly Maddux would continue to be private, funded at $40 an hour plus expenses by Fred and Elizabeth Maddux.

On November 15, 1978, J. R. Pearce and Clyde Olver traveled to New York City. They headed for a five-story brownstone on the Upper West Side, home of Saul Lapidus. Lapidus, a tall, serenely handsome man in his mid-forties, greeted them in the vestibule of the building and sat down on a couch there while the detectives explained the purpose of their visit. Lapidus turned pale and trembling, and quickly suggested that this was a conversation best held in his apartment.

During the next five hours J. R. Pearce would learn more about Holly Maddux's disappearance than he had in the previous eight months.

Saul Lapidus was a businessman and dabbler in real estate who had done well enough to be partially at leisure even before reaching the age when an FBI man takes retirement. His apartment took up the fourth floor of the brownstone, an elegantly decorated space paneled in wood. Lapidus warned the detectives that he might "jump around" in his account, but basically he told them the following. In the summer of 1977, he shuttled back and forth between Manhattan and Fire Island, where his 26-foot sailboat was docked. One mid-August day, at the ferry stop, he ran into Joyce Petschek and Andrija Puharich. Both were well known to him. Petschek was a friend of his former wife, none other than Hilda Brown (at whose home Bob Stevens had reached Petschek). And Lapidus had once been an executive of Intelectron Corp., a medical technology company owned by Andrija Puharich. They chatted, and Petschek told Saul to drop by some night for dinner. A few days later, Lapidus did indeed visit 207 West Walk in Saltaire, and met Holly Maddux for the first time.

Saul Lapidus liked Holly and she felt the same. Soon they were taking walks on the beach, conversing deeply, and more. Holly told Saul all about herself, how she had healed her diabetes, and was getting stronger. She also told Saul about Ira Einhorn. The name was not unfamiliar to Lapidus, as Saul's former wife, Hilda Brown, once had had an affair with Einhorn. Holly said that she was ending her relationship with Einhorn, had already put a deposit on a new apartment. She seemed happy, exercising thirty minutes a day, meditating, eating health foods. But at some point in late August,

Ira Einhorn returned to the United States and began calling Holly, trying to rekindle the relationship. He even promised to father a child with her, a powerful inducement to the nurturing woman of thirty. These promises were mixed with threats of what he might do if she did not return.

It was then September; Joyce Petschek had left Fire Island, leaving her teenage daughter with Holly. Holly also had a guest of her own, a woman named Ruth Fink. After Labor Day, the idyll was over. Holly finally agreed to Ira's entreaties to see him in Philadelphia. First, she returned to New York City with Saul, where she stayed at his apartment for a couple of days. Her plan was to settle things with Ira, then return so she and Saul could take a leisurely boat trip, out into the ocean and then to Block Island, where Saul docked the boat for the winter. But when Holly returned from her two-day visit with Ira, she told Lapidus to postpone the boat trip. She needed to calm Ira down, to "get him off the wall." She explained to Saul that Ira had on occasion flown off the handle, hitting her and once physically throwing her out of the apartment.

Before Holly could return to Philadelphia, Ira, who somehow had obtained Lapidus' phone number, called and asked for Holly. It was around 9:30 P.M., September 9, 1977. Ira was insistent that Holly come to 3411 Race immediately. If she did not return he would heave her possessions into the street—all her clothes, all the antique lace she had purchased in England, and her bank books. Holly became upset. Is Ira prone to such violence? Lapidus wanted to know. Holly said he was. But she was still determined to take the boat trip with Lapidus. She called Ira back, made no progress calming him, and over the next two hours placed calls to several friends in Philadelphia to see if Ira could somehow be soothed. Unable to reach anyone who could do this, she felt forced to return to Philadelphia, promising Lapidus she would be back. "I don't know why this guy has been able to push my buttons for so long," she told Saul.

That was the last time he saw Holly Maddux.

After a few days had passed, Lapidus began calling Philadelphia to find out where Holly might be. He told Ruth Fink that he was thinking of notifying the police, alerting them to the possibility that Ira Einhorn had done something to Holly. Fink told him that the police knew Ira and considered him nonviolent. The police had even used Einhorn as a mediator in gang-war situations.

Around that time Andrija Puharich called. Dr. Puharich had lent Holly a manuscript of his unpublished book on the Space Kids and wanted to know if Saul had it. It turned out that Holly had left it on Lapidus' boat. Lapidus asked Puharich if he could call Einhorn to ask after Holly. Puharich agreed, and called back saying that everything was "cool." Ira and Holly had gotten back together, and Holly had just walked off. Lapidus believed that Holly would not have voluntarily gone away without telling him, but he had no proof to back up his suspicions. He finally let the matter drop, and only two weeks before Pearce's visit, had discarded some clothing that Holly Maddux had left at his apartment.

Pearce and Olver left New York City more confident than ever that they were investigating a homicide. In theory, the Philadelphia police department was also conducting a homicide inquiry, but since it was apparently of insufficient priority to free Detective Curcio from his other duties, the private detectives carried on their efforts. The next step was to check out the people whom Holly Maddux contacted on the night of September 9, when Ira Einhorn allegedly threatened to toss her clothes out on the street if she did not return.

According to Lapidus' phone bill, the first of these people was Ruth Fink, a pleasant, brown-haired mother of a small child. Ruth seemed more conventional than her friends Ira and Holly. She lived in a house in the Germantown section of Philadelphia with her husband, Ted, who had been a friend of Ira's since high school. Ted Fink, a passionate defender of his old buddy, was present for the interview. Ruth said that she had been out that night, and when she returned the babysitter told her that Holly had called. She had not returned the call.

But Ruth Fink provided other information. She confirmed that she had been with Holly on Fire Island, just prior to Labor Day, 1977. It was during the time that Holly was seeing Lapidus and Ira Einhorn was calling her. Ira's calls upset Holly, said Ruth Fink, and Holly would sometimes hang up in the middle of the conversation. Holly wanted to end the relationship, but something kept drawing her back to Ira. In Ruth's view, Holly was not totally sure about leaving Ira. She spoke as if she were finally free of Einhorn, but there was an element of bravado about it, almost as if Holly was trying to convince herself that this was true. Holly certainly liked Saul, but he did not appear to be the love of a lifetime for Holly.

Around the middle of September, Saul Lapidus called Ruth to see if she could find out what happened to Holly Maddux. Ruth contacted Ira, who told the tale of Holly's sudden departure. When Ruth relayed this to Saul, he was dubious. He told Ruth that Ira had been violent with Holly in the past. Ruth said Holly had never mentioned this to her, in all the years they had known each other. At most, she conceded, Ira might lose his temper and hit Holly—but kill her? Never.

Both Ted and Ruth Fink saw Holly as a person who reacted to a tough situation by walking out. She had done this many times in the past—Holly and Ira were always breaking up and reuniting. Maybe Holly was in a commune, Ruth guessed, or maybe she had found someone new. When Ira said that Holly contacted him and told him not to follow her, both Ruth and Ted Fink believed him.

A less sanguine view was offered by Walt Bowker, another person whom Holly called from Saul Lapidus' on the night of September 9. Bowker, an architect, was one of the Synergy Group centered around South Street. When Pearce and Olver visited Bowker, he told them that while Holly was a beautiful person, Ira's behavior to her was atrocious. Ira would put her down in public. In 1977, it was clear that Holly was about to leave Ira, yet he still wouldn't change. It was no wonder that Holly had "had enough of this." While Bowker could not recall Holly's phone call on September 9, he had heard of her returning from Fire Island to see Ira and then vanishing. The length of her absence, and her failure to contact anyone, made Bowker suspicious, and he had even "flashed" on the possibility that Ira could have harmed her. This, even though he had known Ira to be violent only in words, not action.

The other Philadelphia phone number on Lapidus' bill belonged to Curtis Kubiak. This was the architect and former Boo Hoo of the LSD-centered Neo-American Church with whom Ira had been friendly since Free University days. When Pearce called the number, Curt's wife Barbara answered. She immediately understood which phone call Pearce referred to—she had taken the call herself. Barbara Kubiak had been familiar with the surges and eddies in the Einhorn-Maddux relationship, so it was probably no surprise that Holly was complaining about Ira "hassling" her. Specifically, Holly

wanted Curt to go to 3411 Race Street and retrieve her possessions—something Holly did not want to do herself. Referring to her
dilemma with Lapidus in New York and Ira in Philadelphia, Holly
said that she "didn't know how to deal with two people at the same
time." Since Curt was not home, Barbara had referred Holly to Walt
Bowker.

Apparently Holly's attempt to have someone else clear her things
out of the apartment was unsuccessful, because she was in Philadelphia the next day. In fact, the Kubiaks double-dated with Ira and
Holly that weekend.

Pearce tried to get Barbara to agree to a personal interview, but
she backed off, saying she felt "funny" talking about these things.
She would ask her husband. Over the next couple of weeks, Pearce
persisted, and finally, on December 12, Curt Kubiak agreed to be
interviewed.

Since Curt Kubiak and Ira Einhorn had been close friends for
years, Kubiak had been wary about talking to the detectives, especially since they were former FBI men—not an endearing credential to the former LSD priest. For part of the conversation he tried to
draw the detectives into a discussion of the FBI's role in suppressing
radicals in the sixties. Pearce assured him that neither he nor Olver
personally suppressed any radicals in those days, and shifted the
focus to the more salient subject matter of Holly Maddux's disappearance—or murder. By now, Pearce's interviews were focused
primarily on extracting incriminating information about Ira
Einhorn. Much of the time in Kubiak's duplex home in the working-
class area of Kensington was spent with Pearce and Olver bombarding Kubiak with the damaging evidence they had gathered so far.
At one point, when Kubiak repeated Ira's contention that Einhorn
had told the police what he knew, Pearce contended that the asser-
tion was "a load of crap," a self-serving "cop-out" on Einhorn's part.
This had its effect, as Kubiak eventually admitted that he "trusted"
the detectives, though he did not know why.

An obvious explanation for this sudden turnabout is that Kubiak
had come to distrust his friend Ira Einhorn but had not yet come to
grips with this fact. As he spoke, though, his attitude became clear.
In his view, Ira's positive acts in the sixties had recently been overwhelmed by his interest in the paranormal. He had become a "psychic fascist." The other reservation he had about Ira was Einhorn's

behavior toward Holly. Ira was an "egotistical bastard" who verbally abused Holly.

Yet when it came to accusing Ira of harming Holly physically, Kubiak's feelings were scrambled. He had never seen Ira physically violent, and never saw any bruises on Holly. And the last time he saw the pair together, when they double-dated on the night before Holly's disappearance, things seemed fine. Ira and Holly had even joked about Holly's panic-stricken call to the Kubiaks on September 9. Since Holly disappeared, Ira had not manifested any guilt that would indicate he was responsible. While Kubiak was concerned about Holly, and admittedly suspicious of Ira's story, he concluded that there was no proof that Ira Einhorn did anything to Holly Maddux. Just feelings.

Not long before the Kubiak interview, Joe and Bea Einhorn finally had turned over Holly's possessions to J. R. Pearce. In a letter to the Madduxes accompanying the first shipment of clothes, books, and letters—none of which provided information of significant import to the investigation—J. R. Pearce summed up the most recent developments. He concluded with these paragraphs:

> I am sorry if I cannot give you any specific information as to what has happened to Holly. To express any opinion would simply be conveying my personal feelings. Before this is over, Ira Einhorn has to make some explanation. Factually, the indications are that he did not want Holly to leave him, and Holly has told a lot of people that she was desirous of leaving Ira. On the other hand, she returned to Philadelphia, went to his apartment, and went on a double date to a movie with Barbara and Curtis Kubiak and Ira on the night before she disappeared.
>
> Whether Holly voluntarily left to get away from Ira or whether Ira has harmed her is not known at this time. We have not found anyone who knows Ira who describes him as a violent person who would be capable of taking Holly's life. Opinions among my associates are about fifty-fifty, i.e., something has happened to Holly, or she has taken off on her free will, and will show up again when she thinks her problems have been handled.
>
> Our investigation should be completed in the near future and it would appear we have done all we can do in Philadelphia.

Pearce was being extra cautious—he and Stevens both believed strongly by this time that Holly Maddux was dead, and that Ira

Einhorn was the culprit. The next, and what was to be the last, major phase of his investigation would only fortify that suspicion.

Pearce's final investigating would be a return to the scene of the alleged crime.

In December 1978, J. R. Pearce began searching for tenants who had been living at 3411 Race Street at the time of Holly Maddux's disappearance. Since most residents of the building were Drexel students who often leased for a year or less, this was no simple task. With the help of superintendent Harold Johnson, though, he was able to locate some.

The student who had lived in the adjoining apartment on the second floor had no information about Holly and suggested Pearce talk to James Jafolla, who still lived in the building. On the evening of December 6, Clyde Olver visited Jafolla, who lived in the first-floor front apartment. Ira Einhorn was presumably at Harvard and not in the building that day. Jafolla was a physics student working for his doctorate at Drexel; he knew Einhorn and Holly Maddux by sight but never spoke much to either.

The only story Jafolla had to tell of Ira was something that had occurred the previous September. The landlord had ordered work to be done on the area of Einhorn's porch. Ira, in town for a few days between his summer vacation and his Harvard residence, specifically instructed the repairmen not to go near the closet on his porch. When Jafolla, helping out, moved plants and furniture from Ira's porch to expedite the work, he noticed that the closet was locked with a padlock. He had no idea what was in the closet.

J. R. Pearce asked Harold Johnson about this work project and was told that Ira Einhorn had been very sensitive about the project and was emphatic about not having the closet tampered with.

And then Harold Johnson told J. R. Pearce about the problem with the screened-in porch in the rear of Ira Einhorn's apartment.

Some months ago, the tenant below Einhorn had complained of an odor that seemed to be coming from the porch of the second-floor rear apartment. No amount of deodorizing chemicals could eliminate the smell. Johnson had called a roofer to check this out. Johnson could not remember the specifics, but ultimately, no one could figure out the odor's origin. The smell faded, and porch work was done in September to fix possible leaks. Ira Einhorn had been, as Johnson recalled, relieved that his closet did not have to be disturbed.

The owner of the building, Norman Lerner, confirmed that Einhorn had complained about the porch repairs and had specified that the roofers not disturb his things. Lerner, used to Einhorn's demands for privacy, did not think that request unusual. What he did consider odd, though, was that during the previous summer, 1978, Ira Einhorn did not sublet his apartment when he left town. This was the first time in Einhorn's seven-year residence that he failed to do so.

The roofer, John Paulmerio, told Pearce that the roof over the porch had originally been tarred in early 1977. About a year later, he received the complaint about the odor. Thinking it may well have been stagnant water that had leaked in through a fault in the tar, he sent an employee, Frank Bucciarelli, to look things over. Paulmerio's firm retarred the roof in September 1978.

Frank Bucciarelli recalled checking out the foul smell in the winter of 1977–1978. He said that it may or may not have been stagnant water. He had no idea where the odor originated. Since he had never smelled a decaying human body, he told Pearce, he could not identify the smell as such.

J. R. Pearce was friendly with a nearby undertaker, who told him that a human corpse can begin decomposing after as little as two warm days. (Cold weather delays the process.) As Pearce wrote in his report, "the odor is such that it even permeates your hair and clothing."

Pearce's investigation was now proceeding with an ominous inevitability. It was no surprise, but grim confirmation, when the following story emerged, pieced together from interviews of the visitors and inhabitants of the first-floor rear apartment—directly under the apartment of Ira Einhorn.

Two Drexel students, Paul Herre and Ron Gelzer, had rented the apartment in June 1977. Both attended summer session and were about to enter their senior years. After Labor Day, Paul Herre remained in Philadelphia to clean the apartment in preparation for the fall term. He left around September 20 to attend his sister's wedding. Gelzer was in the Powelton Village apartment that weekend. It was he who first noticed the odor. It came from the kitchen, apparently from the closet. Ron Gelzer was a biology student, and his first impression was that it was something that "smelled like blood." Decaying blood. Whatever it was, it was terrible. He ventured into the closet and lifted a transom in the ceiling, and saw what looked like water. Then he went into the backyard to determine what was directly over his closet on the floor above. It was Ira Einhorn's porch. Gelzer approached Einhorn and asked him if he knew of a leak, and Ira Einhorn, unperturbed, said he knew of none.

When Paul Herre returned from the wedding on September 26, he immediately noticed a "gross" smell. As he walked through the living room and into the kitchen the odor became overwhelming, an organic stench stronger and even less tolerable than that of human excrement. Herre went to the Johnsons, who told him that they were suffering from the smell, too—it had insinuated itself into their kitchen and was so offensive that they couldn't eat there. They promised to reimburse him if he cleaned up the odor himself.

Accompanied by Stephanie DeMarco, a friend of both Drexel students, and armed with several cleaning agents, Paul Herre once again ventured into his kitchen, an act requiring a strong stomach. DeMarco was sickened by the smell, which she said, only half jokingly, was like that of a dead body. Paul Herre, mustering up the strength to go into the kitchen closet, did not appreciate the statement, though in later weeks he would scoff at its silliness. Ignoring the stench as best he could, he looked up into the closet—on the top was the transom that he pulled open. In the space between the first and second floor, he could see a brownish stain had come through a crack in the ceiling plaster. It had almost dried, but looked slightly damp. It was obviously the source of the odor.

He washed the area down with ammonia, then other cleaning agents, but after everything dried up, the odor persisted. Then he tried stronger agents—Lysol, pure Clorox bleach. That did not kill the odor completely. Finally, he painted the area to try to seal the odor into the plaster and stuffed the area with Super Odor-Eaters. That seemed to work until a month or two later when heavy rain fell and the ceiling began to leak. The odor returned, and he had to repeat the entire process. Eventually, the odor faded. But as long as Herre and Gelzer lived in the apartment—they had moved out the following spring—they had to stuff the area with Odor-Eaters, and even then one could detect a foul odor near the closet.

The Johnsons' explanation was that it was rotting wood. Herre thought it might have been a dead squirrel caught between the floors. While he lived in the apartment, he never found out what it was. At one point, he even went outside with a tape measure to determine exactly what was overhead of his kitchen closet. It was the closet on Ira Einhorn's screened-in porch.

At this point, J. R. Pearce knew that he was reaching the limits of what a private investigator could do. His interest now was in alerting the police to the degree to which the case had progressed. On first developing the information regarding the odor, he had contacted Detective Curcio, who was not in at the time. Two days later, Pearce called Curcio's lieutenant and told him of the breakthrough. Two days after that, Curcio was finally contacted and told that Pearce would soon hand over his latest report. They discussed whether there might be probable cause to draw a search warrant for Ira Einhorn's apartment.

Supplementing Pearce's report was a four-page summary entitled "Information Possible Circumstantial Evidence" [sic]. More than an outline of the findings to date, it was a cogently constructed argument that Ira Einhorn was the probable cause of Holly Maddux's disappearance.

It turned on contradictions in Einhorn's argument. There was the Unicorn's contention that Holly's disappearance was no worrying matter. Pearce emphasized the unnatural circumstances—Holly's formerly faithful correspondence with family, particularly at Christmastime. (The Madduxes had just spent the second Christmas with no word of their daughter.) Meanwhile, Holly's bank account, with well over $20,000 in it, had been untouched. "QUESTION: If MADDUX had not met foul play," Pearce wrote, "why has she not withdrawn any of this money considering the fact that there is no history of her having any regular employment."

Einhorn told several people that he checked everywhere for Holly after she vanished, yet of all the people Pearce spoke to, only one said Ira asked about Holly. Ira had not inquired about Holly's whereabouts to the Kubiaks, the Finks, or the Johnsons. He did not call Saul Lapidus, a likely escape route for Holly. Ira had not even asked about her at the Ecology Food Co-op, Holly's presumed destination when she walked out his door. "If IRA made effort to locate

HOLLY after she left to go to the store," Pearce wrote, "why had he not inquired if she came to the food co-op?"

Ira insisted several times that Holly phoned him shortly after she left and assured him she was safe. Yet his own parents described him "upset and crying" upon her disappearance—behavior which, according to his friends, was drastically uncharacteristic. Pearce asked: "Again, the question is, 'Was IRA EINHORN on this occasion "hysterical and crying" because he had harmed HOLLY MADDUX?' There is no report that he was this upset over her previous departures."

Then there was Ron Gelzer's story. (Pearce had not yet talked to Herre or DeMarco.) "QUESTION: Were the leaks and the resulting odor in RON GELZER's apartment caused by EINHORN attempting to wash away evidence of attack on HOLLY MADDUX?"

On January 3, 1979, Pearce handed his report to Captain Patterson of Homicide, and to Pearce's satisfaction, Patterson remarked that in order to build a case against Einhorn, the police would use the information as a guide for their own interviewing, to build a case for a search warrant. The next day, Pearce met with Curcio. The meeting was away from the office, so the two could discuss the case without interruption. Pearce made specific suggestions to Curcio as to what he should nail down: the dates of the odor, witnesses who might have seen or heard something around September 12. He also suggested that Curcio interview Saul Lapidus immediately, something on which Pearce himself followed up the next day. Lapidus agreed to come to Philadelphia and spontaneously volunteered to take a polygraph test. This pleased Pearce considerably. "It works to our advantage," he wrote in a letter to Bob Stevens. "Eliminating Saul as a suspect, and the other . . . investigations, are all targeted towards proving Ira Einhorn's previous statements false, and also taking away his possible defense, if and when he is questioned."

Even though Pearce assumed that he would participate only slightly from that point on, it was he who carried on the next stage of the investigation. In January and February, Pearce—not Curcio—conducted the interviews of Herre and DeMarco, and Pearce revisited the Ecology Food Co-op to confirm that Einhorn did not ask about Holly. Pearce also sat in on Lapidus' polygraph test, conducted by Philadelphia policewoman Dianne Riley. Lapidus' test indicated that his story was reliable.

In late February, Pearce met with Joseph Murray, the chief district attorney of the homicide division. Murray was yet another Philadelphia official with whom Pearce had worked previously. Months before, when Pearce first began hounding the Philadelphia police to do something about Ira Einhorn, Murray had thought Pearce something of a crackpot, but by January, when Murray had been given Pearce's reports, the prosecutor was convinced. At a lunch at Wanamaker's the two had discussed what evidence should be presented to get probable cause for a search warrant of Ira Einhorn's apartment. With luck, some of the floorboards in Einhorn's closet would show evidence that Holly Maddux's body had been there in September 1977. "The search, if successful," wrote Pearce in his account of the first meeting with Murray, "could lead to the break to obtain a confession from IRA EINHORN, if he is guilty." In this second meeting with Murray, in February, the district attorney said he had requested that Detective Kenneth Curcio, the policeman assigned to the case, be assigned to a regular day shift to conduct the interviewing that could lead to a search warrant.

A few days later, Pearce sent yet another report to Curcio. In early March, Pearce twice tried to reach Curcio so the detective could accept Liz Maddux's statement about Einhorn's phone conversations—something Joe Murray had requested—but, as Pearce wrote, "efforts to reach Detective Curcio were unsuccessful."

Neither Bob Stevens nor J. R. Pearce has ever claimed that Kenneth Curcio was derelict in his duties. As a member of one of the four squads, his time was consumed by the pressing need to investigate fresh homicides. But official attention seemed essential now, and Pearce arranged a meeting with Commissioner O'Neill on March 7, 1979. Specifically, Pearce was worried that the Drexel students, Herre and Gelzer, would graduate and be gone by the time Detective Kenneth Curcio could clear the time to interview them. Pearce had outlined the situation to O'Neill, and the next day O'Neill had J. R. Pearce return to the Roundhouse once more to meet the new detective on the case, Michael J. Chitwood.

Detective Chitwood was a controversial figure in Philadelphia. A slim man of surprising strength—he stood 6 feet 1 inch while weighing only 170—he had earned the reputation in nearly two decades of service as the local version of "Dirty Harry," a man cited as a brutal inquisitor of homicide suspects by a Pulitzer Prize–winning *Phila-*

delphia Inquirer series. (Chitwood thought this ironic since, in violation of department regulations, he refused to carry a gun.) No
charges were ever formally brought against Chitwood, though his
reputation suffered. For a bleak period after the press attacks, he was
removed from Homicide Division. But his diligence and intelligence
surfaced, as his subsequent yeoman work in hostage negotiation
transformed his public reputation from goon to hero. The Einhorn
case was the first homicide investigation Chitwood had been handed
in a long time, and he approached it with relish.

Mike Chitwood quickly realized that the reports from Stevens and
Pearce were a gold mine. He read them with enthusiasm and
wonder—he thought it unfolded like an Alfred Hitchcock movie.
He couldn't believe that West detectives had originally treated this
like a missing persons case, giving it only cursory attention. When
he finished reading, he had no doubts about Ira Einhorn's role in
the case: "This guy did it," he said to himself. "*This guy did it.*"

Chitwood's job was to officially verify the Pearce information so a
search warrant might be drawn. He was assigned to the case full-
time. In two and a half weeks, he reached the key witnesses that it
had taken Stevens and Pearce over a year to track down. Beginning
with Detective Lane, who had first interviewed Einhorn on the
missing persons case in 1977, and on to Mrs. Maddux, the bank
manager, the food co-op workers, the Johnsons, Genie Berman,
Rick Iannacone, Ruth Fink, the Kubiaks, Ira's landlord, the roofers,
and Ira Einhorn's neighbors who detected the horrible smell, Chitwood retrod the turf first traversed by the private detectives—
ground on which a clear path was now visible. Sometimes new
information tumbled out. For instance, Paul Herre, who had lived
in the apartment below Ira Einhorn's, recalled that he heard sometime in that autumn of 1977 a very loud thumping on the ceiling of
his apartment—like "somebody being bounced against the floor."
This was instantly followed by a "blood-curdling scream." To his
eternal regret, Paul Herre had not done anything about it at the
time—the noise had stopped and he had simply let the matter drop.
But now, for obvious reasons, Herre thought the incident worthy of
mention.

Chitwood also visited Halbert Fillinger, the city coroner, to ask
him about the decomposition process of human corpses. After
briefing Fillinger on the case and discussing various forensic possi-

bilities, Fillinger told him, "When you go to Einhorn's apartment, you're going to find a body there." Chitwood said no way. "Our goal is to get a search warrant, get in there, have the lab technicians tear up the floor and the walls, and take all this stuff," he said. Toward that end, and working with Joe Murray, Chitwood compiled his evidence and finally typed up a thirty-five-page search warrant, loaded with information from his interviews. On March 28, 1979, less than three weeks after having been handed the case, Michael Chitwood gathered a team for a morning's work. It included Chitwood, Captain Patterson, three men from the Mobile Crime Unit, and two technicians from the chemical laboratory. They were armed with crowbars, power tools, cameras, and a warrant signed by Judge Lynn Abraham. At about ten of nine, they rang Ira Einhorn's buzzer.

Seventy minutes later, J. R. Pearce received a phone call. As he later wrote in his mop-up report, the call informed him that "the police had found a body in the trunk in a closet at the apartment of IRA EINHORN, 3411 Race Street, Philadelphia, PA." Pearce arrived on the scene an hour later, witnessing the end of his year-long investigation. Later in the day, Bob Stevens in Tyler received the news and made the painful visit to the Maddux household to tell them the news that they had long dreaded. Then Stevens drove to the office of the late Holly Maddux's dentist, to retrieve the dental records that would verify the body found in Ira Einhorn's closet was indeed Holly Maddux's.

10

"I DIDN'T KILL HER"

When Ira Einhorn was released on bail after his arrest for the murder of Holly Maddux, he attacked the problem at first with the same vigor that he would direct to one of the perpetual global crises he dealt with on his network. This was a *project,* as was the Geller publicity campaign, or Sun Week, or his more recent offensive in alerting the world about the dangers of the Tesla effect.

One component of an effort like this of course is romancing the press. Judging from the skepticism of some of the newspaper articles written since his arrest, Ira had to conclude two brief jailhouse interviews had been insufficient in asserting his innocence. So within forty-eight hours after leaving the Detention Center, Ira was presenting a lengthier version of events to Greg Walter, a *Philadelphia Magazine* reporter who had told Ira he might coauthor his story with Gaeton Fonzi, Greg's colleague and Ira's long-time friend. Walter had called Einhorn on the very night Ira had been released on bail. "It's a *mess,*" said Ira of his situation. He spoke very quickly but sounded far from hysterical. The unspoken assumption in the conversation was Einhorn's innocence. "If I were guilty it would be a lot easier," said the Unicorn. "I could plead insanity or something of that sort, but since I'm innocent it's an impossible situation."

Walter asked Ira how he was bearing this ordeal.

"I am fine," said Ira Einhorn. "Believe it or not, my spirit is very high and I'm feeling very good. I'm looking at my situation as clearly as I possibly can. I'm not depressed in any way. I'm just looking at my options."

They agreed to meet the next day, and on the morning of April 4, 1979, Ira Einhorn conducted the interview at his temporary quarters, Stuart Samuels' apartment. Samuels was the Penn instructor of film studies who had viewed the movie *Hair* with Ira on the night before Ira's apartment had been searched. Einhorn had accepted Samuels' offer to stay at his penthouse in the Alden Park Manor, a luxury building past its prime in the Germantown area of Philadelphia. Ira slept in the living room, a vast, well-lit sunken area with a two-story cathedral ceiling. Without consent of his lawyer Arlen Specter, Ira freely discussed details of the case as he understood it. When Walters would apologize for asking a sensitive question, Ira would assure him that it was all right. "I'm not flinching from anything, my friend," he said. "I can't."

They began by talking about Holly's disappearance. Ira told the same story he had related to others, more or less, since September 1977. On Sunday, September 11, Holly Maddux had left 3411 Race Street, saying she was going to the Ecology Food Co-op. When she did not return, Ira became worried, particularly because Holly was a diabetic who had recently sworn off her medication.

Late in the afternoon, when she didn't come back from the co-op, I called the co-op and asked if Holly was there. Because she so often went to the co-op and spent hours. I was in the bathtub when she left. So, I called the co-op and they said—I don't remember what they said, but that she wasn't there when I called . . .

I put the word out. . . . I told a couple of people who I knew would spread the word around rather than my making a million phone calls. . . . I certainly spoke to the Finks and the Kubiaks . . .

I know I called, by that evening, most of the hospitals and I spoke to. . . . I either spoke to a lawyer or somebody from the police department about filing a missing persons thing. And what I was told was "don't bother." That they don't do anything.

Three or four days later, Ira said, around Tuesday, September 13, he received a phone call from Holly.

She just told me that she was okay, please don't look for her, and that she would get back to me, that she would keep in touch, that's what I extracted from her. I said, "Please call me in a week," she said, I'll keep in touch, something to that effect. I certainly don't remember the exact words. And that's the last I heard from her. . . .

I have a tendency in situations like this, because Holly had disappeared before, to be rather cool about it; she was under an enormous amount of pressure because there was another man involved. There was somebody else she was seeing in New York . . . Saul Lapidus. . . . She had just started to see him. It was a new relationship she had begun at the end of her stay, as far as I know, at Fire Island.

Holly would pick up with people instantly. She was very insecure. Extremely beautiful but very insecure, so she would pick up with people very quickly. And she was also, I'm sure, very pissed off at me. . . .

My feeling was that she had made a decision . . . most of my actions at this point were controlled by two things: One was a phone call from her mother which cooled me out . . . about a month after Holly disappeared. It must have been October. I remember the conversation very carefully because I was very, still very upset. . . . She called me, I would never call her. We don't get along. She called me and said, "We haven't heard from Holly since the beginning of August," or something of that sort. And I said, "No, I've seen her since then." . . . And then we went back and forth, and I said "I'm upset about it, but I don't quite know what to do." And her mother said, "Holly is an adult. She's thirty-one years old, she's old enough to make her own decisions." And I said it's good to hear that. I said I'm feeling very responsible but I don't quite know what to do. And that was it.

Ira's explanation contradicted J. R. Pearce's discoveries on several points. Neither the Kubiaks nor the Finks recalled Ira phoning them in search of Holly. Nor did people at the Ecology Co-op. And Ira's parents said that when he told of Holly's disappearance, he was not "cool," but hysterical. Ira never mentioned Holly's phone call to them. Finally, Elizabeth Maddux's recollection of her conversation with Ira did not include her alleged reassurance that Holly was an adult and can make her own decisions. But Ira had his own things to say—and not for the last time—about the Maddux family of Tyler, Texas.

I'm really tempted to just blast back because they present this picture of this absolutely sweet, secure, incredible family. I was there once and I saw Holly get up from the table and burst into tears because of the incredible way in which the father ruled. He's a tyrant. In fact the mother had told Holly, "Don't ever get involved in a relationship like that." I mean, as if she'd shifted that to me, which is very possible, that she was acting toward me. In fact a lot of what I said to her often, "I'm not your father." I had to keep reminding her.

I'm a very powerful personality. So that even if I would want to be like this, Holly would act with great dependence toward me. . . . But the family is being painted in this incredibly white terms when it is just . . . just crazy. I mean anybody realizing, even if it's a joke, flying SS symbols and having FUHRER [on the license plate] for the last eight years as far as I know. They have three Mercedes. I saw them when I was in the house, he has all the old license plates, he has them hanging in his garage.

Ira used his antagonistic standing with the Madduxes to help explain why he did not cooperate with the family's efforts to search for Holly. These had begun when Lawrence Wells called Ira in November, and Ira took offense at Wells' questions about Holly's bank account. (Later, Wells would deny probing Einhorn on that matter.) To quell that attack, Ira now explained, he personally looked into it, getting somebody to "break the computer code and get into the bank and find out" how much money was in the account, finally giving Wells an accurate report of around $21,000. (How this presumably illegal computer break-in was accomplished Ira did not say.) Ira was furious at having to defend himself against such an accusation.

I was turned off on the parents to begin with and that just did it, 'cause that's totally . . . I mean, I supported the woman for five years, and money has never been an important part of my life. I'm not somebody who has ever lived high, ever. I'm friendly with some of the wealthiest people in the world . . . but it doesn't mean very much to me, that's not my trip.

Ira explained that he had no quarrel with *official* efforts to find Holly—he cooperated when Detective Lane came to his home in late 1977, and later when George Fencl came by—but he wanted nothing to do with investigations controlled by Holly's parents.

I think it was Mr. Stevens came to town and said, "I came into town especially to see you." I was very, very busy—this was in the middle of Sun Week—about March of '78. So Stevens arrives on the scene, he calls me and said he came specifically to see me. . . . And then he tried to get to see me and I said "No." I said I'm not going to cooperate with the family. I said it's been too long, and Holly's made a decision. . . . I said, "I have nothing against you, but I have no intention of cooperating with the family." And I maintained that. I didn't tell anybody not to talk to the police, or thwart anybody, and I think the record will show that. If the record shows anything else I'd like to confront that situation, because I did not in any way *make any attempt to obstruct. I just decided not to cooperate with the family.*

Ira described the search of his apartment, and explained why he had been careful about protecting the contents of the closet in which Holly Maddux's corpse was found. The closet, as far as he knew, held no evidence of a murder, but secret papers concerning psychic warfare.

I'm increasingly a recipient of things that are frightening in terms of psychic warfare and things of that sort and some of it—I've been circulating a lot of it—but I get stuff that only two or three people should see. It's like the argument the government has just had in The Progressive *magazine, of publishing the atomic bomb plans. I'm getting the equivalent at times of things that are that devastating—only they're invisible. It's like this radioactivity that everybody was afraid of. Only when somebody's operating on your mind, there are very few people sophisticated enough to know that something is happening. They would think of it as some sort of physical complaint. So what I decided, I was lecturing one night and made a joke and said, "My God. The stuff I have on my back porch is stuff that the CIA would kill for in a couple of years." And I went home that night and I thought, Jesus Christ, what did I just say? Think about that. So I eventually went out and I bought a way of giving minimal protection. . . .*

I bought the trunk . . . Jesus Christ when did I buy it?—I bought the trunk after I got back from London. It would be around the time when Holly disappeared.

Jesus Christ, all these things look so wonderful for me.

I bought the trunk about the time Holly disappeared. I do not in any way know the exact dates. . . . I can remember calling lots of people about checking on prices and things. . . . I think it was someplace on Frankford Avenue. That will come to me I'm sure. It was not a big event in my life, buying a trunk. . . . I could probably pretty accurately pinpoint the place once I spend some time meditating on it and looking at the Yellow Pages. But I remember making a series of calls. To get a trunk and to find prices, things of that sort . . .

I didn't padlock the closet until a year later . . . the summer of '78. Once again, I was away, I knew I was going to be away for six months. I knew I was going to be in and out, and I knew I had enough money to maintain the apartment. So instead of subletting, I kept the apartment. So whenever I was in Philadelphia, I had access, my work was on my desk . . .

Let me explain to you my procedure. When I go away for the summer I very quickly pack up. It takes a day to pack up the apartment. Because we're subletting. I clear my desk, we just pack everything away and put it in the back closet and in the last four years, of course, I did that with Holly. . . . We went to London in the summer of '77 and everything went into the back closet. My procedure when I came back from the summer [was] to spend a day or so going through things, throwing them away, straightening out papers— and also refreshing what I had out there 'cause I often got requests for past papers most of the time which I wouldn't fulfill because I was so busy, but I'd like to know what I had out there. And that's what I did [in 1978]. I obviously went through a whole series of papers, decided which ones were dangerous, put them in the trunk, and just stored it back there. . . .

Then Ira got to what he considered "the crazy part of the story." It began with Ira's companion in the so-called psychic mafia, Andrija Puharich. According to Puharich, the arson of his Ossining home had been caused by the CIA, which took a dim view of the Space Kids experiments, particularly Puharich's habit of having the young psychics monitor the Pentagon, the White House, and the Kremlin by means of remote viewing. Puharich had recently sent Einhorn a letter saying that intelligence agencies had been spreading a rumor that Ira had killed Holly. (The possibility that these "agents" may have been J. R. Pearce and associates, who while investigating Holly's disappearance frequently identified themselves as FBI men, was something Ira did not consider here.) Ira's guess was that those rumors were part of an effort to stop his crusade of soliciting and spreading information about U.S. and Soviet involvement in psychic warfare. Einhorn claimed he was among the world vanguard in circulating information regarding Tesla technology—used in various ways from Soviet jamming techniques known as the "Russian Woodpecker," to ELF transmissions clouding minds in Timmons, Ontario, even in Russian efforts to control the weather! Ira had not only distributed dispatches on his network about this but had written an article in *Co-Evolution Quarterly* (a magazine founded by Stewart Brand of the *Whole Earth Catalog*) about the Tesla stuff, warning of a "psychic Pearl Harbor." Then there was his recent trip to Yugoslavia, paid for, Ira said, by the Yugoslavian government, which provided him high-level access to their Tesla files. All of this technology was, Ira insisted to the dumbfounded Greg Walter, potentially as dangerous as nuclear weapons. And, as far as Ira could see, his involvement in this might have triggered his present dilemma. A dilemma made more confounding by the fact that its origins were so fantastic—and difficult to verify—that the explanation seemed absurd in terms of a murder alibi.

That's the only thing I can speculate . . . that from our point of view we're dealing with a weapons system that we have no defenses against. That would be the last thing that the CIA—or anyone in the military establishment—would even want us to breathe *about . . . that's only my speculation—but what do you do with that? So I keep putting it out of my mind. . . . I'm not thinking so much about the political implications—it's the fact that I'm facing a trial. I mean,* what will go in court? *. . . What can we say? All we can do in public right now is protest my innocence, which seems rather vacant. I can't come out and point at the CIA. I mean, that'd be crazy. . . .*

"What are you going to do?" Greg Walter asked Ira.

I don't know, I really don't know. . . . I'm in a tough situation. I know that. My life is at stake, basically. I'm not the kind of person who can spend life in jail. I'm a Gary Gilmore. If I would go to prison, life in prison, I would demand the death *penalty, quite frankly. I'm not about to spend my life in jail. It's as simple as that. But, uh, what can I do? I know that getting upset does not help. And I have enough internal discipline and self-possession not to get upset. It's the only way I can answer the question. It's a process of* years *of working with* every *upset that came to my system and cooling it out—to the point where I have myself, almost in terms of total body, pretty well under control. I got an anxiety attack last night before I went to sleep, but it was more like an* energy wave *that came over my body. It was just* incredible, *the energy. I felt I was glowing in the dark, literally. Because having been in jail for six days and all this building up and knowing that it's going to be eighteen, nineteen, hours a day now, I don't know, for the next four years. But I'm used to that schedule. I keep an unbelievable schedule and always have. Not in terms of the office person going in to work, but my phone rings anytime during a twenty-four-hour period. I travel at a moment's notice. . . . And I'm not in* good *shape anymore, but I'm in pretty good shape. And I'm going to get myself back in shape. I'm going to have to be in just tip-top physical condition to deal with it.*

Ira's initial strategy was to portray his plight as a global problem, something that affected everyone's well-being as much as his. He would imply that this was not a case of murder, but a scandalous cover-up demanding investigation. This attitude is implicit in the tone of the fundraising letter for the "Ira Einhorn Legal Defense Fund":

> I am very conscious of the general shock and pain that my arrest has brought about. Due to the nature of the legal situation, I am not able to talk about the facts of the case.
>
> However, I can share with you that I am sick to heart at this interruption of work that I have slowly and patiently created over a period of many years. The psychological shock of such an abrupt transition has left me dazed and totally without a context. I feel as if I have lost my home planet. It would be so easy to give up or disappear.
>
> Yet I know that I must not desert at such a critical time, for the transformation is accelerating rapidly and must be understood if we are to survive.
>
> Thus I am faced with a lengthy and expensive court battle. I have the best legal help available: Arlen Specter. I need your financial support, for my life hangs in the balance.
>
> May this soon be over, so that once again, I might direct all my energy to the transition at hand.
>
> Peace,
> Ira Einhorn

While this did not strike many on the network as an odd missive, and indeed Ira generated a few thousand dollars from the letter, some friends of Ira's were offended by it. Specifically, they objected to the letter's failure to mention Holly Maddux. Generally they did not understand why Ira was dealing with this as a political issue and not a personal legal problem. Even those sympathetic to his claims of conspiracy saw quite clearly that Ira Einhorn, as an individual, was in trouble, and then made their decision to help him or not. If the decision was favorable to Ira, often it was not followed up with the degree of commitment that Ira had hoped for.

Initially, of course, many of Einhorn's friends rushed to his defense. For one thing, they considered tales of psychic warfare not at all "crazy." Though rumor and hyperbole were common in the outposts of fringe science that constituted Ira Einhorn country, true believers claimed a factual basis for the charge that the superpowers, and particularly the Soviet bloc, had funded experiments to consider the military applications of paranormal phenomena. The facts were documented in books like *Psychic Discoveries Behind the Iron Curtain,* as well as dispatches from the likes of the *Washington Post* and Jack Anderson's columns (one Anderson researcher wrote *Mind Wars,* a book about U.S. government efforts in this field). Ira Einhorn himself had recently obtained and circulated a mammoth U.S. Defense Intelligence Agency study, recently declassified, entitled "Soviet and Czechoslovakian Parapsychology Research," in which a researcher for our government claimed that the Communists indeed had programs in psychic phenomena that one day might lead to the development of unstoppable mind-weaponry.

Naturally, many of Einhorn's network buddies, particularly those in the psychic mafia, were ready to believe that his arrest was an effort to suppress the flow of information about such activities. Witness the stirring treatment given to Ira's case in *Specula,* a journal focusing largely on psychotronic weaponry and obscure UFO sightings. Ira's colleague Tom Bearden, in a roundup of the various persecutions suffered by truth tellers of his acquaintance, wrote that Ira

> was suddenly confronted with a decomposed body in a trunk in his apartment. He is now awaiting trial, charged with the alleged murder. And that is so totally incredible, so out of character with the high consciousness and attunement of my friend, that I for one don't believe it for an instant. Particularly since he was working on Tesla material, directly in contact with the Yugoslavian government, and trying to get information out to the public on Tesla weapon effects. At any rate, it appears suspiciously as if the psychotronics investigators/researchers are slowly being eliminated or nullified.

To experienced conspiracy theorists like Bearden, Einhorn's arrest was one of a series of calamities befalling those involved in this particular cause: These included the arson of Puharich's house; the death in a plane crash of Itzhak Bentov, author of *Stalking the Wild Pendulum* and an Einhorn crony; and the mysterious fatal stroke that befell Wilbur Franklin, an Ohio scientist studying the powers of Uri Geller. Surely on the surface, the idea of Ira Einhorn murdering Holly Maddux seemed ludicrous, much more so than the idea of his being one more victim of the "psychic Watergate" he so frequently spoke of. And if you chanced to ask Ira why it was that these government agencies decided to frame him with a murder, rather than simply eliminating him personally, well, wasn't it obvious? They didn't want a martyr.

Even some friends of Ira's who harbored considerable cynicism about the government had to swallow very hard before considering this possible scenario. Michael Rossman, for instance, was a friend of Einhorn's who followed the psychic underground closely, writing about it at length in his book *New Age Blues.* He felt that Ira "was in an absolute critical and pivotal position to bring to the surface what if anything was lurking underneath in that whole domain. There was nobody poking in as many corners as he was." Yet, for Rossman, accepting the CIA-KGB scenario of a frame-up was a dizzying leap to take. It would mean that someone killed Holly in 1977, held on to her body for a year and a half, then planted it in Ira Einhorn's closet. Shades of Houdini! Or, if one accepted Einhorn's claims about psychotronic behavior modification, you could even postulate that Einhorn literally killed Holly, but his actions were caused by some outside agent beaming Tesla rays at his head. The implications could spin your head around. "As soon as you open the door to the existence of the potential technologization of this," says Rossman, "then, you *want* Ira to be guilty. The reason I wanted him to be guilty was that it's just too hard to deal with if he's not guilty."

Most people, though, never bought any of the psychic warfare theories, for reasons Ira understood even as he spelled them out to Greg Walter. It was too bizarre. And the fact was that Einhorn himself presented the theory simply as speculation. His actual explanation was . . . no explanation. One night, he had noticed his windows tampered with. The next day, police search his apartment, look in a trunk he bought around the time she disappeared, and find his girlfriend's mummified body, thirty-seven pounds, still wearing clothes. All the theories in the world could not explain that away.

So when challenged with the ultimate question—"Did you do it, Ira?"—the Unicorn would draw on what he knew was his most effective weapon: his belief in himself. Holding no grudge about being asked the question, he would coolly look his accuser in the eye and answer in the negative. It was a rare person who engaged Ira Einhorn's deep blue eyes in that exchange and walked away thinking that Ira was guilty.

"We were out in the garden of my house, I think it was the spring or summer [of 1979]," says Jeff Berner, a California friend of Ira's, "and I guess we were smoking some of my homegrown. I just really eyeballed him and said, 'Ira, did you do it?' And he says, 'What do you think?' And I said, 'I don't know. But you know. And I would like to know. And let me tell you this, my friend—if you say to me, "No, I didn't kill her," I'll believe you. And if you say, "Yes Jeff, I killed her," I will support you and will write you in prison and I'll send you wonderful books and I'll still be your friend when you get out.' And he said, 'No, I didn't do it.' "

"He never lied in his whole life," says Bea Einhorn. "And he didn't lie to me when I asked him if he killed Holly."

Yes. Even his mother asked him. After his bail, she said the words: "Ira, did you kill Holly?" And Ira Einhorn said, "Mother—of course not. I loved her."

That question was posed to Einhorn time and again. Some friends never did muster up the nerve to ask it, but those who opened the subject were never disappointed. In addition to his naked denial, Ira would pose some cutting questions to the skeptical questioner:

Do you know me as a violent person?

Why would I kill Holly Maddux, a woman I loved?

Even if I did kill her—and I didn't—would I really be so stupid as to leave the body in the trunk in my apartment for so long?

Food for thought, indeed. Ira had been a symbol of nonviolence for over a decade, and even the people who suspected him of occasionally roughing up Holly Maddux could not logically assume that a man known to strike a woman would necessarily qualify as one so deranged as to kill her. Similarly, one could imagine no possible benefit that would accrue to Ira by murdering Holly. Her untouched bank account, as well as Ira's lifelong habit of austerity, ruled out a financial motive. And Ira's apparent patience at Holly's previous departures, as well as their history of an open relationship, indicated that Holly's leaving Ira would hardly provoke a murderous response.

Furthermore, Ira had an excellent point when he noted that only an exceptionally inept murderer would leave the corpse at his home, the most incriminating location possible. For dozens of Ira's friends who had come to think of him as the type of person *they* would call in an emergency—clear-headed, practical Ira—this was a compelling indication that Einhorn was framed. Einhorn buffeted this argument by noting that during the time Holly's body was supposedly stuffed in his closet, he often entertained visitors in the apartment. If Ira was really hiding Holly in the trunk, would he be so reckless? Even when he knew detectives were searching for Holly, and they had involved the Philadelphia police in their investigation?

"Ira was just too damn bright [to leave the body in his apartment]," says Mel Richter, who'd known Ira since high school. "If indeed he had murdered her in a moment of passion, there was sufficient time elapsed so he could have rethought his initial plan and revised it. In the way it was done, *it's not classic Ira.*"

"It doesn't add up," says David Ehrlich, another friend. "Ira was very meticulous. He knew where every book was in his apartment, everything was organized. [How can someone who paid such attention to detail] leave a body? I used to own garbage dumps, and Ira was aware of this—if he had said to me, 'Look, I've got this trunk full of papers, it's confidential, I want to dump this,' I would have done it. We could have driven to the dump and that would have been it. They never, never would have found the body."

When Ira ran through this litany of contradictions, he gained believers. Once he even addressed a classroom full of journalism students taught by his old friend, *Bulletin* reporter Claude Lewis. "It was one of the most interesting classes I ever held," recalls Lewis, "because I told the students he was coming, and they read the newspapers, they knew about him. And I said, 'Ira's going to talk to you and at the end of the class we're going to take a little poll to see whether he's guilty or innocent.' He presented all the facts, and they were weighted in his favor. He had the personality, the spirit . . . he was enjoying the audience. He was so cunning that of around thirty-five students there, there were maybe two people who said he might be guilty. The rest of the class said he was innocent."

But despite the compelling questions Ira raised, a sizable contingent of Einhorn supporters slowly withdrew from the ranks as the weeks passed, particularly as they learned more details of Holly Maddux's disappearance. Just two weeks after Ira won bail, a pretrial hearing was held to determine whether there was sufficient evidence to arraign Einhorn. While Ira sat calmly, assistant district attorney Joe Murray paraded witnesses to the stand—a command performance of the main actors in J. R. Pearce's fateful report.

Besides the key figures of Saul Lapidus, Elizabeth Maddux, Rick Iannacone, and Paul Herre, there was Detective Mike Chitwood, describing the search, and coroner Halbert Fillinger, describing in precise terms the pathetic state of the body found in Ira Einhorn's closet, "an adult human showing advanced decomposition and mummification," which dental records and fingerprints identified as that of Holly Maddux.

Fillinger described the cause of death as "cranio-cerebral injuries to the brain and skull." This clinical description, when elaborated upon, indicated that Holly Maddux was killed in a horrifying manner. The coroner reported that "there are at least ten or twelve fractures and maybe more." Apparently, crushing blows had been delivered to the victim's head from above and from the right and left side. There was a linear fracture running below the left eye socket, a series of other fractures on the left side, a number of irregular depressed skull fractures in front of the right ear, as well as a number of fractures around the orbital area and right lateral aspect, underneath the eye. In addition, there was a depressed skull fracture on the right frontal bone over the right forehead. Also, the lower jaw was fractured, part of it driven in toward the mouth itself. Fillinger guessed that the injuries were caused by a blunt object, such as a board or the base of a lamp. It was impossible to tell how many blows had been given, because "the holes in the skull are so big you can't define how many times one area had been struck." Six was probably the minimum number of blows. In light of these injuries, Fillinger ruled out the possibility of an accidental death.

So much for the "semiaccidental" theory that some of Ira's friends had been formulating, in which Ira momentarily lost his temper and struck Holly once, whereupon she fell backward, hit her head against the bathtub, and fell suddenly dead.

One witness testified who did not appear in any of Pearce's reports, Penny Jeannechild, who swore that at her Free Women's School class, Holly had appeared with a bruise on her face, and told the class that "the bruise had resulted from a physical fight that involved herself and Ira."

Arlen Specter argued that no one actually *witnessed* Einhorn striking Holly, and therefore the testimony from both Lapidus and Jeannechild, that Ira hit Holly, was hearsay. But the judge allowed the testimony. The state was building a strong circumstantial case against Ira Einhorn, the centerpiece being the discovery of Holly's body. In Joe Murray's opinion it was a "lock-solid" first-degree murder case. (He was confident that the charge would not be reduced to voluntary manslaughter in light of Einhorn's dissembling behavior *after* the murder—when, in Murray's view, Einhorn used cruel cunning to hide his crime, proving a cold-blooded consciousness consistent with a premeditated violent act.) It was no surprise when the judge ruled that an arraignment would be in order; a trial was inevitable, with the same devastating evidence. It looked very bad for Ira.

Even some of Ira's closest friends suggested that he might do well to plead guilty. Among them was Jerry Rubin, who after their 1969 argument had reconciled with Ira in the mid-seventies. The day Ira had been released on bond, Rubin—in the wake of a recent EST experience, a big fan of self-confrontation—insisted that Ira could do a great deed for the world by admitting that he had killed Holly in an overdose of male domination; he could proclaim himself an example of this negative character trait, and, after paying his debt to society, he perhaps could found an institute of violence to study the problem. Ira said it was an interesting idea, but irrelevant since he didn't kill Holly.

According to some of Einhorn's friends, Arlen Specter himself advised that Ira's best hope lay in an insanity defense. But Ira was emphatically opposed to that course of action. Claiming insanity would be as disastrous as accepting the accusation that he murdered Holly—either option would discredit his lifetime work. All the effort he had put into legitimizing his ideas would be wasted. His credibility would vanish. No, Ira would continue to insist on his innocence. And his insistence would be calm and matter-of-fact. As if this were happening to someone else.

"I was sitting constantly with this person, and we were having conversations as if nothing had happened," says Julie Samuels, who with her husband, Stuart, had allowed him into their home. "He was acting as if it were the KGB [who had killed Holly]. It was just a farfetched story, but the truth is not many of us in everyday life knew about what the CIA or KGB do. He was insisting he was innocent, and he wasn't going to cop a plea or do anything that implied that he had done it, insane or not. He was dealing with this all the time, his friends thinking, Did he do it? His point of view was that 'People who have known me so well don't know I couldn't do such a thing like that?' "

As the weeks went on, the momentum of Ira's defense effort waned. Arlen Specter, soon to begin his successful run for the United States Senate, turned over the role of lead attorney to Norris Gelman, a less imposing criminal lawyer who had worked for Specter in the Philadelphia district attorney's office. (Besides the negative political implications of defending Einhorn, it seems that Ira was unable to guarantee Specter's top-dollar fees.) The tactics necessary to defend Ira were also discouraging: Despite Ira's occasional boasts that he would expose the frame-up and present the world with a psychic equivalent of a Scopes trial, his lawyers never considered this. "You think the Russians came to Powelton Village and threw a beam on him?" Norris Gelman would later ask, mocking the very premise. Nor did Gelman urge that Ira plea diminished capacity. "The most brilliant defendant that ever hit City Hall, and I'm going to claim he was insane? No way." Instead, Gelman's legal strategy was a traditional "reasonable doubt" defense. This relied on refuting the state's evidence, bit by bit; evidence that could not be refuted would be minimized. The jury would be asked to conclude that the evidence did not indicate, at least not beyond reasonable doubt, that Ira Einhorn killed Holly Maddux. While Ira's lawyers insisted that the case was not "open-and-shut," and Ira had a fighting chance, the comfort this provided was less than, say, gushing optimism.

Ira's network dispatches stopped cold. This was a severe disappointment. The past few years had been the busiest yet for the network, an enterprise that was finally gaining international attention. Ira felt he was circulating information that would eventually permeate the newspaper front pages. Giving up was painful, but obviously Pennsylvania Bell would not fund an accused murderer. Ira wrote his friends that "I am in the process of transforming my life, so that I might continue my work in another fashion. The network has come to an end, and I am saddened by that fact. These past nine years have brought me in touch with the leading edge of planetary thought. I will continue to identify with that thought in ways more private."

Ira Einhorn's carefully nurtured public profile was permanently marred. He was no longer a welcome fixture at La Terrasse. Tensions grew between Ira and many of his friends. George Keegan, one friend who maintained ties—it was Keegan and his wife, Kathy, to whom Ira entrusted the books and houseplants from the Race Street apartment Einhorn was forced to vacate—recalls Ira's visits during that period. "We would take a walk down the street and some people that he knew didn't want to say hello to him," says Keegan. "Ira slowly began to realize that people had had it with him. People whom he normally would have walked up to and exchanged a big hug now approached him warily, no communication. I could see the hurt in Ira. It was very hard to accept that his work, his life as he had built it, was gone." Even George Keegan, worried about the effect on his eight-year-old daughter, finally suggested that Ira not hang out at the Keegans' house so much.

Stuart and Julie Samuels also became uncomfortable with him. When they moved to a new home, the unspoken agreement was that Ira remain at the old apartment for the brief remainder of the lease, and then find his own lodgings. Einhorn asked the Samuelses only if they would leave a television for him. Ira failed to lock the door one day, and the TV set was stolen. Alone in this giant penthouse, Einhorn paced the empty rooms, careening with thoughts of self-destruction. He visited the Samuelses at their new house, idly talking to Julie Samuels on nights when Stuart taught his film courses, but Julie became uneasy with the friend she had so recently described, under oath at his bail hearing, as a member of her family. "I'd be stuck with him for the whole night, and I couldn't talk anymore," says Julie Samuels. "There was nothing more to talk about. So although I never confronted him directly, he knew that something was definitely amiss in the way I was perceiving him now."

Uncomfortable in Philadelphia, Ira headed to California. Even as he left, he had an almost comic reminder of the mistrust he had engendered amongst his friends. George Keegan, to whom Ira promised to lend his car while he was away, drove Einhorn to the airport. When Keegan opened the trunk of Ira's green Toyota to get the luggage, he gasped with horror. Globs of a thick, sticky substance dotted the trunk well. "It's *honey,* George," Ira explained. He had been transporting some gallon jugs for a beekeeper friend, and one had leaked.

Sandy White, an old friend from the Powelton Piles, picked up Ira at the San Francisco airport, and for a few days he stayed in her houseboat in Sausalito. Then he roamed down the coast, finding shelter at Esalen Institute, his stomping grounds in the sixties, and later the site of Physics and Consciousness sessions in the seventies. While there, he worked with a psychic named Jenny O'Conner, attempting by paranormal means to get to the bottom of his troubles. "Jenny channels through this entity called the Nine, a mass energy entity from the planet Sirius, giant reflectors of ourselves," Ira explained to a friend. (According to an Esalen biographer, Jenny's methodology was to "sit down in a room, make herself comfortable, take off her shoes, drink canned cola, and smoke cigarettes while people asked questions of the Nine." The answers came instantly, with Jenny recording them on legal-size notepads.) While Jenny "helped me get down through some deep layers of my psyche," Ira said, "nothing definite came up."

California seemed to reinvigorate Ira. According to the account of Jennifer Birkett, who was then an adventurous, twenty-two-year-old spiritual traveler, Einhorn generated considerable personal power while at Esalen. Birkett was a recent college graduate from Canada who had on impulse taken off for California and found herself at Esalen, nude in the hot baths by the cliffs overlooking the Pacific, peaking on a psychedelic called MDA, happily merging with the environment. Suddenly, Ira Einhorn's shadow blocked the ray of sunlight she was basking in. Their eye contact was long and, in her mind, awesome, a "telepathic encounter." They dressed and began walking on the high bluffs. She confessed she'd taken MDA and he was "totally accepting." He explained who he was, said he was giving a workshop at Esalen on "thought-form physics." He was, he told her, "deeply involved in the counterculture movement and consciousness research but also deeply troubled." He told her of his arrest, and his confusion in the aftermath. Birkett later recorded the next moment of their encounter in her journal:

"Do you think I murdered her?"
  I feel electrified by his question and the presence, but deeply calm. For an eternity I gaze into his fathomless blue eyes, letting my attention be drawn into the center of his being. I just kept looking through him. There wasn't anything like that there. There just wasn't anything like that there. I say nothing with words, just letting

the peace I feel with him be my only response. He looks deeply into me again. I am scrutinized lovingly and completely by this bear of a man with a shock of silver gray hair, the most incredibly blue, penetrating eyes.

As far as she could perceive, this was an extraordinary being, scandalously charged with a crime he did not commit. *No*, every fiber of her being wanted to cry out, *you did not murder*. She conveyed this trust to him, and they arranged to meet soon after in the Bay Area. By then the vulnerability he had shown at Esalen had been replaced by a positive energy as he drove around to see various friends, explaining his situation to them. There was lunch at Palo Alto with Jacques Vallee, the French UFO expert whose computer conferencing company Ira had been consulting with. Then up to Berkeley, for a conference with Mike Rossman. From there they went to San Francisco, to the Café Trieste headquarters of Jack Sarfatti, a self-styled "New Age physicist" who was for a spell the guru of Northern California quantum theory, advising the likes of EST founder Werner Erhardt on subatomic issues. Calmly relating his circumstances, Ira found sympathetic ears at each stop on his tour. "He certainly didn't *act* as if he did it," recalls Sarfatti.

Though he was skeptical about Ira's claims of innocence, Sarfatti helped organize a public meeting for Ira to address at a friend's home on Russian Hill. By now, Ira was fully re-energized. "He wanted to talk to all his friends here to give his position," says Sarfatti. "He was very calm, very together. Extremely strong, psychologically." Saul-Paul Sirag, another physicist who attended the meeting, agrees with Sarfatti's assessment. "We were all very suspicious of him at that point, but the thing that impressed me was his incredible nonchalance considering the enormity of what he'd been charged with . . . he seemed to be in great spirits." From Ira's point of view, the meeting went quite well, but Sirag left the meeting confused, and became even more baffled at a trivial incident that occurred when he left.

"I had gone to the meeting with my girlfriend at the time, Barbara Honneiger [later notorious as the Reagan White House insider who leveled sexism charges at that administration and was dismissed as a "low-level munchkin"], and we walked off in one direc tion and he went in another," recalls Sirag. "I guess Barbara and I were arguing mildly, and Ira turned back and heard us bickering, and he said—as if this were a joke, but it was still weird—'Beat her up.' " Under the circumstances, Ira's jocularity fell flat.

Still, Ira returned to Philadelphia charged up. He told Stuart Samuels how great he had felt in California. People didn't run away from him there. Not long after this liberating visit, he made a return trip to California, driving his Toyota cross-country. This was possibly a tonic to what depression might have come from a hearing held in May, on the admissibility of some of the evidence against him. Despite the efforts of Einhorn's new lawyer, Norris Gelman, a judge ruled that the search warrant of Einhorn's apartment was valid. The pretrial motions would continue, but since Gelman was an attorney in the pending MOVE case, involving the siege and ultimate shooting that occurred when police stormed the radical group's headquarters, Einhorn was granted the first of several postponements.

Meanwhile Ira kept moving. Despite his status as released on bond pending a murder trial, he considered himself free to travel abroad. He embarked on a drive to Canada, via Woodstock. Michael Green, a former Tim Leary disciple who knew Ira vaguely from the skirmishes of psychedelia, accompanied Ira on the first leg of the trip. "It's not every day, as the Aquarian Age goes along, that you find one of your compatriots accused of killing his girlfriend and sticking her in a trunk," admits Green, who sat back and let Ira weave his odyssey. "We went through the business, the frame-up, as he called it. The rap was, he was doing stuff that *They* didn't want done. They, the big They. The CIA does not want people like him going over and starting to make links with hip Yugoslavian scientists, psychic discoveries behind the Iron Curtain, and astral spying squads. He said the whole thing was a setup, don't worry about it."

In Montreal, Einhorn's friends included, among others, Charles and Barbara Bronfman. The Seagram heir and his wife were among the Unicorn's staunchest supporters. They had supposedly put up the cash for his bail and visited him soon after his release when he was living at the Samuels'. Ira would visit Canada several times in the next twenty months.

But the Unicorn did not limit himself to the North American continent. Though his passport was taken when the police cleared out his apartment, Ira procured another. He flew to England. Unfortunately, preceding him by several weeks was a long article in the *Village Voice,* which presented the facts of his case in an unflattering manner. As a result, he had to face yet more truth tests. One was administered by playwright Heathcote Williams. "I asked him whether he did it," says Williams. "He looked me straight in the eye and said no." As he had in California, Ira startled people by his confidence and nonchalance in the face of horrendous charges. "I got the feeling that the whole thing was an inconvenience to him," says Heathcote Williams. "That the work was important and this was kind of a nuisance."

"He was making no secrets about [his legal problem]," says Richard Adams, who knew Ira in London, "but he wasn't anxious to talk about it other than to say that the *Village Voice* was just prejudging him, that it wasn't true. I think Ira was essentially a truthful man— he was well liked over here."

When Ira returned to Philadelphia, he was more settled in his new existence as a branded man. He did not hammer away at the KGB-CIA conspiracy theory as much. For a while he postulated the ugly premise that people in Tyler, Texas—perhaps even Holly's father!—were somehow involved in the presumed frame-up. He asked his friend George Andrews to check out the possibility that Fred Maddux was a high officer in the American Nazi Party, and that the Nazis were somehow involved in planting Holly's body in his closet. Andrews was shocked at the request, but dutifully ascertained from his sources that Fred Maddux was not a member of any organized Nazi or neomilitary right-wing group. In response to another of Ira's requests, Andrews could draw no connection between Holly's disappearance and recent UFO sightings in Tyler.

As months went by, Ira's identification of those who framed him became more and more vague, ultimately settling into statements to the effect that *he* knew who they were and would reveal them at the proper time. Meanwhile, following the lead of his lawyers, he looked for vindication less by a satisfying explanation of what had occurred than by a refutation of the charges against him.

In November 1979, Ira Einhorn received some good news on this front. After months of urging from Ira's defense team, the prosecution finally handed over the results of the FBI laboratory's forensic study of the materials from Ira's closet. The conclusion was that neither the floorboards nor any other matter underneath the trunk tested positively for blood and/or human protein. In Ira's view, this proved that Holly's body had not been in his closet since September 1977, as the prosecution claimed. As far as the Unicorn was concerned, this development vindicated him totally.

"There's no blood in the apartment, they found no blood in the entire apartment!" Ira crowed to *Bulletin* columnist Claude Lewis. They were discussing the case over dinner at Casa Vecchio, an Italian restaurant in West Philly. "How can you fracture somebody's skull twelve, thirteen times, and not have any blood? It's crazy, it becomes crazier." He went on, explaining how many fingerprints besides his and Holly's were found in the cardboard boxes in the closet. How the pubic hair of someone other than him was found in the trunk. How the prosecution had misbehaved in not releasing the information sooner. How the prosecution now had to argue that he had killed Holly outside the apartment, and only then put her in his closet.

"That's what the prosecution is going to be asking people to believe," he said. "I mean, anybody can lose their temper. I've never met *anybody* who's not capable of murder . . . any male who's been involved with a woman, any woman who's been involved with a male has felt murder in their blood." He laughed the trademark Einhorn laugh, that boisterous high-pitched giggle. "So one is not making a plea on the basis of that," he continued. "One would make a plea on the basis, in effect, that I'm a reasonably intelligent being, and if I would take the trouble to drain blood from the body, I certainly wouldn't put it in a trunk in my apartment. I certainly wouldn't put it there when I knew the police were investigating and when I knew a private *detective* was investigating!"

"You're suggesting," said Lewis, "it would be impossible to drain the body of blood in the apartment and not get blood on any—"

"Yes, I would think so," answered Einhorn. "How did the blood get out of the body? I don't know how to drain blood from the body! Certainly I'm bright enough to learn how to do anything. But that's not something I bothered"—Ira laughed again—"to learn about. I couldn't tell you how that's done."

Ira paused while the waitress asked if they wanted coffee. He informed her that the table hadn't received bread yet nor had he gotten his side order of spaghetti. "The skull was supposedly fractured, six to twelve—multiple times," he continued, after the interruption. "You can't tell me blood didn't squirt all over the place. And no matter how careful you are, you wouldn't be able to get it all up!"

Ira asserted that "with this new data, the ball is in my court." He praised Norris Gelman and the rest of his defense team, speaking as if the case was all but dismissed. It might take a year or so, he admitted, but the conclusion was now foregone.

"What this has given me is a new lease on life," he said. "I feel totally free. I feel like a citizen of the world. I can go settle anyplace. Because I'm going to do a book on all this."

Ira was referring to his efforts, along with a book packager named Ian Summers, to sell a proposal that would reveal Ira Einhorn's side of the story. "I intend to write a book directed to a mass audience, for it is obvious that my case has enormous mass appeal," Ira wrote. The proposal promised "an inside view of someone who lives on the edge of thought, but I will never become overly abstract or philosophical." Though he did vow to focus on the murder, which of course he denied committing, he warned that the book would not speculate on who actually *did* kill Holly Maddux. "This ambiguity will not detract from the value of the book," he assured his potential publishers, "for so much of the public interest in this case hangs upon the ambiguity of my present public *persona*."

While in Montreal during the Christmas season, Einhorn massmailed the FBI report to potential supporters. His cover letter summarizes his hopes and state of mind at the end of 1979, his most difficult year:

Friends,

Enclosed you will find an FBI report. . . . We have waited 8 months for this report, due to us by law. It took a court order to place it in our hands. You may draw your own conclusion from this behavior. It is what I have struggled against during the last 8½ months of difficult uphill battle.

I was conspired against in the most hellish way; so many of my friends could not grasp the conspiracy, for it is beyond normal ken. For this there can be no blame or recriminations as the press played right into the hands of those who wished to silence me. This is not the time to name them who are guilty of murder—that will come. For now there is only the courts and the media. For the first time I need your help. I am innocent of all charges and you have part of that proof in your hands. To prove that statement in a court of law will not be difficult, but it will be expensive. Please help me if you are able.

The media will soon carry more of the story, and my own book will clear up a lot of unanswered questions. Three years ago some members of my network stumbled upon information relating to matters of the gravest national security. In the face of threats and other dire consequences, we all refused to change our way of open sharing of information. I would do the same thing again, for if we fail to risk, we cannot protect the open society that is presently under siege on all sides . . .

I look forward to resuming many interrupted interactions.

But the clouds did not disperse. The dull concatenation of pre-trial hearings and motions continued. From the grip of this legal vise, Ira attempted to reconstruct his life as best he could. With the network down, he landed a job, of sorts—a book review sine-cure. A long-time buddy of Ira's named Harry J. Katz had recently started a small weekly newspaper. Ever since the early sixties, when he had tried to establish a Playboy Club in conservative Phila-delphia, Harry J. Katz had a well-deserved reputation for contro-versy. Most recently, Katz had been a defendant in a libel trial arising from his column about an imaginary trip to Mexico, during which a feminist *Inquirer* writer masturbated him under the table at a dinner for Betty Friedan. (The jury did not appreciate this brand of satire and Katz lost the case.) Harry J. Katz thought it would be a splendid idea to have a famous accused murderer commenting on the latest offerings from the world of books. Ira Einhorn took the job seriously, rebuilding his library with new review copies, and meticulously meeting his weekly deadlines with commentary on books ranging from *A Confederacy of Dunces* to *Thy Neighbor's Wife*. In one of his columns, he devised a slogan that would demonstrate he had not lost his talent for cultural prescience: "Money," Ira wrote, "is the long hair of the eighties."

Ira moved into a new apartment, far away from Powelton Village where he had once been cock of the roost. It was a nondescript one-bedroom apartment in a modern high-rise called Morgan House, about a mile from the neighborhood in which he grew up. "He needed a place to live," says Ira's lawyer Norris Gelman, who had an apartment there himself. "I told him it was a good building." Ira's friend Ted Fink was surprised when he saw Ira's new digs: "It was a far contrast from anywhere he'd lived before," he says. "It was modern, well furnished, basically immaculate—it was a Jewish apartment." The giveaway: Instead of Ira's signature floor mat, the apartment had a real bed.

Ira also found a woman with whom to share the apartment. Her name was Jeanne Marie Morrison. She was twenty-two years old, a quiet redhead from a conservative Republican family in Virginia. Her father, Julian Morrison, a long-time journalist, was soon to join the Reagan administration as chief speech writer for the head of the Veterans Administration. Of the six Morrison children, only Jeanne Marie, the oldest child, had gravitated to the life-style of drugs, unconventional morality, and aversion to authority. (In that respect, her family situation was similar to that of Holly Maddux, another free-spirited daughter of conservative stock.) Ira reportedly met her at Barbara and Charles Bronfman's estate in Charlottesville, Virginia; Morrison had gone to college there, but had dropped out. The young woman was subsequently swept away by Einhorn and moved to Philadelphia with him. Friends of Ira's remember her as very quiet, deferential to Einhorn; when Ira would speak of defending himself of the murder charge, Jeanne Marie would listen approvingly, much in the way they recalled Holly Maddux's behavior in the early stages of her relationship with Ira.

Jeanne Marie got a waitressing job at Pick-A-Deli, a restaurant in a nearby shopping center. Einhorn, of course, did not have a regular job, unless you counted his weekly book review. Always a cinemaphile, he went to the movies often. He also kept track of developments on the Tesla front, particularly in regards to a Canadian group called the Planetary Association for Clean Energy, which saw Tesla's theories as a solution to the energy crisis as well as a threat when used to bend minds or control the weather.

Still, it was impossible to carry on the charade that all was well. For one thing, no publisher made a serious bid on Ira's book. Though Einhorn and Ian Summers had conducted several long sessions with top publishing executives who couldn't seem to hear enough of Ira's personal presentation of the story, the project was doomed by Einhorn's insistence on proclaiming innocence without a convincing alternative explanation. "If Ira had committed the murder, [the publishers] felt they had a great book," says Summers. "As long as Ira said he didn't do it, the book didn't deliver." Another problem was Ira's prose: The proposal was the usual Unicorn stew of convolutions, boasts, and crypticism. The fizzled book project was a double blow, as Einhorn not only hoped that its publication would vindicate him but that a six-figure advance would help him fund his undercapitalized defense.

Even fewer friends were coming to Ira's aid as time went on. When he attempted to once again escape Philadelphia temporarily, returning to the same Nova Scotia farmhouse where he and Holly Maddux had lived through good times and bad, the vacation was difficult. The Cape Breton Islanders had heard of his arrest, and not realizing that he was legally free on bond, called the Mounties to arrest this presumed fugitive. The misunderstanding was cleared, but Ira, who had Jeanne Marie in tow, found that the farmhouse would not be rented to him. They took a cabin on the other side of the harbor, a ferry ride away from Englishtown, but after only a few nights his new landlords discovered his circumstances and asked him to leave. Eventually a man rented him a cabin for the summer.

When he returned to Philadelphia in the fall of 1980, he must have known that it would be the last winter he would ever spend there.

From the very first few days after his arrest, when he told Greg Walters that he was like Gary Gilmore in the sense that he would rather die than be imprisoned, Ira Einhorn had considered the possibility of fleeing. In June 1979, on the back of the form letter he sent to generate funds for his defense, he wrote a personal note to his friend Craig Samms in London:

> You can help as of course I will play it straight, forcing me, probably, to eventually have to flee. The shoe is now on the other foot and soon I'll be arriving at your doorstep. I'm not about to go to jail for life for a crime I did not commit. I may need a British passport. That is being worked on, so go slow and make very discreet inquiries. What you could work on is a place where I could disappear for a few years, a country house, a room on a large estate, a cottage in some safe far-off

place. I prefer Northern Europe and I'm open to anything. I should have enough money to live quietly for two to four years and friends will add to that. A hideaway in the middle of London might be the most elusive. Go slow, trust only those you can totally count on, and above all be silent. You should read this and then destroy it. I'll come to London as soon as I am certain it is jail or flight. . . . As soon as I make a decision I'll be heading your way. I have a safe place to stay and my own passport. I will not be a fugitive for a while. I'll discreetly call you, and then we're off. Love to all, Ira.

When Ira knocked on Samms' Portobello Road door in 1979, he was not yet a fugitive. But he probably was scouting out locations in case he did decide to forfeit bond. "He talked about places like Iceland and Finland, he asked me questions about European locations, but basically, I don't know how to be a fugitive," Samms says, insisting he made no efforts to fulfill the instructions in Einhorn's letter.

It required no great intelligence, though, to perceive the high probability that Ira Einhorn might flee before his trial. Ira would often assert that under no circumstances would he go to jail. He said this in a lunch with George Leonard at a Mill Valley restaurant, and he repeated this to his parents in family discussions. Even as he spent hours preparing his defense with Norris Gelman and other lawyers, Ira had to be considering the odds of being convicted. As the trial date in February or March 1981 approached, those odds seemed poor indeed.

For one thing, Ira's nemesis in court was Barbara Christie, to whom Joe Murray had assigned the prosecution. She was the most aggressive prosecutor in the district attorney's office, a workaholic bantamweight black woman who, in the awestruck description of one colleague, "pisses ice water." With Barbara Christie there would be no breaks, and no bend. She attacked each defense motion with unalloyed fury, eschewing collegial courtesies common even in major criminal cases. Norris Gelman accused her of purposely withholding information: He implied that at one point, she maliciously refused to turn over the FBI lab findings, and that when she photocopied J. R. Pearce's report, she intentionally failed to hand over certain key pages, including the ones that spoke of Gwendolyn Coleman, the woman who thought she had seen Holly after the date of the alleged murder. Though nothing came of those charges, the trial judge found sufficient cause to force Christie to present sworn affidavits justifying her behavior in these matters.

Ira Einhorn knew that Barbara Christie's pit-bull persistence could spell doom for him, and he envisioned diabolical schemes to get her kicked off the case. At one point he went as far as to ask investigative reporter Gaeton Fonzi to scrounge up dirt on Christie. "I need some info on the QT about the madwoman DA Barbara Christie who is prosecuting/persecuting me," he wrote. "*Anything* you dig up will be appreciated."

The clincher in Ira's decision may have been a new series of tests performed on the floorboards, the rug, and the plaster sitting underneath the steamer trunk in which Holly Maddux's body was found. It is debatable how crucial these materials would have been in the trial. When the FBI's tests on them showed no positive traces of organic matter, Ira portrayed them as pivotal. But Barbara Christie undoubtedly would have seized on the assessment of the FBI chemists, given in a long pretrial hearing in February 1980, that the negative results on the floorboards and plaster did not preclude the possibility that blood or human protein might have been in the materials at an earlier point, dissipating in the eighteen-month interval between the alleged murder and the body's discovery. In any case, no amount of tests on floorboards, rugs, and ceiling plaster underneath the trunk overwhelms the unavoidable fact that Holly Maddux's body was *in* the trunk.

Nonetheless, even Ira's slight advantage of the FBI tests was wiped clean by the results of the new tests by a laboratory in Willow Grove, not far from J. R. Pearce's office. Using different methods, these chemists found that there *was* human protein in the materials. Those who knew Ira at that time say he took this news very hard. When Harry J. Katz, Ira's gadabout publisher, discussed the case with him, he was frank in his assessment.

"H-J-K-One," he said to Ira.

"What's that?" Einhorn asked.

"You're going to be making license plates for the rest of your life," said Katz. "That's my request for a vanity tag."

Katz had never been a person to hold things back. "Ira," he said, "you don't stand a chance in the world, whether you did it or not. Look at you—you're an old hippie Jew wearing a dashiki with sandals, with body odor. You're fat, you're a weirdo, you make

Charlie Manson look like a faggot, and you're going to go in front of a jury of your peers? They'll say that dirty, smelly, fat, aged, hippie Jew killed a little, blond, *shiksa* cheerleader from Texas! Ira, trust me, the law's for lawyers. They are going to fry you!"

Any Philadelphian knows to regard speeches from Harry J. Katz with a fistful of salt. Still, by that time, Ira Einhorn's conclusion about his chances of acquittal was well in tune with Katz's assessment. During December 1980, Einhorn's visits began to take on an unspoken pathos of farewell. It was two months until his trial date. He ceremoniously dropped off his underlined set of Proust to a writer he'd befriended in 1978. On Christmas Eve, Ira appeared at Steve Harmelin's house, teasing his friend's two daughters that "I bet you expected Santa Claus." Harmelin was a Central buddy, now a corporate lawyer, who was steadfast in supporting Ira; his wife, Terry, was treasurer of Ira's defense fund. "It was a wonderful evening we had," Harmelin recalls. Meanwhile, Ira was confiding to his own family that he no longer believed he would receive a fair trial. Bea Einhorn recalls it clearly: "He said, 'Mom, I don't have a chance.'"

By then, Jeanne Marie Morrison was making unspoken farewells of her own. She spent the Christmas holiday on a ski trip with her family, and for the first time in years the atmosphere was not strained with tension. Her departure came suddenly, though, after a call from Einhorn. "Evidently he was furious because he was expecting her and she hadn't called him," says Jeanne Morrison, Jeanne Marie's mother. "And Jeanne Marie's response was to come down to my bedroom, absolutely as white as a sheet after being on the phone with him. She said, 'I've just gotta get to the train station right away.' She was absolutely beside herself. So her father took her to the train station."

Around that time, Jeanne Marie recorded a dream in her journal. While driving a car, she spotted a woman hitchhiker. After passing the girl by, she saw the same hitchhiker on the road again. She stopped and picked up the stranger. The girl got in the car and tried to tell her something, tried desperately to give her a message. But Jeanne Marie couldn't make out the urgent message. But she did know who the hitchhiker was: Holly Maddux.

In the first few days of 1981, Ira placed an ad in the newspaper, offering his Toyota for sale. On January 6, a New Jersey man paid him $4,400 for the car. That same day, he withdrew $500 from his bank account, leaving a balance of $9.94.

He called Ian Summers with a request. "Ian, I don't know who else I can trust—I want you to be my mail drop," he said.

Summers refused to take the risk. "Why are you going into exile?" he asked his friend.

"They got me," said the Unicorn. "It's all a frame-up, but they got me."

During the second week of January, Bea Einhorn called Morgan House and asked Jeanne Marie where her son was. "She said, 'I haven't seen him,'" recalls Mrs. Einhorn. "She was lying, of course . . . a couple of days later, I called again, and there was no answer."

Jeanne Marie Morrison had gone back home to Virginia, with some of her and Ira's possessions boxed. She was arranging to sell a Persian rug of hers before making a flight to England on January 14, where she would meet Ira Einhorn. Ira had probably left the country through Canada and taken a Montreal-to-London flight. He called Jeanne Marie on January 13 to let her know he had arrived in Europe. He was scheduled to appear at a pretrial hearing the next day, but he would not fulfill this commitment. He was overseas again, only this time he had no intention of returning.

There would be no trial to resolve the question of Holly Maddux's murder. The Unicorn had fled. He had begun a self-imposed exile. From the start he had insisted: *I'm not about to spend my life in jail. It's as simple as that.* Now, facing a long stretch of incarceration after a trial that he knew would lead to a negative verdict, he set out to begin a new life. There would be no hope of returning. But at least he could go to a library, eat a good meal, have sex with a woman, and preserve the status of a man convicted of no crime.

Seven years later, he would still be free.

11

THE DARK SIDE

To the friends of Ira Einhorn, his clandestine departure was a cruel betrayal. Many had been hoping that the engines of justice would contrive a neat answer to the conundrum they had been struggling with since Holly Maddux was discovered in Ira's closet: How could this happen? Was Ira Einhorn really the person he seemed to be? Some reckoned his escape an act of cowardice, or worse—an admission of guilt.

Others noted that this was not necessarily the case. After all, Einhorn had been consistent in his grim contention that he could not accept a long jail term for a crime he insisted he did not commit. In his estimation, the evidence against him, as well as the circumstances under which the trial would be conducted, was overwhelmingly negative. Had he stayed, he would have been convicted. In that light, his fleeing the country and forfeiting his bail was akin to a committed draft dodger fleeing to Canada, rather than facing incarceration. Not a pure choice; still, an honorable one.

How one viewed his escape was ultimately as subjective a matter as how one viewed his claim to innocence. But even those who had concluded that Ira Einhorn, whether by accident or by a temporary descent into violent insanity, had killed Holly—these people now constituted a solid majority—had no explanation for the central contradiction. As the high school friend had exclaimed, *this was not classic Ira.* So the questions lingered.

Was Einhorn indeed an avatar of planetary consciousness who believed that the world would save itself only by eschewing greed

266

and violence? Was he a fraud, mouthing the platitudes of the sixties while secretly flouting those halcyon ideals? Or was there some other, more troubling explanation . . . that Ira Einhorn, while ostensibly trying his best to do good works, had been a tinderbox ready to explode, and the failure to see it was the failure of all who knew him?

Ira's friend Steve Harmelin, who had adored him since high school and stood up for him under oath when Einhorn was arrested, posed the dilemma: "I often wonder if Ira was the moon that I saw the bright side of," he said, "and whether there was just a whole other dark side of the moon that I never knew."

Seven years after Ira Einhorn's departure, the question of his "dark side" has never been resolved. The answer demands a deeper study of Ira Einhorn's personality, an examination not only of his conscious deeds but the style with which they were accomplished; a look behind the words to discern the revelations they offer; and the exposing of some of his most secret actions. While Ira Einhorn left behind innumerable fragments of his public persona, his private self turns out to be oddly obscure. Only by lifting that curtain of careful image making can one discover the Unicorn that even his closest friends had only glimpses of. When the curtain is lifted, we may understand the disappearance of Holly Maddux, the pattern of Ira Einhorn's life, and perhaps a deeper understanding of the way Einhorn formed a symbiotic relationship to the times he lived in.

How can we do this? First by contemplating the obvious. The core of the problem had always been in clear sight. Even those who knew Ira only casually were well aware of this most glaring of character flaws—his ego. Though he included the wisdom of Zen among the many topics on which he could discourse fluently, Einhorn had never mastered the abandonment of self that Buddhists advocate. To the contrary, Ira Einhorn's ego was a force to be reckoned with even in the briefest encounters, an ego of breathtaking stature, a Gibraltar of self-images.

The roots of this egomania were easy to discern: As Ira Einhorn himself noted any number of times, Bea Einhorn had instilled an unusually strong sense of self-esteem in her son. This was to act as a safety net in his early social explorations, a fail-safe mechanism he could count on to be there when his high-wire misbehavior got too outrageous. How his confidence ultimately spiraled to the heights of Icarus is anyone's guess. Perhaps it was Einhorn's ability to draw energy from readings. But certainly by high school—when he trashed the distinction between egghead and jock—the basic elements of the Ira Einhorn ego had already been introduced.

It would grow to awesome proportions. Like dwellers of a city near an active volcano, or any similarly daunting natural phenomenon, those in proximity to Ira Einhorn's ego had to make accommodations to it or conscientiously avoid it. There certainly was no ignoring it. In any room, no matter how stellar the cast, Ira would contend for center of attention. He would routinely unleash a dazzling fusillade of powerful or well-known names he was in contact with, inside information he had access to, and the elevated means of understanding that he had attained. He had an odd way of twisting his apocalyptic vision so that he could speak of the world's inhabitants in the first-person plural, yet somehow be personally excluded from the category. *Things are happening so fast that people don't know how to deal with the situation,* he'd declaim, with the implicit understanding that Ira Einhorn himself had no difficulty comprehending the disorienting complexity of world events.

The very *unspokenness* of this superiority could make it more infuriating, because you could not put your finger on it. Ira had a way of appropriating the high ground for his opinions and attitudes, simply because they were Ira's, and by that measure correct. He would borrow your vacuum cleaner, and if you asked him, months after the loan had passed, if he might see fit to return the vacuum cleaner he would casually reply that, oh, the vacuum cleaner was broken, and change the subject . . . if you persisted, tried to elicit at least some clarifying comment on the missing vacuum cleaner, he would regard you with some disappointment— you actually *care* about a vacuum cleaner? And you, bound in your material possessions, would shrink a little, thinking *of course* vacuum cleaners are but dust in the great mandala of existence. And if you resented the fact that you were out one vacuum cleaner, you kept it to yourself.

Ira Einhorn handled formal rejections in much the same spirit. It was seldom *his* failing, but the inadequate qualities of the rejecter that led to those problems. Once, writer William Irwin Thompson (who had compared the Einhorn personality to the Cuernavacan weather) refused Einhorn permission to attend sessions at Thompson's New Age conversation pit, Lindesfarne. In fact, as Thompson recalls, "I told him he was full of shit." And what did Einhorn do? "His way was to become patronizing and condescending," Thompson recalls. "To [imply] I was a benighted person with neurotic hangups, a gifted person with blocks, who would never amount to much because he had all these strange blockages to the evolutionary momentum of the human race. That I was beyond salvation."

The premise underlying that attitude was that Ira Einhorn was somehow a greater being, not bound by common limitations. This much was clear from his school days, when he rejected the conventional means of learning—attending classes, fulfilling the required readings—for a self-designed curriculum. The premise was also in evidence by Einhorn's almost obsessive struggle against the confinement of being pigeonholed. A few months of common labor convinced him that he was destined for something better, and years of further development helped him create a virtually inexplicable niche for himself, so he finally did not have to be like everybody else.

His closest friends bear testimonial to his assumption of superiority:

"Ira always lived as if the rules didn't apply to him, and for an extraordinary amount of time he got away with that," says Ira's friend Mike Hoffman. "He got away with it because he convinced people of his very special quality. Which he had. The intensity he put into all the reading and thinking and the willingness to go out there farther than anyone else to follow some train of thought. . . . God knows where it would lead, but he would follow it. It was part of the risk he took with himself for kicking loose of all the traces."

"Ira really was [to himself] the center of the universe," says his friend Ralph Moore, who ran the Christian Association at Penn. "He would have an 'ends justifies the means' attitude that says, 'My agenda is the legitimate one here.' And sometimes he was considerate in not being heavy-handed about that, but it was very clear that he would leave when he wanted to leave, he would say what he wanted to say—he was his own mover."

"Ira psychologically had no superego," says Stuart Samuels. "One of the reasons that his smell was so bad, despite people literally telling him about it, was that it didn't matter, because as far as he was concerned, he was larger than the world. So it didn't matter if he smelled. Ira was totally egocentric, so anything you said would always turn back on his knowledge of it, his point of view. It was always from his perspective."

Often, Ira's erudition, charm, and social swashbuckling diffused his more off-putting aspects. "What I saw Ira do most was take over, wherever he was," says Jeff Berner, a California friend of Ira's. "Dominate every social scene, take over every room, use every environment and every space fully as his own. He was one of the few people I've allowed to do that in my own home. And I didn't mind because by the time he left, I was richer." Thus friends and associates accepted Ira's ego as part of a package which, on balance, was marvelously entertaining, intellectually provocative, and righteously motivated. Best of all, if you joked about it, Einhorn would be the first to laugh with you, chortling heartily with his warm, infectious Ira laugh. While self-absorbed, he was seldom pedantic. He would rail about macrobiotics for half an hour, and you could, as one friend did, finally interrupt him by saying, "Great, Ira, now let's go and get a hamburger," and Ira would say, "Sure," without missing a verbal beat. In that sense, perhaps the ego did have a sense of the Zen comic to it. From a certain angle, it could be looked at as so huge that it was big enough to good-naturedly devour itself.

Viewed straight on, though, Ira's ego could be alarming, and more than a few people shared the opinions of William Irwin Thompson, who claimed that "There are some people whose auras I don't like, and I didn't like to be around him." Dave Dickstein, a Powelton Village figure who for a time held the mortgage on the Piles, called Ira a "social psychopath. . . . I think the definition of that is someone who believes that he can make up his own rules. His idea about society was that he had a special role to play. He probably would manipulate anyone for anything. He just happened to find the right niche at the right time."

A large ego, however, should not necessarily reflect poorly on the causes that egotists work to advance. Ideas of personal freedom, resistance to repressive government, ecological action, and even exposure of news of paranormal phenomena were among the ideals that Ira Einhorn put himself on the line for. While there were always plenty who insisted that Ira's works in this area were simply the hustles of a left-wing con man, that analysis does not hold. Certainly other areas would have proven more fruitful if Ira's focus was solely self-aggrandizement and personal gain. It is true that the loose atmosphere of the counterculture allowed him a tolerant, well-situated pulpit from which to issue quirky gospel, but ironically, his greatest successes came not from within the borders of Woodstock Nation but as a diplomat from that state of consciousness to foreign regions of the Establishment. In his role of diplomat, he urged his contacts to accept the ideas from his home nation, to promote the transformation he believed would come. If he were a con man, this was indeed an altruistic scam.

No, the confusion and dissonance stemmed not from his ideas, not even from the self-centered manner in which he behaved while forwarding those ideas, but from his private actions and attitudes, running counter to those ideals, and ultimately ruining Ira Einhorn's mission, and Ira Einhorn himself. The enemy was inside the Unicorn. And it could be identified most damningly in his relations with the opposite sex.

The beginnings of Ira Einhorn's sexual career are more than adequately documented. In the mid-sixties, apparently around the time he was teaching at Temple University, he sat down for a long interview with a journalist compiling a book to be called *Sexual Appetites on Campus*. This document was an attempt to mask mildly pornographic sexual histories in the guise of contemporary sociology. Though Einhorn was offered and given anonymity, identified by a pseudonymous first name (Seth), his age lowered by a couple of years and his location unspecified, Ira cheerfully told the interviewer that there was no need for the precautions, an offer the interviewer declined on grounds that "college administrators . . . are not yet liberal enough to approve teachers giving lab courses in sex in their own bedrooms."

Seth/Ira is described in the book as

> a collector of books and women, somewhat more of a connoisseur in the first instance, but in either case a glutton for exploring delights between the covers. . . . His movements are quick and direct, which also characterizes his approach to the opposite sex. A time-motion study of his amours would make an interesting research project for a

doctoral thesis. . . . It is perhaps significant that Seth professes to believe it is "normal" for boys of his age to have slept with 200 or 300 different women. Whether this is rationalization for a compulsive Casanova syndrome, whether he is trying to prove something to himself, I cannot say, but I am certain Seth is not average. He is exceptional both in intellectual capacity and the capacity for what I would be tempted to term sexual excesses.

According to this interview, Ira lost his virginity at the ripe age of thirteen. On an overnight trip of a summer camp, a nineteen-year-old counselor seduced him. "I'm still grateful to her for the initiation—knowing this older girl wanted to sleep with me reinforced my self-confidence and made me feel important," said Seth/Ira. "I've liked nineteen-year-old girls ever since," he added. It was another year before Ira would sleep with another girl, but from then on, it was a steady regimen of one woman after another. With most Ira followed a methodical pattern of progressive advances—breasts, genitals, heavy petting, and after "a long time"—a month—sleeping with them. He participated in a couple of "gang-bangs" but did not have a taste for that. Interestingly, he told his mother about the gang-bangs. "I've never kept anything from her that she's asked about," Seth/Ira said.

He estimated ten lovers through high school, but things accelerated dramatically when he entered college, when he found conditions favorable to pursue a sex life on a par with Henry Miller's Paris years. A devilish White Negro to the middle-class coeds, he was a gourmet at the smorgasbord. But something was missing in his interactions. "I was a sophomore or junior in college before I began to have a tendency to want to talk to the girl who was momentarily in my bed, to give her the feeling that I was really interested in her," he said. "Until you develop this sort of interaction, sex is a narcissistic thing. You're really just having an affair with yourself. You're experiencing yourself, not the girl. She's an object, an id, a projected image of yourself. You may be having sex with her, but, in effect, you've never met her. I guess I slept with seventy girls before I began to get interested in them as individuals."

Even though this turning point presumably occurred several years before this admission, Seth/Ira's clinical description of his physical methods and techniques betray the contention that the speaker has overcome lust and has passed into a realm beyond exploitation, where man and woman meet as equals. To the contrary, the young Unicorn appeared quite self-centered in his interactions:

I've never used prophylactics. . . . I don't worry about it too much. The girls use contraceptive measures most of the time. . . .

I couldn't live very long with someone who didn't enjoy cunnilingus or wouldn't perform fellatio on me. (This remark was followed by a description of his technique to manipulate a reluctant partner into performing the trick in question.)

I don't like to sleep with virgins. I have a few times and it was a mess. I much prefer to pick up a girl who is adequate in terms of sexual experience and will perform without constantly having to be told what to do. . . .

If a girl was important to me and wanted to get married, sure I'd indulge her whim! . . . It's a corny custom we should have outgrown ages ago, but if it will make a girl feel better you may as well humor her. . . .

Because of our heritage of a two-faced attitude towards sex, very few people are capable of healthy promiscuity, enjoying sex as you would a good meal and then forgetting about it. (A classic Ira Einhorn statement, with the unspoken understanding that the speaker is among that elite "very few.")

Despite a shrewd contention that "men have not grown up as much as women in the last six or seven years," there is no evidence that Ira Einhorn's actions are in any way consistent with feminism. Put bluntly, the interview is not only an account of a Casanova but a portrait of a raging sexist.

It is true that promiscuity was a particularly ambiguous evil in the era in which Einhorn thrived and swived. "In the time and culture in which Ira established whatever record he established, things were a lot looser sexually," explains his radical California colleague Michael Rossman. "The sexual plagues had not yet struck, and we were coming off a cultural era in which widespread sexual behavior had been considered normal in certain circles and even admirable. Ira never presented himself as a cocksman in a crude sense, either in terms of boasting or in terms of implication, by the number of notches on his belt. He expressed that more in terms of the variety of activity that he enjoyed, a variety of pleasures with a lot of people."

Yet could it be fairly said that Ira was fulfilling his mandate as a sensitive, evolved being when, for instance, he lectured at a small Southern women's college in 1969 and, in the recollection of the faculty member who invited him, "ended up in bed with a number of students before he left"? Or when he attended a New Age convention in Washington and ran a virtual assembly line of women into his room? Is a routine hunt for quick sexual partnership— enjoying sex as you would a good meal and then forgetting it, in Ira's words—an unselfish act? Any number of postfeminist memoirs of the counterculture, looking at the situation from the woman's point of view, tell quite a different story.

The fact is that Ira Einhorn's encounters with women were most often conducted by the Unicorn at great advantage. He would exploit his edge in confidence, his superior worldliness, and his considerable brainpower to overwhelm his prey, who sometimes would be barely out of adolescence. "It was something in his energy" which dazzled women, says his friend George Keegan. "He would walk in on you and there was no way you could escape. You had to listen to what he was saying." In one case, when Ira was in his midtwenties, he carried on a long affair with a sixteen-year-old; his alternating periods of tenderness and cruel disregard toward her were brutal. Another time, he wrote of his affair with a girl only weeks out of high school. Professing concern about the effect it would have on the girl, he refrained from traditional lovemaking, though he schooled her thoroughly in alternate means of satisfaction. Finally, he wrote, "I have one rather hurt little (in age) creature on my hands: a creature who has given me delightful hours while she has been sucking my ass, balls, and prick with the kind of passion that really turns me on."

Einhorn's sexism did not stop with his predatory promiscuity. Women within his acquaintance are uniformly agreed that, planetary consciousness or not, the Unicorn was a blatant chauvinist in many ways. Some women felt that Ira had two modes of dealing with those of their gender without outstanding intellectual credentials: He would try to bed you or he would ignore you. "Ira was mostly interested in himself," says Tom Bissinger. "Unless he was actively pursuing a woman—then he could be all attention. Until he got the woman." Melanie Myerson, who knew Ira in the seventies, agrees: "My feeling about Ira was that if he could make a conquest, another notch on his belt or whatever you wanted to call it, then he kind of tolerated you, even if you never saw him again. But if you didn't, you were really no longer of any interest."

Also, despite his admiration for and friendship with formidable women like Hazel Henderson, there is evidence that Ira Einhorn had mixed feelings about the idea of women in forceful roles. When his friend Judy Wicks told him she was assuming the post of manager of La Terrasse, Ira Einhorn advised her against it. "You just won't be able to handle it," he told her. "That's a job for a man." Wicks was surprised at the reaction, because he had previously been supportive of her activities in publishing an alternative guide to Philadelphia. This was a sign that Ira really was more comfortable with women in subservient positions. "If I did something non-threatening, like publishing a little book or something, it was fine [with Ira]," she says. "But if I did something like manage a restaurant where he was a customer, then that was threatening to him."

Many spouses of Ira's friends would complain about Ira's rude behavior toward them. Sometimes this came in the form of ignoring them. Or he would treat them like servants. Jane Moore, wife of Ira's friend Ralph Moore, felt the latter. One day in the mid-seventies, Ira and Holly dropped by, and in the process of taking their coats, Ralph asked if they wanted some tea or coffee. Ira looked coldly at Jane Moore and said, "Tea, please. And make it steeped. I prefer steeped tea, not bag tea." Ralph Moore recalls that it was couched more as an order than a request, and after they left, Jane said to him, "I don't want that pig in my house anymore."

Others noted this imperious attitude, and wondered whether Ira really liked women much at all. Whether Ira's constant rondelet of bed partners rose from an obsession with the chase, and the reputation that he earned as a womanizer. Whether his constant seductions stemmed more from domination than desire.

"I don't think he was a very sexual person at all," says a woman who would sometimes tumble casually with Ira. "Not that he didn't talk it up, but I think he was one of those people who are on power trips, not on sex trips. They want people to do things to them, they want people to serve them in various ways."

Though some of Ira's lovers claim satisfaction, the accounts of others of the hundreds of women to which he claimed conquest indicate that his lovemaking could be perfunctory, even disappointingly so.

"To hear Ira talk about sex, he has taken women to the edge of their sexuality, he's made their elbows have orgasms," says one of

Ira's sex partners in the mid-sixties. "When it came right down to it, the four or five women I knew [who slept with him] didn't think so. You didn't really get the feeling that a sexual experience was taking place. It was like there was nobody home there. It was something like territory conquered and then done with."

"It was much more mental than physical, although he was kind of like a bear, a big teddy bear," says a woman whose experience with Ira was in the seventies. "The sex was secondary to the merging of energies."

A friend of Ira's, who also fancied himself a world-class Sybarite, once heard one of those demythologizing accounts, and was profoundly shaken. "Gee, that doesn't sound like my Ira," he mused, and the woman, who had sampled Ira's favors a few times over the years, said to him, "Well you better believe it—I loved him dearly, but he was not interested in pleasing a woman." But the friend could not bring himself to accept it, and set up a test. "I tapped the resources of the harem I had developed over twenty years," he recalls, selecting "an extremely attractive twenty-year-old blonde, a real adventuress" for the experiment. She agreed to meet Ira and "spend some time" with him on the friend's recommendation, and the friend made damn sure to be in the bedroom for a "clinical analysis of Ira, whether or not he was some impotent little boy who was parading around as a man." The friend's conclusion: No way. "He struck me as being a strong, loving, bull of a man," he says. "He was fucking her royally. And I jumped in now and then, because, how can you resist?"

Upon hearing this story, the woman who first told the friend about Ira's somnambulic performance remained skeptical. "I always got the feeling he was more interested in the men, and he was playing cut and divide between the men and the women," she says.

This certainly had been the case between Ira and his friend Michael Hoffman. "Forget your middle-class morality," Einhorn wrote Hoffman at one point. "Rear back on your hind legs and tell Diane to shut-the-fuck-up and leave you alone, [or] you'll leave her." With that attitude, it was not uncommon for spouses to sense Ira as a rival for their affection.

"There was something about Ira that was always trying to split up the yin and the yang, the male and the female," says Sandy White, who knew Ira for over a decade. "It was sort of a chauvinist game."

Einhorn would break up couples, she says, in order to get closer to the male partner, seducing him with ideas.

This does not necessarily mean that Ira Einhorn acted out any sort of homosexual motive. (For the record the only indication that Einhorn had physical experience in this realm was his account, speaking as "Seth," that at age seventeen, he had been orally serviced by another man—"I didn't find it particularly appealing," he said, judiciously adding that "homosexuals don't threaten me.") More likely, Ira's actions were part of a general pattern of controlling behavior.

Perhaps in service to his goals of domination, he kept control of himself as well. A realm of Ira was always unapproachable. "Ira was [warm in some regards, but] not in the regard where you need to feel needed and emotionally understood, in dealing with difficult things in one's internal life," says Michael Rossman. "In that sense, Ira's sensibility was quite exteriorized ... he had projected an invulnerability."

Just as Ira often implicitly excluded himself from the confused state of the hoi polloi, he seemed to have willed himself out of the common maladies to which humans are prone.

"The main thing that struck me was his lack of emotional involvement, and that he didn't want to discuss it, even though he wanted to discuss everything else. It was always sort of intellectual, one step removed, never about himself personally," says Judy Wicks, the co-owner of La Terrasse. For a brief spell when she first came to Philadelphia, she had been involved with Einhorn. "He wanted to know me, and he wanted to know how I felt about everything, but I never remember him ever talking about his own feelings. He's an extremely controlled person, everything he did was thought out and calculated. He liked having the upper hand and doing something for others, and not feeling like he was dependent on anybody. I thought that got to be weird. I even said, *Don't you ever get angry, or sad, or express any kind of emotion? Don't you really have feelings for things you do and for people?* He didn't even want to talk about that. He was very, very closed."

The exceptions to this controlled behavior were rare, and seldom discussed by the Unicorn. They seemed to be focused on the very few times that Ira Einhorn let slip his above-it-all aura of guruhood and allowed himself to fall prey to the most bittersweet of human maladies: love. Ira had perhaps four love affairs that developed into something more than idle physical pleasure and first-person anthropology. Despite the differences in the women, the circumstances, the age and development of Einhorn himself, and the cultural milieu of the relationships—which spanned a period of fifteen years—there were alarming similarities in those four affairs. Each time, Ira Einhorn found himself obsessively fixed on a woman who, tired of being smothered by his dominating ego, rejected him. And in at least three of those four times, Ira Einhorn reacted in a manner inconsistent with the person he stood for, betraying at least part of himself as something beastly.

He responded with violence.

This is what the friends of Ira Einhorn, and even the police at the time of his arrest, did not know. The true heart of Ira Einhorn's darkness has not been exposed to date: If Ira Einhorn killed Holly Maddux in a rage at the time she made it clear she was leaving him, the act would not have been an isolated instance of violence.

On September 11, 1977, Ira Einhorn and Holly Maddux were in a room, a room of their apartment, third-floor rear, 3411 Race Street. No outsiders witnessed their interaction. Ira Einhorn says that the key event was Holly's casual announcement that she was going to the store, an errand from which she never returned. Holly Maddux, of course, is dead, and will never tell her version of what occurred that day. Speaking in her behalf, the Commonwealth of Pennsylvania contends that Ira Einhorn viciously and fatally beat her. While circumstantial evidence may be compelling, in and of itself it is seldom satisfying. It calls out for context and precedent. Why now, after a lifetime of espousing nonviolence, would Ira Einhorn burst free of his remarkable self-control and act so completely out of character?

The grounds of inquiry change when we understand what happened in other rooms at other times.

Fifteen years before the death of Holly Maddux, there was another room, a dormitory room at Bennington College. It was 1962. This was the time, as Ira Einhorn's letters show with almost comically overheated sentiment, that his passions were fueled by gluttonous reading and a dizzying freedom in his personal interactions. Graduated from college, not yet enrolled in graduate school, urged by Morse Peckham's paternal enthusiasms, and picking his way into visions of a culture where youthful energy and ripe ideas merge, Ira cut a figure of wolfish intensity, charming many he met, but most of all absorbed in himself. So it was that when he met Rita Siegal in early 1962, their relationship was more a function of what he imagined it to be than what it actually was.

Rita was a Bennington girl from Long Island, smart and direct in her speech. She was a dancer, with a fine dancer's body. At the time she met Ira in early 1962, she was having trouble with her self-esteem. "If anyone would pay me a good word, or pat me on the head, I would just lap it up," she recalls now, with the perspective of a quarter-century of reflection. "So I was real needy. So that's where the relationship came from, he patted me on the head and showed me some interest. And then I respected his intelligence, he seemed very intelligent to me." But never, according to Rita Siegal, did she consider it a towering relationship, the key union in her life. This contrasts to Ira Einhorn's perception at the time:

"I hope that the beauty of Rita's love will be able to sustain me in all the agonies of those restless days ahead!" he wrote. "When I'm with her, all disappears—and no matter how she acts the calm of 'knowing' descends upon me—all becomes joy and light. Long live love!"

Siegal considered these ejaculations part of the syndrome of Ira's romantic projections. He lived in a world of ideas, and apparently those ideas leaked into his head in crazy ways. It was almost as if he viewed life, his own reality, as some fictional construct in which he could project his view of things, as a novelist controls the environment of his protagonist. "Eventually he got into all these fantasies," says Siegal. "But I never really took it very personally somehow, because he was so far removed from reality. The quote, great romance of the century, was what was in his head and he was fantasizing, but that wasn't what was happening at all. I never got the feeling that this was a love relationship. I got the feeling it was a sick relationship."

Yet, perhaps because of Rita's insecurity, she allowed the relationship to continue through the spring and into the summer. Rita planned to work during the term break, at a lab in Hanover, New Hampshire, and she invited Ira to live with her. This was despite her realization that Ira Einhorn was an exceedingly strange person.

Indeed, Ira's behavior was increasingly, disturbingly weird. His lack of contact with any institution except his own free-style academy of literature and thought had unleashed any bounds that might have even slightly modified his behavior. Exulting in the words of thunderous loners, individuals who set their own rules for behavior—Nietzsche, Lawrence, Henry Miller, the Marquis de Sade—he fell into primal reveries. Some of his outbursts gave Rita the frights.

"It was as if somebody were talking about something, and dreaming about something, and fantasizing about something, and all of a sudden he would become the thing itself," she says. "And he would start glaring at you, and leering at you."

Rita Siegal felt at those times that if she remained stationary, Ira Einhorn might do violence to her. "I could see when he'd be clicking into crazy, and I'd just run, physically get out of there. I was fast . . . he couldn't catch me. Who knows what he would have done if he'd caught me. It was like that."

As the days went on, with Rita working and Ira poring over dozens of texts borrowed from the Dartmouth library, she began to feel more and more uncomfortable. She wanted to leave, but was afraid to. She felt trapped. She was convinced that Ira was capable of horrible things. At one point he had actually shown a bizarre propensity for torturing small animals. "[He would] take a kitty-cat into the shower and listen to it scream."

This is what Ira Einhorn was writing in late June 1962:

> Sadism—sounds nice—run it over your tongue—contemplate with joy the pains of others as you expire with an excruciating satisfaction. Project outward the vision of inward darkness. Let no cesspool of inner meaning be concealed. Reveal the filth that you are. Know the animal is always there. . . . Beauty and innocence must be violated for they can't be possessed. The sacred mystery of another must be preserved—only death can do that.

Rita Siegal figured that her job would soon be over; she would return to Bennington and be free of him. "I just wanted to get out gracefully," she says. "Survive." But the caldron of Einhorn's mind was bubbling furiously, as he probably was beginning to realize that Rita was determined not to continue the relationship. On July 24, he wrote that "Death may join us where life fails." On July 28, obviously frustrated by her looming rejection, he penned another tirade:

> Rita and I have come to an impasse—I can no longer tolerate either her selfishness or lack of faith. To give and give some more is my desire, but not to one so unthinking as her. My dreams are realizable and will not be snuffed out by the fear of anyone—I too have a right to a life of my own and to that I will dedicate myself. She lacks faith and the ability to respect another: Without these qualities, no matter what she is, she is as nothing. Come September and all is over. The pieces will be picked up and all started anew. The progress of my soul must not be crushed by the failings of a selfish young woman. So good-bye my love and good luck to my replacement—may he be more willing to be taken advantage of.

In Rita Siegal's recollection, she had returned to Bennington by then and had informed Ira Einhorn that the relationship was over. He found her there, in her dormitory room. On July 30, Ira had just read, and been enchanted by, a sadomasochistic classic, *Venus in Furs*. He was moved to express his feelings upon turning the final page:

> We so carefully hide the blackness of our soul from all those around us (even ourselves) we forget so easily the impulses of power which unconsciously control so many of our actions! A book like *Venus in Furs* reminds us of what we are—blackness and light. To beat a woman—what joy—to bite her breasts and ass—how delightful—to have her return the favor in our sensitive areas. How is life to be lived? That is what the book asks unknowingly. Should we subjugate or be subjugated. Realize our darkness or at least become aware of it. Can I love Rita as she is or must I break her spirit. Does she provide me with what I want. Often I think not. Investigate—plunge deeply—leave no stone unturned. You are one of the rare free spirits do not be saddled by one who isn't. Life to be lived at its full must be lived freely. Let nothing stand in your way to getting what you can not even the illusion of love which you know to be so transitory.

As Rita remembers it, Ira came to her dorm room. Rita made it clear that he was not welcome. "I probably said, 'We need to end this thing,' " she says. It was then that she perceived that silent click that told her that Ira had shifted into a darkly determined being. The shift was difficult to explain. "It wasn't like he lost his reality," she says. "He totally knew what he was doing."

Unlike other times this had occurred, she had nowhere to run.

"He just went over and locked the door," she says. "It was quiet, premeditated. It wasn't a rational buildup of temper at all. It was almost like, you watch one of those supernatural movies on television, and eyes change. Like a werewolf. It was like that truly. And so I knew when that happened, I was in the room with a madman."

The room was not large, and there was only one door. "I could have gotten out if I had been a more assertive person," says Rita Siegal, thinking back to when she was nineteen years old and young Ira Einhorn was approaching her with madness in his eyes. "I could have screamed. But I didn't. I suppose I could have jumped out the window, but I was afraid of getting cut. The man was strong."

Ira Einhorn moved steadily toward her. He did not rush his movements. For a brief while, Rita Siegal tried to fight him off, but then she let go. Ira Einhorn's hands were around her neck, choking her. And then she passed out.

On July 31, 1962, Ira Einhorn wrote: "To kill what you love when you can't have it seems so natural that strangling Rita last night seemed so right."

Michael Hoffman recalls reading another of Ira's accounts of the incident. "He talked about how, watching the color of her face change, something clicked at the last minute and he looked up, he let go."

Ira: "Insanity, thank goodness, is only temporary, and when the nightmare lifts one must face the truth."

Ira later told Rita that he returned to the room soon after he left it, to see if she was still alive. She did not recall that visit. She awoke with his fingermarks still visible on her throat, and spent the night in the school infirmary. She says that she preferred no charges against the man who assaulted her but did arrange with the college that Ira thereafter be banned on campus.

Perhaps the strangest thing of all was Ira Einhorn's reaction to what could have been a disastrous night. He tried to will it to insignificance. Others may have sought help after almost killing a woman, but Ira seemed to regard it as a step in a struggle for self-realization. He did not even seem to think that it need affect his relationship with Rita, and a full month after the incident he wrote that "I want to love Rita (my entire being cries and needs the love we could have) but it is so difficult to anticipate the shifting of her unstable sands. Afraid, trapped, unsure, insecure . . . but beautiful in the desire which entirely grips her (even though she can't admit it to herself) to realize what she has . . ." As if her refusal to commit to him was based solely on unfounded timidity.

Ira saw the incident as an existential act in an intellectual tradition. He did not see it as a human failing, or a reflection of his own social problems.

Michael Hoffman, one of the few who knew of the Bennington incident, still is dazzled by how Ira handled the knowledge of his violence. "Everything Ira talked about, he theorized. So he would mention Raskolnikov. And then he would talk about some archetypical thing that would have driven him to do it." It puzzled Michael Hoffman to no end. "I never saw him mean or violent to other men," he says. "He certainly was never violent with me. I mean, Ira could have pulverized me. He was always very gentle with me, I could always tell him to fuck off. All he would answer, he'd look at me, give me his charming smile, and say, 'Why? Why are you angry?' But this [incident] I found very scary. And I'd say to him, 'What would you have done if you killed her?' He said, 'That would never happen, something would stop me.'"

Blinded by ego, he considered himself invincible. Unbound by the rules of common man, he felt no reason to abide by laws and limits.

Amazingly, Ira still pursued Rita, who says she did her best to avoid him. Since they had friends in common, they would sometimes see each other. At least one more time, the relationship flared, at the home of mutual friends Mark and Tama Zorn. Rita's recollection is hazy, but Mark Zorn recalls coming in the room and seeing Rita bruised. "As far as I knew he just hit her in the eye," says Zorn. "A black eye." Ira himself, talking as "Seth" in the aforementioned interview, described an event that seems to fit that circumstance. "I probably made some dirty crack," he said, "whereupon she insulted me terribly, I forget how, and I walloped her across the face, leaving a big welt." Though Ira felt badly about hitting her, he prefaced this admission by saying that "I think people should be able to hit each other occasionally within the context of a structured situation where the violence is understood and accepted."

So ended Ira's relationship with Rita. Even though, as far as Siegal was concerned, the relationship was "very much one-sided on his side" and "more a flip kind of thing for me." Einhorn considered it perhaps the major relationship in his life to date, and thought about Rita extensively for years afterward. Late in 1962, he wrote Hoffman of "the melancholy that had plagued me like a silent specter ever since Rita left for good. . . . I still love Rita but my spirit does not brood over lost glory or rage about with a fine frenzy; it has learned to sit and wait—to care and not to care and to be assured of others who will pursue the mystic union of flesh with the same ardor as the one I lost."

For the next few years, Ira sought that mystic union rather indiscriminately. His relationships followed a pattern. The initial encounter would put him in raptures, and he would subsequently pursue the woman with such intensity that within a few weeks, or even days, both partners would be exhausted, ready to move on. Other affairs were more casual—light lovemaking as a result of geographical coincidence, or purely sexual pickups. It was not until 1965 that he met another woman who fired his imagination—and drew his emotions out—as deeply as Rita had.

The outcome would occur in yet another gruesome scene, in yet another little room.

Her name was Judy Lewis, and she was a student at Penn. Her instructors describe her as magnetic, vital, very tall, very pretty. Her hair glowed with auburn highlights, and for Ira this was particularly enchanting because he had long harbored a fetish for redheads. It is, Ira once said, "an attribute which has the same effect on me as marijuana—delicious ecstasy."

Ira was growing into his role as culture hero, but had not yet established his public beachhead as a Free University instructor. Judy, seven years younger, might have seemed malleable enough for him to dominate. Yet, though she was experiencing some emotional stress of her own, she was independent, and certainly intelligent enough to engage him. Ira set aside the progression of short affairs he had been having, and became obsessed with Judy Lewis.

"Ira was so intense that when you got involved with him, he would get inside your head," says Michael Hoffman, who was on the Penn faculty at the time, and observed the Einhorn-Lewis affair as a friend of both. "You would have that kind of relationship—inside of one another's heads. He was particularly that way with women because he needed to dominate. . . . It was not a placid relationship, it was obviously a very passionate one, and at a certain point I think she wanted out. Because I think like a lot of other people, she finally felt mind-fucked by the guy."

"She was very interested in him, because of his mind, basically," says Jill Bressler, a close friend of Lewis's. "And he got more and more possessive. Underneath all of his business, I think he's extraordinarily defensive. She was not allowed to do anything except be with him, and I think that she wasn't the kind of dependent female that he was used to or that he needed. I remember she used to talk about how he would insist on staying up all night long and talking, and if you wanted to go to sleep that was disloyal. She began to get a sense of his intensity, and his emotional violence. He was grasping and tenacious and nuts."

As he had with Rita, Ira Einhorn had constructed a fantasy scenario in which Judy Lewis was a woman he wanted to share his life with. He ignored evidence that the longer the relationship lasted, the less eager she was to continue. Ira poured his heart into reams of copy about Judy—her beauty, her depth, and her selfish refusal to give everything to him.

"Joy would erupt," he wrote in September 1965, "if Judy could only learn the simple acceptance of the magic which flows between us." Ira even figured out how deep were his ties with her—if willing, she could provide him the "absolute trust my mother's strong relationship imposed on my psyche." He asked himself: "Do I wish to master a woman sufficiently so that she will take care of me as my mother did?" But these ruminations faded in the heat generated by his emotions. He alternately cursed Judy and crowed over her. Intermingled with these exultations were his reports about the anguish in his soul, and the excruciating headaches he was suffering. "I have a strange lightness about the head which is beginning to frighten me," he wrote in September 1965. "There seems to be a strong possibility that I may eventually be permanently psychotic!"

It was no wonder that Judy Lewis became terrified at the Unicorn's mad intensity. But as Rita Siegal had discovered, leaving an obsessed Ira Einhorn was no simple matter. "You just didn't walk away from Ira and say, 'Fuck you, Mac,'" explains Mike Hoffman. "To leave Ira, to do *anything* with Ira, was something you really needed to think about and talk about. It was a big thing."

It took months before Ira finally came to realize that Judy Lewis really wanted to end it. Not see him. Generally, he tried to disregard what she said. Ira would construct explanations that saw her demurrals as vacillation; he would mentally produce evidence that Judy really wanted to extend the relationship. And if she didn't? Ira had some ideas about that, too.

The Unicorn in November 1965:

> The violence that flowed through my being tonight . . . still awaits that further dark confirmation of its existence which could result in the murder of that which I seem to love so deeply. The repressed is returning to a form that is almost impossible to control. . . . There is a good chance that I will attempt to kill Judy tomorrow—the rational awareness of this fact brings stark terror into my heart but it must be faced if I wish to go on—I must not allow myself to deviate from the self-knowledge which is in the process of being uncovered!

The next day brought no violent scenes, but week after week the problem deepened: Judy attempting to let Ira know things were over, and Ira refusing to let things go. Even as he slipped toward the unspeakable, he examined his own behavior with a morbid self-consciousness. At one point he made a note to himself to quiz his mother on details of his behavior in infancy. "So much of my deviancy could be explained in terms of an impotent, uncompleted rage," he noted. Underneath this clinical curiosity, though, something horrible was brewing underneath the upbeat demeanor he showed his public.

By March of 1966, Ira was writing that "I feel as if things are about to culminate in the creation of an involvement that will allow me to do the work that will enable me to become more of what I am or as a result of this partial madness I will bring my world crashing down about me." At times, he was specific about how he would bring the world down—he fantasized about murdering Judy Lewis. On March 14 he wrote, "How ridiculous the thought of killing Judy appears, yet I held it in my mind just four short hours ago—this particular ability of man is both his horror and his joy." He was seething:

> Violence creeps over my body as I reach toward the destruction of Judy, a hopeless victim in this infernal entanglement which seems to be draining the life's blood of both of us . . . the foolish ambivalence

of our desires still tosses us beyond the recall of reason to a point of suspension on which we hang in perilous balance threatening to destroy or be destroyed in an instant of reckless action—we must come together or die.

On March 17, 1966, that instant of reckless action occurred. According to Judy Lewis, who recounted the incident to Philadelphia detective Mike Chitwood thirteen years later, Ira had been insistent on a meeting. The rendezvous was to be at her apartment, for coffee and nothing else. Ira arrived, full of ideas why the relationship should be resumed, but Judy did not want to continue. The argument broke off momentarily when she left the apartment to get something for the coffee.

Ira Einhorn's reconstruction of the scene came in an unpublished poem entitled "An Act of Violence." It tells of his lingering over coffee in the shadow of the relationship's finality. It tells of her departing for milk, cynically noting that it is "a rare performance of duty for one she loves." It tells of her returning with milk and donuts. The coffee is served, as Ira musters up courage for some unnamed act. But then he seemingly discards the notion, and puts on his jacket, ready to leave.

Suddenly it happens.

Judy Lewis apparently had her back turned at that point, and thus did not see that Ira Einhorn had started toward her with a weapon in his hand—a Coke bottle.

Bottle in hand I strike
Away at the head . . .

The glass broke and Judy began bleeding. He wrestled her down to the floor, holding her by the neck; she felt her head hit against the table as she fell. Ira was strangling her. She felt herself going limp . . . and lost consciousness.

In such violence there may be freedom.

The next thing Judy remembered was seeing her neighbors, who had come into the room, attracted by the commotion. She told them to call the campus police. Ira Einhorn, of course, was gone.

He was alone with his thoughts:

Where am I now after having hit Judy over the head with a coke bottle, blood on my jacket and pants—then making some feeble attempts to choke her. She wanted to live, that has been established. . . . I'll be able, if she does not have me arrested, to go back to living a normal life. Violence always marks the end of a relationship. It is the final barrier over or through which no communication is possible.

As was the case with Rita Siegal, Judy Lewis spent the night in the school infirmary, nursing the bruises from Ira Einhorn's attack. Also as in the case of Rita Siegal, no charges were preferred, but assurances made that if the assault were repeated, Ira would face legal repercussions.

Once again, Ira Einhorn had gone out of control. And once again, in the aftermath of a shocking act of violence, he displayed absolutely no remorse. Though he admitted his action was "ridiculous," he seemed to feel it a liberating response to a woman too "selfish" to accept him. As if he were some sort of Nietzschean Ubermensch, he saw the act solely in terms of the Unicorn—how it affected *his* growth, how it freed *him* from moping. As if he were willfully oblivious to the reality of the situation: He had almost killed a woman, again.

Michael Hoffman, more appalled by this attack than by the Bennington incident, would grill Ira on the matter, with little satisfaction. "He would sort of disengage himself from himself when he talked about these things. He didn't take responsibility. He didn't have the same kind of guilt that you or I would have, in that he didn't say, 'Jesus Christ, how could I have done that terrible thing?' He would talk about how it had grown out of the nature of the relationship. How it's not really possible to have the kind of full, rich, sharing relationship that a man and a woman needed to have. And somehow that would be part of the explanation."

Others might have been scared at the dark side of their personality taking over. Not Ira Einhorn. "He had probably the most elaborate defense structure I've ever seen in anybody," says Hoffman. "He would literally walk in after doing something like that and want to discuss the reasons for its having been done from a psychoanalytic point of view, a sociological point of view, its place in history

... so that he immediately had a very elaborate structure to put it in."

But Ira Einhorn would never—never—look at his morbid handiwork and, realizing it might reoccur, ask for help.

"Not to me, he didn't," says Mike Hoffman. "And I think he would have been as likely to ask me as any other man. We were very tight."

When Ira did address the dark side of his nature, it was in tones of a romantic hero, almost boastful of his violent tendencies, as if they were a badge of his significance. (Some in Ira's circle came to know he had been violent with women; however, only a very few knew the extent of the violence.) From California, the summer following the Coke bottle attack, Ira discussed the direction of his life in a letter to Hoffman: "Rita and Judy practically destroyed, Peckham unable to go any farther! I need the confrontation of my monsters lodged in some external being—to meet and see what haunts me—to face it and fight it every day without it disappearing.... I live quietly and calmly with real joy on the edge of a volcano that might explode into nova-like being at any moment ... when it happens, beware!"

But increasingly, even that degree of self-examination was becoming rare for Einhorn. After his experiences with the two vital, intelligent women he adored, Rita and Judy, he seemed to settle on what friends came to know as the classic Ira Einhorn woman— shy, gentle women of classic beauty, most often blondes or redheads. Women of very low confidence. Women he could easily dominate. No longer did Ira Einhorn seem to have any taste for the struggle.

"He liked to be challenged in his guru capacity," says Rose Rutman, friendly with Ira in this period, "but in his capacity of personal friend or lover he didn't like to be challenged. Because he would pick these wimpy, brainless women. The people he actually got to move in with him were antithetical to the [more intellectual] kind of people he seemed to want as friends."

It is possible that Ira subconsciously realized the dangers that came when he lost such struggles; maybe he feared that a reoccurrence would end with a dead woman in his arms. In any case, the experiences of Rita and Judy—where he launched furiously into one-sided romances that consumed his being—were not to be repeated. "Perhaps the repressed has not been cared for," he mused. "It could linger in wait like a caged animal awaiting the moment when it will unleash a wave of anger that will spell destruction—for myself rather than another, I would hope."

Ira had been seeing other women even as his passion over Judy had reached a violent boil, and his scorched-earth relationship with the opposite sex continued. Privately, he despaired of ever finding a woman who could satisfy him. "I'm slowly beginning to realize the enormity of the problem which my development has created in respect to women," he wrote not long after the abrupt breakup with Judy, "The interaction with Rita is just an example of how difficult, even at that age and with such a magnificent partner, any final linking is to be. Judy provided in her striking beauty a repository for always wandering projections, and the strength of our deathlike struggle is a good indication of how impossible my quest is to be. I refuse to admit the inevitable—that I can live without a woman (my mother). Until I accept this my productivity will be intense, like my countless infatuations, but sporadic. . . . I'm faced with a hell that is somewhat relieved by my incredible energy which is so capable of constantly creating that joy which is deeper than sorrow."

As the mayor of Powelton, Ira found women as plentiful as ever. A womanizer in the sixties, especially one with guru credentials, found no challenge at all in bedding women within minutes after meeting them. One day, after figuring out that he had, in his times, been brought to orgasm by at least 200 women, he fancied that more amusement might be produced by several women at once. Indeed, Ira was the sponsor of the first official Powelton Village orgy, described by some participants as a rather self-conscious event that ultimately did the trick for Ira and others who adventured all the way.

But even as Ira became more firmly convinced that polygamy was his natural state, he did yearn for one special woman, someone with whom he could share a long-term union. He seemed to find what he was looking for in June 1968. On a plane to San Francisco, he met gorgeous yet almost preternaturally docile twenty-two-year-old Kim Owens.

Owens, whose blond perfection led people to think her Scandinavian (though her melodic accent stemmed from her childhood in

Hawaii), was instantly struck by Einhorn, who regaled her during the transcontinental journey with his friendships with Jerry Rubin, Allen Ginsberg, Alan Watts, and Baba Ram Dass, the heroes of the sixties. As Einhorn's escort, she would meet them all. "I was very quiet, a very shy person, definitely involved in the counterculture," recalls Kim Owens. "Hearing this man who was very powerful and intellectually sure of himself, and very much accepted by all these people who I had only heard about . . . I was really in awe of him."

Before the summer was over, she had moved into the apartment in the Piles with him, her main reservation being an uncertainty over why such a well-spoken, powerful figure would deign to live with *her.* "I think she probably saw Ira as an authoritarian or father figure," says Dave Peterson, who shared the apartment with them during that period. "I don't think it was an equal relationship in terms of dominance or control. I think he dominated and controlled the situation." Ira did little to boost Kim's confidence, particularly when he made it clear that he considered it his prerogative to freely sample other young women of the counterculture. In theory, she could conduct similar explorations, but Kim Owens was fairly traditional in that respect, and could not consider—had no desire to consider—that option. By October, she drew on a fund of money she had inherited and flew to Boston. "I was there about a month," she said, "and flew back to see him, wished he would marry me, make a commitment, or something. That didn't work. I left for Boston again."

For two years, that cycle held. Kim Owens was stuck on a pendulum, in love with Ira, but unable to reconcile herself to his insistence on promiscuity. Just as Holly Maddux, another shy and striking blonde with money of her own, would later leave and return, furious at the Unicorn's domination.

From Kim Owens's point of view, the troubles did not stop with Ira's other women. She found herself in the role of a virtual servant—cooking, cleaning, assuming the organic/domestic duties of a good hippie housewife. When in the presence of Ira's intellectual cohorts and famous friends, she slunk to the background, a bauble for which the Unicorn was envied. On occasion he would be verbally abusive—"He would mostly just put her down, or make fun of something she was doing or saying," says Dave Peterson. Kim was often frustrated by Ira's deep immersion in the intellectual life—

even in the most stunning natural settings, he seemed more interested in the pages of books than his surroundings. She had to beg to get him to go on a picnic. And he never betrayed vulnerability, was always so *controlled*. "That's what frightened people, that's what gave him his power," she says. "I felt that he would hold in his feelings. He didn't share those things, if things bothered him. He was always a bit above it."

When the Woodstock festival was held in August 1969, Kim was excited and ready to go. But Ira refused. Apparently he had no desire to be a foot soldier in the counterculture, in mud and squalor. Kim said she would attend anyway—she even arranged a ride for herself—but then the Unicorn played his trump card. "If you go," he said, "then *I'm* free this weekend." Unable to deal with the certainty that he would see another, Kim Owens did not go to Woodstock.

Yet the romance, while not flourishing, went into its second year, and kept going. Ira might not have considered Kim an intellectual match, but he came to feel for her. He wrote page after page of erotic poetry with Kim as protagonist. But she was not his only carnal object. "He would always say, and this was particularly when he went with Kim, that he had to get laid two or three times a day," recalls Rose Rutman. "Those were his needs and that it just had to happen. That his sexuality was an expression of his power and his need was so great, that he had so much power." But that "need" was something that Kim could not compromise on.

He would tell her he saw other women, and she would break down. Her unhappiness toward Ira's other lovers grew to paranoia, and it reached the point where one day she saw mussed pillows and the closet door ajar, and immediately assumed another had been in their bed—she quickly headed for another airport escape, leaving in tears, to Ira's insults. At another point, she read his diaries, and though certain people were identified only by astrological symbols, she figured out he was writing about women he was having sex with. "I remember tearing apart those diaries," she says, "throwing them around and splitting on a plane, far away." Apparently this reached Einhorn—"It was like cutting his finger off," she said. After that action, even Bea Einhorn, who normally adored Kim, called to admonish her. "She asked how could I do that to him, when his diaries were so important," Kim recalls.

What Kim Owens remembers most clearly about her two years with Ira Einhorn is her tears. This happened most often when Ira flouted his other women to her, something she later identified as deliberate "mind-fucking." During that period, "I cried," she says. "Really cried. It tore me apart."

As far as she can recall, the pain was physical only once. They were painting the apartment and the tired old dispute about other women came up. This time, Ira struck her in the face. Though momentarily stunned, Kim Owens was sufficiently feisty to respond, but instead of retaliating directly, "the argument went to the walls." They wound up throwing brushes and wrecking the room, and soon they were laughing at their slapstick. The incident was diffused.

But the troubles continued. In early November 1969, Ira took Kim along to a weekend seminar he was presenting with a guerilla theater troupe, at Shippensburg State College in western Pennsylvania. The trip took a sour turn when Kim lost track of Ira and found him in the back of an auditorium with another woman. Then, on the way to the train station on icy roads, the car spun out of control. Ira suffered only a split lip, but Kim was badly hurt, temporarily paralyzed from the waist down. Ira stayed by her side until the ambulance came, administering breathing exercises. She spent ten days in the hospital, another month in bed, and several more on crutches. Ira was touchingly gentle with her.

Actually, he was figuring that the relationship had reached a decision point. Just days before the accident, he was experiencing breeding pains. Seeing a cute puppy, he pictured Kim holding his baby. Now he sent healing vibes to Kim's hospital room and wrote that he could understand their troubles. He yearned for security, the knowledge of another's love. Yet, he wrote, "I still must be free to touch all others when the need is there." He added, though, that this need was on behalf of those unnamed others since, as a greater being, "[my need] has almost disappeared."

Though during the few weeks of the new decade, there were the same breakups and reconciliations, Ira had reconsidered the idea of marriage. Just as the unicorn of legend was captured by a virgin, the Unicorn was willing to give up his titular bachelorhood for Kim Owens's pure devotion. A date was set, but astrological considerations intervened. "The day we planned to get married, we had three major oppositions on our chart," explains Kim. Jimmy Hammerman, who moved into the apartment when Dave Peterson got married in 1968, recalls another obstacle: "He wanted to get married on TV," he says, "and she thought that was a load of crap."

In the early spring, though, the talk of marriage simply dissipated. It seems that on Ira's part there might have been cold feet, complicated by the preparations for Earth Day. On Kim's part, marriage seemed contraindicated by the specter of coping with constant adultery. In Bea Einhorn's recollection, the couple had actually taken out a marriage license before Ira finally changed his mind. "I don't think I can handle this," he told his mother. "If I look and talk to another girl she gets very upset. I've been looking and talking to girls all my life."

Jimmy Hammerman had been witness to innumerable Ira-Kim fights and breakups. He guesses that the eventual split was Ira's fault. "Here was Kim Owens, a very nice lady who was devoted to him, and then when push came to shove, when it came right down to it, he throttled the whole situation. He was a kid. A great brain, but emotionally he was very immature." Hammerman guesses that if Einhorn was aware of this immaturity, it was only "in his deepest secret recesses." More likely, he chose not to deal with it.

In any case, one tearful escape by Kim Owens that spring proved to be final. Oddly, she did not immediately hop on an airplane but took shelter for a short while in an abandoned apartment elsewhere in Powelton. She cleaned out the place and lived there a week or two. Ira came over once to give her some mail and saw her on the street once, thinking her "a beautiful creature that I hardly knew." Soon she was gone, off to join Wavy Gravy and the Hog Farm commune in San Francisco. Within six months she would write him to tell of her marriage to another member of the Hog Farm.

Unlike the breakups with Rita and Judy, Kim had gotten away clean. Just why Ira's dark side did not erupt is a matter of conjecture. One explanation might be that though Ira cared for Kim, his passion was not obsessive, as it had been in the other cases. Also, in the anticipation of Earth Day, and the excitement of signing a Doubleday book contract, Ira had other concerns to deflect his attention. The most charitable reason is that Ira had come to grips with the "monsters" within him. His wistful reflection soon after Kim's departure seems to indicate some awareness of this:

Sadness just washing over as I fully experience the loss of Kim—she's gone and the knowledge rips into me—hovers and swirls, bites, erodes, and then the sadness again . . . the light must come through as we/it goes on its way. Now what do you feel—anger, loss, resentment—arising from the pit of your stomach. Let it rise—detach yourself from it—feel fixation . . . instead of living out the violence of anger and resentment. . . . Emotions are the past—they hold, they pull, they grab—mind flows!

The outburst over, I feel ready to go forward. There really is no sense in seeing K again. Pain on both sides. I'll go back on this decision again and again, but it is obviously the best one.

Two years later, when Ira Einhorn met Holly Maddux, he sensed himself ready for another deep relationship, perhaps deeper than Kim's, and more reciprocal than Judy's or Rita's. With his history of violence, it would have been logical for him to worry about the dangers if he should be rejected. He seemed to recognize his dark potential, at least as he pondered it in December 1972, two months after meeting Holly. The two were already fighting, but Ira reasoned that hurt would be a necessary component for their growth. "I need to be worked with," he admitted. "Helped—shocked . . . failure would once again mean the agony of losing a mate—how to release myself from that agony is just as important as having Holly as mate. . . . I've learned, but I can still feel the possibility of shock on the edge—watch carefully. It would be easy, so easy to indulge that pull that would hurl me back into the past—ten years work can be destroyed in a day!"

That statement would prove prophetic.

12

THE UNICORN'S SECRET

When Holly Maddux left Ira Einhorn in Europe in mid-summer 1977, it was unclear whether or not they would ever rekindle their relationship. The understanding was that Holly would find her own place to live, a course more to Holly's liking than Ira's. This didn't mean that Holly might not change her mind, as she had in the past, and move back in with Ira. There was no reason for Ira Einhorn to panic. Yet within days he was beginning to suffer depression and anxiety. Perhaps he intuited that this time Holly Maddux meant it—she was rejecting him, as the others had done in the past. As he traveled in Scandinavia, this possibility hung over him like a mocking specter. He had lost *control* of the relationship; knowing this caused mental havoc.

"I think of her with others, and anger and hurt comes," he wrote only a few days after they parted. "Yet I want to love, not possess. . . . Let her find someone else who will give her a child—tinges of wanting to hurt and punish her also crisscross with this theme." He vowed to ponder the subject as he traveled.

Holly was very much on his mind as he moved through Norway and Sweden, saw friends, slept with other women. One night he dreamed of her. They were in a public place, perhaps a movie theater, and they kissed tenderly, forgetting the people around them. He woke with a good feeling, and spent the next day missing her, writing her a letter proposing marriage, "kids included." This

296

was the enticement he had used to draw her back the previous summer.

This time Holly did not jump at the offer. Ira phoned her, Oslo to Fire Island. She told him that she had already arranged an apartment of her own. This resolve was followed by a letter that, while warm, steered clear of the treacherous issues between them. Instead Holly offered chatty descriptions of her encounter with Rick Iannacone, and the precarious status of the large jade plant at 3411 Race.

Ira tried to shrug off these warning signs, and made his plans to fly back to the States. He was in high spirits when he returned on August 21, a Norwegian pullover sweater for Holly in hand. But when he phoned her at Joyce Petschek's house in Saltaire, he found her still determined to live apart. The hour-long phone conversation was, in his word, a "horror." He was stung by her reaction, as if he had been bitten by a pet he had raised from birth. "She is adamant about her space," he wrote. "No want *me*: I feel so rejected and lost." He called her twice more that day: The first time she told him she had no privacy to speak, but during the second call she was, in his view, "softer." He felt that maybe, if given some space, she might come around.

Rick Iannacone, who had sublet Ira's apartment, had not expected Ira back until October. He asked if he could stay until September. So Ira traveled to Andrija Puharich's house in Ossining, where more psychic work was being done. Ira began to experience some very strange feelings. He believed that suddenly he had accumulated the power of healing. He marveled at the heat and energy that flew off his hands. In the midst of practicing his new white art, he kept slinking back to the phone to call Fire Island. They were emotional calls, with Ira urging Holly to probe deeper into what went wrong. She admitted "resentment" toward him but Ira was sure it could be overcome. Despite his urging, though, she would not give Ira a date for her return from Saltaire. Ira's feelings were swinging in a wide pendulum. He described himself as "a bird paralyzed by fear," frozen by his inability to continue life without her. Sometimes he would be sure that their problems would be overcome. Other times, he conceded that her love was "hesitant," and they would be better off making a clean break.

One morning he awoke in his room at the Turkey Farm to a deep aching. As he bathed, he pondered his situation. He had lost Rita, then Judy, then Kim, and now Holly? His former lovers appeared clearly in his mind, but he had trouble seeing the woman who was now slipping away from him. And he worried about his "accumulated karma." He wrote that "shards of violence accompany the frustration of my titanic will." But he vowed to fight the impulse to call Holly. As if aware that the ache within him could be ruinous, he concluded that he must find something that would consume him. Perhaps the Tesla work would do.

But something happened at Puharich's; he left suddenly. From the Turkey Farm, he took a bus to Woodstock to stay with Stuart and Julie Samuels in their summer home. As Stuart Samuels remembers it, Ira's departure from Ossining was dramatic: "He had a big fight with Puharich. Puharich literally told him to get out. It wasn't a philosophical thing, it had to do with style—Puharich's women, Ira's women, I don't know. What I do know is, here was a man who in one week had the two most important people in his life reject him totally. His intellectual connection and his life connection, both going off to somewhere else."

Samuels had never seen Ira Einhorn behave so erratically. During the week he stayed in a small cabin in back of the Samuelses' contemporary retreat, he seemed like a paranoid rudely disgorged from a Russian novel. Extremely uptight, and aggressively, obsessively, chasing women. He was, no doubt, trying to compensate for his losing battle to convince Holly to join him in Woodstock, but his equilibrium was upset; his usual omnivorous intensity came off as threatening behavior. He met a woman in town, but intimidated her by his near-desperate insistence on instant sex. "That made three rejections in a week," says Samuels. The Unicorn was making a spectacle of himself, and people were talking about him.

Marty Carey, a Woodstock artist and former Yippie, had known Einhorn since the sixties. Over the years he and his wife, Susan, sometimes found Ira too much to take, but generally they tolerated him and considered him a friend. On this Labor Day weekend, however, Ira was intolerable. Ira's effervescent personality, which usually rumbled and rocked like some exhilarating vintage locomotive, had finally jumped the tracks. The Careys went to a small gathering one evening and Ira, demanding the attention of everyone, ostentatiously performed a "healing" on Julie Samuels. "His need to be the center of attention was so strong," says Marty Carey. "Here we all are, sitting in this room watching a movie, and he just started performing, doing this healing ritual."

Sue Carey, seeing the plump guru lying on the floor in the rapture of alleged energy emissions, joked that he looked like a beached whale. Always skeptical of Ira, she decided to press the point, and that night, she, Marty, and actor Peter Coyote spent hours grilling Ira on what he did, who he was, and why he was always talking about his international connections, about Tesla rays, about his network financed by the phone company. They never did find out. "Somehow I figured if I could get him to talk about his feelings, I could find out what he did," says Sue Carey. "And I was unsuccessful." He was so evasive that the trio wondered whether he was some CIA agent run amok.

Stuart Samuels and his crowd were acquainted with a medium who went by the name of Astrid, and that weekend she was conducting a reading that Ira and the Samuelses attended. "There must have been forty or fifty of us sitting around a table," Samuels says. "Ira stepped forward to have an interchange with Astrid. And Astrid freaked. Astrid just said there was evil. There is horror. And you could see it in the room, there was redness in his face, and this *aura*. Astrid picked it up, just terrified."

Ira laughed it off.

All the while, he kept calling Holly. "The whole point was to make her feel guilty," says Samuels. "He was trying to get her to come up to Woodstock."

On one of those calls, Ira Einhorn found out that Holly was seeing another man on Fire Island. This revelation came only after intense coaxing. Holly told him that she was going to be in New York for a while. In the near future, she explained, there would be no "us." Perhaps they would get together for a one-day trip—but, Holly insisted, they would not have sex. No, she was not living with someone. But, Holly admitted, there *was* a someone.

Ira was devastated. Trying to write the conversation down, he was unable to come up with a word strong enough to convey his hurt at knowing "that her sweetness is going to another. Sucking another prick, licking another asshole." He tried to calm himself, reasoning that if he went slow, started from the beginning, he might win her again. But something deep inside Ira would not be stilled by his nostrum. He could hold his demons temporarily, but how long could he hold them?

I can feel the frustration trying to rage, but the buttons won't push. I'm through to the other side, but it would be easy to fall back.

He called her later that day and demanded to know—*would* she be living with someone when she went to New York? Holly stalled, wanted to know why he wanted to know. He *had* to know! So she said it. *Yes.*

And again, Ira tried to calm the storms within. Separations had happened before. But he admitted that "perhaps this [separation] holds a different meaning."

Pulled back into our old form—the violence and frustration and wanting again.

It was almost as if Ira Einhorn had come face to face with his dark side. Now that Holly had forced him into this crisis, he had to choose between the idealistic principles he often expounded and the hypocrisy of his behavior—the selfishness that flouted those principles. The warmth he felt for Holly—the *love*—had chipped away at his invulnerability, his armor of superiority. Who knows—if this had a lasting effect, the *Ubermensch* might turn out to be a *mensch* after all! Ira might finally be in touch with the true spirit of the era he cherished, a man with the heartfelt tenderness that complemented the "transformation" he so fervently promoted. Love would not be a mere concept for Ira—it would be something *lived*. But that generous surrender was apparently beyond him. The monster inside him that screamed *me* would not be stilled. Holly's independence was therefore treachery. Her rejection was his loss of face. Her leaving would be Ira's calamity. And by his ultimate refusal to allow Holly Maddux the human sovereignty to make her own decisions about her own life, he would cast himself into an enemy of the glorious transformation he hoped would be his generation's legacy on Earth.

On September 3, Ira convinced Holly to come back to Philadelphia on Tuesday the sixth. Holly was careful to impose ground rules of how far things would go, rules to which Ira agreed. It was to be a brief trip, with no lovemaking. On the eve of their reunion, Ira awoke with Holly on his mind—maybe they could have a baby!

Julie Samuels had watched Ira closely during his stay in Woodstock. "I think that the strangeness was that he really was recognizing she was serious this time," she says. "She had tried to leave him so many times and was not able to. She always came back, there with this moth-to-the-flame kind of thing." But this time Holly meant it, and the fact of it changed Ira. By the time he left Woodstock, off to Philadelphia to meet Holly, Julie Samuels felt, for the first time, that Ira *valued* Holly. "I'd never felt that before. You could really feel he loved her," she says.

If Ira had agreed that their meeting was to avoid the physical component, he had little intention of following those rules. He bought flowers on his way to pick her up on the train. He drove her to a motel, and it was clear that his motive was not access to a swimming pool. Restrictions or no, he reported "clothes off it all melts as we unite again and again."

But she still insisted on seeing the other man.

The next day, they returned to Philadelphia; Ira reclaimed 3411 Race Street from Iannacone. This was the day when Ira would try to win Holly back with wild promises. They would have a baby. And Ira would agree to monogamy. Monogamy! *Ira Einhorn* promising monogamy. Perhaps more than anything, this signaled Ira's desperation. The man who thrived on control now had no control over the situation. His promises startled Holly but did not change her mind. Holly Maddux had grown too much to fall back now. No. She would not give up the other man because of Ira Einhorn's desperate vows. The man from Fire Island had invited her to sail with him, and the two were going on a trip.

This defiance stunned Ira. As if Holly Maddux's rejection was a sound too high-pitched for human ears, Ira Einhorn could not register the fact that she had slipped from his grasp. There had to be some misunderstanding!

Suddenly realize that I had not been understood. [She] wants to keep seeing Fire Island [man]. Our relationship is primary, special . . . twelve days on a boat is crazy. A honeymoon with another lover. Don't want to argue my cause: sense her deep confusion—she is so afraid . . . it will take much courting to help her step into the light of our love. . . . I feel the difficulty of being objective in any way that is not false: essence speaks—end it—I voice the feeling—tears—hurt—it feels clear but wrong.

The visit ended inconclusively, and certainly not the way Ira Einhorn hoped it would. On Thursday, Holly went back to New York, to the man with whom she would spend what Ira derisively—

and masochistically—called "a honeymoon." In Ira's mind, Holly had pledged to return after the weekend. But from New York she called the next day to say that she would not come back.

I freak and pull a number—call her in N.Y.—heavy.

It was Friday, September 9. Ira's calls showed he was far beyond any plateau of acceptance. He had indeed "freaked." These were the threats that if Holly did not come home—immediately—he would toss her belongings on the street. This was the night that Holly Maddux was so concerned about Ira's threats that she called several friends to see if he could be calmed down. But Ruth Fink was out that night. Walt Bowker wasn't around. And Barbara Kubiak said that her husband, Curt, wasn't home. It would have to be Holly Maddux who soothed the raging Unicorn. To "get him off the wall," as she told a worried Saul Lapidus.

"I don't know why this guy has been able to push my buttons for so long," she said. She implied that the time where Ira Einhorn pushed her buttons was at an end. As she left Lapidus to board a train at Penn Station, she expressed no qualms about her safety.

There is no evidence that Holly Maddux ever knew about what Ira Einhorn had done to Rita Siegal, or Judy Lewis. Or that after strangling Rita, he had written "To kill what you love when you can't have it seems so natural." Nor is there evidence that she was aware of Ira's words after hitting Judy with the Coke bottle: "Violence always marks the end of a relationship," he wrote then. "It is the final barrier over or through which no communication is possible."

Holly Maddux apparently calmed Ira Einhorn down somewhat when she arrived in Philadelphia on Saturday, September 10. Ira reported forging an arrangement with her for the foreseeable future—they would spend two nights a week together. That night, they double-dated with the Kubiaks at a twin-screen movie theater in Pennsauken, New Jersey, just across the river from Philadelphia. Since Curt and Barbara had seen the movie Ira wanted to see, *Star Wars,* the couples separated and saw separate films. Ira Einhorn enjoyed the exploits of Luke Skywalker and Princess Leia. The four drove back to the Kubiaks', and then Ira and Holly, for the last time, drove back to 3411 Race Street where they argued once again about her leaving Philadelphia to see Saul Lapidus.

The Unicorn could not let her go.

*   *   *

Exactly what happened between the time Ira and Holly returned to the second-floor rear apartment on Saturday night and the afternoon of Sunday, September 11, 1977, will never be recounted beyond question. Ira Einhorn would always insist that Holly went off to the Powelton Ecology Food Co-op and never returned. Even his private journal, which recounts them at odds on that Sunday morning—fighting again about Holly's leaving—records that she left to make a call and go to the co-op. Those who have seen that document say Ira reports that after she failed to return he checked her things and found everything there except her money. He worried about her absence.

He also reported this activity: *work on messy place.*

Another sentence in his short entry for that day mentioned his taking a drive with two women friends, one of them named Jill. A simple statement. He did not mention any details, nor was there evidence that he ever mentioned to anyone what occurred on that drive. But Jill Hamill, one of the women in question, remembers the incident quite clearly.

It was that day, the day that Holly Maddux allegedly disappeared off the face of the earth, that Ira Einhorn asked Jill Hamill to help him permanently dispose of a large steamer trunk sitting on the back porch of his apartment.

Ira had known Jill and her friend Sharon since the spring. The two young women, barely out of high school, lived in a Philadelphia suburb, and had been given Ira's name as a contact in the world of the paranormal, a possible guide. Periodically, Ira would entertain the two girls for sessions where they presumably practiced psychic arts such as meditation and astral projection. Holly was never present when the girls would come to the apartment.

This was the first time Jill and Sharon visited since Ira had left for Europe that May. They met not in his apartment, but took a spin in Jill's car, to the West River Drive along the Schuylkill River. According to Jill, Ira seemed different. "He seemed like he had a sense of urgency," she says. "He said he wanted to ask us something."

"Sure, ask away," the girls said. "We've asked you a million questions."

"I'm in some really, really deep trouble," said Ira Einhorn. "I've got a steamer trunk that has some very, very valuable documents in it. They're documents that belong to the Russians, and I need to get rid of it."

He wanted them to put the trunk in Jill Hamill's 1976 Plymouth Volare and take it to the river. They would dump the trunk in the Schuylkill.

Jill Hamill says that she had a bad feeling about the request. "He almost had us convinced to get this thing . . . He wanted me to drive my car to the Schuylkill River. And I believe it was either Kelly Drive [on the east side of the river] or the West River Drive, because I had asked him exactly, 'Where do you want to take it?' Anyhow, Sharon and I were looking at each other like, this is really weird. I mean, why did he want to get rid of something like this?"

As it turned out, a visual survey showed that Jill's car would not handle the trunk, and the girls were spared the task. Jill was greatly relieved.

The trunk remained in Ira's apartment.

Bea Einhorn remembers the call she received from Ira, ostensibly on the following day, the twelfth of September. "You know, Mom, I'm upset," he said. "Holly didn't come home last night." Mrs. Einhorn asked whether Ira called the hospitals, and he said he did. He said he called all her friends. He also said that he was going to report her disappearance to the police. According to Bea Einhorn, Ira was nearly panic-stricken, as emotionally affected as she had ever heard him. "He said, 'Mom, she didn't take anything. She didn't have any money. Where *is* she?' "

At that time, though, Ira had *not* called Holly's friends. According to Nicole Hackel, manager of the Ecology Co-op and known there as a friend of Holly's, Ira had not even checked for Holly at her presumed destination. On the other hand, Ruth and Ted Fink were calling *Ira,* conveying Saul Lapidus' worries that something had happened to Holly. Ira regarded her departure as sudden, but certainly not tragic. There was no reason to think that she would not turn up.

The now-frantic Saul Lapidus thought Ira's viewpoint as overly optimistic—or worse. He recruited Andrija Puharich to call Ira. In Puharich's recollection of the conversation, the normally cheerful Ira was strikingly gruff:

"Ira," Puharich said, "I understand that Holly came down to see you."

"Yeah, she was here and she left."

"Do you have any idea where she went?" asked Puharich.

He said, "*I* don't know where in the hell she goes, she always disappears."

"Anyway," Puharich now says, "he didn't want to talk about Holly, and he shut me off. He was very terse. He wasn't trying to be communicative at all. He just said she left. So I told Saul, and Saul said, 'My God, I bet she's been killed.' At this point I said, 'Come on, Saul. You know Ira wouldn't hurt a fly.' "

It was within hours after that phone call, on the fourteenth of September, that Ira reported to the Finks that he had gotten a call from Holly, affirming that she was fine, she wanted to be left alone, she would call in a week. He told Ruth Fink to pass that news on to Lapidus. But Ira was mysteriously selective in mentioning this call to others. He did not share her alleged all-is-well message with his mother, who certainly would have welcomed the news. Nor did he mention Holly's call two weeks later, when he described his worry about Holly's vanishing to two friends after they had seen a late showing of *I Never Promised You a Rose Garden*. Sitting in H. A. Winston's restaurant in Center City Philadelphia, Ira told them how worried he was that Holly had left—*and he had never heard a thing.*

His behavior during that period was, to say the least, uncharacteristic for Ira. Normally upbeat, stoic in the face of difficulty, and loath to show signs of vulnerability, Ira Einhorn was crumbling. Never in any of his previous bouts of depression—even in the obsessive love affairs he'd borne in the sixties—had he allowed personal matters to mar his façade. Generally, he attempted to maintain a good front, but for weeks it was a difficult battle, with memorable lapses. David Ehrlich, a friend who regularly treated Ira to steam sessions at the Camac Bath Club downtown, was stunned at Ira's condition when he saw him after Holly's disappearance. "He was visibly shaken and completely lacked composure of any sort," Ehrlich recalls. "He was on the verge of tears."

For the next few months, Ira was prone to erratic behavior. At an art opening not long after Holly's disappearance, recalls Susan McAninley, who'd known Ira for years, he seemed "very upset, distraught." "I'm disgusted with everything," he told her. "I'm going to change my life completely. I think I'm going to get interested in pornography." One day, out of the blue, he asked Kathy

Keegan to cut his hair, and to complete the transformation, he shaved his beard off. This was tantamount to proclaiming himself a different person. He did not offer an explanation for the change. Once he had done it he almost immediately regretted it and quickly grew back his trademark ponytail and Santa beard.

His most irrational act came when he flew to London in November. His ticket had been paid for by the Orb Foundation, the sponsor of the Iceland Conference, where papers would be presented regarding psychic phenomena and developments on secret Tesla projects. Ira was scheduled to speak November 5 at London's Commonwealth Foundation and then fly to Iceland. In the weeks before the conference, he bickered with the organizers, making sure his expenses would be paid. He received his guarantees. But when he flew from Philadelphia to London on November 1, he disembarked the aircraft, hoping to find someone to meet him, despite receiving a telegram from Joyce Petschek some days before telling him to go to her house independently. After a few minutes at the airport, he called Joyce's house. Andrija Puharich, already in town, got on the phone with him. Where, Ira wanted to know, is the limousine to pick me up at the airport? This seemed a ludicrous request—Ira Einhorn, whose idea of acceptable travel accommodations included sleeping on the floor, asking for a personal limo?

"Ira, get a cab for Christ's sake and get out here," Puharich said. "Stop this shit about a limousine."

"I don't like the way you guys are treating me," said Ira.

Puharich told him that they would be waiting for him at Joyce's. But Ira did not hail a taxi. He marched back into the airport and cashed his prepaid ticket, which included round-trip flight to Iceland and the return to Philadelphia, using the money to purchase a first-class seat on the first plane back home. Through Pan American, Joyce and Andrija sent him a note: "Ira, turn around," it implored. "We are expecting you at the house. Major that you come. We love you." He ignored it. He luxuriated in the comfort of the first-class lounge, gobbled "mountains of food," and was absorbed by the love affair between Gene Hackman and Candice Bergen in the on-flight movie, *The Domino Affair*.

It was not as if Ira totally lost his mind in those months. He saw other women, wrote his Tesla article for *Co-Evolution Quarterly*, lunched with phone-company friends at La Terrasse, bought a new

Toyota Corolla, visited Jerry Rubin in New York, and forged a relationship with Jonathan Moore of Harvard's Kennedy School of Government, which ultimately would result in his becoming a fellow there the following autumn. But as reflected in his private writings, he was severely depressed. He even considered suicide.

SEPTEMBER 15: *So difficult to get up.*

SEPTEMBER 17: *Feels so lonely.*

SEPTEMBER 19: *Can't shake the H depression.*

SEPTEMBER 21: *Feeling the loss of H very strongly.*

SEPTEMBER 24: *Depression overwhelming at times.*

OCTOBER 5: *Holly and Ira—fifth anniversary: What a way to celebrate— at my lowest ebb—suicidal.*

OCTOBER 8: *An angel lingers in my mind.*

OCTOBER 24: *Much depressed—a bit of wanting to end it all—getting much more difficult to sustain the entire mess.*

OCTOBER 29: *Got into a low today: allowing myself to be yanked back by my feelings—easy to exacerbate and go off the deep end.*

OCTOBER 31: *H weighs: I have been very depressed lately. No desire to move in the morning.*

NOVEMBER 6: *H will be with me for a long, long time.*

NOVEMBER 17: *So little desire to live, yet not ready to kill myself. What am I waiting for?*

NOVEMBER 20: *Brooding over H. Thinking on suicide again.*

NOVEMBER 26: *So out of it. No desire to live.*

NOVEMBER 27: *Miss H so much. No will to do anything: must regain the will to live.*

He dreamt of Holly frequently. He wrote poems about her—one, subtitled "A Last One for H," was called "Suicide." In another poem he wrote about his "self-dissolved life." He suffered headaches, and a sound in his head kept buzzing, driving him to distraction. (This internal noise was a chronic difficulty for Ira: During the previous summer he had told an interviewer of "the sound that has been around for about ten years, it often drives me crazy, and it seems to be doing something I can't understand." He said that though the "high-pitched hum, or buzz" was always present to some degree, at times it filled his room, "so much that people can't walk in the door!") But he did not give in, and one day, he wrote that he "finally began the difficult and heart-breaking task of cleaning H's stuff out of the closet: It's time to end my depression and begin a new life."

In early December, he reported being past the nadir of his emotions. He began to participate in his activities with more enthusiasm, not just walk through them. The energy was returning. While dozing a few days before Christmas, he felt an enormous surge of energy. Holly came into his mind. His inner sound became deafening—he felt as if his skull would split open. And he heard voices raised in ethereal song: *We're guarding you.*

A few days later he wrote a friend: "Great suffering just undergone for three months. Now out of it and much stronger. Another path of learning. Not one I would consciously choose. Celebrate in '78. Love, Ira."

There are two ways to view Ira's emergence from the "great suffering" described here. The first poses Ira as a jilted lover whose girlfriend left him, inexplicably failing to contact her family or the man she had agreed to vacation with. Then she dropped off the face of the earth, only to reappear in Einhorn's closet eighteen months later, just hours before the police—alerted to the crime by J. R. Pearce's independent investigation—entered 3411 Race Street. Not only was Ira unable to come up with a shard of concrete evidence to support any such scenario—be it CIA, KGB, or some other Byzantine strike force—but even such a fervent conspiracy believer as Andrija Puharich (who claims that the CIA has several times attempted his assassination) judges that what Ira Einhorn was doing in that field was not important enough to provoke a reaction of such extreme from any intelligence agency. Of all people, Puharich was most intimate with the nature of the information Ira was circulating about psychic warfare, and most sensitive to efforts to suppress its circulation.

The other course is to assume that Ira Einhorn murdered Holly Maddux. Then one must deal with the less outrageous yet still mystifying question of why the corpse remained where it was. Later,

Ira would cite the discovery of Holly Maddux's body in his closet as a reason to believe that he did *not* kill her. Would I be so stupid, he would ask, as to leave the most incriminating evidence where it would implicate me? Assuming Ira was behaving logically at that time, the answer is no.

But if Ira Einhorn had lost control on the evening of September 10 or the morning after, had gone after Holly Maddux with the same murderous intensity with which he had attacked Rita Siegal and Judy Lewis when they, too, had rejected him, furiously pounding the skull of Holly Maddux until it shattered in not one, but at least six, and as many as fourteen cranial locations . . . then there is no compelling reason to think that Ira Einhorn would behave logically. Standing over the lifeless body of Holly Maddux, he would have realized that he had murdered not only the delicate angel he so cherished but his own future as well. And more. The gruesome spectacle would have blown to pieces the great secret he long kept with some success from his cohorts, but with greater effectiveness from himself: He was not the person he appeared to be. The sixties were something spoken, not practiced. His lifelong effort to enhance human life was a lie, because the Unicorn, at the bottom of his soul, was something he had always stood against: a negative life-force.

After the fury of breaking the skull underneath Holly Maddux's fine blond hair had subsided, Ira would have had several options. Perhaps the most expeditious would have been calling the police, or at the very least, a sharp lawyer of his acquaintance like Bernard Segal. Ira Einhorn had been under emotional stress at losing his lover; possibly he could claim this as a mitigating factor to murder. A few years in jail, and Ira might begin to put the tragedy behind him. Yet Ira could consider no such damage control: Admitting to such a heinous act would not only leave his career in ashes but it would fly in the face of the implicit yet ludicrous assumption on which he had operated for years—that he was somehow above the failings of common humanity, invulnerable and wiser.

Another logical alternative would have been to carefully cover up the murder. It appears that certain steps were taken in that direction. As Ira later pointed out, it would certainly be difficult after such a brutal killing to thoroughly clean the apartment of blood, and no visitor to the apartment thereafter had ever noted bloodstains. Yet a cleaning of that sort would not have been impossible, and few have ever had such incentive to do a household job so well. Nor would it have been impossible for Ira to drain the blood from Holly Maddux's body in the bathtub, and then stuff the corpse in the trunk he had purchased. The dates of the newspapers found later in the trunk, contemporaneous with Holly's disappearance, indicate that he may have done just that. In a feeble attempt to stifle the smell of death, Airwick deodorizers were placed in the trunk and closet.

But why would Ira not follow through with the cover-up? Why didn't he dispose of the trunk? It appears that he tried this initially, asking his friends Jill and Sharon to aid him in the task. But apparently, even if he made subsequent efforts to try to dispose of the body, he eventually gave up. Some of Ira's friends still cannot reconcile this failure with the Ira they knew.

After the arrest, there was some macabre speculation about why Ira left the trunk in his closet, where its contents would leak into the apartment of Paul Herre and Ron Gelzer, and for a while generate a sickening odor. Some said that Ira could not bear to be separated from Holly. "He is a social activist who fell into the world of Edgar Allan Poe," says Allen Ginsberg, referring no doubt to the haunted protagonist of "The Tell-Tale Heart." Another friend of Ira's, a renowned physicist, opined that Ira with his "chicken-skinny legs" could not single-handedly move the object and was too proud, or too cautious, to ask for help. A few others have guessed that it was Ira's arrogance that allowed him to leave Holly Maddux's body in the tiny apartment; entertaining guests, even sleeping with women on the mattress that sat a few feet away from the closet, was a sort of statement of superiority, Ira crowing that he felt no compulsion to follow rules. Comparisons have been made to the Leopold-Loeb killings or the movie—Hitchcock's *Rope*—inspired by the incident, where two arrogant young men are exhilarated by serving cocktails on a trunk, inside of which is the corpse of the man they murdered.

A more cogent explanation of the Unicorn's behavior arises from the sincerity with which Ira Einhorn defended himself after his arrest. When Einhorn pleaded his innocence to his friends, they felt, despite the overwhelming evidence, that he was telling the truth. Perhaps, he only *believed* he was telling the truth. It is possible that after killing Holly Maddux, Ira Einhorn willfully convinced himself that the event did not happen. The act was too much at odds with the person he believed himself to be. The consequences of facing up to that reality were too dire to contemplate. As far as Ira was concerned, it was *impossible* for Ira Einhorn to kill Holly Maddux, especially in such brutal fashion. The act could not be reconciled with his self-image. After some feeble attempts to dispose of the trunk, he not only literally but figuratively shoved the horrible scene into the closet. Any further attempt at disposal, involving accomplices after the fact and other grim logistics, would have required him to focus too closely and too long on a personal catastrophe that he could not face.

If that was the case, then Ira Einhorn reinterpreted the grief he felt at murdering a woman he loved: He mourned her sudden departure, not her murder. Toward this self-deceptive end, he formalized his fiction by writing the Holly-went-to-the-store tale in his personal journal. (This might have been a step toward an alibi as well, since Ira would sometimes let others read his journals; he later claimed to writer Greg Walter that his journals would prove his innocence.)

But Ira's self-deception was not complete. (Psychologists record that denials of this sort never are.) His behavior during that troubled aftermath, as well as the months that followed, was not consistent with that of a person who had seen a lover leave under such strange circumstances. For one thing, the near-suicidal degree of Einhorn's depression was out of kilter with the circumstances. It was as if, despite his willful efforts to convince himself that a murder had not occurred, part of his consciousness maintained a marker. While Ira seemingly developed a capability in his daily dealings to ignore the reality of Holly Maddux's body in his closet, he was simultaneously vigilant in protecting his secret from discovery.

Perhaps this dissonance became easier to maintain under the influence of Ketamine, Ira's "serious" drug of choice during the last couple of years before his arrest. Ketamine hydrochloride is a sister drug of PCP, or "angel dust." The drug acts on the cortex and creates "dissociative anesthesia," a strong dissociation from one's environment. The drug's only recommended use for humans is as a surgical anesthetic administered by a physician. Otherwise it is considered an extremely dangerous substance; among its side effects are vivid imagery, delirium, irrational behavior, and extreme responses to various stimuli. (These responses include violence. It does not appear that Ira Einhorn took the drug in the days preceding Holly Maddux's disappearance, but some experts say that the drug's reactions might be delayed, so it would be possible that one component of an extended, irrational outburst of violence might have been a result of Ketamine use; however, we have seen that he was capable of violence long before he became interested in this drug.)

One of Ira's sources for the drug was a Philadelphia psychiatrist who would occasionally inject Ira with Ketamine, then administer the drug to himself, whereupon the two would sit quietly while the effects of the drug were experienced. "He would lie on the couch, lie down for an hour and talk," says the psychiatrist, who estimates a typical dosage at a half to three-quarters of a cubic centimeter. When Ira told Evan Harris Walker, a scientist working for the army who appeared at several psychic conferences, about his use of Ketamine, Walker told him it was "nasty stuff to be working with," that it had troublesome effects on people. "It doesn't matter what happened to other people," said the Unicorn, as if he were not prone to mortal consequences. Another of Ira's friends, after hearing Einhorn's enthusiastic talk of "out-of-body experiences" with Ketamine, warned Ira strongly against the drug. This friend is convinced that Ira's "state of complete dissociation," in regard to his denial of the murder of Holly Maddux, is inextricably linked to his use of Ketamine.

When confronted with the fact that the body of Holly Maddux was in his apartment, Ira—if he had indeed blocked out the horrible scene of her murder—would have been able to react as if he, like one of Hitchcock's more benign protagonists, was suddenly a victim of a frame-up. Since he had already developed a voracious suspicion that powerful forces were attempting to dog his attempts at circulating crucial information, it was natural for him to concoct a CIA-KGB plot against him. "A feverish mind like Ira's tends to see conspiracy where there is a concatenation of mistaken silences," says Christian de Lait, a scientist on Ira's network. Ira himself would claim that "The paranoid has the incredible ability to create coherence out of chaos," invoking with approval Charles Manson's quote, "Total paranoia is total consciousness."

In any case, Ira was able to behave as though he were the non-violent person he had always presented himself to be. On any given day, Ira might be asked about the pretty blond woman he had been hanging out with for the past five years. "Where's Holly?" people would ask him, and Ira would more or less repeat the same account. He would offer his reasons for her sudden departure: She had been depressed, she had been sick, she was a lost soul. He would often evoke considerable sympathy from his listeners, moved at the spectacle of an obviously caring man troubled at the sudden departure of his lover. Not everyone was moved, though. Several people were perturbed at how casual he seemed when speaking about his lover's disappearance—his tone would be matter-of-fact, almost as if he didn't care. And at a New Year's Eve party attended by the Synergy people, someone came up to Ira, perhaps a few drinks too full, and said, "Ira, I bet you killed Holly." But Ira was able to laugh it off.

Nineteen seventy-eight was a good year for Ira Einhorn. The network was thriving, focusing surely on the worldwide interest in Tesla-style technology, release of semiofficial documents of UFO sightings, and future-shock accounts of computer conferencing. Ira himself became a player in the latter field as a key consultant for Infomedia, a company that ran a computer system called PLANET. Infomedia was headed by Einhorn's friend Jacques Vallee. Ira traveled that year with a computer teletype terminal that he used to maintain asynchronous communication with fellow futurists around the world; at little provocation he would amaze onlookers with this display of electronic magic. He convinced Pennsylvania Bell to use the network and indoctrinated Alvin Toffler in the wonders of computer conferencing.

Locally, Ira was more visible in 1978 than he had been in years. For much of the spring, Ira spent much time organizing the Philadelphia festivities for Sun Day, a national appreciation of alternative energy. The effort was not as mammoth as was Earth Week, but nonetheless significant, and this time Ira Einhorn was clearly in charge. This did not mean that he had acquired an attention for detail and scut work in the interim; Ira built a staff and let them do the envelope licking and arranging while he networked with celebrities, wrote bardic tributes to solar energy for the newspapers, and hit up his corporate-executive friends for donations. ("I went around to fifteen executive friends," Ira later explained, "and I said"—clapping his hands to show his control over the business elite—" 'Give me a thousand dollars,' and they gave me a thousand dollars.") Ira accepted supporting proclamations from the city and the state, but his efforts at luring President Jimmy Carter to personally bless Sun Day fell short; Carter aide Midge Costanza forwarded the Unicorn's request to the president's director of scheduling who declined, conveying Carter's "warm appreciation for inviting him" as well as his "very best wishes to you, particularly for a most successful program."

This occurred around the time Einhorn was deflecting the advances of the private detectives who implored him to cooperate with the investigation into Holly Maddux's disappearance. He told them Holly wanted to be left alone, although he confided to one friend that he believed Holly might have run into "foul play."

Sun Day meetings were often held in Ira's apartment, also the scene for weekend visits, sessions of Go, and frequent seductions—a sign that Ira was unconcerned about visitors gathering olfactory evidence of what was decomposing in his closet. Yet visitors apparently were not given free reign while in the apartment. Kathy Keegan, who was executive director of the Sun Day event, suggested to him that he open up the porch area. "Don't go near there!" Ira shouted. Keegan recalls that "He got real upset. At the time I thought it was pretty strange he would do that to me."

Sandy Rubin, a friend of Ira's, came over to 3411 one night. Ira was in the kitchen with the phone and computer while Rubin was in the living room. With Ira busy, she began looking for the bathroom on her own. "Never having been there, I didn't know where it was," she said. "So I just opened the door." She had opened the French door to the porch, and then the door to the closet.

"I was overcome by the smell of formaldehyde," she says. "I know it was formaldehyde because I used to be a medical technician. And there were these huge green bags in the closet. Huge green trash bags. And the overwhelming smell."

Ira Einhorn must have heard her open the door. "What are you doing?" he yelled.

"I'm looking for the bathroom."

"It's not there!" said Ira, in a harsh, menacing tone of voice that Sandy had never heard him use before. "Close that door!"

Sandy Rubin still shudders when she recalls the scene. "Did you ever have a split second when you feel you're in danger?" asks Sandy Rubin. "Just an eerie feeling you can't explain. The tone of his voice made me feel I was in danger."

Sun Day was a success: It garnered publicity for solar causes and provided a platform for prosolar speakers. It also strengthened Ira Einhorn's claim as a person who could make things happen, in the seventies as well as the sixties. *Philadelphia Daily News* columnist Chuck Stone called Einhorn "Philadelphia's tireless activist and warm-hearted humanist. . . . If Henry Thoreau were to return to earth he would be reincarnated in Ira."

That spring, Ira received word of his appointment as a fellow at Harvard's Kennedy School of Government. Only six or seven people, "actively involved in the political process and the shaping of public policy," are appointed each semester to that elite post, which requires teaching a noncredit seminar and hobnobbing with members of the political aristocracy who frequently drop by. According to Jonathan Moore, then the director of the school's Institute of Politics, some advisers had suggested that previous choices had been top-heavy in "middle-of-the-roaders"; presumably Ira Einhorn would balance the selection. "A number of people recommended Ira to us, from the academic, church, and private sector," Moore says. "By the time we actually got him in the process of being interviewed, we had a very thick file of strong recommendations." Before moving to Cambridge for the autumn semester, though, Ira had the summer before him. This year he decided to spend his vacation in the Harvey Cedars area of Long Beach Island, New Jersey.

Unlike every other year he had gone away for the summer, Ira Einhorn did not sublet his Race Street apartment in the summer of 1978.

On Long Beach Island, Ira lived in the second-floor rear apartment of a private home; the highlight of his space was a deck overlooking part of a marina. He arranged for the local phone company to rewire the telephone connections so he could use his computer terminal at night. By day, he would amble to the beach, spending his time with a crowd of Philadelphians who owned houses facing the bay.

Rikki Wagman and her husband, Howard, owned one of those houses, and both became close to Ira that summer. As always, Ira's charm and energy were impressive, but the Wagmans noticed the peculiar character that Ira's energy had taken. It seemed jittery, not quite controlled. "He was high-spirited and hyper," says Rikki Wagman. "Very hyper. If it wasn't for the enormous amount of food he'd eat, you'd think he was on speed."

Ira would routinely visit the Wagmans in early evening. Rikki would cook him a dinner, and later in the evening Ira and Howard Wagman, who in his work as an importer seldom met such unusual and erudite figures, would talk far into the night. More accurately, Howard would listen to Ira's monologues, amazing tales of his incursions into the corporate world, national security issues, and paranormal phenomena. His politics seemed out of character for someone who looked so much like a hippie—he was extremely concerned about the Russian advances in psychotronic weapons, and warned that liberal Democrats had to wake up to the threat. And then there were times when what he said went beyond politics. He once pointed to a scar on his stomach and explained that extraterrestrial invaders had come in the middle of the night and planted devices in his body. Normally, this was the kind of talk that one would dismiss without a second thought, but when Ira Einhorn got going, he could have you believing, at least until you thought about it afterward. This was partly because you *wanted* to believe in mysterious and sometimes wonderful phenomena. And it was partly because of Ira's enthusiasm in telling the tale. You could see this in his eyes.

"The eyes were special," says Rikki Wagman. "They were wild. They had all this excitement in them. But what Ira did to his friends was give you a feeling that he was your protector. You just felt safe around him. I did." But Wagman admits that though "Ira had a wonderful quality as a teacher, there was never a personal level. There was always that distance."

Ira's social life was active on Long Beach Island. He not only had flings with fellow summer residents (though there was a moment of tension when he tried to woo the girlfriend of the Wagmans' teenage son) but he sometimes imported women he'd been seeing previously. Late in the summer, Einhorn briefly pursued Mary Schoonmaker, a woman he had met at Hazel and Carter Henderson's house in Princeton. (It was Mary Schoonmaker who in early August accompanied Ira to Puharich's farm after it had been destroyed by fire.) One weekend, Hazel, Carter, and Mary visited Ira on Long Beach Island. Something odd occurred.

Mary Schoonmaker is an expert at foot massage. "When I'm

sitting and talking to someone, I rub their feet," she explains. "Somehow it grounds me." So while sitting in Ira's living room, talking about some abstract subject, she naturally began to rub Ira's feet. "And I just remember . . . suddenly being filled with a fearful feeling," she says. "I just remember being filled with something distasteful. And I remember crawling across the rug on all fours away from him, all the way to the farthest corner, and sitting in the corner in a fetal position, with my legs up. Just sitting there and shaking. And he was *yelling* at me, 'What's wrong? What's wrong? What is it?' And he said, he kept saying, 'Did you see something? What did you see? Tell me what you saw!' Well, anyway, that put a damper on our relationship. Poor Ira. And I just felt very guilty about it, because I didn't know what it was."

Mary Schoonmaker says that "I've never had any experience like that before or since."

When the summer ended, Ira headed to Cambridge, while still paying rent on the second-floor rear apartment at 3411 Race Street. (In September, Ira took specific pains to assure that the men the landlord sent to work on the apartment's rear porch did not disturb the locked closet.) His domicile while at the Kennedy School was a small suite in the North House dormitory complex on Linnaean Street. He furnished it with a sleeping bag and some paintings, notably a Tibetan mandala, borrowed from a friend. A few weeks into the semester there was a formal dedication of the Institute's new building. Ira attended the event in black tie, rubbing elbows with the likes of Ted Kennedy ("a good, but tired man," Ira wrote his mother), Jackie Onassis, and Massachusetts governor Michael Dukakis. Ira also insinuated himself into a controversy over the naming of the building's library in honor of a man involved with the South African governor. "Ira was mildly helpful" in mediating the issue between demonstrators and administrators, recalls Jonathan Moore.

Ira made an impact of sorts on Harvard. He moderated several programs, one called "New Age Politics" with antinuclear activist Helen Caldicott and Esalen director Michael Murphy on the panel. Another was a conversation between him and Hazel Henderson, called "Reflections on a Dying Patriarchy." His own seminar was called "The Hierarchy Is Surrounded," described in the course catalog as "an intensely personal look at how a networker functions." It was the Free University's "Evenings with Ira Einhorn" revisited, this time with the Establishment's blessing. His special guests included Bill Cashel of Pennsylvania Bell.

The *Crimson* was quick to lionize this most unusual fellow, who looked like a hippie, claimed friendship with Jerry Rubin and the corporate elite, and boasted that "My new consciousness was reinforced by LSD, dope, and the loving I was doing." Ira also took the opportunity to give the university's leaders some tips on running America's premier educational institution. "A little more hugging could do Harvard a lot of good," he said, complaining about an excess of regimentation. "There's simply no time to interact, relax, to enjoy yourself," he complained. Then, smiling at the female reporter, he added that "It's like you have to schedule your fucking."

Apparently Ira had no trouble with the latter task. He was a popular figure on the Harvard campus. Susan Bencuya, a receptionist at the Institute of Politics, once went to Ira's room for a private poetry reading. "I asked him whether he had made any friends with the students at Harvard," she recalls. "He went into the bedroom and came out with this lady's underwear and said, 'Yeah.' I wasn't going anywhere near the bedroom after that!" Though Bencuya liked Ira and agreed to stay in touch with him after the semester, some things about him made her feel uneasy—his sexism, and his predilection for a drug she had never heard of, called Ketamine.

While in Cambridge Ira reactivated a friendship with Gunther Weil, whom he had known from the days of LSD activism. Weil had been a key figure in Timothy Leary's Millbrook period; now he was a psychotherapist who also had an interest in producing a film based on Robert Anton Wilson's conspiracy-paranoia masterpiece, *The Illuminatus Trilogy*. Naturally, says Weil, "Ira wanted to be a consultant." He suggested people who might get involved, particularly actress Ellen Burstyn, an acquaintance of Ira's. (Ellen Burstyn says that she never acted on Ira's request to make the film.)

Among the other institute fellows that semester, Ira generated an *esprit de corps*, according to Karen Burstein, also a fall 1978 fellow. "He tried to create among us the sense that we were part of a group. He was friendly with everybody, very open," she says. "The thing that struck us was not so much his intelligence but his gentleness, the way he treated people. He was very considerate." The fellows would meet on a regular basis, sometimes with an influential speaker like Edwin Reischauer, Paul Warnke, or Senator Robert Packwood. After the meal was served and the speech was made, formalities would loosen. Sometimes discussions could get heated. "Ira tended to be a peacemaker," says Burstein, now auditor general of New York City. "He gentled situations. He didn't raise his voice. He calmed things out."

The closest Karen Burstein came to Ira was on a day when she had been feeling down. Ira noticed and convinced her to drop everything and go to an Indonesian restaurant with him. During dinner, he told her why he was almost compulsively having to sleep with women. He once had a girlfriend he really loved, but she left him. Her name was Holly. Karen Burstein thought the conversation odd: Even though the subject matter was confessional, Ira's account was totally lacking in sorrow.

After a triumphant semester, Ira's farewell to Cambridge was felicitous—he played Santa Claus at North Hall's Christmas party. The only sour note occurred when he spun his car out on the ice, totaling the Toyota. When he returned to Philadelphia, he bought a new one. With a $6,000 stipend from Harvard, various lecture fees, finder's fees from his publishing connections, foundation grants, and other odd consultancies, the man who newspapers once called "Ira the Freeloader" was more than solvent.

As 1979 began, Ira's career was at a new plateau. During his tenure at the Kennedy School, he had freely used the stationery and the mailing address to win a new set of contacts, some of whom assumed they were dealing with a Harvard professor. He had met dozens of power brokers, influential academics, and people who pulled political strings behind the scenes. He was entered into any number of important Rolodexes as an unorthodox, entertaining, and possibly helpful contact into future studies, paranormal phenomena, radical management styles, and the counterculture. His stock in the lecture circuit was definitely a buy.

All during his stay at Harvard, though, private investigator J. R. Pearce had been investigating Holly Maddux's disappearance. Ira's attitude toward Pearce's effort was disdainful. "It feels like a Bogart movie," he complained. He professed to be unconcerned about the whole matter. "H made a decision," he wrote. "It didn't make me happy, but one year later I'm out the other side of it and that is where I want to stay."

Meanwhile, in the apartment downstairs from Ira's on 3411 Race, the new tenant wondered why his cat, Ashes, kept going to the closet in the kitchen—the one underneath the porch of the second-floor rear apartment above—and making such a fuss.

In late January 1979, Ira wrote Susan Bencuya about his reentry into the "real" world outside of Harvard. He described himself as "a bubble in a stream of play, humor, and much activity." Einhorn also dispensed some advice about love. "Romance is nonconstant," he counseled. "Remember that as you put the pieces together—getting along, caring for, and just being there (companionship) are the keys to a relationship that lasts." Then a self-reflective note: "Romance is the cream on the top of the bottle and I often think I lick too many bottles."

Though he missed having a steady woman, he felt he was not ready for one. Of the several women he was seeing with a degree of frequency, one in particular pleased him, but as they became closer, Ira found himself becoming more cold to her. Late one Saturday night in January, she tried to evoke affection from him. But he was preoccupied. Why not come to bed? she asked, and Ira said no. She wanted the light out, and Ira said no. She said she was going home and asked Ira to drive her. No. She left anyway. A few weeks later, when visiting another of his temporary lovers, Ira was piqued when the woman pulled away from him. He withdrew himself, began to read, and after extracting an apology from her, went home. "So ends another quick one," he wrote of the incident.

Ira's mind was on more global concerns. In February, he focused on Yugoslavia, Nikola Tesla's native land. Einhorn's idea was to set up a joint committee between that country and America specifically to sponsor a Tesla exhibition in the States and generally to improve relations between the two countries. Ira's partner in these activities was a Yugoslavian-born scientist named Bogdan Maglich, who had been appointed as a special representative of President Ford to a Yugoslav national celebration in 1976. As a side benefit of this effort, Ira Einhorn would be, as he put it, "the unofficial U.S. ambassador to Yugoslavia." Maglich himself thought Einhorn brilliant, impressed "by his breadth, by his knowledge," he says. "I thought that he had great political potential." In late 1978 and early 1979, Maglich and Einhorn began recruiting prominent people to join them on the board of the Tesla Foundation, and letters were sent to the likes of statesmen George Kennan and Averell Harriman.

Meanwhile, Maglich had written a letter to the president of the Yugoslav Nikola Tesla Society, on behalf of "Mr. Ira Einhorn of the Institute of Politics, Harvard University" so Ira could visit the society and the Tesla Museum in Belgrade to begin organizing a conference based on Tesla's ideas. The letter mentioned the interest of Philadelphia's Franklin Institute science museum, which Ira had tentatively secured. The president of the Tesla society, Dr. A. Marincic, replied that he was very pleased to be working with Harvard University and extended a welcome to Einhorn.

Ira left for the trip in mid-February, starting in London, where he stayed at Joyce Petschek's house. Then he flew to Paris, where he continued an affair he had been having with a French woman in the process of divorce. On February 27, he arrived in Belgrade, where the Yugoslavian government treated him like a state official, entertaining him royally and assigning him the same interpreter used by their minister of defense. Ira was disappointed by the architecture and air quality of Belgrade, but he was happily surprised at the proliferation of attractive redheaded women on the streets. In the next few days, Ira was given access to the papers in the Tesla Museum as well as the resources of the Tesla Society. The Yugoslavians obviously regarded his and Maglich's proposal for a bilateral committee and a Tesla Foundation with great enthusiasm. By the time Einhorn left, he had become close enough with the interpreter for the man to admit his belief in UFOs to Ira.

Ira enjoyed the movie on the way back to Philadelphia: *Foul Play*.

In mid-March, when unbeknownst to Ira, Detective Michael Chitwood was assigned to the homicide case involving Holly Maddux, Ira was in full swing with Tesla, network activities, computer work, and a crowded social calendar. He flew off to the London conference sponsored by the shah's nephew, gave a quick hello to friends abroad, and was back four days after he left, just in time to keep his appointment to speak for the London Group. Sitting in Ross Speck's cozy living room, the Unicorn proclaimed that "I am glandularly very optimistic. I like life, I enjoy life. It's very difficult to get me depressed."

That weekend, Ira had a house guest, a woman named Claire Hooton, who until recently had been involved with an acquaintance of his. He had called her out of the blue and invited her to take the train to Philadelphia and stay the weekend. He picked her up at

Thirtieth Street Station and delighted in showing her the landmarks of the city he loved. They went by the park, by the river where he once had considered dropping the steamer trunk that now sat in his closet, and then back to 3411 Race. Claire looked around the apartment, at the teletype terminal on the kitchen table, the mat on the floor, the books, and was particularly struck by a large picture of a hauntingly beautiful young woman. She was doubly intrigued when she learned that the oversize baby picture hanging in the bathroom, where a male would see it while urinating, was of the same person. Ira explained that the woman was his former girl-friend, now off traveling somewhere.

As the woman walked around the apartment, she noticed the French door at the rear. "You have a porch!" she said. "How delightful."

But before she got any closer Ira cut her off. "It's locked," he told her, and the porch was unmentioned for the remainder of the visit.

That night they went to dinner and a movie, returning about one-thirty. Ira wanted to make love, but Claire did not, so she stretched out on the mat to go to sleep while Ira, inveterate insomniac, sat at his desk. He was stripped down to his briefs, and Claire could see the massive bulk of his back as he bent over his work. Without warning, something happened that she had never experienced before, and would not again. "As I lay there," she recalls, "the whole atmosphere of the place turned spooky. It was like a black . . . *thud.* Something was in the air—an awesome terror. Like no terror I had ever had."

Ira was still hunched over his desk. Nothing had moved in the apartment. There was no apparent provocation, no trigger for her panic. But Claire Hooton lay on the mattress in mental agony, tormented by a fear she could not identify.

Ten days later, Michael Chitwood rang the buzzer of the second-floor rear apartment at 3411 Race with a search warrant in hand. "Search what?" Ira asked him. Mike Chitwood went directly to the closet on the outdoor porch.

The Unicorn's secret had been uncovered.

13

THE FLIGHT OF THE UNICORN

On January 21, 1981, a week after Ira Einhorn skipped bail, Judge Paul Ribner summoned Ira's lawyer and an assistant district attorney to see what might be holding up the recovery of the fugitive. Assistant DA Joseph Canuso, standing in for Barbara Christie, was apologetic.

"It's not easy to find a planetary enzyme, Your Honor," he said.

"Find a *what?*" asked Judge Ribner.

"A planetary enzyme."

The judge, obviously not familiar with the writings and speeches of Ira Einhorn, suggested that Einhorn might object to that nomenclature.

"That's what he referred to himself as, Your Honor. They're not my words, believe me."

"Well, if he referred to himself that way, then I agree with you—it's not easy to find a planetary enzyme," said Ribner. "The point is, I want him." Ribner instructed agents of the commonwealth to be tough in pursuit, particularly in warning the "prominent people" among Einhorn's friends that any aid they might provide Einhorn would result in charges filed against them. The court had been made to look foolish, and an alleged murderer was free. The authorities were not to rest until the Unicorn was back in custody.

Later that day, Joe Murray assigned Sergeant Richard King to assist in tracking down Ira Einhorn. It was already clear from searches of Einhorn's apartment, as well as a fruitless visit to Bea and Joseph Einhorn's home, that the suspect was no longer in Philadelphia. King obtained the rental forms from the Morgan House, Einhorn's postarrest residence, and unsuccessfully tried to contact the reference provided—Charles Bronfman of Montreal, Canada. The Bronfmans had recently separated, and the woman who answered the phone at Barbara Bronfman's home said Mrs. Bronfman was on vacation. King had better luck in tracing the identity of the woman with whom Einhorn had been living. This was Jeanne Marie Morrison. From her employment application at the Pick-A-Deli restaurant, he learned that she was not, as some of Einhorn's friends had described her, a woman of French origin, but a daughter of Falls Church, Virginia, a comfortable suburb of the nation's capital. A coworker at the deli told King that Jeanne Marie was quiet and hadn't spoken much about the man she'd lived with. But in December, she had mentioned a few times that she'd been thinking of leaving him. After going home for Christmas, though, she said that she would try to work it out with the guy. And then she was gone.

Jeanne Marie's mother, Jeanne Morrison, was quite understandably taken aback when Sergeant Richard King of the Philadelphia police informed her that her daughter had quite probably assisted an accused murderer of jumping bail before his trial. All she knew of the man her daughter was living with was that he was old enough to be her father—that had been bad enough. It had been one of a number of continual problems with her eldest daughter, who had been an all-too-willing victim, she told King, of "bad friends and drugs." This did not sit well with Mrs. Morrison or her husband, who were devout believers in conservative politics and morality. Mrs. Morrison had known that Jeanne Marie had left the country of late and had left many of her possessions with her sister Susan—but she had thought, perhaps wishfully, that this meant that she was leaving this man. Obviously, this news was unwelcome. Sergeant King did not make things any easier when he told her, with what seemed ungracious frankness, that the man her daughter was with had killed his previous girlfriend, locked her in a closet, and lived in the apartment for more than a year with the body in the closet.

Much distressed, Mrs. Morrison called her daughter Susan, a year younger than Jeanne Marie, and found that Jeanne Marie's departure had been more dramatic than she suspected. Susan had been under the impression that her sister was helping a boyfriend flee under some phony tax case or something. She still had the possessions that Jeanne Marie had dropped off, which included furniture, clothes, Ira Einhorn's Go board, Jeanne Marie's diary, and the Persian rug that Jeanne Marie had told her to sell.

The last two items were significant to Sargeant King and Drew Carr, the FBI man who was also working on the Einhorn disappearance. Mrs. Morrison would not release the diary, insisting on reading it herself to see if it contained information that might track her daughter and the fugitive she was apparently aiding. She approached the book with trepidation, partially because, however necessary, she was aware that the act was an invasion of privacy, and partially because she had reason to believe that the contents would alarm her. They did. Apparently begun on a trip to London where she had helped Einhorn case Europe as an escape route, the diary expresses Jeanne Marie's doubts over whether she should continue the relationship with Einhorn. (It also included her unsettling dream about Holly Maddux.) She recorded his near-constant assault of disparaging words, an unrelenting attack on her self-esteem. "A lot of verbal abuse, from A to Z . . . she was worth nothing, and was really reminded of it day after day from what I can get," Mrs. Morrison recalls. "And there were times when he handled her very roughly, physically." It may not have occurred often, and it never took the form of outright beating, but rather shoving, grabbing her by the neck, a sort of unfocused mishandling. Since Jeanne Marie was only 5 feet 2 inches and slight of stature, the 227-pound Einhorn must not have had difficulty adjusting her physical position at any given time.

One can only imagine how a mother would feel reading that, knowing that her daughter was now in a state of mutual dependency with this man, whose previous girlfriend was murdered in such abhorrent fashion.

Thus panicked, both Mrs. Morrison and her daughter Susan agreed to cooperate with the plan suggested by King and Carr. This involved the other item, the Persian rug. Both the proceeds from its sale and a tax refund that Jeanne Marie had been expecting were, upon her instructions, to be sent to a friend of Ira's named Roger Voisnet. This young man had first met Ira when Einhorn had spoken at his Ohio college in the early 1970s, and had been thrilled at the Unicorn's presentation. Voisnet had subsequently become involved in the alternative energy movement, working with Ira on that cause. When Sue called Voisnet, though, saying that she had money from the Persian rug, he insisted that he had not heard from Ira for over a month, but if he did he would contact her. A mail cover on Voisnet was ordered, to intercept any correspondence from Einhorn, who presumably was to be in touch concerning the fund from Einhorn, who presumably was to be in touch concerning the fund from the rug or the taxes. But nothing came of it.

Sergeant King and FBI agent Carr had no idea at the time—and the story has been untold to date—but in early 1981, Ira Einhorn and Jeanne Marie Morrison were apartment hunting in Dublin, Ireland. They had suffered no hitches in crossing the Irish Sea from England; those making the passage are not required to show pass-ports or other identification. Ireland seemed the perfect place to resettle. Besides it being an English-speaking country, it had the ultimate amenity for a fugitive: No extradition treaty existed between Ireland and the United States.

It was around February 1 that they set out for the Rathmines section of Dublin, south of city center, a middle-class residential quarter with rows of roomy brownstones often arranged so that owners would have bed-sitter apartments for rent. Specifically, they were responding to a newspaper ad that posted an apartment for rent at 22 Greenmount Road, a three-story row home on a quiet block. It was raining, and the house numbers were not clear, so Ira and Jeanne Marie rang the bell of the corner house, number 26. Dennis Weaire, a thirty-nine-year-old physics professor at the Uni-versity College of Dublin, answered and told the waterlogged pair that the house they were looking for was a few doors down the street. They turned away, but then Weaire, noticing the American accent of the heavyset, bearded fellow, had second thoughts. There was an unoccupied flat in the upstairs portion of *his* house; he had not been actively trying to rent it. Perhaps these Americans would be interested in using it. He called them back and offered them the flat as a temporary quarters. They agreed. They introduced them-selves to Weaire; his wife, Collette; and teenage son, Gavin. Their names were Ira and Jeanne Marie Einhorn.

The third-floor flat was decent if not princely. There was a living room with cooking facilities, a bathroom, and a back bedroom. A bay window looked onto Greenmount Street. In the living room was a day bed, a low table, and a large chest; the kitchen was an L-shaped counter under which sat the appliances and stove. A double bed dominated the bedroom, which, with its simple-patterned wallpaper, had a homey if somewhat prosaic feel to it. Even though Jeanne Marie decorated the rooms with pleasant drawings she had produced, there was no way to disguise the temporary, furtive atmosphere of the flat.

Jeanne Marie, with her jeans and long red hair, seemed to the Weaires a familiar student-type. But Ira Einhorn was more difficult to buttonhole. He claimed he was a writer, and he spent his days upstairs, presumably working on his opus at the living room table. He did not discuss the subject matter of his book and was extremely protective of the manuscript, which was never in sight when he left the premises. On the other hand, he could be garrulous and entertaining. Not infrequently, he would drop into the Weaires' cozy sitting room on the first floor and chat on any number of subjects. Dennis Weaire found that he was quite capable of an intelligent conversation about physics, though eventually the professor was turned off when Einhorn insisted that the annals of science should accommodate paranormal phenomena. Since there was no television in the upstairs flat, Einhorn would occasionally view the Weaires' TV; the American visitor took special pleasure in early comedy films, laughing lustily at Marx Brothers antics. He sometimes would notice books on the shelves, and when the Weaires offered to lend him some, he took advantage. One of the first tomes he asked for was Dostoevski's *Crime and Punishment.*

As weeks went by, Einhorn did venture out into Dublin, mostly at night. He visited libraries, joined a cinema club, participated in a discussion group examining *Finnegans Wake.* He would dine at restaurants, fancying in particular a modest Italian bistro on Dame Street called Nicol's. But generally, he led a reclusive life. He never had visitors. His mail was not voluminous. The bulk of his time was spent upstairs, presumably writing. He also—once he established that none of the Weaires had the slightest idea or interest in playing Go—set up a board and ruminated solo on various Go scenarios.

Collette Weaire, an effervescent woman who considered herself a student of human nature, could not help but observe the unusual dynamics between Jeanne Marie and her "husband." The girl was obviously discomfited by living abroad. She was looking for jobs in the computer field, but had difficulty, especially since for some reason she was unable to procure her college transcript from the States. Then, despite not finding employment, Jeanne Marie began to maintain a schedule that kept her away from Greenmount Street during the day. She explained to Collette that Ira did not like her around when he was writing, so she spent the time visiting art galleries. She said that sometimes she would simply sit on a park bench, for hours. Collette could not help but suspect that something was wrong between the couple, no surprise since Einhorn seemed to dominate the poor girl. He would belittle her in front of the Weaires, telling her to go find something to do with herself, or maybe go back to the States. Collette Weaire's suspicions were confirmed when, after she had gotten to know the American girl better, Jeanne Marie said to her, "You know, we have no relationship at all now." The mystery was why she didn't leave him.

As Einhorn became more familiar and more trusted by the Weaires—he was scrupulous about discharging his debts and performing any household favors asked of him—he opened up somewhat, too. He had experienced some difficulty in his home country, he said, intimating that his involvement in the antinuclear movement had earned him disfavor. He had been framed for a crime, and the book he was writing on the third floor of 26 Greenmount Street would clear his name. This admission seemed plausible and did not diminish Einhorn in the Weaires' estimation. In fact, even though all had agreed that the living arrangement would be temporary, and in theory Ira and Jeanne Marie were still searching for a flat in the nearby quarters of Ballsbridge and Ranelaugh, no deadline was set for their departure. Certainly by April, the Weaires had no compunction about leaving the house, and the care of the family dog, in the hands of the Einhorns when they traveled to visit friends in America.

Before they left, Ira casually mentioned that it would not be a good idea to mention his name to anyone in the United States. (Lately, he had been flirting with a pseudonym, claiming that his first name evoked too much of a reaction—too many thought him connected to the Irish Republican Army. His new name was to be

"Ian Morrison." He was apparently unaware that this was also the name of the head of the Bank of Ireland.) If his enemies in America found out his location, he might be captured. Collette agreed but silently vowed to look into the matter while in the United States, to examine once and for all the credibility of this odd tenant.

Mrs. Weaire told the story to the friend she was visiting in Chicago. The friend contacted a *Sun-Times* reporter, who called the desk at the *Philadelphia Inquirer,* and it was then that she learned exactly why Ira Einhorn had left the United States. On April 14, when Dennis Weaire joined his wife in Chicago, she excitedly spilled the story to him—the man living in their house was an accused murderer!

Dennis Weaire called the Irish Consulate in Chicago, who told them to tell their story to the FBI. On April 16, Weaire went to the FBI office and identified a picture of Ira Einhorn as the image of the person living in his house.

It would appear at that point that the flight of the Unicorn was soon to be terminated, doomed by his carelessness in using his real name. Although it is true that no extradition treaty existed between the United States and Ireland, often when such is the case, these matters are handled informally. A foreign traveler does not have the right to remain in a country indefinitely and can be placed on an airplane and exported. On the other terminus of the flight would be authorities prepared to take the fugitive into custody. But the Republic of Ireland, a nation consumed with troubles between its northern neighbor and the British government, was not inclined to bend the rules on extradition cases. In 1981, the extradition situation between the United States and Ireland was particularly muddied, since the United States was refusing to extradite an Irish fugitive with IRA ties who had escaped from an Irish prison.

Still, one would have expected the FBI to do something about a positive identification of a fugitive wanted for murder. But when Dennis Weaire returned to Dublin on Sunday, April 19, no one was there to meet him, as the FBI office in Chicago had promised. No agency seemed to know anything about the situation.

The Weaires did not want to come face-to-face with an alleged murderer without protection. They stayed at Collette's father's house that night. It was not until Tuesday, April 21, that they were able to convince Irish authorities of the validity of their story. After apparently checking with American and Irish diplomats, the police decided that they had no standing to arrest the accused murderer, or hold him for any reason. All they could offer Weaire was to accompany him home and observe as he threw out his tenant.

Accompanied by a sergeant from the local Garda precinct, Weaire finally arrived at his home at 1 P.M. that day. Ira Einhorn was in bed. Weaire roused him and said he had half an hour to pack and leave. A very startled Einhorn tried to discuss the matter, but Weaire refused. After Einhorn left, the professor moved his family back. He changed the locks on the door. That night, Jeanne Marie called, begging Weaire to listen to her side of the story. He would not, but said she could come by the next day.

Jeanne Marie was in tears when she came the next afternoon. She professed that Ira was innocent and seemed chagrined that the Weaires thought otherwise. "How could you believe such a thing of him?" she asked.

Meanwhile, no one in Philadelphia had been told about any of this. It was not until May 8 that Sergeant Richard King heard that a couple in Ireland had spotted Ira Einhorn. The news came from Drew Carr, the FBI agent in charge of the Einhorn case in Phila-delphia—apparently *he* hadn't heard about the sighting until after Einhorn had been allowed to go free. King was boggled by the foul-up, but was unable to get much information, let alone action, from overseas. It was not until September that the Irish police sent back word that officers had interviewed the Weaires and dusted the area for fingerprints, which confirmed that indeed, Ira Einhorn had been there. But where was he now?

On October 14, 1981, Richard King flew to Dublin to investigate personally. King's first efforts were to contact Irish authorities to determine what could be done if he actually *found* Ira Einhorn. "This was an inquiry that no one seemed to want to answer," he noted in his report. After being shuttled around in the bureaucracy, King finally got the answer—Ira Einhorn was not to be arrested. The United States and Ireland were in the process of drafting an extradition treaty, and at the time of ratification—months away—more significant steps would be taken. Meanwhile, King was told specifically, "Do not molest Einhorn—he is not to be touched."

King called his office and told them, "I'm coming home—I'm just wasting my time here." King left Dublin on October 20 with the frustrating knowledge that his quarry was probably still there. Though Garda officials promised to check out all possible leads, King had no confidence that they had any motivation to help out. Indeed, they did little in subsequent months. When King retired from the Philadelphia police in 1984, Ira Einhorn still sat atop the local most-wanted list, and it was Richard King's greatest professional regret that the Unicorn was still loose.

For the next few years, the search for Ira Einhorn was utterly fruitless. After King retired, the onus of the dragnet was passed to Richard DiBenedetto, the extraditions officer of the district attorney's office. DiBenedetto was a sly investigator who, from years of extracting fugitives from jurisdictions ranging from South Carolina to Zambia, knew both the advantages and limitations of dealing with other agencies when retrieving Philadelphia criminals. Ira Einhorn, DiBenedetto knew, was unlike the vast majority of those he was charged to recover. A typical case for him would be a car thief who, he'd discover, had a sister in Buffalo. A call to the police, who would visit the sister's home, more often than not would yield his quarry. From there, it would be a routine extradition arrangement between New York and Pennsylvania. The criminals were largely flotsam of a troubled social system, and their efforts to slip through the weave of a legal latticework bigger than their imaginations was almost poignantly pitiful.

Einhorn, though, was something else. With benefits of education and apparently some degree of brilliance, he had won influence from people who stood above the spheres in which detectives and extradition officers moved. It was a world of scientists, educators, renegade intellectuals, and wacky occultists. Not to mention some hideously rich people. Finding Einhorn was a fascinating quest. There was no way that Ira would return to the United States, where he could be netted by something as routine as an automobile check. But DiBenedetto was not sure whether he was in Ireland, or had moved to another country. Even though Einhorn was a high-priority fugitive, the city of Philadelphia did not have the funds to send Rich DiBenedetto on a world tour in search of the Unicorn—and even if it did, how would success be assured? DiBenedetto could maintain the required due diligence only by frequent Interpol inquiries, and pressure on people with whom Ira Einhorn was likely to have kept in touch.

Unfortunately, the urgency recommended by Judge Ribner immediately after Einhorn's flight had not been heeded. Few of Einhorn's associates had been contacted. Using Einhorn's correspondence and address books, which had been confiscated the same day Holly Maddux's body was discovered, DiBenedetto began calling Ira's friends and colleagues, none of whom seemed to be in touch with the fugitive. If he could get to whoever was supporting Einhorn, he figured, he would have his man. He did not know for sure who those supporters were, but he was most suspicious of two wealthy women who seemed to have played a role in the life of Ira Einhorn: Joyce Petschek and Barbara Bronfman.

Collette Weaire had told interviewers that Einhorn had spoken of at least one wealthy benefactor, a woman whose name she recalled as "Petscher." To DiBenedetto this sounded like Petschek, who had residences in London, Italy, and Fire Island, New York. He was never able to interview Petschek personally, though, and when he sent investigators to question her, she said that she was no longer in contact with Einhorn. Confronted more recently, she repeats her denial, saying Einhorn represents an era of her life that she closed the book on some years ago. However, she implies that in her view Einhorn should not be subjected to bothersome publicity. "I don't see how your book will help Ira," she says. "He's had to rebuild his whole life."

Barbara Bronfman was another challenge to DiBenedetto. Collette Weaire also recalled hearing Einhorn speak of "a wonderful Canadian woman who was helping him." Certainly Bronfman was wealthy. In 1982 she had divorced Charles Bronfman, citing his involvement with another woman (he remarried several days after the divorce); Charles Bronfman's personal wealth was valued in excess of a *billion* dollars, and quite probably Barbara Bronfman did well in the settlement. But since there was no evidence that she was using that wealth to aid Ira Einhorn, Rich DiBenedetto had no justification to go beyond his jurisdiction to interview her.

What DiBenedetto did not know was that sometime around 1983, Barbara Bronfman had called Ian Summers, the book packager with whom Einhorn had been trying to sell his story. "I was very surprised to hear from her," says Summers, who had never met the woman before. "But she did track me down, and she . . . needed to see me and wouldn't tell me what it was about. But I knew what it was about. I knew it had something to do with Ira."

According to Summers, they met at an expensive Italian restaurant. Summers found Bronfman an attractive woman in her forties. He felt she was feeling him out, seeing if she could trust him with something. And then she came out with it. A manuscript had one day mysteriously appeared at her doorstep. It concerned the experiences of a woman who worked in a sleazy massage parlor; the woman was part of an expatriate couple living in Dublin, Ireland.

Summers got to the point: "Is it written by Ira?"

"I don't know," said Bronfman.

Summers asked her what she wanted from him.

"Well, I'd like you to sell the book," she said.

Summers bore down. "What's gonna happen to the money if there's no author? Do *you* want the money, Barbara? Is it your book?"

Barbara Bronfman was implacable. "Well," she assured Summers, "somehow I think the money will get to the people who need it."

Though Summers tried to press her for an admission that it was Ira's book, she refused to confirm it, denying that she was in direct contact with him. No reason was given why Barbara Bronfman, upon unexpectedly receiving an anonymous book manuscript, would approach Ira Einhorn's quasi-agent and ask for help in getting it published, with the confidence that the money would go to the author. She simply said that Ian Summers would have to make a leap of faith. So he accepted the manuscript and promised to read it. But not before he satisfied some curiosity he had about Ira Einhorn and this woman who had married into one of the world's richest families.

"How peculiar that someone of your status and your husband's status would have befriended this man," he recalls saying to her. "What was in it for you? What did you like about Ira that made you really go this far?"

And she said, "Ira was the best friend that anybody could ever have."

When Summers took the book home and read it—it was entitled *A Year in the Life* and credited to one "Grace O'Malley"—he realized two things. First of all, it was unpublishable, a mildly sordid account of the underbelly of Dublin life, with little redeeming value in the writing. Second of all, he was convinced that it was written, at least in part, by Ira Einhorn. Some of the language was reminiscent of Ira's, and the obtrusive sociological observations in the book were prime Einhorn. "If Ira were telling the story, this is the way he would have told the story," says Summers.

The manuscript, produced with a low-cost dot-matrix computer printer, has details that may well have paralleled certain circumstances of Ira Einhorn's life in Ireland. Though the identities were well masked, beginning with the obvious pseudonym (any Irish person would instantly recognize "Grace O'Malley" as the name of a legendary sixteenth-century figure, the "Pirate Queen" of the island's western coast), some aspects of the novel seem strangely familiar. The American-born protagonist and her boyfriend live in the Rathmines neighborhood, and the bus route she takes from city center to her apartment is the same that Jeanne Marie Morrison used to travel from downtown Dublin to the Weaires' house on Greenmount Street. More telling is the nature of the relationship between the expatriate couple. "Daniel" is thin whereas Ira is heavy, and Daniel is an artist whereas Ira is a writer. But Daniel's behavior toward women recalls that of Ira Einhorn at his worst.

"When I got home," the fictional protagonist writes of a typical domestic scene, "he'd be in bed painting. . . . I'd come into his room to say hello. He'd throw off the covers, spread his legs with a silly grin on his face and a hand fluffing his balls. I'd sigh and blow him, or get the oil and jerk him off, or let him fuck my mouth, or let him fuck my cunt, or let him fuck my tits, feeling obligated to allow him my pleasure, trying to suppress my resentment of the obligation. . . . Daniel, and my own performances in bed with him, had convinced me that there must be something wrong with my sexuality."

Vulgar language aside, this could be an extract from Holly Maddux's diary of life with Ira Einhorn.

Summers never did tell Barbara Bronfman his opinion of the book. She never called back.

Many of Einhorn's friends doubted that Ira could successfully avoid capture, no matter where he chose to run. It seemed inconceivable that someone as public as Ira could bear the anonymity of life on the run. As the months, and then years, passed since his illegal departure from Philadelphia, some people assumed he might be dead. Those bent toward conspiracy theories—a few of these people had always assumed that Ira had been in the employ of an intelligence agency—wondered whether the CIA or FBI was helping him avoid capture. (There is no evidence that Einhorn was an agent of any intelligence agency, and those investigators who have worked on the Einhorn case report that their efforts were not hampered by interference from higher up.) Other followers of Einhorn's career enjoyed fantasizing what disguises he might be assuming, what exotic locations he might be haunting. Rumor had him working in the Sun City casino in South Africa, or living as a guest of the Yugoslavian government. A high school friend opined that, knowing Ira, he would be exactly where one expected *not* to find him—working as an accountant in Minneapolis, perhaps.

How Einhorn would be received if he ever returned, voluntarily or otherwise, was a different matter. Some of those who had supported him most staunchly after his arrest felt betrayed that he solicited their support for a trial made moot by his retreat. "Even though I testified at his bail hearing," says one friend, "I think that his skipping bail severed my obligation to protect him anymore. He should stand trial. He should not be wandering around." Two days after Ira's departure, Claude Lewis wrote in his newspaper column that "a lot of people sacrificed a great deal of time and energy for him. Even when, by right, faith should have failed, they stood with him. When the news arrived that Ira didn't show up for court . . . a lot of people felt numb." A few months later, Lewis reported that Einhorn's friends were now "as scarce as hen's teeth." He came down particularly hard on Ira for leaving his mother liable for the remainder of the $36,000 bail bond.

The subsequent years of silence have focused the pain on those left behind to ponder the meaning of the Unicorn's betrayal. This was not a standard domestic killing, but something that unsettled the souls of those familiar with the principals. To some, it stood as a troubling eclipse of some of the finer values curried in two decades of liberation and self-realization.

Jerry Rubin, the former Yippie and Chicago Seven defendant, puts the matter bluntly: "Ira betrayed everything I stood for and possibly everything that he stood for," he says. His argument is that if the evidence is to be believed and Ira killed Holly, Einhorn's violence negated fifteen years of talk about nonviolence, proplanetary motivations, and positive transformations. "The ultimate crime," Rubin says, "is that Ira betrayed the sixties."

Others have come to the same conclusion. "In a way, Ira was a counterfeit of everything he successfully pointed me towards, things that became the best values in my lifetime," says Michael Woal, who was close to Ira in the sixties.

But one cannot separate Ira's dark legacy from the person who committed more positive deeds in the sixties. Even as Ira arranged his Be-In, educated the Episcopal bishop on the wisdom of flower children, and organized the Powelton Help Center, he was a man harboring a secret—he had nearly murdered two women. This was not open knowledge. But some people had heard rumors that he was violent to women. Many more had witnessed him verbally abusing women he was involved with. Almost anyone could see he was unmistakably predatory in his approach to women he wanted to make love to. And one would have to be blind to miss the fact that behind his disarming friendliness lurked an ego that did not operate in sync with the egalitarian spirit of the times. Charisma was his tool, but it was also his weapon.

But few questioned him on these contradictions. Michael Woal is not sorry he did not. "I acted like all the others there. I never confronted him. I don't think anybody did. We just said, 'Oh, that's Ira.'"

Who knew? Who knew that when Einhorn wrote, in a 1970 publication of the Catholic Art Association called "The Prophetic Generation," "Violence is the simplest mode of contact—it allows touch without formality, providing us access to the other through direct unritualized action," that at the time of publication he had almost killed two young women and was a threat for worse? Who knew that when Einhorn, in a campaign speech in his 1971 mayoral run, declared himself a brother of Charlie Manson and said, "Psychopaths like myself emerge when societies are about to change," that he actually might be a psychopath? Who among Ira's business friends knew that when he entertained them with stories of UFOs and psychic Watergate, that those extraordinary scenarios would be part of his murder alibi? People let Ira slide because he was Ira, and because it was a time to let things slide, if you seemed to be on the right side. And in a sense, Ira's weaknesses were not far removed from those of others who carried the same mantle. Ego was not a rare commodity in the social history of the past two decades. And a general difficulty of the sixties was the thin line between indulgence and freedom. At the time this did not appear so problematic; only afterward have the tales of sexism, of manipulative charisma, seeped in. The values were worth living up to, but it was too easy to give them lip service and take what one needed from the decade. The dissonance was built-in.

Ira Einhorn's psychological karma is his own; one cannot blame that on a generational movement that meant well but could not deal with evil within its circles. But it is also true that the sixties gave Ira Einhorn his focus, his prominence, his rap, his confidence, and his slack. Slack that he used to the detriment of others. In times that boasted themselves as a historical turning point in history, times larger than life, it was easier to convince oneself that you were larger than life. Especially someone like Ira, who entered the decade already swimming in a sea of Nietzschean self-importance.

"Ira is an example of the illusions we pull on ourselves," says Reverend Ralph Moore, who came to know Ira well in his capacity as the director of the Christian Association on the Penn campus. "In each of us there is the capacity to explore and push and develop self-images of righteousness and power. It's one of the positive and creative aspects of spirituality in general that we continue to keep ourselves down to size, and not think better of ourselves than we ought to think. And rely on feedback, criticism, human community as to the way we grow—rather than, in isolation, develop a fantasy of heroic personality [for ourselves]. And Ira is a fantasy of heroic personality. . . . Since this did happen, it gives us an opportunity to ask other questions: How far should any of us go unchecked? And this means not only in societal relations, but personal ones, even with lovers."

The same questions plagued others who had been close to Ira. The Synergy Group, whose members had bonded with both Ira and Holly, had been particularly stunned by both her disappearance and Ira's arrest for her murder. "I spent about a year going through the grief process," says George Keegan. The reverberations dealt not only with what Ira had done but to what degree the others might have prevented the tragedy. One night, Keegan recalls, the entire Synergy Group had tried to hash out their emotional confusion. Once they had believed that Ira was the way they saw themselves—peaceful and loving. That was why their first instinct on hearing of Ira's arrest had been to say, "No, not Ira." But now facts were coming out, and they were deep in the process of reanalyzing what they knew of Ira Einhorn. Underlying the session was a collective guilt—they had seen how Ira behaved with Holly and were uncomfortable with how little they had done to stop things. It was a tumultuous meeting, with almost unbearable truths unearthed. As Keegan recalls it, at one point, someone furious at Holly's death piped up that "If he did that to Holly, he should be put in jail forever."

And the fellow's wife said to him, "Who the fuck are you to talk? You beat up on *me!*"

"Ira was the most traumatic thing that happened to us as a group," says George Keegan. "We were all young, idealistic . . . we were out to save the world. We saw what our parents had done, and we had this kind of New Age philosophy that someone's just got to go out there and do it, pull humanity out of the muck and go on to a better future. And I guess in a way we got a little arrogant. Somewhere in there we forgot that we are really fragile human beings."

Keegan has identified Ira Einhorn's great failing. The Unicorn was competent as an intellectual, a leader, a far-watcher, a networker, or an oracle, but he could not allow himself to become a human being. To admit that he was like everyone else would have been an admission of vulnerability that was beyond him. He could answer the door naked without hesitation, but when the time came, he could not stand naked as a person, and admit that he *needed*. Despite the thousands of books he read and the thousands of people he impressed, the love he craved was that of a single woman. But none of his friends report him capable of acknowledging this mortal trait. Perhaps he considered it too mundane for one in his situation. When he had been unable to cope with this problem previously— those times he had been rejected by Rita Siegal and Judy Lewis— instead of accepting, he struck out. It seems he did the same thing with Holly Maddux. And when that was over, he could not subject himself to the humiliation of being the defendant in a mere domestic killing. For Ira, the circumstances had to have global implications—the CIA, the KGB, the Nazis. Grandiose, bigger than life. For Ira Einhorn, life-size was too small.

"When murder happens, it's a stain," says Ira's friend Tom Bissinger, still stinging from Ira Einhorn's legacy. "A blot on the earth. I would have preferred for him to come to trial. We all wanted to think it didn't happen. But there was no way to conclude he didn't do it. I can only assume the worst. And keep in mind that a woman died here. Holly's dead, and that's the tragedy. I was hoping that he was not going to leave a trail of karma, but [by fleeing] he did. He left a big, big mess. He has put a lot of people through hell, with no suitable ending. Justice has not been served. We're all left hanging. It's hard to think otherwise than he blew it."

The dark side of the Unicorn had cast its shadow on the sixties itself, and the New Age that followed.

In early 1986, despite the fact that it had been almost five years since he had heard of anyone spotting Ira Einhorn, Rich Di-Benedetto's interest in his fugitive had not waned. Einhorn had become sort of an obsession for DiBenedetto. The extraditions officer had continued his phone survey of friends of Ira Einhorn. He would receive uniform denials—Ira, they would insist, never contacted me. But the investigator would press on, preparing himself for the day, which he considered inevitable, when the high-and-mighty Ira Einhorn, with all his cleverness, would find himself under police custody.

DiBenedetto had come to believe Einhorn was probably still in Ireland. The only concrete indication he had of this was the confirmation that in 1984, Jeanne Marie Morrison had renewed her passport at the American Embassy in Dublin. No one had questioned her at the time, and she had given an apparently phony address in Cork. But DiBenedetto hoped that his bosses would soon release the funds for him to go to Ireland himself to search for Ira Einhorn. He planned to travel after the extradition treaty between Ireland and the United States was finally activated. The treaty had been drawn and ratified, but a legal snafu in Ireland—its legislature, the Dail, had not properly approved its language—prevented its enforcement. The Dail was slated to vote late in the year, and then, if Ira Einhorn was still in Ireland, he could be sought and arrested. Of course, finding Einhorn would be no picnic—who knew if he still was in Dublin?

That mystery was suddenly, and temporarily, resolved in late May, when DiBenedetto got a call from Dennis Weaire. He had seen Ira Einhorn. Weaire, who had left University College and was now teaching at Trinity College, the hoary institution in both the physical and spiritual centers of Dublin, met his wife one day for lunch in the faculty cafeteria. And Collette had spotted him! He was just coming in, accompanied by a Trinity faculty member. His hair was still long, tied back in a braid, but he had no beard. In the past half decade, he had gotten heavier and grayer. There was no question, though, that this was Einhorn. "My God, Ira," she said, "what are you doing here?" She turned to her husband, a few steps away, and bleated out whom she had just seen. Ira turned on his heels to exit, but Dennis Weaire, furious that this outlaw had the temerity to dine in Weaire's place of employment, followed Einhorn out the door and down the stairs, shouting at him to get out. Ira was understandably uncomfortable with the turn his lunch hour had taken and asked if they could step outside for a minute.

"I just want to be left in peace," he told Dennis Weaire.

Weaire had recognized Einhorn's companion as a German professor named Gordon Carr, and the next day, he went to Carr's office. Carr registered astonishment at Weaire's claim that his friend was an alleged murderer named Ira Einhorn. He knew the fellow as Ben Moore, an intelligent fellow to whom he'd been giving German lessons. In exchange, Ira was educating the professor about matters of philosophy and science.

Rich DiBenedetto realized, even as he heard Weaire's account of the conversation, that his best chance to pursue Ira Einhorn might be fading by the minute. If Weaire had not confronted Einhorn, an investigation could have been conducted discreetly, and the Irish police could have maintained a loose surveillance until the extradition treaty went into effect. Now, Einhorn knew at the very least that Weaire had fingered him, and any careless confidence he might have assumed during his five years of successful hiding would be dissolved. By the time DiBenedetto could convince someone in the Garda to visit Carr, his fears were confirmed—the German professor said his friend Ben Moore had just called him to say he was going away for a couple of weeks. It was, Carr said, an unusual announcement, in that Moore previously had never felt it necessary to notify him of his whereabouts.

DiBenedetto, as usual, could not count on much help from the Garda in following up on the sighting. Information eventually filtered back that Garda officers had stopped by the address that Carr had given for Ben Moore—and saw no one. By then, it was midsummer, and the opportunity was blown.

Late in 1986, another break came. Jeanne Marie Morrison had returned to the United States. Her family regarded the return as a near miracle when the phone rang one day with the prodigal daughter on the line. She was in New York, newly arrived to her home country, and terribly upset—looking through back issues of newspapers in the public library, she had seen her father's 1984 obituary. When reestablished in the bosom of her family, she told her story. She had not, she asserted, been living with Einhorn for over two years. Rather than leave him outright, she had made herself "a pain in the neck" to him, so that he would welcome her departure. In this, her escape was reminiscent of the careful exit of Kim Owens from Ira Einhorn's life—and a blessed contrast from the farewells given to Rita Siegal, Judy Lewis, and Holly Maddux.

Jeanne Marie had been afraid to return directly to the States, so she worked in Dublin, at odd jobs, out of contact with family and friends, a quasi-fugitive for almost two years after she left Einhorn. She had even, she said, made some money by her artwork, a pastime that had given her increasing comfort in her years of exile. Though her mother sensed that she harbored considerable fear of her former traveling companion, Jeanne Marie Morrison was vocal in her belief that Ira Einhorn was innocent. "Mom," she said at one point, "he's *not* a monster."

Though she maintained a sense of loyalty to Ira Einhorn, Jeanne Marie realized that in order to dispel a precarious legal position, she would have to cooperate to some degree with the police. In exchange for a guarantee of immunity, she agreed to an interview with Rich DiBenedetto and other authorities. She revealed details of her life with Ira Einhorn, but none that would lead to his present location.

Apparently, Einhorn's brush with Weaire had indeed led to his leaving Ireland. Around Jeanne Marie's birthday in May 1986, she had a party that Einhorn attended—the first time, she said, she had seen him in months. Not long after—around the time of the Weaire confrontation—he had called her, saying that he was leaving his apartment. Anything she wanted, she could go and collect. She and some friends cleared out the apartment for him. A few weeks later, he appeared on her doorstep and asked if he could stay for a few days. When he left, he did not reveal his destination. That, she insisted, was the last she heard of him.

DiBenedetto pressed her as to Einhorn's contacts. She professed relative ignorance. Einhorn was protective of the particulars of his subterranean existence, she said. He lived a disciplined, quiet life. He purchased many books, and had an account with Blackwell's of Oxford. Under his assumed name, he conducted limited correspondence with noted authors, including letters to classicist Guy Davenport and mathematician Rudy Rucker. As Ben Moore, he attended some poetry readings in Ireland and was acquainted with some Irish poets of repute, such as Seamus Heaney. He held no job, but did research, and worked on a book. He would not let her see his mail. She did not handle the money. DiBenedetto persisted—who was sending money? Eventually Jeanne Marie gave the police a name: Barbara Bronfman.

This did not necessarily mean that Morrison's identification was accurate; it is possible that it was a guess on Jeanne Marie's part, or an attempt to mislead. Nonetheless, the comment intensified DiBenedetto's desire to look into the matter more deeply and speak to Ms. Bronfman directly. But in the next year he was frustrated in this quest. There is only so much an American authority can do to investigate the actions of a citizen-resident of another country, particularly when the citizen has the lofty status of a Bronfman. He had to suffice with reports from his more deferential Canadian counterparts.

Even if he had spoken to her, it would be questionable whether the dialogue would be fruitful. When asked about Ira Einhorn, Barbara Bronfman begins by saying that she does not know his whereabouts but then states that "I'm not going to confirm or deny anything." She explains that "I'm a very private person as far as my friends are concerned," and adds that "this is a very sensitive matter for me." Finally, the woman bearing the surname of Canada's richest family offers this pronouncement concerning Ira Einhorn: "The main thing I can say is that I miss him very much because he was a great friend. He enriched many people's lives, including mine."

Ms. Bronfman speaks of the side of Ira Einhorn that charmed and presumably enriched hundreds of people in his peculiar odyssey. If his behavior in Ireland during the 1980s was any indication, this charm has continued unabated.

The circle of friends who knew "Ben Moore" considered themselves lucky to know him. It was never explained why a worldly American who looked like a vestige from the hippie era was living a life of relative luxury in Dublin, but people assumed that he was independently wealthy and perhaps had run into trouble in the States due to his political beliefs. Some cynics opined that he was a CIA agent, working on a study of the Irish, but most simply accepted him as a font of intellectual energy.

He lived in a roomy two-bedroom apartment at 61 Pembroke Street, in one of Dublin's best neighborhoods. Down the block was the Irish headquarters of IBM; from his fourth-story window, Ira Einhorn could see the American flag flying outside his native country's embassy, only two blocks away. Ira's building, known as Halcom Court, was a stately, Georgian, four-story former mansion, onto which was built, in the rear, a stucco addition whose lower ceilings allowed for six stories of apartments, two or three to a floor. An elevator opened directly into Ira's apartment, one of those in the rear section of the building. When renting the apartment, he had described himself as a writer. The rent was about 300 Irish pounds monthly, well into the local high-middle-class price range. Ira had transformed it from its rather sterile furnishings—bland plastic-covered furniture, and wood-paneled built-in shelves and bureaus—to an unusual arrangement in which the sofa and chairs were moved out, and the room was engulfed with lush plants. Zodiac signs were etched into the windows. An upstairs neighbor was once startled when, knocking on the door for some errand, Ben Moore took some time before answering, explaining that he had been sitting nude before the window, welcoming the sun into the apartment. (Either caution or a newly developed sense of modesty prevented Einhorn from answering the door in that state.)

Ben Moore on occasion would entertain guests at the apartment, where presumably he was working on a book. He spent much of his days at home, though in summer he would venture out to nearby Herbert Park. His interests seemed to focus on pagan history, particularly on the Roman Empire, and he was building a collection of early texts, including pre-Christian Bibles. He and his presumed wife, Jan Moore—who was of course Jeanne Marie Morrison—had rented a word processor.

Ben and Jan Moore became friendly with Toby and Deidre Hall, a couple who lived off a small alley behind the building, and eventually fell into a group of artists and intellectuals. Ben Moore became a guiding force for these people, both in Dublin and during weekends in a quasi–New Age retreat in nearby Avoca, south of the Dublin mountains. Some of these friends would regularly go to the Moore apartment for an informal philosophy seminar that was set up as a free-for-all discussion session on Hegel, Descartes, Kant, and other mental giants. This strange, somewhat overbearing American dominated the sessions. Since he was so fascinating, the other participants did not object.

He became especially close to Diurmid Boyd, a even-tempered painter, who found him inspiring. "I could tune into his social aspects," Boyd says, conceding that Ben Moore's graces did not include a mode of personal revelation. Still, Boyd was dazzled by his friend's erudition and energy.

If Einhorn was homesick for America, Philadelphia, or Powelton Village, he cloaked the depression magnificently. He did organize a Thanksgiving dinner for a few other expatriate countrymen, but it was a festive event. He served no morose nostalgia with the turkey he cooked. "He didn't seem troubled," says Glenda Cimino, an American-born small-press publisher who knew Ben Moore in Dublin. "He seemed to be the sort of person who was an intellectual explorer, a learner, excited by books and ideas. He didn't seem inclined to depression."

Some of his friends could not help but notice another side of him. "Being with him had its scary elements," says Boyd. "He was a formidable presence, due to his intensity." A few female acquaintances disapproved of his domination of the woman called Jan Moore. "I couldn't bear being in their company because he ran her down so completely," says one friend. "It was a cold, calculated wearing down," she adds, all the more onerous because "he blocked himself off emotionally." Ben and Jan slept apart, and he saw many other women. He once boasted that three or four different women had asked him to father a child with them. Another time, he made a clumsy pass at a woman who had recently dyed her hair, seductively asserting that he could sniff a redhead a mile away.

Margaret Wright, the superintendent at Halcom Court—despite acknowledging that Moore was so trustworthy she would leave the building in his care on occasion—thought him uncomfortably manipulative. After Jan left him, he had many young girls to the apartment. Then he had an apparent affair with a seemingly respectable married woman who had an infant daughter. Worse, Mrs. Wright's daughter had once heard him say that he didn't object to slapping a woman; and she told her mother that at one point, during an argument with a woman, Ben Moore indeed struck her. "There was something about him that wasn't right," says Mrs. Wright. "Evil. My daughter felt he was the devil."

But that was the minority opinion about Ben Moore. Most people felt, as they had felt with Ira Einhorn, that this was a special being, one of the elect. "To me, he was a positive person," says Toby Hall, who shared his interest in Celtic and pagan studies. "I've never met a more useful person for society. As far as the United States is concerned, they could do with a guy like that for president." When Ben Moore suddenly vanished one day in May 1986, leaving a note for Mrs. Wright citing "domestic reasons" for his departure, and instructing Jan and some friends to clear out the apartment, people ascribed the event to his overall mysteriousness. As if he were some fairy godfather sent to Dublin for their instruction and amusement, suddenly called to service in another region.

When months later, they learned the identity of Ben Moore, and the crime he had been accused of, they could not bring themselves to believe it. They were immersed in the same air of unreality as Ira Einhorn's friends had been, seven years before, when the news of Holly Maddux's murder first exploded their illusions about the Unicorn.

Epilogue

Beatrice Einhorn lives with her son Stephen in an apartment outside of Philadelphia, not far from the neighborhood where she raised Ira. Joseph Einhorn died not long after his son fled the country. Ira's mother has no question but that her son is innocent—indeed has never committed an act of violence in his life—and has hopes that the "real" killer will one day be caught, thus ending the family nightmare.

Until his death in May 1988, Fred Maddux and his wife Elizabeth remained in the rambling house on the south side of Tyler. Their son John lived with them; their other three grown children have left Tyler—but remain in Texas. Among the grandchildren surviving Fred Maddux is a little girl named Holly.

Morse Peckham lives in a comfortable home in Columbia, South Carolina. He no longer teaches but still writes, currently involved in an ambitious multivolume study of human behavior. He has not seen Ira Einhorn since 1973.

Holly Maddux's high school friend Toni Erwin lives in Tyler with her family, including her husband, Bill Ferrell, who dated Holly in the early sixties. Lawrence Wells is a federal attorney in Austin, Texas. Holly's first boyfriend, Richard Olver, works for the United Nations. Her boyfriend before Ira, Alan Torledsky, works for a construction firm in Florida.

Many of Ira's friends during the sixties have lives with conventional trappings, yet are still influenced by the values of those years. Grant Schaefer, for instance, who ran the first head shop in Powelton Village, now sells real estate for Century 21. Michael Hoffman is the head of the English department at a California college; Michael Woal also teaches. Of those known as Yippies, Jerry Rubin promotes events at New York's Limelight nightclub, Abbie Hoffman remains active in politics, and Allen Ginsberg is still Allen Ginsberg. The first poem in his recent collection, *White Shroud*, contains this stanza:

> *Did the Ecologist chop his girl with an ax in Philadelphia*
> *& hide her corpse a year in the trunk?*
> *What does that red-haired boy half-naked on the sidewalk*
> *with his Frisbee think of that?*

Andrija Puharich returned to the United States some years after the arson of his home. He claims he has been a target of four assassination attempts by the CIA. He lives in North Carolina and lectures frequently, selling specially designed wristwatches that deflect the harmful ELF rays that he says are constantly bombarding us.

J. Robert Pearce, the detective instrumental in solving the case, died in December 1987. Robert J. Stevens, the Tyler detective whom the Madduxes hired, is still in practice. Michael Chitwood, who conducted the search of Einhorn's apartment, is the police chief in Portland, Maine.

Powelton Village is striving to maintain its character in the face of gentrification and further encroachment by Drexel University. La Terrasse is still thriving, still owned by Ira's friend Eliot Cook. Judy Wicks, the former manager, has opened a restaurant on the same block. The Lerner Court Apartments on 3411 Race Street still stand. The second-floor rear apartment has been renovated, and the area that was formerly a porch is now an enclosed room. In 1987, it was used as a bedroom for the two Drexel students who rented the apartment, unaware that they were sleeping only inches from the spot where Holly Maddux's body was discovered.
A block away from 3411 Race stand two holly trees, planted as a memorial to the dead woman by neighbors who knew her. No plaque commemorates her there. In Tyler, Texas, the headstone on her grave simply lists the years of her birth and death.

Neither Rita Siegal nor Judy Lewis want circumstances of their current lives disclosed. Both believe that Ira Einhorn is capable of more violence and want to put their previous involvement with him behind them.

Ira Einhorn is still a fugitive, undoubtedly living abroad. It is anybody's guess where he might have gone after leaving Ireland in 1986. There is no statute of limitations for murder.

A NOTE ON SOURCES

The main source material for *The Unicorn's Secret* consisted of more than 250 personal interviews of those connected to the case in various ways. In almost all cases, the names used in the book are the real names of the people involved; only in very few cases have names been changed to protect the privacy of those involved (these are the people referred to in the book as Kim Owens, Rita Siegal, Judy Lewis, Jill Hamill, and her friend Sharon). In cases where people's names have changed subsequent to the events described, I have generally used the names they went by contemporaneously.

Other sources included public and private documents and published materials. Philadelphia publications such as the *Inquirer*, the *Bulletin*, the *Daily News*, the *Daily Pennsylvanian*, the *Drummer*, *Psychedelphia Period*, *Yarrowstalks*, and *Philadelphia Magazine* were invaluable.

SELECTED BIBLIOGRAPHY

Acton, Jay. *Mug Shots.* New York: Meriden, 1972.

Anderson, Walter Truett. *The Upstart Spring: Esalen and the American Awakening.* Reading, MA: Addison-Wesley, 1983.

Bearden, Thomas E. *The Excalibur Briefing.* San Francisco: Strawberry Hill Press, 1980.

Blair, Sam. *Earl Campbell: The Driving Force.* Waco, TX: Word Books, 1980.

Blum, Ralph, with Judy Blum. *Beyond Earth: Man's Contact with UFOs.* New York: Bantam, 1974.

Breznitz, Shlomo, ed. *The Denial of Stress.* New York: International Universities Press, 1983.

Einhorn, Ira. *78-187880.* New York: Doubleday Anchor, 1974.

Fuller, John G. *Arigo: Surgeon of the Rusty Knife.* New York: Thomas Crowell, 1974.

Glover, Robert W., ed. *Tyler & Smith County, Texas: An Historical Survey.* Tyler, TX: American Bicentennial Committee of Tyler-Smith County, 1976.

Goleman, Daniel. *Vital Lies, Simple Truths: The Psychology of Self-Deception.* New York: Simon & Schuster, 1985.

Kernberg, Otto, M.D. *Borderline Conditions and Pathological Narcissism.* New York: W. W. Norton & Company, Inc., 1975.

Keyes, Ralph. "The Free Universities." *The Nation,* Oct. 2, 1967.

Lewis, Zella, ed. *The Proud Century: Tyler Public Schools 1882–1982.* Tyler, TX: Tyler Independent School System, 1982

Matalene, H. W. "Morse Peckham." Unpublished essay.

McCormick, Bernie. "Don't Trust Anybody Over 40." *Philadelphia Magazine,* May 1970.

McNamara, Charles. "A Faint Cheer for Gratis U." *Philadelphia Magazine,* December 1967.

McRae, Ron. *Mind Wars.* New York: St. Martin's Press, 1984.

Melick, Weldon Douglas. *Sexual Appetites on Campus, Vol. II: Men.* New York: Award Books, 1968.

Monsul, Mari. "A Village Called Powelton." Unpublished thesis, 1977.

Ostrander, Shiela and Schroder, Lynn. *Psychic Discoveries Behind the Iron Curtain.* New York: Prentice-Hall, 1970.

Peat, David. *In Search of Nikola Tesla.* Bath, England: Ashgrove Press, 1983.

Peckham, Morse. *Beyond the Tragic Vision: The Quest for Identity in the Nineteenth Century.* New York: Braziller, 1962.

Puharich, Andrija. *Uri: A Journal of the Mystery of Uri Geller.* New York: Doubleday Anchor, 1974.

Randi, James. *The Truth About Uri Geller.* Buffalo, NY: Prometheus Books, 1982.

Rice, Edward, and Garney, Jane. *The Prophetic Generation.* Rensselaerville, NY: Catholic Art Association, 1970.

Rittenhouse, Carline, and Dolenski, Leo M. *Bryn Mawr College.* Bryn Mawr: Bryn Mawr College Libraries, 1985.

Robbins, Al. "Blinded by the Light." *Village Voice,* July 23, 1979.

Rossman, Michael. *New Age Blues: On the Politics of Consciousness.* New York: E. P. Dutton, 1979.

Rubin, Jerry. *Do It!* New York: Simon & Schuster, 1970.

Thompson, William Irwin. *At the Edge of History.* New York: Harper & Row, 1971.

Walter, Greg. "Holly." *Philadelphia Magazine,* December 1979.

Weissburg, Michael P., M.D. *Dangerous Secrets: Maladaptive Responses to Stress.* New York: W. W. Norton & Company, Inc., 1983.

Wilson, Graham. "Interview with Ira Einhorn," parts 1 and 2. *New Life,* Summer–Fall 1977.